Judicial Power and Canadian Democracy

Judicial Power and Canadian Democracy

EDITED BY PAUL HOWE AND PETER H. RUSSELL

Published for the Institute for Research on Public Policy

by McGill-Queen's University Press
Montreal & Kingston · London · Ithaca

© McGill-Queen's University Press 2001
ISBN 0-7735-2131-3 (cloth)
ISBN 0-7735-2225-5 (paper)
Legal deposit first quarter 2001
Bibliothèque nationale du Québec

Printed in Canada on acid-free paper

Founded in 1972, the Institute for Research on Public Policy is an
independent, national, nonprofit organization. IRPP seeks to improve
public policy in Canada by generating research, providing insight and
sparking debate that will contribute to the public policy decision-making
process and strengthen the quality of the public policy decisions made by
Canadian governments, citizens, institutions and organizations.

IRPP's independence is assured by an endowment fund, to which
federal and provincial governments and the private sector have
contributed.

McGill-Queen's University Press acknowledges the financial support of the
Government of Canada through the Book Publishing Industry
Development Program (BPIDP) for its activities. It also acknowledges the
support of the Canada Council for the Arts for its publishing program.

Canadian Cataloguing in Publication Data

Main entry under title:
Judicial power and Canadian democracy
Chiefly papers originally presented at Guiding the Rule of Law into the
21st Century, a conference held Apr. 16–17, 1999 at the University of
Ottawa.
Includes bibliographical references.
ISBN 0-7735-2131-3 (bnd)
ISBN 0-7735-2225-5 (pbk)
1. Judicial power–Canada. 2. Judicial review–Canada. 3. Canada. Canadian
Charter of Rights and Freedoms. 4. Canada. Supreme Court. I. Russell,
Peter H. II. Howe, Paul, 1966– III. Institute for Research on Public Policy.
IV. Guiding the Rule of Law into the 21st Century (1999: University of
Ottawa).
KE4775.J83 2001   347.71'012   C00-901326-1

This book was typeset by Typo Litho Composition Inc.
in 10/12 Baskerville.

Contents

Acknowledgments   vii

Introduction   ix

Contributors   xvii

PART A: SETTING THE STAGE: THE JUDICIARY'S
ROLE IN CANADA AND BRITAIN

Judicial Politics in Canada: Patterns and Trends
Frederick Vaughan   3

A British Bill of Rights: Incorporating the European
Convention on Human Rights   *Kate Malleson*   27

PART B: ARE JUDGES TOO POWERFUL?
DEBATE AND DIALOGUE

Courts, Legislatures and Executives in
the Post-Charter Era   *Hon. Beverley McLachlin*   63

We Didn't Volunteer   *Hon. Bertha Wilson*   73

The Activist Constitution   *Lorraine Eisenstat Weinrib*   80

Courts Don't Make Good Compromises
Rainer Knopff   87

The Charter and Legitimization
of Judicial Activism   *Sébastien Lebel-Grenier*   94

The Provincial Court Judges Case and Extended
Judicial Control   *Pierre Patenaude*   99

The Charter Dialogue between Courts
and Legislatures   *Peter W. Hogg and
Allison A. Thornton*   106

Dialogue or Monologue?   *F.L. Morton*   111

Reform's Judicial Agenda   *Peter H. Russell*   118

A "B" for Prof. Russell   *E. Preston Manning*   123

PART C: JUDICIAL AUTHORITY, ISSUES
AND CONTROVERSIES

Merit Selection and Democratization of Appointments to
the Supreme Court of Canada   *Jacob S. Ziegel*   131

Wrestling with Rights: Judges, Parliament and the Making
of Social Policy   *Janet L. Hiebert*   165

Interest Group Litigation and
Canadian Democracy   *Gregory Hein*   214

Public Opinion and Canada's Courts
Joseph F. Fletcher and Paul Howe   255

Section 33, The Notwithstanding Clause:
A Paper Tiger?   *Howard Leeson*   297

Acknowledgments

Many of the papers in this collection were first presented at *Guiding the Rule of Law into the 21st Century*, a conference that took place April 16 and 17, 1999 at the University of Ottawa, sponsored by the Institute for Research on Public Policy in partnership with the Centre on Governance at the University of Ottawa and the Political Law Development Initiative. Conference co-organizer Gregory Tardi was integral to the event's success.

The short papers in the collection first appeared in *Policy Options*, under the editorial direction of William Watson. The longer papers were originally published in IRPP's serial publication *Choices*, with research assistance from Murray Mincoff and page layout by Chantal Létourneau. Suzanne Ostiguy McIntyre provided valuable administrative coordination for the entire project.

Translation of the texts that originally appeared in French was carried out by Scribe d'Aujourd'hui.

Introduction

Are judges too powerful? It is a question that has preoccupied Canadians for some time now. Rarely does a month go by without one court decision or another making headlines in newspapers across the country. Canadians unaccustomed to scrutinizing the work of judges have found themselves assessing the merits of judicial authority as it runs up against some of the traditional practices and conventions of Canadian democracy.

The broad contours of the debate are familiar enough. After a difficult and protracted round of constitutional negotiations spearheaded by Pierre Trudeau, the Canadian Charter of Rights and Freedoms came into force in 1982. His purpose was twofold: to put in place constitutionally entrenched rights protections for all Canadians and, in response to the sovereignist movement in Quebec, to establish a pan-Canadian symbol of national unity. While this bold initiative hardly passed unnoticed onto the political scene – least of all by Quebec, which refused to sign on – it is fair to say that the full implications of the Charter for the balance of power between the different branches of government were underestimated by many observers at the time.

Trudeau, for his part, tended to speak of rights and freedoms as if they had an obvious and unproblematic content, and was untroubled by the new powers being given to Canadian judges. His chief lieutenant, Justice Minister Jean Chrétien, took a slightly different, though still optimistic, view. Chrétien recognized that defining rights and their implications for policy could be a contentious and acrimonious process, but believed that assigning this task to the judiciary was an effective way to depoliticize it. "I think we are rendering a great service to Canada," Chrétien suggested in 1981, "by taking some of these problems away from the political debate and allowing the matter to be debated, argued, coolly before the courts with precedents and so on."[1]

Neither Trudeau's nor Chretien's sanguine expectations have been borne out by developments since 1982. Inevitably, disputes arose about the meaning and scope of rights and freedoms, which are set out in the Charter in broad, general terms, and the judiciary was called upon to settle these disputes. And, just as inevitably, the courts' decisions – contrary to Mr. Chrétien's expectations – turned out to be highly controversial. Sometimes the judges interpreted a right or freedom more narrowly than some had hoped, and sometimes more liberally than others had expected. In both cases, judicial decisions on the Charter became the stuff of politics.

If it is undeniable that the introduction of the Charter signaled the start of a new era in Canadian political life, it is also fair to characterize this as an important step in a long, evolutionary process rather than an abrupt change of course. For judges exercised considerable influence on the Canadian political scene well before the Charter came into effect. As in other common law countries, the judiciary had always played a law-making role through its interpretation of statutes and establishment of legal precedents. In the modern period, judges had been important players in policing the administrative state. They had also had occasion to strike down legislation on constitutional grounds in their capacity as referees of division of power disputes between the federal and provincial governments. In the Charter era, judicial power has been expanded further, as the courts are now responsible for interpreting a codified charter of rights, which has drawn them into sensitive areas of public policy involving important and contentious social values.

In making this transition, Canada has kept pace with a global trend that has been steadily gaining ground for several decades. Following World War II, there was a push throughout the Western world to ensure that the atrocities visited on the peoples of Europe and elsewhere would never recur by formally enshrining commitments to human rights. To that end, many European countries included bills of rights in their postwar constitutions. At the international level, covenants recognizing universal political and civil liberties, as well as social and economic rights, came into being. Canada was slow to follow suit with a domestic analogue until the Diefenbaker government passed the Canadian Bill of Rights in 1960. This, however, was an ordinary statute only, applying to federal, not provincial, areas of jurisdiction, and was therefore a relatively weak tool of rights enforcement. The patriation of the constitution with a Charter of Rights (and a new section, outside the Charter, recognizing and affirming the rights of aboriginal peoples) took the process further, as the rights of Canadians were constitutionally entrenched and made binding on both the federal and provincial governments. But the binding was not as tight as it might have been, as all the rights and freedoms in the Charter were subject to a general limitation clause (Section 1). Many, moreover, were subject to an override clause (Section 33) which allows legislatures to protect legislation from judicial review for a five-year period.

This attempt to strike a balance between judicial authority and legislative prerogative, a uniquely Canadian inspiration, has not kept the critics at bay. A lively debate has unfolded that is played out in this collection of essays. That debate is wide-ranging with important claims and issues at stake. There are, however, some elements of the post-1982 arrangement that are generally uncontentious. For most of the rights enumerated in the Charter, there is a core meaning and some basic policy implications on which virtually all Canadians would agree. It is at the periphery of rights definition that disagreements break out. Some critics find fault is in the expansion of rights to include interests and privileges that hardly seem inviolable, a process made possible by the general language in which Charter rights are necessarily expressed. Others take judges to task for shying away from broader interpretations that would bring more claims under the umbrella of rights protection. Both sets of critics sometimes question, though usually not simultaneously, whether judges alone should be responsible for rights enforcement or should share the task with elected officials more responsive to the popular will.

Different court decisions raise the ire of different groups. Feminists, for example, have been critical of rulings that have afforded persons accused of sexual assault access to victims' private records and sexual histories. Anti-smoking groups (and many others too) were appalled at the victory won by RJR-Macdonald in 1995, when it asked the Supreme Court to declare federal legislation restricting tobacco advertising unconstitutional on the grounds that it infringed on freedom of expression. Trade unions have decried rulings that have excluded their collective bargaining rights from the protections afforded by Charter's guarantee of freedom of association. Moral traditionalists railed at the 1998 *Vriend* decision, in which the Supreme Court instructed the Alberta government to include protection for homosexuals in its human rights legislation; while Aboriginal claims to territory and natural resources upheld by the courts have sometimes triggered angry reactions from non-native populations.

Traditionally inclined to keep to their chambers, judges have begun to defend themselves publicly against a barrage of negative publicity. In an interview two years back in *The Globe and Mail*, Antonio Lamer, Chief Justice of the Supreme Court at the time, voiced concern that "as a result of virulent or harsh comments by the press or the public, the most popular thing to do might become the outcome" in judicial rulings.[2] Of course, it is not only the public and press who have been giving judges a rough ride. In an odd incident – hardly typical but perhaps emblematic of the times – Alberta Court of Appeal Justice John McClung wrote a scathing letter to the *National Post* criticizing Madame Justice Claire L'Heureux Dubé for the commentary she had attached to the Supreme Court's 1999 ruling in the *Ewanchuk* case.[3] Though L'Heureux Dubé refrained from responding in kind, the episode nonetheless illustrated how difficult it has become for judges to remain above the fray. They speak out much more than in the past, generally avoiding comment on specific cases, but expounding at length on the general principles that guide them in their work. The judicialization of politics – the adjudication of contentious social issues by the courts – is engendering politicization of the judiciary, just as prescient observers had predicted in 1982.

While the courts have come under fire from critics located at different points on the political spectrum, in recent times it is those on the right who have been most outspoken. Leading the charge has been the Reform Party, now the Canadian Alliance, which contends that certain minority interests – homosexuals, feminists, and Aboriginals above all – are consistently winning favourable judgements that run counter to the will of the majority of Canadians. The Charter, which should be used simply to protect the basic democratic rights and freedoms that all Canadians value, has been stretched beyond recognition by a Canadian judiciary engaging in liberal and unwarranted interpretation. Judges are overstepping their bounds; steps must be taken to pull them back in line and make them more accountable to the Canadian public. Which brings us back to our initial query: are judges too powerful?

If the question is simple enough, the responses it engenders often are not. Many arguments have been marshalled on both sides of the debate and a wide range of evidence brought to bear. The Institute for Research on Public Policy, in the hopes of disseminating some of these perspectives more widely in order to facilitate constructive public debate, sought out leading experts in the field of judicial politics to provide their insights and commentary on this important issue. The result of this effort was a collection of essays, long and short, published at various points over the past couple of years. This material is now brought together in a single volume.

The book is divided into three sections. Part A contains two papers that provide useful background to the Canadian debate over judicial politics. Frederick Vaughan sets the stage with a succinct historical review of the Canadian Supreme Court, from its founding in 1875 to the present day. Kate Malleson, a British legal scholar, offers an overview of developments in Great Britain that led to the recent incorporation of the European Convention on Human Rights into British domestic law and outlines the anticipated impact on the role of the British judiciary. It is an interesting case for Canadians to consider since our political arrangements are so closely modelled on the Westminster system.

Part B contains a set of shorter essays that cut to the heart of the debate: has the judicial branch become too powerful, making policy decisions that are the rightful preserve of elected officials? These pieces, originally commissioned for IRPP's *Policy Options*, come from a distinguished group of academics and practitioners who offer their considered, and sometimes adamant, opinions on the matter. Two Supreme Court justices – Chief Justice Beverly McLachlin and former Justice Bertha Wilson – not surprisingly spring to the defence of judges everywhere by invoking some of the important principles that underpin and legitimize judicial authority. Lorraine Weinrib sides with the judges, defending the Charter as an embodiment of modern, progressive values reflecting basic principles dear to most Canadians. Others, including Rainer Knopff, Sébastien Lebel-Grenier and Pierre Patenaude, are unpersuaded, citing a host of problems with the dispensation established in 1982: the inability of courts to effect compromises between contending positions, the conflicted motivations that led to the adoption of the Charter in the first place, and the suspect interpretation of constitutional documents by an unbridled judiciary.

In the hopes of bridging the divide, Peter Hogg and Allison Thornton present an argument that has captured a good deal of attention lately. Neither courts nor legislatures, they contend, have the upper hand. Instead, the two are engaged in an ongoing dialogue that gives both some say about how rights will be respected in legislative decisions. Ted Morton responds with a more skeptical appraisal, suggesting that the dialogue is dominated by the courts and decidedly one-sided. Peter Russell and Preston Manning square off too, agreeing on certain basic reforms that would help assuage the concerns of court detractors, but differing over important details. In these conversations between judicial critics and sympathizers, many pivotal arguments are concisely presented. It is a valuable and substantial précis of the contending positions.

Part C presents a series of longer papers that originally appeared in IRPP's serial publication *Choices*. While these too do not shy from the broad normative issues that permeate any discussion of judicial politics, their primary focus is more empirical, their subject matter more narrow. Jacob Ziegel addresses the issue that is most often raised about the Supreme Court: the appointment procedure. Currently it is the Prime Minister, with counsel from selected advisors, who gives the nod to his preferred candidate. Ziegel, drawing on examples from other jurisdictions, argues that this method of selection should be supplemented with either a nominating committee, Parliamentary confirmation hearings, or both.

Janet Hiebert takes us inside the legislative branch of government to look at the efforts of elected officials to interpret and respect the Charter. Her analysis reveals that judges are not the only ones who are Charter-sensitive. It follows that it would be reasonable to assign legislatures a greater role in Charter interpretation and enforcement. Hiebert outlines ways this might be done.

The issue of interest group litigation is taken up by Gregory Hein, who reports the results of an exhaustive analysis of Federal and Supreme Court cases dating back to 1988. His findings run counter to common wisdom. It is not only aboriginals, gay rights groups, feminist organizations and other so-called special interests that turn to the courts. Instead, it turns out that many different groups, corporations chief among them, use litigation to pursue their goals. Hein's is a valuable counterpoint to prevailing wisdom on this important aspect of the debate.

Public opinion on the Charter of Rights and the role of the courts is the subject of Joseph Fletcher and Paul Howe's contribution to this volume. Drawing on a public opinion survey commissioned by IRPP, the authors discover that the criticisms directed at the judiciary, and played up by the media, have failed to resonate with the Canadian public at large. Canadians remain highly supportive of both the Charter and the role of the courts in ensuring its observance. It is an important point to bear in mind as the debate over judicial politics rages on among the chattering classes.

And finally, Howard Leeson provides a historical review and assessment of the notwithstanding clause. This clause, section 33 in the Charter, was meant to provide some of the balance advocated by court critics by allowing governments, for a period of five years, to keep in force legislation found to be inconsistent with the Charter. But for reasons that are not entirely clear, the clause has fallen into disuse. Leeson, who was a participant in the negotiations that led to the adoption of the Charter, recounts the discussions and debates around section 33 and offers his assessment on its future status.

In short, there is a variety of perspectives on offer in this collection and a diverse set of topics addressed. All, however, come back to the question of judicial power. Are judges too powerful and if so, what might be done about it? It is an issue that is unlikely to fade from public view anytime soon. Though some have been predicting a change of course for the Supreme Court under the new Chief Justice, Beverly McLachlin, an about-face seems unlikely. As elsewhere, the Canadian courts will go through periods of greater and lesser judicial restraint, but the presence of the Charter means there will always be cases coming down the pipeline that will generate significant controversy. As the debate continues to unfold, this collection should provide readers with a deeper understanding of the principles and perspectives shaping positions on both sides of the issue.

Paul Howe
Peter Russell

NOTES

1 Minutes of Proceedings and Evidence of the Special Committee of the Senate and of the House of Commons on the Constitution, Issue no. 48, Jan 29, 1981, p. 110.
2 Kirk Makin, "Lamer hits at judge-bashing," *The Globe and Mail*, February 6, 1999, p. A4.
3 *National Post*, February 26, 1999, p. A19.

Contributors

JOSEPH F. FLETCHER
Department of Political Science,
University of Toronto

GREGORY HEIN
Intergovernmental
Affairs Officer
Government of Ontario

JANET L. HIEBERT
Department of Political Studies
Queen's University

PETER W. HOGG
Dean, Osgoode Hall Law School,
York University

PAUL HOWE
Research Director
Institute for Research on
Public Policy

RAINER KNOPFF
Department of Political Science
University of Calgary

SÉBASTIEN LEBEL-GRENIER
Faculty of Law
Sherbrooke University

HOWARD LEESON
Department of Political
Science
University of Regina

KATE MALLESON
Department of Law
London School of Economics

HON. BEVERLEY MCLACHLIN
Supreme Court of Canada

E. PRESTON MANNING
Member of Parliament,
Calgary Southwest

F.L. MORTON
Department of Political
Science
University of Calgary

PIERRE PATENAUDE
Faculty of Law
Sherbrooke University

PETER H. RUSSELL
University Professor Emeritus
University of Toronto

ALLISON A. THORNTON
Blake, Cassels and Graydon

FREDERICK VAUGHAN
Department of Political Science
University of Guelph

LORRAINE EISENSTAT
WEINRIB
Faculty of Law
University of Toronto

HON. BERTHA WILSON
Scholar-in-residence
University of Ottawa

JACOB S. ZIEGEL
Professor of Law Emeritus
University of Toronto

PART A

Setting the Stage:
The Judiciary's Role in Canada
and Britain

Judicial Politics in Canada: Patterns and Trends

FREDERICK VAUGHAN

INTRODUCTION

In recent years Canadians have begun to hear dark warnings from edi-torial writers and academics about judges overreaching their authority. The Supreme Court of Canada, it is said, has become an "activist Court," especially since the adoption of the Canadian Charter of Rights and Freedoms in 1982. Indeed, it seems that hardly a day goes by without some comment or criticism to the effect that under the Charter courts are usurping the role of the legislatures. Rather than enunciating what the law is, the critics contend, the Supreme Court has begun to make law.[1] Some judges have overstepped their proper role, these writers say, by redefining (among other things) the nature of the family to include same-sex relationships and by striking down the Criminal Code regulations on abortion. The call to restrain judges from engaging in this kind of judicial activism has begun to reach a chorus. The Reform Party was especially quick to respond to this cho-rus and called for the establishment of a parliamentary committee to "review decisions of the Supreme Court and advise the House when any decision appears to violate the purpose for which Parliament passed legislation or the original intent of the Charter of Rights and Freedoms." In addition this parliamentary committee would "advise Parliament whether any legislative action is necessary, including the use of the notwithstanding clause, to restore the legislation or the ap-plication of the Charter to its original intent." Such a committee would also vet candidates for the Supreme Court in terms of their "qualifica-tions and judicial philosophy."[2]

The purpose of this paper is to present a descriptive account of judicial politics in Canada and to assess whether our courts, especially the Supreme Court of Canada, have become as activist as the critics suggest. Have our judges begun to impose their own values, through their interpretation of the law, in defiance of the will of the legislators who make the laws? This question has become critical since 1982 when the courts were handed the Charter of Rights and Freedoms which gave them a new and wider mandate in areas touching directly controversial matters of public policy. The *Constitution Act, 1982* obliges our judges to become more activist than previously. But have they gone too far in interposing their own private perceptions in contentious areas of public policy? I shall attempt to answer this question by, first, reviewing the role the courts have played throughout our history, as well as the events that led to the adoption in 1982 of the Canadian Charter of Rights and Freedoms. Second, I shall review the trends that have emerged since 1982 in several areas of public policy where the Supreme Court has rendered controversial judgments in applying the Charter to contemporary events.

THE COURTS AND THE CONSTITUTION OF 1867

What has come to be called "judicial activism" is little more than the sharp edge of what is known as "judicial review," i.e., the act by which judges assess the validity of legislation or government regulations. The term "judicial review" is American in origin and the practice has been, until recently, predominantly an American one. The judiciary under the American Constitution has assumed, since late in the nineteenth century, an expansive interpretation of the Bill of Rights and, hence, has generally been in the forefront of contentious public policy issues. But the history of the American practice of judicial review comes down to us steeped in controversy. It would be difficult to imagine Chief Justice John Marshall, the great defender of judicial review, party to such modern decisions as *Brown v. Board of Education* (1954), which set the contemporary court on the fast track to judicial supremacy.[3] The Supreme Court of Chief Justice Earl Warren and its reliance on "sociological jurisprudence" would never have appealed to Marshall. There has been a growing concern throughout the literature on the courts in the United States that judges have begun to usurp the role properly belonging to the legislators.[4]

Judges in Britain, by contrast with their American counterparts, have been by tradition more deferential to the will of Parliament. There are in fact no grounds (until the most recent legislation incorporating the

European Convention on Human Rights into British domestic law) for British courts to declare acts of Parliament unconstitutional or *ultra vires*. But this does not mean that British judges have been obliged to sit mute in the face of injustice. For the great Blackstone clearly enunciated the ancient rules of equity which oblige the judge to make up for defects of the law's application in specific cases; since laws by definition must be universal and expressed in general language, Blackstone noted, there runs the likelihood that a given law will be applied unjustly if not trimmed to suit the specific circumstances. But even here Blackstone cautioned restraint: "The liberty of considering all cases in an equitable light must not be indulged too far, lest thereby we destroy all law, and leave the decision of every question entirely in the breast of the judge. And law, without equity, though hard and disagreeable, is much more desirable for the public good than equity without law; which would make every judge a legislator, and introduce most infinite confusion; as there would then be almost as many different rules of action laid down in our courts, as there are differences of capacity and sentiment in the human mind."[5]

The Canadian courts have tended to follow the British tradition of restraint or deference. But because of the federal nature of Canada's constitution, with spheres of legislative jurisdiction divided between the two levels of government, our courts have always been more directly involved in the politics of the country than British courts. And there can be no disputing the fact that the Judicial Committee of the Privy Council (Canada's final court of appeal until 1949), played an "activist" role in re-ordering the terms of the Canadian constitution. Through a series of binding decisions, the Judicial Committee restricted the authority of Parliament to legislate for the "peace, order and good government of Canada," to matters of "emergency" or "national importance." At the same time it expanded the powers of the provinces to legislate in matters relating to "property and civil rights" and restricted the federal authority over "trade and commerce." To no one's surprise, the serious re-ordering of the terms of the *Constitution Act, 1867*, undertaken by the Judicial Committee, met with a mixture of approval and disapproval in many quarters throughout Canada, especially from those who thought that "Macdonald's constitution" was being eviscerated.[6] As W. P. M. Kennedy observed in the 1930s, the Judicial Committee refused to see in the *British North America Act, 1867*, "anything of a constitutional nature or to be guided by its historical origins...They have applied to it arbitrary rules of construction which have at times robbed it of its historical context and divorced its meaning from the intention of those who in truth framed it."[7] Very few commentators today subscribe to Kennedy's assessment of the work of the

Judicial Committee. For however questionable some of the Judicial Committee judgments have appeared to certain observers, it would be difficult to imagine Canada today being governed by a powerful Parliament armed with the authority to ride roughshod over the wishes of provincial legislatures. There can be no question, however, that it was the "judicial activism" of the Judicial Committee that re-ordered the terms of the Constitution Act, 1867, and gave our constitution a more genuinely federal character. In this sense, the courts, especially the Judicial Committee of the Privy Council, have been active in determining the scope and powers of our constitution from the very earliest years.

It is important to note that the criticisms directed at the Judicial Committee rarely challenged the right of that body to exercise judicial authority over cases arising under the terms of the Constitution Act, 1867. Indeed, the path Canada has followed from the very beginning, like almost every other federal state, has been to resolve disputes over jurisdiction through judicial review.[8] But as Canada emerged out of the shadows of the old colonial order, it was not long before voices were heard calling for a termination of appeals to the Judicial Committee. Those calls, however, were never to abandon the use of the courts as instruments of constitutional adjudication. Rather, they were to allow our own Canadian courts, especially the Supreme Court of Canada (established in 1875), to become the final court of appeal in all matters affecting Canadian disputes. These voices fell on deaf ears until the Judicial Committee ruled as *ultra vires* certain acts of the national parliament that were designed to lift the country out of the Great Depression. This proved to all, even to some of the most inveterate JCPC supporters, that Canadian courts comprised of Canadian judges with knowledge of Canadian problems must have the final say in important constitutional matters. As Howard McConnell has written: "After most of the New Deal statutes were invalidated by the Privy Council, the controversy passed from the judicial to the political forum and Canadians were confronted starkly with the question of whether they should – or could – establish an ultimate court of appeal in Canada."[9]

THE COURT AND ADVISORY OPINIONS

One of the great ironies of the Canadian debate over the role to be played by the courts of law in the constitutional life of the country is the fact that from the very earliest years there was the clear provision that the Governor in Council (the federal Cabinet) could refer virtually any matter to the Supreme Court for an "advisory opinion." Under rule 53 of the Supreme Court Act, the Supreme Court is required to answer all questions asked by the Governor in Council "as in the case of a judgment upon an appeal to the Court." The Court is granted "special jurisdiction" under this provision covering "important questions of law or fact" over a wide range of issues. This practice, known as the reference procedure, has been used many times from the earliest days up to and including the present government of Jean Chrétien. Indeed, between 1867 and 1966, 35 percent of all constitutional cases heard by the Supreme Court or the Judicial Committee were reference cases; between 1967 and 1986 the number dropped to 15 percent.[10]

The practice of referring cases to the courts for advisory opinions is not new in Anglo-Saxon jurisprudence. As Huffman and Seathoff have shown, there was a long history in English judicial practice of sending questions to the courts for their view.[11] Indeed, the *Judicial Committee Act, 1833*, specifically provided for such opinions.[12] However, the practice of referring questions to the Supreme Court of Canada was initially resisted, especially by the provinces. These concerns later abated partly because the provinces established their own reference procedures. A provincial government can refer a question – which can involve either federal or provincial legislation – to its own provincial court of appeal and appeal that judgment to the Supreme Court of Canada.

Given the provinces' early concerns, the matter was not finally resolved in favour of the practice until the Judicial Committee ruling in *Reference Appeal*[13] in 1912. Since that date it has, by and large, won the approval of constitutional commentators. As Peter Hogg has commented, "the reference procedure enables an early resolution of the constitutional doubt" on important occasions.[14] Hogg's only regret is that "the Court has not made sufficient use of its discretion not to answer a question posed on a reference."

By contrast with the United States, where the Supreme Court is restricted to considering actual cases arising under the Constitution,[15] our courts are virtually dragged into the political fray by the reference procedure. And, what is more, there appears to be no way the Court can refuse to hear reference cases, though, as Hogg has noted, it does have a measure of discretion to reject questions that are overtly political. The full Court must answer the questions put to it and do so expeditiously.

There can be little doubt that on most occasions reference cases have been very useful. But in a few notable cases they have been used to get our parliamentarians out of embarrassing or difficult positions, as we see briefly in several instances. The Criminal Law Amendment Act, 1968–69, contained the provision for a person accused of drunk driving to obtain a sample of his or her breath for purposes of self-defense. The Act stated that the accused was to be given a sample "in an approved container." This provision was intended to provide an accused person the means of obtaining independent analysis for purposes of self-defence. Unfortunately, the government of the day was unable to come up with an "approved container," as prescribed by section 120. So when it promulgated the Act, the government simply deleted the provision requiring the police to provide the sample. Thus the final Act lacked the safeguard guaranteeing an accused the means of self-defense as intended by Parliament. Civil libertarians throughout the country poured scorn on Justice Minister John Turner. Turner responded by sending the case to the Supreme Court on reference. Turner asked the Court whether the government could promulgate the Act without the protection of section 120. This only aggravated the matter because there was a case in the courts of British Columbia challenging the breathalyzer law on the grounds that it violated the Canadian Bill of Rights. Turner did not ask the Court whether the failure to enact section 120 of the Act violated the Bill of Rights. Many Canadian civil libertarians thought that this failure was critical.

To the surprise of many Canadians the Supreme Court of Canada (which included the great civil libertarians Emmett Hall and Bora Laskin) ruled in favour of the Minister of Justice. The federal government has never, to this day, made an effort to find an "approved container." And thus Canadians accused of drunk driving remain without recourse to a sample by which they might defend themselves as Parliament had intended. Canadians can only guess what the outcome might have been had the British Columbia case been permitted to make its way to the Supreme Court and assessed on its merits under the Canadian Bill of Rights.

In 1980, the federal government under Prime Minister Pierre Trudeau was determined to bring about a constitutional amendment that, among other things, would permit Canadians to amend the British North America Act, 1867 without going to Westminster. And Trudeau made it clear that he was prepared to proceed unilaterally, without provincial approval. He was adamantly opposed by eight provincial governments. Three – Manitoba, Newfoundland and Quebec – referred the question of unilateral patriation to their courts of appeal. The results were mixed and confusing. All three appeals to the Supreme Court of Canada were consolidated into one. The Court rendered its judgment on September 28, 1981. It ruled that by going to Westminster without the unanimous consent of the provinces, the federal government would be acting legally but *unconstitutionally*, in the conventional sense. Armed with this decision, Trudeau reconvened the provincial premiers at a federal-provincial conference in November. The result of these new consultations was (over Quebec's opposition) the Constitution Act, 1982, complete with a Charter of Rights and Freedoms which armed our judges with new constitutionally entrenched powers to oversee legislation both federal and provincial.

And finally, in the 1998 reference to the Supreme Court on Quebec secession, the Court's decision served both to defuse a climate of constitutional uncertainty and to put a little order into ensuing discussions and debates concerning Quebec's right to secede from the federal union. In many respects, it was a model of how the reference procedure can work to defuse important, contentious constitutional disputes. The Canadian constitution says nothing about the right of a province to secede from the confederation. Hence a debate arose throughout the country concerning the Parti Québécois government's plan to press ahead with secession after a favourable referendum vote. The Supreme Court ruled that the constitution did not allow a province to secede unilaterally, that is, "without principled negotiation with other participants in Confederation within the existing constitutional framework."[16] The Court further ruled that a vote favouring secession, "by however strong a majority, would have no legal effect on its own and could not push aside the principles of federalism and the rule of law, the rights of individuals and minorities, or the operation of democracy in the other provinces or in Canada as a whole."[17] At the same time, the Court noted that "A clear majority vote in Quebec on a clear question in favour of secession would confer democratic legitimacy on the secession initiative which all of the other participants in Confederation would have to recognize."[18] As to what constituted a clear majority and a clear question and what form negotiations would take, the Court threw those matters back to the politicians.

Despite the muted dissatisfaction with the reference procedure that continues to emerge from time to time in the legal literature there is no indication that the Parliament of Canada is about to amend the Supreme Court Act in the near future to eliminate rule 53. All the evidence points to the continued use of this device especially in controversial constitutional matters. The Supreme Court showed in both the patriation and the Quebec secession references that it could serve a very useful function in controversial matters.

In sum, while Canadian courts in the past demonstrated a pattern of judicial deference to the will of the legislature, their role in division of powers and reference cases did offer some scope for an early judicial activism of sorts. Thus, the judiciary has always played an important role in the constitutional life of the country, though in the past it did so anonymously, and judges only rarely met with criticism. But the quiet and anonymous life of judging in Canada began to change with the introduction of the Bill of Rights in 1960 and, especially, with the adoption of the constitutional Charter of Rights and Freedoms in 1982.

THE AFTERMATH OF WAR AND THE PUSH
FOR A BILL OF RIGHTS: 1945–1960

With the end of World War II there arose throughout the entire Western world a call for judicial enforcement of basic political and civil liberties. The Nuremberg trials of the principal Nazi criminals and the increasingly outrageous details of the Holocaust drove public sentiment in the direction of codes or bills of rights that national governments would judicially enforce.[19] This movement was encouraged by the adoption of the Universal Declaration of Human Rights in 1949 by the United Nations. Canada and Canadians were not immune from these international sentiments. Indeed, most Canadians were confident throughout the 1950s and 1960s that they were in the forefront of the movement to foster human rights. Many of the provinces responded within their own jurisdictions by adopting "human rights" codes. Some, such as Ontario, went so far as to undertake a formal judicial inquiry into the condition of human rights in the province.[20] It comes as a shock, therefore, to learn that the Canadian federal government under Louis St. Laurent and other ranking members of the federal Liberal Cabinet were deeply suspicious of statutory codes of rights and judicial enforcement. According to archival documents recently uncovered by William Schabas, of the Université du Québec à Montréal, "the real story was that there was a conscious strategy within the Canadian government to obstruct the universal declaration." Contrary to the official line that Canadians were fed by the Department of External Affairs, "the new documents show that the role Canada played was more subversive than supportive, with little if any regard for human rights in the External Affairs Department at the time."[21] Quebec Premier, Maurice Duplessis, was especially reluctant to sign on to a document guaranteeing freedom of speech and peaceful assembly, rights that ran the risk of threatening his province's determination to restrict the activities of groups such as the Jehovah's Witnesses. So the Department of External Affairs under Lester Pearson put it out that Canada's resistance to the Declaration in the draft stages arose out of concern over the invasion of provincial jurisdiction. Canada was finally cajoled into signing the final document once it was made clear that not to do so would place Canada with those nations, like the Soviet Union, who had made "human rights" a dirty term. Canada's reluctance to become a signatory to the United Nations instrument guaranteeing basic human rights reveals the depth of suspicion that existed throughout the higher levels of the Canadian political and civil service establishment of the day, a suspicion that was to resurface later in attempts to secure a domestic bill of rights.

In the late 1940s, members of the Canadian bar began to urge the adoption of a constitutional charter of rights modeled on the United Nations Charter. This appeal was stimulated in no small way by such matters as the wartime handling of Japanese-Canadians and concern over the National Emergency Transitional Powers Act of 1945, which declared that a condition of emergency still existed throughout Canada giving the federal Cabinet all the draconian powers it had under the War Measures Act. A furore erupted when it became clear that the government was prepared secretly to interrogate and detain citizens without access to the legal protections guaranteed by the common law.[22]

The concern for the rights and liberties of Canadians has remained an issue since that time. John G. Diefenbaker entered Parliament in 1945 with the promise to have Parliament enact a bill of rights preventing the infringement of basic civil rights. The debate in the law reviews and the public press reached a peak in the 1950s with three cases from Quebec involving freedom of speech, religious liberty and the right of peaceful assembly, the famous "Padlock cases."[23] In these cases, the Supreme Court wrestled nobly with the basic issues of civil liberties but appeared handicapped by the absence of clear statutory authority by which to strike down patently unacceptable government actions to restrict the rights of citizens. It was becoming evident by the late 1950s that a groundswell of support existed for a federal bill of rights. John Diefenbaker swept to power in the general elections of 1957 and 1958 with a promise to enact a such a bill.

THE CANADIAN BILL OF RIGHTS: 1960–1982

Despite opposition within his own party, Diefenbaker's determination won out and on August 8, 1960 the Parliament of Canada unanimously adopted The Canadian Bill of Rights. The unanimous vote is often trotted out as confirmation of the depth of support for the Bill of Rights, but the record shows that suspicion or fear of a statutory bill of rights still lingered, for almost 60 members of Parliament absented themselves from the vote on third reading of the bill. They simply could not bring themselves to vote in favour of the document, but they feared for their reputations in voting against a bill supporting basic rights of citizens in a democracy.

The Diefenbaker Bill of Rights was a pale imitation of the bill desired by many Canadian civil libertarians, for it applied only to federal areas of jurisdiction. The provincial and municipal levels of government were formally excluded from the reach of the act, an important omission since many of the issues that fall under the category of political and civil liberties lie within provincial areas of jurisdiction. As well, the terms of the Bill of Rights were ambiguous and imprecise; they did not give the courts the explicit authority to strike down offending practices or legislation. The Act simply enjoined the courts of Canada to "construe and apply" offending legislation "so as not to offend the terms of the Act." All in all, the Bill was ridiculed by legal specialists as virtually useless.

And so it proved to be with one notable exception: the *Drybones* case of 1970.[24] In this case the Supreme Court of Canada for the first time struck down a provision of a federal statute – the Indian Act of 1947, which had made it an offence for a native person to be drunk off a reserve. The Court ruled that the provision offended the equality guarantees of the Canadian Bill of Rights. Canadian civil libertarians celebrated this decision as the harbinger of things to come. But such was not to be the case. For the Supreme Court soon retreated into a more passive disposition and never used the Bill of Rights as effectively again. Indeed, the author of the *Drybones* decision, Chief Justice John Cartwright, formally repudiated the line of reasoning he had taken in that case in *Robertson and Rosetanni v The Queen*.[25] Thus, Canada's first efforts to extend judicial protection to basic civil liberties were less than impressive.

Growing dissatisfaction with the Supreme Court under the Bill of Rights fueled the call for a new one that would give our courts a clearer mandate to strike down acts of Parliament which were in violation of basic civil liberties. But there was another force, too frequently overlooked, moving Canadian public opinion toward more judicial protection of civil liberties. The central role being played by judges in the United States during the early years of the civil rights movement and the ensuing television coverage available to Canadians contributed in no small part toward public acceptance of a more directly involved judiciary. Lawyers and judges were seen as the white knights of the downtrodden. It was television through fictional and factual accounts of lawyers and judges championing the cause of civil liberties – from "Perry Mason" to court-ordered school integration – that prepared the Canadian public for an increased role for our judges. As well, operating at another level, was the influence of those academic lawyers who had pursued their graduate studies in the United States during the heyday of the civil rights movement. These teachers, returning to Canada, did much to sensitize future lawyers and judges to the benefits of judicial protection of basic rights and the virtues of a written constitutional bill of rights.

THE MOVEMENT TO ENTRENCH THE CHARTER

Pierre Trudeau, as Minister of Justice, seized the occasion with the promise to entrench a bill of rights, one that would not only cover the

actions of the federal government but the provincial spheres of jurisdiction as well. Needless to say Trudeau's efforts to carry out this
project over the next decade and a half were greeted with a flurry of
controversy. Many in the press and in the academy came out with guns
blazing. Those who opposed the Bill of Rights of 1960 rose to denounce Trudeau's efforts to entrench a bill of rights in the Constitution. But this time the Canadian Bar Association put its considerable
weight behind entrenchment (previously, most members of the Association were unenthusiastic about involving the court in such matters).[26]
As J.-G. Castel, editor of *The Canadian Bar Review* wrote soon after the
adoption of the new constitution in 1982: "...in recent years, the
federal government and many of those concerned with human rights,
especially the Canadian Bar Association, came to the conclusion that
the best way to protect basic rights and freedoms including minority
rights was to entrench them in the Constitution."[27]

The public and academic debates over the Trudeau Charter of Rights
predictably brought out all the arguments that greeted the Diefenbaker
Bill of Rights two decades previous. The general thrust of the opponents was the same: a statutory bill of rights would increase the power
of judges and would result in "judicial supremacy"; it would also infringe upon the duty of parliamentarians to be the champions of rights
and freedoms. The old critics were more adamant than ever because
they viewed the new Charter as a certain step in the direction of the
"judicialization of politics" in Canada. There can be no mistake about
it, the new Charter of Rights and Freedoms was a considerably more
powerful instrument than the old Bill of Rights, for the Charter was
constitutionally entrenched, becoming a formal part of "the fundamental law of the land," and gave judges the power to declare offending acts
and procedures "unconstitutional." As Mr. Justice Gerald La Forest
wrote shortly after the adoption of the Charter, "[W]e really entered
into a new stage of constitutional development when the Charter became law, a stage that will involve a new way of looking at law and the
rights of the individual."[28]   But La Forest did not believe that our
judges would use the new Charter as actively as American judges have
done. He was persuaded that they would be constrained both by the
Canadian psyche and the inherited British tradition of restraint.

The essential differences between the Bill of Rights and the Charter
of Rights and Freedoms cannot be over-emphasized; they are formida-
ble and important. The latter gave the Court a much broader and powerful role in the protection of fundamental rights and freedoms. The
first important difference between the two instruments is that the
Charter is a formal part of the Constitution and can be amended only
by the explicit amending formulas contained in the Constitution. As

well, it extends to all governments, federal, provincial and municipal, unlike the Bill of Rights which covered only the federal area of jurisdiction. Furthermore, the terms and language of the Charter are stronger than the Bill of Rights and give judges a clearer mandate to strike down as unconstitutional acts of Parliament and legislatures and their agents, something they never had so explicitly before.

The Charter's judicial mandate, however, is formally circumscribed by two legislative "escape hatches": section 1 states that "The Canadian Charter of Rights and Freedoms guarantees the rights and freedoms set out in it subject only to such reasonable limits prescribed by law as can be demonstrably justified in a free and democratic society." And section 33 permits Parliament or a legislature to "expressly declare in an Act of Parliament or of the legislature...that the Act or a provision thereof shall operate notwithstanding a provision included in section 2 or sections 7 to 15 of this Charter." It goes without saying that the courts have a role in determining whether any limits on rights under section 1 are "demonstrably justified." Indeed, the Court has already laid down the basic ground rules for section 1 adjudication. In *R v. Oakes*,[29] the Supreme Court set down a two-step test that governments must meet: The government must show that the exemption is justified by a "pressing and substantial" objective; and the legislative means chosen must be "proportional" to the objective. The "notwithstanding" clause, on the other hand, provides for no judicial scrutiny.

These "escape hatches," however, have not resulted in a deferential Court. Despite the fact that the Supreme Court has on occasion upheld the use of section 1, it has not, as we shall see, shied away from a vigorous application of the Charter. At the same time, the Parliament of Canada and the provincial legislatures have been generally reluctant to use the notwithstanding clause. Politicians at both levels of government tend to feel that the people at large do not want them to avail themselves of this provision too readily.

THE COURT AND THE NEW MANDATE: 1982—PRESENT

The new mandate given to the Court in 1982, it must be remembered, was a major part of Trudeau's vision to unify Canadians around a distinctly Canadian concept of citizenship. In no small part this movement was designed to defuse the nationalist sentiment in Quebec by articulating a pan-Canadian national identity and by drawing the attention of all Canadians to a "higher" set of values. Americans had their Bill of Rights, now Canadians would have their very own Charter of Rights and Freedoms. And all evidence points to the enthusiastic popular acceptance of the Charter. No matter how controversial some Charter decisions have been, there can be no question that Canadians have embraced the Charter. Clearly, the Charter has provided Canadians with an indigenous point of national coalescence.

But the Charter has also, of course, increased the power of the judiciary. By way of a brief statistical overview of Supreme Court decisions and a look at a few equality cases and legal rights cases, we shall see how aggressively the Court has begun to embrace its mandate under the Charter.

Statistical Trends since 1982

As Peter Russell has pointed out, "Statistics about courts and judges can at best give only an indication of broad trends in the work of the courts and the inclinations of judges."[30] But such studies do help to show overall trends in the "success" or "failure" of the various items in the Charter, keeping in mind that a litigant's "failure" can be a "win" for the people at large, or *vice versa*. A statistical review of the "success rate" of Charter cases goes a long way to dispelling the notion that the Court has gotten out of hand since the Charter's introduction and needs to be reined in. For the statistics show that, despite an initial burst of activity in the early years, the Court has not been wielding the Charter as a broad sword.

When the Charter was adopted in 1982, some observers thought that it would transform the Supreme Court of Canada into a "Charter court"; that it would deflect the Court's attention away from its traditional role as referee of the Canadian federal system; that the Charter would unleash a flood of litigation so as to overwhelm the Court's docket. The annual statistics for the Supreme Court's docket from 1982 to 1992 show a different pattern: only 18 percent of the decisions rendered by the Court were Charter decisions. That number includes a low of zero percent for 1982 [when there were no Charter cases] through a high of 31 percent in 1990. All in all, looking back over the past 14 years of Supreme Court decisions, the Charter has accounted for just under 25 percent of the Court's work.[31] The most recent statistical study reveals a remarkable continuity in the Court's workload: "Actions of executive branch officers, mainly the police, rather then legislation continue to be the target of just under one-half of the Charter challenges coming before the Court."[32] This no doubt reflects, as Russell remarks, "the fact that two-thirds of Charter cases involve the legal rights sections of the Charter."[33] Overall, the success rate of 31 percent is higher in legal rights cases (Charter sections 7 to 14) than in fundamental freedoms (section 2) or equality rights (section 15) cases, where the success rates are 20 percent and 22 percent respectively. The overall success rate of Charter cases over the years from 1991 to 1997 is 31 percent.[34] The statistics also show another more or less consistent trend: "the four most frequently litigated Charter provisions at the Supreme Court level are section 7 (principles of fundamental justice), section 8 (search and seizure), section 10(b) (right to counsel), and section 11(d) (right to an independent and impartial tribunal)."[35]

Big M Drug Mart and "Purpose" and "Effect"

Despite the fact that quantitative analyses tend to show that the Court has been reasonably restrained in its Charter decisions, there can be no denying that in a number of cases it has been very active. But this should come as no surprise, for from the very beginning of the Charter's life the Supreme Court justices themselves understood that they were called upon to exercise a new and more active role in the life of the nation. In the very first Charter decision, Justice Estey observed that "with the Constitution Act, 1982 comes a new dimension, a new yardstick of reconciliation between the individual and the community and their respective rights."[36] And as Justice McLachlin said in an address to law students several years later: "The Charter...has changed the life of judges dramatically."[37] She went on to say that "the Court will take an expansive approach to defining the rights and freedoms guaranteed by the Charter and will not hesitate to tackle substantive issues even where limiting their role to procedural concerns is a viable alternative."

On the bench, both Justice Bertha Wilson and Chief Justice Brian Dickson served notice in one of the early Charter cases – Big M Drug Mart[38] in 1985 – of exactly how the Court would look at matters raised under the new mandate. Big M Drug Mart challenged the federal Lord's Day Act which prevented the company from opening its stores for business on Sundays. Big M Drug Mart argued that it was being forced by the statute to close on a designated Christian day of worship and that this violated the "the right to be free from conforming to religious dogma,"[39] guaranteed by the Canadian Charter of Rights and Freedoms. Chief Justice Dickson in a majority judgment ruled, after a lengthy review of Lord's Day Acts or their equivalent, to strike down the federal statute.[40] In doing so, he noted that the Charter would be interpreted with a view to evaluating an impugned statute in terms of its *purpose* and *effect*. "Either an unconstitutional purpose or an unconstitutional effect can invalidate legislation," he explained.[41] Justice Wilson picked up on this and elaborated: "In my view, the constitutional entrenchment of civil liberties in the Canadian Charter of Rights and

Freedoms necessarily changes the analytic approach the courts must adopt in such cases....While it remains perfectly valid to evaluate the purpose underlying a particular enactment in order to determine whether the legislature has acted within its constitutional authority in division of powers terms, the Charter demands evaluation of the impingement of even *intra vires* legislation on the fundamental rights and freedoms of the individual." She concluded that "placing the analytic focus on the effect of legislation impugned under the Charter rather than on its purpose will impose a less heavy evidentiary burden on the plaintiff. Once the plaintiff can point to an actual or potential impingement on a protected right, it will not matter that the underlying legislative purpose is subject to conjecture. In this case at bar the effect of the Lord's Day Act is to compel adherence to the Christian Sabbath by requiring the uniform observance of the day chosen by the Christian religion as a day of rest. It is this effect which infringes upon the freedom of conscience and religion guaranteed by the Charter."[42]

Equality and the Charter

One of the most important cases decided by the Supreme Court under the Charter, which had wide implications for public policy and which caused considerable public reaction, was the *Morgentaler (1988)* case.[43] The Court majority led by Chief Justice Dickson and Madame Justice Wilson agreed that the Criminal Code provisions restricting access to abortion to therapeutic abortion committees of hospitals violated a woman's right to security of the person. The Court ruled on procedural grounds and explicitly invited the Parliament of Canada to come up with a more equitable law. The effect of *Morgentaler* was to make Canada the only western nation not to have laws governing abortion.

The purpose of the Supreme Court's judgment in *Morgentaler* was clearly to return the issue of the regulation of abortion to Parliament to rewrite the legislation. Parliament attempted to do so in 1991, but the Criminal Code amendment which passed the House of Commons was defeated in the Senate on a tie vote. Thus, the failure to provide regulations governing abortion procedures cannot be laid, in the final analysis, at the door of the Court; Parliament has failed to act to correct the mistakes of the impugned legislation. In this instance, at least, it would appear that the "activism" of the Court simply reflects Parliament's willingness to sometimes let the Supreme Court make difficult public policy decisions.

If one looks, however, at Charter section 15 cases, such as equality between the sexes, gay rights, and so forth, one begins to see a pattern if not exactly a trend. In the first instance, the Parliament of Canada deliberately left out sexual orientation from the enumerated items protected by the Charter. The Supreme Court, however, in *Egan v. Canada* read homosexuality into the Charter's "equal benefit of the law" provision on the grounds that "sexual orientation...falls within the ambit of section 15 protection as being analogous to the enumerated grounds."[44] And very recently the same Court overturned the Alberta appeal court decision and read homosexuality into the Alberta Individual Rights Protection Act despite the fact that on two distinct occasions the Alberta legislature, after debating the matter at length, formally voted to exclude homosexuality from the reach of the IRPA. What was especially notable about the *Vriend* decision was the fact that the Supreme Court ruled that a legislative *omission* bears judicial disapproval on the same basis as the legislature's positive acts. In other words, according to the Court, the legislature can offend the Charter by failing to do something just as much as it can offend the Charter by an explicit act of legislation. The Supreme Court majority led by Justices Cory and Iacobucci argued that by excluding sexual orientation from the IRPA, the Alberta legislature sent a message to the community that it was acceptable to discriminate against people on the grounds of sexual orientation. Nor, said the Court, was the breach of section 15(1) of the Charter saved by the "reasonable grounds" provision of section 1. As a remedy, the Court ordered that sexual orientation be "read into" the IRPA. But this was not the only time that the Supreme Court has ruled on the failure of a public body to act. In *Eldridge v. British Columbia*, the Court held unanimously that the failure to provide sign language interpretation for deaf patients violated the equality provisions of the Charter. In cases where an identifiable group claims unequal treatment, gays and deaf people in these two instances, the Supreme Court has shown a tendency to use the Charter as an instrument to correct the matter.

It is interesting to note in connection with the *Vriend* decision that when Alberta Premier Ralph Klein mused publicly that he might invoke the "notwithstanding" clause of the Charter, he quickly withdrew his threat when the public proved to be unsupportive. The negative reaction by the people of Alberta to the use of the notwithstanding clause seems to point to a general reluctance of the public to support the use of the override provision of the Charter. Calls by the Reform party for the federal government to use the notwithstanding clause to overturn a British Columbia court decision involving the possession of child pornography were likewise met with mixed reaction, if not outright public disapproval. Something is clearly happening in public opinion in this matter: there seems to be some concern about judicial activism, while at the same time there is a general reluctance to see governments move in too quickly to curb court activists by way of the notwithstanding clause.[45]

Those skeptical of the new role of the courts since 1982 perhaps realize that judges are not wholly to blame. When one looks at the Charter mandate given to the courts, what can one expect but that judges would interpret their mandate in a generous or liberal manner? After all, the Charter imposes a duty on judges to uphold the "equal protection and benefit of the law," a phrase that is at best general, at worst vague. And, as Chief Justice Antonio Lamer himself has said, the Supreme Court of Canada is "struggling" under the burden of trying to interpret the equality provisions of the Charter of Rights and Freedoms. "If you read the judgments coming out of this court," the Chief Justice said very recently, "I think it is apparent that we are struggling....And the courts below are struggling. There is so much social impact....How far do we go in terms of seeing that everyone is equal?"[46] There can be little doubt that it is in the area of equality rights that the Court, on its own admission, has created a certain confusion.[47] In the now famous "equality rights trilogy" of cases of 1995 – *Miron, Egan,* and *Thibaudeau* – the Court left a cloud of confusion, for "there is no clear majority position in these cases," as one critic noted.[48] In *Miron,* a case where a common-law spouse sought the benefits of her injured husband's insurance policy, the Court ruled that the "exclusion of unmarried partners from accident benefits...violates section 15(1) of the Charter."[49] Yet in *Egan,* a case involving a same-sex relationship, the Court ruled that while "sexual orientation" is protected by section 15, the denial of spousal benefits was not a form of discrimination.[50] And in *Thibaudeau,* the Court held that the requirement that child support payments be declared as income does not violate section 15(1) of the Charter: single custodial parents are not discriminated against by the Income Tax Act.[51]

Justices of the Supreme Court itself have attempted to resolve what Justice L'Heureux-Dubé has called "the divergent approaches" to section 15. She has urged her colleagues to revisit the "fundamental purpose of section 15 and...to seek out a means by which to give full effect to this fundamental purpose."[52] The divergence among the judges was somewhat mitigated by three equality cases of 1997 in which the Court clearly made an effort to come to a clearer perception of what offends the equality section of the Charter.[53] In *Eaton v. Brant,*[54] a unanimous Supreme Court ruled that the Brant county school board did not violate the equality provision of the Charter by placing a child in a special education class because the child did not suffer any adverse affects despite the fact that he was being treated differently. And in *Eldridge v. British Columbia,* the Court ruled that the failure of the BC Medical

Services Commission to provide sign language interpreters violated the Charter because the child suffered adversely from the failure to provide the service. In *Benner v. Canada (Secretary of State)*,[55] the Court considered the case of a man required to undergo a security check before being granted Canadian citizenship since he was born before February, 15, 1977 and his mother was a Canadian citizen. If his father had been a Canadian citizen he would not have been required to undergo the security check. The Court ruled unanimously that the itizenship Act[56] violated section 15 of the Charter.

Legal Rights

While it can be said that, in many respects, cases arising under section 15, "equality rights," have proven to be the most difficult for the Court and have received the most publicity, the majority of Charter cases coming to the Court have arisen under the provisions guaranteeing "legal rights." All statistical studies of the Court's workload testify to this.[57] One hundred and forty-three out of one hundred and ninety-five Charter cases between 1982 and 1992 were legal rights cases. A review of these cases shows that the Court has not hesitated to use the legal rights provisions of the Charter "to develop new constitutional codes of conduct for Canadian police officers."[58] But despite the preponderance of activity in this area of the law and the impact on policing in Canada, the general public has been relatively undisturbed by these developments. By contrast, the United States Supreme Court rulings in *Escobedo v. Illinois (1964)*[59] and *Miranda v. Arizona (1966)*,[60] touching the right to counsel and self-incrimination, occasioned a flurry of public anger.[61]

The Canadian Charter of Rights and Freedoms protects a wide range of legal rights under sections 7 to 14: everything from "life, liberty and the security of the person," through "unreasonable search and seizure" and "the presumption of innocence" to the "right to the assistance of an interpreter." In addition, legal rights under the Charter have arisen under analogous federal criminal statutes, such as the Criminal Code and the Narcotics Control Act.

It should come as no surprise, therefore, that so much litigation arises under this lengthy list of protections and guarantees. In many respects, the Charter has provided judges at all levels of the Canadian judiciary with a new set of tools with which to make a difference in criminal matters, even to prompt major changes in criminal procedure. But no level of the judiciary has responded to this new challenge more enthusiastically than the Supreme Court of Canada, especially in the early years. In *Hunter v. Southam*,[62] just two years after the adoption of the Charter, the Court struck down a provision of the Combines Investigation Act as "unreasonable search and seizure," ruling that the officer authorizing the searches was not sufficiently independent of the investigatory authority and that the grounds for the search were too weak. And in *Therens*,[63] the next year, the Supreme Court ruled that breathalyzer evidence obtained from an accused who had not been advised of his right to counsel could not be used against him at trial. The following year, the Supreme Court threw out a murder conviction because the accused was too intoxicated to appreciate the consequences of her waiving the right to counsel.[64] And in *Oakes*[65] the same year, the Court nullified a twenty-five year old provision of the Narcotics Control Act on the grounds that it shifted the burden of proof in some instances to the accused. A year later in *Manninen*[66] the Court quashed a robbery conviction because the police had not offered the accused a telephone when he asked to consult with his lawyer.

In cases involving an accused person's right to counsel and not to be compelled to testify against himself or herself, the Supreme Court has been especially innovative. In *R v. Hebert (1990)*,[67] for example, the Court ruled that since the accused was tricked into making incriminating statements to an undercover police agent, the statement was obtained in breach of section 7 of the Charter. The Court effectively created a new right not enunciated in the Charter, on the basis of the section 7 provision relating to "the principles of fundamental justice." The Court ruled that the "right to silence" was a "basic tenet of the legal system."[68]

Nor was the Court reluctant to come to grips with highly contentious issues such as the "rape shield" provisions of the Criminal Code. Rape shield provisions prevent a person charged with sexual assault from cross-examining a complainant about her past sexual activity. In *Seaboyer*[69] the Supreme Court ruled that the rape shield provision of the Criminal Code violated both section 7 and section 11(d) of the Charter guaranteeing an accused "the right to full answer and defence." The outcry among feminists groups over this decision resulted in Parliament replacing the Criminal Code rape shield provisions with even tougher ones. In an attempt to meet the Supreme Court's ruling in *Seaboyer*, however, the new law gives the trial judge discretion to include or exclude evidence from the past sexual history of the complainant.

Finally, when one looks at criminal matters in the Canadian courts one finds a certain confusion. The Supreme Court of Canada upheld the breathalyzer law and has consistently upheld the reverse onus features of Canadian criminal law relating to drunk driving offences.[70] The Court has been willing to allow random spot checks for drunk drivers – which clearly violate section 9 of the Charter guaranteeing that no one should be "arbitrarily detained" – as a "reasonable limit" and "demonstratively justified." And the Supreme Court recently upheld the right of teachers to search without a warrant students and their lockers for drugs.[71] Yet in a British Columbia case involving police searches the Court sent back for retrial an accused on the grounds that the police failed to get a search warrant before entering the man's house. In this case, the police followed a trail of blood to the accused person's residence. Prior to the Charter, the Court would have allowed the search on probable grounds. The Court ruled, however, that the police are required by the Charter provisions relating to search and seizure to obtain a warrant. This and other Court rulings have led Harvie and Foster to conclude that "the Canadian Supreme Court has created broader procedural protections for the accused than now exist in United States jurisprudence."[72]

CONCLUSION

The foregoing review reveals that Canadian courts, while always prominent in the Canadian political process, have indeed, become more "activist" since the advent of the Charter. And the general public, due to a greater press coverage, has become more vocal in its criticism of the courts. On several recent occasions Canadians have become emotionally excited over judicial rulings such as the British Columbia Supreme Court's decision relating to the possession of child pornography,[73] as well as the Supreme Court of Canada's recent ruling in *Ewanchuk*, where the Court overturned two lower court decisions upholding "implied consent" in a sexual assault case. Not a few women writers, such as Lysiane Gagnon and Barbara Amiel, heaped scorn on the *Ewanchuk*[74] judgment. Wrote Gagnon: "It is absurd to believe, as the court does, that human sexuality is black and white and that there is no 'third option' between 'yes' and 'no'; absurd to expect that consent must be given at every step even if a woman sends out positive signals....absurd to assume that there can never be implied consent in the complex dance of seduction."[75]

  The only thing one can say about trends in judicial activism in the Supreme Court of Canada is that there is emerging a consistent trend towards a liberal judicial philosophy, especially in matters relating to abortion, feminist causes, sexual orientation and the protection of the criminally accused. These advocacy areas have, clearly, benefitted most from the application of the Charter. The general conclusion to be drawn from this review is that the "Charter has served as a catalyst for a new era of judicial activism unparalleled in

Canadian history." But it is difficult yet to agree that this activism has been "on a par with contemporary American practice."[76] We can safely say that the Supreme Court of Canada has emerged after a decade and a half of Charter litigation less aggressive than it first signaled in the early years, but nevertheless prepared to strike out boldly on occasion. One thing is certain, as long as the Charter of Rights and Freedoms remains a part of our constitution and central to the mandate of the Supreme Court of Canada, the Court will continue to be active in shaping the character of Canadian society.

NOTES

1 The leading critic of the Supreme Court's activism is F. L. Morton, a political scientist at the University of Calgary. See his "The Charter of Rights: Myth and Reality," in *After Liberalism: Essays in Search of Freedom, Virtue, and Order*, William D. Gairdner (ed.) (Toronto: Stoddart, 1998), p. 33.

2 See Preston Manning, "Parliament, Not Judges, Must Make the Laws of the Land," *Globe and Mail*, June 16, 1998, p. A23.

3 See, Gary McDowell, *Equity and the Constitution* (Chicago: The University of Chicago Press, 1982).

4 See, Mitchell Muncy (ed.), *The End of Democracy? The Judicial Usurpation of Politics* (Dallas: Spence Publishing, 1998).

5 George Sharswood (ed.), *Blackstone's Commentaries on the Laws of England* (Philadelphia: George W. Childs, 1866), p. 62.

6 See Eugene Forsey, "In Defence of Macdonald's Constitution," *Dalhousie Law Journal*, Vol. 3, no. 2 (October 1976), p. 529.

7 W. P. M. Kennedy, *Essays in Constitutional Law* (Oxford: Oxford University Press, 1934), p. 85.

8 I do not intend to imply that the issue of judicial review in Canada is not controversial. See Barry Strayer, *Judicial Review of Legislation in Canada* (Toronto: University of Toronto Press, 1968) for a critical discussion of the roots of the practice in Canada.

9 H. W. McConnell, "The Privy Council and the New Deal Cases," *Osgoode Hall Law Journal*, Vol. 9, no. 2 (November 1971), p. 221.

10 See James L. Huffman and MardiLyn Seathoff, "Advisory Opinions and Canadian Constitutional Development," *Minnesota Law Review*, Vol. 74, no. 6 (June 1990), p. 1251.

11 Huffman and Seathoff, "Advisory Opinions and Canadian Constitutional Development," pp. 1255–56.

12 See Barry Strayer, *The Canadian Constitution and the Courts*, 3rd ed. (Toronto: Butterworths, 1988), pp. 125–31.

13 See Sir Lyman Poore Duff, *Reference re Criminal Code* [1912] 43 S.C.R. 434 at p. 451.

14 See Peter Hogg, *Constitutional Law of Canada*, 3rd ed. (Toronto: Carswell, 1992), pp. 214–16.

15 It is worth noting that seven states do permit the practice of seeking advisory opinions of their courts. See Huffman and Seathoff, "Advisory Opinions and Canadian Constitutional Development."

16 *Reference re Secession of Quebec* [1998] 2 S.C.R. 217.

17 *Reference re Secession of Quebec* [1998] at p. 221.

18 *Reference re Secession of Quebec* [1998] at p. 220.

19 See Sir Kenneth Roberts-Wray, "Human Rights in the Commonwealth," *International and Comparative Law Quarterly*, Vol. 17 (October 1968), p. 908. "It required the gross excesses attendant upon the second of the two world wars to shake us out of our complacency," p. 914. See also, S. A. deSmith, "Fundamental Rights in the New Commonwealth," *International and Comparative Law Quarterly*, Vol. 10, nos. I and II (January 1961), pp. 83 and 215.

20 See James C. McRuer, *Report of the Royal Commission of Inquiry Into Civil Rights* (Toronto: Queen's Printer, 1969).

21 Lisa Fitterman, "Canada's Reticent Role Revealed," *The Gazette*, Montreal, December 5, 1998, p. B3; and William A. Schabas, "Canada and the Adoption of the Universal Declaration of Rights," *McGill Law Journal*, Vol. 43, no. 2 (August 1998), p. 403. Schabas notes that "at its extreme, Canada's attitude bordered on hostility" (p. 406).

22 See, F. R. Scott, "Constitutional Adaptations to Changing Functions of Government," *Canadian Journal of Economics and Political Science*, Vol. XI, no. 3 (August 1945), p. 334.

23 For a brief discussion of civil liberties, see Hogg, *Constitutional Law of Canada*, Part III, pp. 765–69.

24 *The Queen v. Drybones* [1970] S.C.R. 282.

25 *Robertson and Rosetanni v the Queen* [1963] 41 D.L.R. (2d) 485. See Michael Mandel, *The Charter of Rights and the Legalization of Politics in Canada* (Toronto: Thompson Educational Publishing, Inc., 1994), pp. 22–24 for a discussion of this case.

26 See A.S. Pattillo, Past President of the Canadian Bar Association, *Globe and Mail*, April 29, 1970, p. 5: "The Court of Last Resort Should not Get Mixed up in the Legislative Process."

27 J.-G. Castel, "The Canadian Charter of Rights and Freedoms: La Charte canadienne des Droits et Libertés," *The Canadian Bar Review*, Vol. 61, no. 1 (March 1983), p. 1.

28 Gerard V. La Forest, "The Canadian Charter of Rights and Freedoms: An Overview," *The Canadian Bar Review*, Vol. 61, no. 1 (March 1983), p. 23.

29 *R v. Oakes* [1986] 1 S.C.R. 103.

30 Peter Russell, "The Supreme Court and the Charter: Quantitative Trends –
Continuities and Discontinuities," *Canada Watch*, Vol. 6, nos. 4, 5 and 6
(October 1998), p. 61.

31 Russell, "The Supreme Court and the Charter," p. 63.

32 Russell, "The Supreme Court and the Charter," p. 64.

33 Russell, "The Supreme Court and the Charter."

34 See, Patrick J. Monahan, "The Supreme Court's 1997 Constitutional
Decisions: A Statistical Overview," *Canada Watch*, Vol. 6, nos. 4, 5 and 6
(October 1998), p. 102.

35 Monahan, "The Supreme Court's 1997 Constitutional Decisions," p. 102.

36 Justice Willard Estey, *Law Society of Upper Canada v. Skapinker* [1984] 1
S.C.R. 357 at p. 366.

37 Justice Beverley McLachlin, "The Charter of Rights and Freedoms: A Judicial Perspective," *University of British Columbia Law Review,* Vol. 23, no. 3
(1989) p. 579.

38 *R v. Big M Drug Mart* [1985] 1 S.C.R. 295.

39 This is the interpretation placed on the Court's decision in *Big M Drug Mart*
by Chief Justice Dickson *in R v. Edwards* [1986] 2 S.C.R. 713 at p. 754.

40 For a critical assessment of the Court's ruling in this case, see Rainer
Knopff and F.L.Morton, *Charter Politics* (Scarborough: Nelson Canada,
1992), p. 185–86.

41 *R.v. Big M Drug Mart* [1985] at p. 344.

42 *R.v. Big M Drug Mart* [1985] at p. 361.

43 *R v. Morgentaler* [1988] 1 S.C.R. 30.

44 *Egan v. Canada* [1995] 2 S.C.R. 513 at p. 517.

45 See the *Globe and Mail* editorial, "Reconciling Rights and Democracy,"
February 4, 1999, p. A14. See also, Gordon Gibson, "Gordon Wilson Signs
his NDP card," *Globe and Mail,* February 2, 1999, p. A15. Gibson muses:
"What if the problem people deplore here has nothing to do with the
court, but lies in the sacred cow of the Charter itself, which is increasingly
wreaking legal havoc in the area of sexual mores?"

46 See, "Lamer Worries Potential Backlash Might Sway Judges," *The Sunday
Daily News*, Halifax, February 10, 1999, p. 10.

47 See, Justice L'Heureux-Dubé's comment on the confusion of approaches
to section 15 in *Egan v. Canada* at p. 541.

48 See, Debra M. McAllister, "Litigation Trends in 1997 Supreme Court Jurisprudence," *Canada Watch*, Vol. 6, nos. 4, 5 and 6 (October 1998), p. 68.

49 *Miron v. Trudel* [1995] 2 S.C.R. 418 at p. 420.

50 *Egan v. Canada* [1995] 2 S.C.R. 513 at p. 521.

51 *Thibaudeau v. Canada* [1995] 2 S.C.R. 627.

52 *Miron v. Trudel* [1995] at p. 541.

53 See *Eaton v. Brant County Board of Education* [1997] 1 S.C.R. 241; *Benner v. Canada* (Secretary of State) [1997] 1 S.C.R. 358 and *Eldridge v. British Columbia* [1997] 3 S.C.R. 624.

54 *Eaton v. Brant* [1997] 1 S.C.R. 241.

55 *Benner v. Canada* (Secretary of State) [1997] 1 S.C.R. 358.

56 Citizenship Act, R.S.C., 1985, c. C-29, section 3(1).

57 See F. L. Morton, Peter H. Russell and Troy Riddell, "The Canadian Charter of Rights and Freedoms: A Descriptive Analysis of the First Decade, 1982 - 1992," *National Journal of Constitutional Law*, Vol. 5 (1994–1995), p. 1.

58 Morton, Russell and Riddell, "The Canadian Charter of Rightsand Freedoms," p. 13.

59 *Escobedo v. Illinois* [1964] 378 US 478.

60 *Miranda v. Arizona* [1966] 394 US 436.

61 For a good discussion of these American cases, see Christopher Wolfe, *The Rise of Modern Judicial Review: From Constitutional Interpretation to Judge-Made Law* (New York: Basic Books, 1986), pp. 294–98.

62 *Hunter v. Southam* [1984] 2 S.C.R. 145.

63 *R v. Therens* [1985] 1 S.C.R. 613.

64 See *Clarkson v. The Queen* [1986] 1 S.C.R. 383.

65 *R v. Oakes* [1986] 1 S.C.R. 103.

66 *R v. Manninen* [1987] 1 S.C.R. 1233.

67 *R v. Hebert* [1990] 2 S.C.R. 151.

68 *R v. Hebert* [1990] at p. 184 per McLachlin J., for the majority.

69 *R v. Seaboyer* [1991] 2 S.C.R. 577.

70 See *R v. Whyte* [1988] 2 S.C.R. 3 where Chief Justice Brian Dickson for a unanimous court upheld section 237(1)(a) of the Criminal Code which places "the onus of proof on the accused" in drunk driving cases.

71 See "Supreme Court Rules in Favour of Surprise Locker Inspections," *The National Post*, November 27, 1998, p. A5 for a summary of the Court's judgement.

72 Robert Harvie and Hamar Foster, "Ties that Bind? The Supreme Court of Canada, American Jurisprudence, and the Revision of Canadian Criminal Law under the Charter," *Osgoode Hall Law Journal*, Vol. 28, no. 4 (Winter 1990), p. 779.

73 See, *R v. Sharpe*, British Columbia Supreme Court, New Westminster Registry, Docket no. x050427. The full judgment can be viewed on the internet: www.courts.gov.bc.ca.

74 *R.v. Ewanchuk*, February 25, 1999, Supreme Court of Canada, File no. 26493.

75 Lysiane Gagnon, "The Complex Dance of Seduction," *Globe and Mail*, March 6, 1999, p. D3. See also Barbara Amiel, "Feminists, Fascists and Other Radicals," *The National Post*, March 6, 1999, p. B7.

76 Morton, Russell and Riddell, "The Canadian Charter of Rightsand Freedom," p. 8.

A British Bill of Rights: Incorporating the European Convention on Human Rights

KATE MALLESON

On November 9th, 1998 the Queen gave royal assent to the Human Rights Act which incorporates the European Convention for the Protection of Human Rights and Fundamental Freedoms into UK law.* The Act came into force October 2000. This paper examines the legal and political context in which the Act was passed nearly fifty years after the UK signed the Convention and seeks to assess the likely effects of incorporation both on the protection of human rights and the future relationship between Parliament, the executive and the judiciary.

THE BACKGROUND TO INCORPORATING THE EUROPEAN CONVENTION

Prior to the Human Rights Act, the UK enjoyed the dubious distinction of being the last signatory state to the European Convention on Human Rights which had not incorporated it into domestic law or created an equivalent bill of rights. This apparent lack of enthusiasm for the Convention would, at first sight, appear to be at odds with the UK's early role in its creation. Having played a leading part in drafting the Convention, it was the first state to ratify it in 1951 and thus might have been expected to move quickly to incorporate its provisions into

---

* A list of the rights and freedoms incorporated in the Human Rights Act can be found in Appendix 1.

domestic law. But as cabinet papers from that period reveal, there was serious division in the government over the desirability of the Convention with strong resistance to the enterprise from some senior members of the post-war Labour Cabinet who felt that the Convention would threaten the creation of a planned economy.[1] The Lord Chancellor, Lord Jowitt, regarded it as "a half-baked scheme to be administered by some unknown court" which would allow the UK's European allies to jeopardize its whole system of law. He described the Convention as a document from which any student of the UK's legal institutions "would recoil with a feeling of horror."[2]

This opposition succeeded in watering down the Convention's effectiveness in a number of important respects. The original draft included a mandatory right of individual petition to the European Court of Human Rights, but as a result of British opposition the application of this provision was made optional for the signatory states. The UK duly declined to adopt it and the right of individuals to seek redress at the European Court of Human Rights in Strasbourg was not granted to UK citizens until 1966. In addition, the British government persuaded the other participants to limit the scope of the substantive rights by omitting any rights to property, education or political freedom.[3]

The explanation for this strong tradition of resistance to the Convention and the European legal machinery lies in the long and persistent attachment in British legal and political culture to the principle of parliamentary sovereignty and an unwritten constitution, both of which would be threatened by incorporating a bill of rights. In addition to being constitutionally dangerous, such a move was also regarded as unnecessary on the grounds that the common law provided an equally effective vehicle for protecting human rights. Together these beliefs, which had hindered the full embrace of the Convention at its inception, brought together significant sections of the political left and right for nearly half a century in blocking its incorporation into domestic law. It is only in recent years that a number of legal and political developments have come together to undermine the traditional coalition of interests which united against incorporation.

The UK's Human Rights Record

The original purpose behind the European Convention on Human Rights was to create a tool which would hinder the repetition by some future despotic state of the human rights atrocities committed by Nazi Germany. For the British politicians and officials who participated in its creation, its function was primarily to check the potential abuse of power by the government of another European country rather than to provide protection for British citizens against breaches of human rights by their own government. The consistent position of successive British governments was that it was inappropriate for an international court to review the common law and statutes of the UK. In addition, there was concern that individual petitions would result in the "politically immature" citizens of the British Colonies being confused about where sovereignty lay. The effect would be that their loyalty would be shaken and agitation more likely to occur.[4] The imperialist confidence in the superiority of domestic law in protecting the citizens of the UK and all its overseas territories today appears breathtakingly arrogant. When in 1966 the UK government conceded the right of individuals to petition the Court the decision was taken without reference to Cabinet and it was evidently not anticipated that the change would lead to searching scrutiny of the UK's human rights record and the inadequacy of its domestic remedies.[5]

Thirty years later, the position could not have been more different. In the intervening years the European Court of Human Rights had come to maturity and by 1996 had held the UK to be in breach of the Convention on 37 occasions, placing it near the top of the league of offending states. Thus, by the 1990s, whilst by wider international standards the UK could continue to claim a generally good human rights record, within Europe the history of claims against the UK government at Strasbourg had begun to tell a somewhat different story. Moreover, the cases which went against the UK at the European Court of Human Rights could not be dismissed as technical or trivial since many of them involved the most basic Convention rights, including the right to life (the killing of suspected IRA terrorists in Gibraltar), freedom from torture (the "hooding" of detainees in Northern Ireland),[6] arbitrary detention (four to seven day questioning of terrorist suspects in Northern Ireland) and the invasion of privacy (telephone tapping).[7] In addition, many of the cases involved some of the most vulnerable members of society, such as prisoners, mental patients, detained suspects and children. The steady stream of cases against the British government in Strasbourg inevitably came to undermine traditional confidence in the ability of existing legal processes and cultural norms to protect human rights in the UK. This view was reinforced in 1995 when the United Nations Human Rights Committee declared that the British legal system did not "fully ensure that an effective remedy is provided for all violations of the rights contained in the Covenant."[8]

In addition, the position of Parliament as the natural protector of human rights was significantly undermined by the fact that a high, and growing, proportion of successful claims consisted of challenges to recent legislation. Of the 37 adverse findings between 1975 and 1995, 24 were in relation to legislative provisions. By 1997, the director of the civil rights group, Liberty, claimed that all seven cases decided by the Court against the UK the previous year related to legislation.[9] Many commentators in the 1990s argued that ancient rights which had traditionally been held up as symbols of British justice had been overridden by Parliament.[10] The effect was to undermine the value of the common law as a mechanism for upholding human rights: "The common law presumption in favour of individual liberty crumbles like dust in the face of a statute which erodes that liberty."[11] Rights of citizenship, free speech, assembly and peaceful protest and the right of a defendant to remain silent in criminal proceedings had been eroded by statutes. In particular, the emergency terrorist legislation passed in response to the troubles in Northern Ireland, attracted a high degree of criticism as being ill-considered reactions to public outrage which put political expediency before human rights. The strengthening power of the executive *vis-à-vis* Parliament and the large parliamentary majorities of the Conservative administrations in the 1980s bolstered the claim that Parliament could not be relied upon to scrutinize government legislation from a human rights perspective or to reject that which it found to be in breach of basic rights. The collective result of these changes was that by the mid-1990s, Britain was commonly described as suffering from a human rights deficit.[12]

As concern about the UK's human rights record grew, the coalition of supporters for incorporation became broader and more vocal. Campaigning organisations such as Liberty and JUSTICE were joined by growing numbers of academics and practising lawyers. A few prominent individuals in the legal establishment, most notably Lord Lester, were instrumental in changing the climate of complacency about the UK's human rights record and advocating a bill of rights.[13] In addition, the high profile miscarriages of justice cases such as the Guildford Four and the Birmingham Six, which came to light in the late 1980s and early 1990s, exposed serious police malpractice. This indirectly added fuel to the cause for incorporation by highlighting the fact that the British justice system was not immune from the risks of abuse of process. The traditional claim that Parliament and the British legal culture of fairness fully protected the human rights of those in the care or control of the state was no longer sustainable in the light of those cases.

In addition to the limitations of parliamentary effectiveness in securing human rights, the weaknesses of the common law were becoming increasingly obvious, particularly in relation to cases involving intrusive scrutiny by the media into individuals' private lives. The use of sophisticated surveillance equipment and powerful telephoto lenses attracted increasing concern. The inadequacy of the courts to protect people from such invasive techniques was highlighted in 1991 by the case of Gordon Kaye, a well-known actor who was photographed and interviewed in his hospital bed whilst seriously ill and unfit to give his consent. In the subsequent action brought by Kaye against the newspaper which published the story, Lord Justice Bingham, now the Lord Chief Justice, drew attention to the failure of the common law "to protect in an effective way the personal privacy of individual citizens."[14] Although by the mid-1990s the courts were beginning to develop an embryonic law of privacy through the law on breach of confidentiality, most lawyers agreed that this was neither an appropriate nor adequate way to ensure the proper protection of a basic human right.

Thus a consensus slowly emerged in the legal establishment and the civil rights community that the common law alone was no match for the expanding power of the media and the executive and could not be left to provide the necessary safeguards against abuse.[15] In 1990, the Institute for Public Policy Research drafted a bill of rights for Britain based on the European Convention on Human Rights and the International Covenant on Civil and Political Rights.[16] The following year, Liberty published a Charter of Rights, which drew on a wide range of international conventions and human rights instruments, including the anti-discrimination clauses of the Canadian Charter of Rights.[17] The availability of such documents from other countries was, in itself, a significant factor in the growing acceptance of the desirability of a domestic bill of rights.

International Developments

In the early years after the ratification of the Convention, the divergence between the UK and the other signatory states on the question of incorporation was partly explicable as a product of the different civil law traditions of continental Europe. In the 1950s, almost all the common law world outside the US functioned without an entrenched bill of rights. Moreover, the US could be distinguished on the grounds of its very different political and legal culture, both in terms of the stricter separation of powers and the judicial review role fulfilled by the Supreme Court. Despite the precedents of Magna Carta in 1215 and the Bill of Rights in 1689, the argument that a bill of rights was an alien concept for Britain was widely accepted.[18] However, during the 1960s this argument was already being weakened by the gradual adoption of bills of rights throughout the Commonwealth countries, the political and legal systems of which were closely modelled on that of

England. By 1980, a total of 24 Commonwealth countries had adopted codes of fundamental rights based on the European Convention.[19] By the mid-1990s, Canada, New Zealand, Israel, Hong Kong and South Africa had also all adopted some form of bill of rights.[20]

The spread of rights documents throughout the common law world affected the debate on incorporation in the UK in two ways. First, it provided models for civil rights bodies and lawyers to draw upon in drafting proposed bills of rights for Britain. Second, it represented a global trend toward the incorporation of human rights documents which left the UK increasingly isolated. The Canadian experience in particular, having been in operation since the early 1980s, was increasingly viewed as providing support for the argument that entrenching a bill of rights did not necessarily herald a legal or political revolution but could be incorporated into a common law system as an evolutionary step in the development of a more rights-based approach.

Changing Political Perspectives on a Bill of Rights

The fact that the Human Rights Act was introduced by a Labour government would suggest that incorporating the Convention was traditionally a policy of the political left. But paradoxically, it was Conservative politicians who first showed an interest in the idea in the 1960s and 1970s, in response to the policies of the socialist administrations of that period. In particular, the nationalization of industries under the Labour government generated support for a bill of rights amongst the right as a means of protecting existing property rights. The Conservative politician, Lord Hailsham, later Lord Chancellor, regarded a bill of rights as a potential mechanism for curbing the oppressive power of what he termed the "elective dictatorship."[21] However, support for incorporation amongst members of the Conservative party quickly waned on taking office again in 1979 and was implacably opposed by the Thatcher and Major governments throughout the 1980s and early 1990s.[22]

In recent years, there has been some resurgence of support for a bill of rights amongst Conservatives in the light of the growing power of Europe. Ferdinand Mount, former policy adviser to Margaret Thatcher when Prime Minister, has argued that incorporation would counter the erosion of the English legal system by European institutions by allowing English judges to build up a body of case law which was appropriate to UK needs and circumstances and so "rescue and revitalise the common law tradition."[23] Interestingly, the same point was promoted by the Labour government in its consultation paper which introduced the proposals for the Human Rights Act in 1997:

"British judges will be enabled to make a distinctly British contribution to the development of the jurisprudence of human rights in Europe."[24] Though some Conservative supporters may be reassured by this claim, those on the political right in general remain opposed to the promotion of a rights-based culture and the potential threat which it poses to the full development of free markets. The historical link between a bill of rights and the policies of the political left in the US has entrenched hostility toward incorporation in the UK amongst many Conservatives.

The attitude of the Labour party to a bill of rights, has, until relatively recently, been hardly any more enthusiastic. Throughout the 1960s and 1970s, Labour governments remained opposed to incorporation on the grounds that judges could not be trusted with the task of upholding rights. The record of the judges in such areas as labour disputes, in which they were widely perceived to be hostile to trade union interests, led commentators such as Professor John Griffith to recoil from the prospect of transferring the task of protecting human rights from Parliament to the judges.[25] The erosion of parliamentary sovereignty was, and remains, the strongest ground of objection amongst many on the political left. This mistrust of the judiciary as potential guardians of human rights was not confined to socialists but was widespread amongst liberals both in and out of the Labour party. For example, Lord Lester, a lifelong supporter of a bill of rights, originally argued in the 1970s that English judges could not be trusted to apply a bill of rights in a "progressive and liberal spirit" and he argued therefore that the bill should not be enforceable in the courts but rather that a Constitutional Council should be used to make recommendations about the compatibility of legislation.[26] Similarly, Liberty, in its People's Charter, proposed that a parliamentary scrutiny committee rather than the courts would have the primary role of enforcing the bill. Just as some Conservatives had recognised the potential of a bill of rights to curb socialist policies in the 1970s, for the same reason the Labour party did not intend to risk its policies being hindered by an obstructive judiciary.

The consequence of these objections was that the support which was voiced for incorporation during the 1980s came almost exclusively from liberals occupying the centre ground of the political spectrum at a time when this group was relatively powerless in British politics. The domination of the New Right under Margaret Thatcher and the conflict within the Labour party between Old and New Labour largely isolated traditional liberals in either party. Thus although from the 1970s a number of bills were introduced in Parliament to incorporate a bill of rights, there was never sufficient support for these to be enacted. In

1984, Lord Lester wrote that if incorporation depended on obtaining a political consensus it would not happen in the near future since the Labour party remained firmly opposed to it.[27] Over the following decade, however, that elusive consensus began to emerge. The defeat of the socialist wing of the Labour party in the power struggle of the early 1990s removed the most ardent opponents of the change. In 1993, then Labour leader John Smith first supported the policy in a speech to the constitutional reform group, Charter 88. Smith's successor, Tony Blair, followed his lead and expressed his clear backing for the change on being elected party leader. In 1995, forty years of opposition to the reform was finally abandoned when incorporation was officially adopted as Labour party policy.

The shift within the Labour party and those on the political left in general toward a bill of rights is explained largely by the changing perception of the British judges' record on human rights throughout the 1980s and 1990s. During this period, the senior judiciary had shown itself increasingly willing to exercise its powers to review the legality of administrative action.[28] In 1994, Lord Griffiths highlighted the human rights basis for the judges' role in scrutinizing and checking administrative action: "The judiciary accepts a responsibility for the maintenance of the rule of law that embraces a willingness to oversee executive action and to refuse to countenance behaviour that threatens either basic human rights or the rule of law."[29]

On a number of highly publicized occasions during this period the decisions of Conservative ministers were quashed by the higher courts leading to the widespread view that the radical policies of the Thatcher administration had, for the first time, weakened the natural alliance between the judges and the Conservative party.[30] Professor John Griffith, in the 1977 edition of *The Politics of the Judiciary*, his critical review of the politics of judicial law-making, originally argued that the views and beliefs of the judges as reflected in their judgments most often correlated to those of the Conservative party. By 1997, however, Griffith had removed the association of the judges with the Conservative party and relegated their conservatism to that of a small c.[31] The judges themselves played down the political nature of any conflict between the Conservative government and the judiciary, stressing, firstly, that their task was limited to reviewing questions of law and procedure rather than policy and, secondly, that the majority of judicial review cases went in favour of the government. Some members of the senior judiciary did, however, acknowledge that the greater willingness on the part of the judiciary to scrutinize the actions of government during the 1990s had partly arisen because one political party had been in power for an exceptionally long period.[32] Commentators outside the judiciary also argued that the large Conservative majority, combined with the loss of political direction within the Labour party, left Britain with a vacuum in the political centre ground into which the judges were drawn, reluctantly or otherwise, to fulfil the role of a quasi-opposition.[33]

Whatever the explanation for the increasing judicial activism in the 1980s and 1990s, its effect was to change the mood of the political left toward the judges as potential guardians of human rights and to erode the longstanding resistance to incorporation. In addition, opinion polls during the 1990s all showed consistently strong support of up to 80 percent amongst the public for incorporation.[34] For a party which had lost four elections in a row and faced political oblivion if defeated at the fifth, the demonstration of public support for incorporation was a prerequisite for its inclusion in the manifesto. The Labour party's commitment to the reform was also strengthened by the fact that incorporation was not an isolated policy but one part of a much broader package of constitutional reform covering devolution to Scotland and Wales and the reform of the House of Lords. For these reasons the election of the Labour government in 1997 meant that incorporation was almost guaranteed and the following year the Human Rights Bill was successfully passed over 30 years after the first such bill had been considered by Parliament.

Changing Judicial Attitudes toward a Bill of Rights

Perhaps the most striking change in the public debate on a bill of rights in Britain has been the conversion of the judiciary to the cause for incorporation. Traditionally, almost all the senior judges expressed their opposition to a bill of rights on the grounds that it would force them to cross the Rubicon between law and policy and so undermine the basis of their independence. One notable exception to this consensus was Lord Scarman who first set out the case for incorporation in 1974 and remained committed to the reform in the years that followed.[35] During the 1970s he was something of a lone voice in the judiciary, but throughout the 1980s and 1990s a number of senior judges began to indicate their support for the change. By 1997, the reform was actively supported by a number of top ranking judges, including the Master of the Rolls, Lord Woolf, the Lord Chief Justice, Lord Bingham (and by his predecessor the late Lord Taylor) and Lords Ackner, Lloyd and Slynn. Some, such as Lord Denning, underwent a change of heart on the matter.[36] Others, more recently appointed, brought their support for incorporation with them to the bench. Paradoxically, many of the new generation of the senior judiciary who supported a bill of rights were appointed by the Conservative Lord

Chancellor, Lord Mackay, who remained implacably against incorporation as being an inappropriate expansion of judicial power. His replacement by the Labour Lord Chancellor, Lord Irvine, after the
general election in May 1997 meant that there was, for the first time, a
strong consensus in favour amongst the senior judiciary.

A number of different factors can be identified as contributing to the
very marked change of attitude towards incorporation amongst the
judges. A key consideration was the growing concern about the relative
impotence of Parliament to protect human rights in the face of the expanding power of the executive. Lord Bingham stressed that at a practical level Parliament no longer had the time to correct derogations from
human rights.[37] Less publicly, other judges acknowledged an equal
lack of inclination. Many shared the opinion of Lord Williams, a leading barrister and now a member of the government in the House of
Lords, who commented that judges had been forced to adopt powers to
review administrative decision making because Parliament has been
"too busy, too supine or too fearful" to define the limits of government
power with regards to human rights issues.[38] In addition, the growing
willingness of the judiciary to scrutinize the legality, rationality and fairness of official decision making had weakened the argument that the
judges did not have the experience or outlook necessary to undertake
the more active and purposeful decision making required in the field
of human rights law. The relatively passive and restrained approach to
law-making and interpretation which had prevailed amongst English
judges in the 1950s and 1960s had long been eroded by the time the
Labour government published its proposals for incorporation in 1997
to a receptive judiciary. With the support of the judiciary assured, another longstanding hurdle to incorporation was removed.

CONSTRUCTING THE MODEL OF INCORPORATION

With a very large majority and broad support for incorporation, the
new Labour government was confident of a relatively easy passage for
its Human Rights Bill. The controversial question had shifted from
whether incorporation was a good idea to what form it should take – in
particular, how to reconcile the requirements of parliamentary
sovereignty with a meaningful structure for embedding, if not entrenching, human rights into the UK legal system.

Parliamentary Sovereignty and the Judiciary

For answers to this problem, the government looked abroad to the experiences of other countries which had successfully incorporated a bill

of rights.[39] In the period before the bill was introduced a debate arose both within government and amongst the supporters of incorporation outside over the merits of the different systems. The US, although one of the oldest and best known examples in the common law world, was never a serious contender as a model for the UK since the Supreme Court's unqualified powers to strike down unconstitutional legislation were generally considered incompatible with the constitutional arrangements in Britain. For this reason also, the South African arrangements in which the new Constitutional Court has similar powers were generally rejected despite being much closer in other respects to the UK legal system.

Much stronger support was shown amongst some lawyers and civil libertarians for the Canadian model as being a good compromise between the demands of parliamentary sovereignty and the overriding importance of human rights. The strongest competitor to the Canadian model was the *New Zealand Bill of Rights Act 1990*, which gives the courts more limited power to interpret legislation in a way that is compatible with the Bill of Rights but with no power to strike down provisions which contravene it. This model was rejected as "toothless" by some commentators but preferred by those who gave priority to the need to retain full parliamentary sovereignty. A third option which gained some support was the Hong Kong model which distinguished between legislation enacted before and after the 1991 Bill of Rights Ordinance, previous legislation being subordinated to the Ordinance and subsequent taking precedence.[40] Ultimately however, the government rejected all variations which gave the courts any powers to set aside primary legislation as being a fundamental breach of parliamentary sovereignty:

To make provisions in the Bill for the courts to set aside Acts of Parliament would confer on the judiciary a general power over the decisions of Parliament which under our present constitutional arrangements they do not possess, and would be likely on occasions to draw the judiciary into serious conflict with Parliament.[41]

Having rejected the stronger models of incorporation, the government did not, as expected, adopt the New Zealand approach. Instead, it devised a formula which followed none of the existing models and which purports to offer a uniquely British solution to the problem. Under section 3 of the Act the courts are placed under a duty to interpret all legislation in accordance with the Convention "as far as it is possible to do so." Where this cannot be done, the higher courts are empowered to make a "declaration of incompatibility."[42] The Act then provides for a fast track procedure by which the government can amend the offending legislation in order to make it compatible with the Convention.[43] In the meantime, the Act remains law. However, the consultation paper envisaged that a declaration of incompatibility would "almost certainly prompt the government and Parliament to change the law."[44]

Thus parliamentary sovereignty is preserved, while at the same time the conditions are provided for courts to identify provisions which breach the Convention and for these to be brought into line speedily. This relatively unstructured approach to such an important element of the constitutional arrangement would be anathema to any country with a written constitution. But for Britain, the solution is in keeping with the nature of its unwritten constitution, since it provides the conditions in which new constitutional conventions can emerge. The Act is premised on a number of political assumptions: first, that Parliament will strive to ensure that new legislation is compatible with the Convention; second, that the courts will strive to limit the use of declarations of incompatibility to those few cases where it is absolutely impossible to interpret in a way which is compatible; and third, that Parliament and the government will respond promptly to correct the breach in those rare cases. If, after a period of time this pattern is consistently followed, the responses of all branches of state will become identified as generally binding constitutional conventions and will have a force which is not evident from the words of the Act itself.

The disadvantage of this relatively loose arrangement is, of course, that shared by all constitutional conventions, that no formal sanctions exist should the parties fail to "play the game." The danger posed by the use of this non-binding approach to the amendment of laws ruled incompatible is that it leaves a potential constitutional vacuum into which legislation might fall. If an Act has been declared incompatible but is not amended, courts will be left with the task, in future hearings in which the law is relied upon, of enforcing legislation which they have held to be in breach of fundamental human rights. In such circumstances the moral legitimacy of the law itself, and the judges' decisions based upon it, would inevitably be undermined. Although in most cases it is unlikely that such an impasse would arise between the government, Parliament and the judiciary, there are some obvious danger points, in particular, in relation to the passage of emergency terrorism legislation. It is this area which to date has caused the UK government particular conflict with the European Court of Human Rights. In 1988, for example, the Court ruled that the detention of suspects for a period of four to seven days under the Prevention of Terrorism Act 1984 was in breach of the Convention. In response to the decision, the UK exercised its right to derogate from the provisions and has not, to date, amended the offending legislation.[45] With this precedent in mind, it is quite possible that a government might respond in a similar manner to a declaration of incompatibility in relation to terrorist legislation by the domestic courts. In 1998, the Criminal Justice (Terrorism and Conspiracy) Act was passed in the space of a few days in response to the bombing at Omagh in Northern Ireland. Its provisions, which make it easier to convict an accused person of belonging to a proscribed organisation, have been criticized by civil rights lawyers as potentially in breach of the Convention. If they are successfully challenged once the Human Rights Act is implemented, it is hard to imagine that the government which was responsible for introducing the Act would move swiftly to amend it.

One way in which such conflict can be avoided is by ensuring that legislation which is in breach of the Convention is not passed in the first place. The Act seeks to reduce the danger that a recently passed act is ruled incompatible by requiring that the minister responsible for a new piece of legislation must make a statement to Parliament that in his or her view the bill is compatible with the Convention or that he or she cannot provide such an assurance but the government wishes to proceed nonetheless.[46] The consultation paper anticipates that a negative declaration may be made when, for example, the interpretation of the Convention in that area is unclear or contradictory. Such occasions are clearly intended to be rare and the provision is based on the assumption that most ministers would wish, if possible, to be able to make a statement of compatibility. One effect of this attempt to encourage ministers to ensure that legislation is "declaration proof" before passing it may be to promote greater coordination between the judiciary and the government about the possible human rights implications of proposed legislation. If judges are consulted about the human rights implications of government policy at the early stages of its formulation the risk of incompatible legislation finding its way onto the statute books will be considerably reduced. Whether or not this role will be considered appropriate for the judiciary remains to be seen. At present the government intends to carry out the screening process through a parliamentary committee, although there is a strong lobby outside government in favour of the creation of a human rights commission to fulfil this function which may yet prevail.[47]

PUBLIC AUTHORITIES AND CONVENTION RIGHTS

Although the Act does not give the judges the power to rule legislation unconstitutional, it hands to the courts the task of ensuring that the

Convention is complied with in public decision making. In an unexpectedly wide and imaginative section, the Act makes it unlawful for a public authority to act in a way which is incompatible with a Convention right.[48] Moreover, the government has made clear that public authorities are intended to be defined widely, including, for example the Church and the privatized utilities such as gas and water companies.[49] The Act also defines the courts themselves as public authorities which has generally been taken to mean that judges will be under a duty to apply and develop the common law in conformity with the Convention. Some commentators have suggested that this provision will have the effect of indirectly extending the application of the Convention to the law regulating private individuals and institutions as well as public bodies.[50]

One effect of including all courts in the category of public authorities is that those whose rights have been breached will be able to argue their case in all levels of courts in all proceedings. The government's intention, as stated in the consultation paper, is to import Convention rights into the day-to-day business of the courts: "This will make it possible for people to invoke their rights in any proceedings – civil or criminal – brought against them by a public body or in proceedings which they may bring against a public body. The Government prefers a system in which Convention rights can be called upon as they arise, in normal court proceedings, rather than confining their consideration to some kind of constitutional court."[51]

The effect of this approach is that every court from the lowest magistrates court to the House of Lords, every government department and every public or semi-public institution across the country will, for the first time, need to consider whether its procedures and decision-making are being carried out in accordance with Convention rights. The significance of this change is indicated by the fact that implementation of the legislation was delayed for over a year to allow for a human rights training program to be carried out for judges and magistrates at a cost of £5 million – over twice the current annual training budget of the judiciary.

While the scrutiny of administrative action will not in itself be a new undertaking for the judges, since the role of the judiciary in reviewing administrative action is now firmly established, the expansion in the scope of the courts' role in this area is unprecedented. To date, the courts have generally limited their review to the question of whether administrative action is legal, rational and in conformity with the requirements of natural justice. They have explicitly rejected any claim to have a role in reviewing the merits of the policy being implemented. In the seminal case of *Brind*, the House of Lords rejected an application by a group of journalists to review the Home Secretary's decision to restrict the broadcasting of the voices of members of proscribed organisations with terrorist links. The court held that the Home Secretary's decision to exercise his discretion in that manner under the Broadcasting Act was both legal and rational and could therefore not be challenged in the courts. The judges held that for them to consider whether the decision amounted to a breach of Article 10 of the European Convention on Human Rights, the right to freedom of expression, would amount to incorporating the Convention by the "back door" and would thus be a judicial usurpation of legislative powers.[52] If the same case were brought in the year 2000 the court would be required to consider the merits of the decision in the light of Article 10 and to decide whether the restriction imposed by the Home Secretary was "necessary in a democratic society."[53]

The expansion of the judges into policy areas which have traditionally been the preserve of the executive or Parliament brings with it the inevitable potential for conflict between the branches of government even without any formal erosion of parliamentary sovereignty. However, such conflict is not unprecedented. Tension between the judiciary and the executive has arisen periodically over the years.[54] During the 1980s, relations between the senior judiciary and the executive were strained over the government's introduction of mandatory and minimum sentencing provisions and the extension of rights of audience in the higher courts to solicitors. One notable feature of such past conflicts, however, is that they have generally been limited to policy changes which relate to the administration of justice. By convention it is this area alone in which law lords participate as legislators in the House of Lords and senior judges engage in public debate. In the post-Human Rights Act era it is possible that the intervention of judges in other policy areas in their judicial decision making may lead to conflict, or at least the appearance of conflict, between the branches of government in areas which are not strictly limited to the administration of the legal system and which have traditionally been regarded as outside the legitimate concern of the judiciary. Whether or not such conflict arises will partly depend on the impact which the Convention rights have, in practice, on the courts' decision making.

Implications for the Development of Human Rights Law in the UK

The dominant and most controversial subject in the current debate on the Human Rights Act concerns the extent to which it will have any significant impact on the courts' decisions. In one respect the consultation paper which introduced the proposals gives the impression that the Act is not intended to reform radically the state of human rights law in the UK. The title of the paper, "Rights Brought Home," emphasises that the primary purpose of the legislation is to make more accessible the rights which British citizens have already enjoyed for nearly 50 years. By allowing those rights to be enforced in the domestic courts, individuals who allege a breach will be saved the considerable time and cost of going to Strasbourg for their cases to be decided in the European Court of Human Rights. But the notion that the Act merely brings rights home obscures the more profound effects which the government also clearly envisages for the legislation. In a recent and related government consultation paper on changes to the legal system, the Human Rights Act is described as representing a "radical extension of the jurisdiction of the courts in the UK."[55] The Lord Chancellor has also made clear that the Act was designed to facilitate a significant shift in legal culture towards a more rights-based approach to justice. In November 1998, the Lord Chancellor's Department released the text of a letter written by Lord Irvine to all full-time judges explaining his hopes for the legislation in the following way: "With proper training and planning, I am confident that all courts and tribunals will be able to give full effect to the rights recognised by the Convention and to make their distinctive contribution to fostering a culture of awareness of, and respect for, human rights throughout the whole of society."[56]

Whether or not the Act has the effect intended by Lord Irvine depends ultimately on the willingness of the judges to adopt their new power to take account of Convention rights in interpreting legislation, developing the common law and scrutinizing the decisions of public bodies and officials. An indication of their likely future practices can be gleaned by examining their past and current approach to human rights. For those anticipating a proactive approach, the omens look good, since the courts have clearly signalled their willingness to incorporate a rights-based approach in their decision making. There are a number of different ways in which the Convention currently finds its way into the courts despite the fact that it is not yet part of domestic law. First, it can be used in the process of statutory interpretation where legislation is ambiguous, since it is assumed by the courts that Parliament would not intend to legislate in a way which is inconsistent with the Convention unless it clearly indicated that intention. The number of cases in which the Convention can be used in interpreting ambiguous legislation is relatively limited, but nevertheless the courts have increasingly allowed such arguments to be made where applicable.[57] Second, Convention arguments have been used in court where the common law is uncertain or has gaps, as an aid to guiding the courts' decision making.[58] Similarly, in judicial review cases the courts have sometimes been willing to take into account human rights standards as being relevant to the legality, rationality and compliance with natural justice of administrative action.

The courts have also developed experience in indirect application of the convention through the application of European Community law. Such law, which takes precedence over conflicting domestic law, is required by the European Court of Justice at Luxembourg to comply with the Convention. Thus in applying European law in the UK, British judges are indirectly applying the Convention. One additional effect of the UK courts' growing familiarity with European Community law is their increasing willingness to apply the European law principles of "proportionality" and "legitimate expectation" which are essential tools of interpretation for a bill of rights and which were quite alien concepts to the judges twenty years ago.

Thus, for the Human Rights Act to fail to have the intended effect of enabling Convention arguments to permeate legal reasoning the judiciary would need to apply a brake to a process of adaptation which is already firmly underway.[59] Nor is there any doubt that such cases will come before the court in significant numbers. The organisation Liberty has suggested that there are at least 70 key areas of public life where current practices may breach human rights and be open to challenge. The areas in which it is currently anticipated that challenges are most likely to be made are Article 5 (arrest and detention), Article 6 (fair trial provisions) and Article 8 (the right to privacy). The right to life provisions of Article 2, are also expected to lead to a number of challenges to the rationing decisions of health authorities in allocating their limited resources.

However, the willingness of the courts to open its doors to rights-based arguments does not mean that their decisions will inevitably be different as a result. The record to date suggests that the courts may take a generally conservative attitude to the interpretation of the scope of the rights. In a review of 316 cases between 1975 and 1996 in which the courts had accepted Convention arguments it was found that in only 16 the outcome could be said to have actually been influenced by the rights.[60] The authors of the research conclude that the courts were inhibited by common law practices and procedures which had advanced little over the last 25 years. Whether or not the Human Rights Act will release the courts from those restrictions remains to be seen. Ultimately the approach will be determined by the political and legal culture of the courts. Although the judges are obliged to "take account" of the existing jurisprudence of the European Court of Human Rights they are not bound by it. Moreover, much of the existing jurisprudence is contradictory and many gaps exist. Equally, the judges are not bound by their previous decisions reached before the Act on the construction of legislation since the new requirement to interpret legislation so as to uphold Convention rights may mean that an earlier interpretation of legislation must be overruled.[61] This means that the judges are free to build a new body of case law taking into account Convention rights in whatever way they see fit.

In some areas concerning blatant discriminatory treatment the indications are that the courts will make full use of the Convention to change the law. In the case of *Smith*, for example, in which four gay plaintiffs challenged the decision of the army to dismiss them on the grounds of their sexual orientation, the judges expressed regret that they were not empowered to quash the decision as a breach of the Convention. If the *Smith* case, or an equivalent, is reheard after implementation of the Act, the decision is extremely likely to be reversed. In the field of criminal justice the courts may be less predictable. In considering some legislation, such as the recent abolition of a defendant's absolute right of silence, the courts are very unlikely to hold the provisions to be in breach of the fair trial requirements of Article 6, since the senior judges have clearly signalled their support for the change.[62] In others, such as the reduction of the prosecution's duty of advanced disclosure, the courts may be more receptive to the claim that the provisions breach the fair trial provisions, since the judges have expressed support for the imposition of a wide duty of disclosure. In provisions where due process or freedom of expression have been curbed in response to the threat of terrorism, the courts may well be unwilling to uphold a challenge since their record in this area suggests that the judges have generally been willing to accept such restrictions as being "necessary in a democratic society."[63]

Thus, despite the rejection of a model which would give powers to strike down incompatible legislation, the Act clearly provides the courts with the opportunity to reshape the law in the light of the Convention rights. Although the enthusiasm of the judges to undertake this new task is likely to differ from one area to another, there can be little doubt that real and significant change will occur as a result of the Act which has implications outside the narrow confines of the legal world and raises questions about the future of the judiciary.

IMPLICATIONS FOR THE COMPOSITION AND APPOINTMENT OF THE JUDICIARY

The combination of the power to make a declaration of incompatibility and to police the decision-making of public authorities unquestionably amounts to a significant shift of power to the judges, as Lord

Irvine himself has acknowledged.[64]   The open-ended nature of the Convention rights means that judges will now become the guardians of fundamental democratic values. As the consultation paper made clear, the Convention is a "living document" which must be interpreted in the light of changing social conditions. It is the judges who will be called upon to decide between such conflicting rights as privacy and freedom of expression, as well as the competing demands of individual rights and collective needs. The role of determining which of these different interests should, at any one time, be given priority is a quite different judicial function from that of resolving disputes between two parties by applying rules to facts as has been the traditional task of British judges.[65] This increased power which the judiciary is being given will have knock-on effects on its role and function. If it is to determine the values of a democratic society, questions about who the judges are and how they are chosen take on a new significance.

The Politics of the Judicial Appointments Process

In the years since the Second World War, it has been widely claimed that the judicial appointments process operates outside the political system. This does not mean, of course, that judges come to the bench devoid of political views. The debate about the extent to which those views influence judicial decision making has been a long and controversial one.[66] But there is broad agreement that the party political allegiance of judges no longer has a role to play in the appointments process. Constitutionally, judges up to and including the High Court are appointed by the Queen on the advice of the Lord Chancellor, while judges above the High Court are appointed by the Queen on the advice of the Prime Minister who acts on the recommendation of the Lord Chancellor. By convention, the Queen plays no part in the decision and the Prime Minister is guided by the Lord Chancellor and does not seek to influence the political make-up of the judiciary. The Lord Chancellor, in turn, appoints on the basis of merit rather than political patronage. This claim is supported by a review of the recent appointments to the senior judiciary. Those selected by the Conservative Lord Chancellor, Lord Mackay, included a significant number of lawyers with strong liberal reputations whilst the first two Law Lords appointed by the Labour Lord Chancellor, Lord Irvine, have reputations as conservatives.

In the light of the expanding policy making role of the judges, there must now be a question mark over whether this convention of non-partisan appointment can survive. The idea that future Prime Ministers will continue to be willing to leave the choice of the senior judiciary to the Lord Chancellor once the judges are called upon to decide on questions which may affect government policy is clearly open to doubt. The ability of a convention to withstand political pressure to erode it depends on it being both old and clearly defined. The convention of nonpartisan judicial appointments is neither. Appointment on the basis of merit alone is a post-war phenomenon – before 1945 it was quite normal for judicial appointment to be given as a reward for political support. Moreover, the exact boundaries of the convention have never been clearly set out. In the 1980s, for example, it was revealed that, in at least one instance, Margaret Thatcher rejected the first choice of her Lord Chancellor, Lord Mackay, and this was apparently regarded as constitutionally acceptable both by the Lord Chancellor and by Parliament.[67] Since neither Lord Mackay nor any other Lord Chancellor has been prepared to reveal the exact nature of the advisory process, it is hard to determine exactly what is and is not an acceptable involvement in the selection process on the part of the Prime Minister. Thus, since the convention is both relatively new and relatively uncertain, the potential for its erosion is clear.

Moreover, the increasing interest in the political views of the judges will not be limited to the politicians who appoint them. Once judges reach decisions which choose between basic competing values in society, the apolitical nature of their decision-making will be called into question by the public. As one newspaper editorial recently suggested "It will be impossible for the public to view judges as impartial interpreters of the law – they will be caught up in the partisanship of politics."[68]

Increasing Openness and Accountability in Judicial Appointments

The potential increase in politics in the appointments process as a result of the new role of the judiciary is widely regarded in a negative light as a threat to judicial independence. More positively, it can be regarded as a necessary increase in public accountability. One effect of greater politicization of the judiciary will be that the judges will be obliged to accept the requirements of greater openness. To date, very little is publicly known about the politics or beliefs of the judges who are appointed to the higher courts. This lack of transparency has been justified on the grounds that it preserves judicial independence. However, the argument that judicial independence requires the complete removal of judicial candidates from any form of public scrutiny had come under attack even before the Human Rights Act was passed. The media has in recent years become increasingly vocal in its criticism of the appointments process. In 1998, the appointment of Lords Hobhouse and Millett attracted unprecedented coverage in both the quality and popular press, which criticized the fact that the men were chosen in secret.[69] Whether reflecting or forming public opinion (or both), such scrutiny inevitably impacts upon public confidence in the current arrangements.

A further example of the change in the level of public interest in the politics of the judges was indicated by the media interest attracted by the Pinochet case in November 1998.[70] The backgrounds and reputations of the five Law Lords who heard the case were scrutinized in detail in the press, radio and television coverage amid much speculation about the liberality or conservatism of their views.[71] One effect of the intense scrutiny of the case was that the proportion of the British public who knew something about the judges who sit in the highest court in the UK increased dramatically. Future human rights cases may not attract the international interest of the Pinochet case, but in Britain the precedent of full media coverage and public debate is likely to be followed. As a result, questions about the views and attitudes of the senior judges will find their way onto the political agenda.

The Unrepresentative Backgrounds of the Judges

One effect of increasing public scrutiny of the judicial appointments process is a growing interest in the composition of the judiciary. Traditionally, the judiciary has countered criticism of its unrepresentative make-up with the argument that it is a body of experienced specialists selected purely on the basis of their legal skills. Nevertheless, the striking homogeneity in the background of the judges has attracted criticism over many years and as the policy-making role of the judges grows the claim that the make-up of the judiciary is not a matter of general public concern will become unsustainable. As the power of the judges expands, the debate on the composition of the judiciary is bound to intensify. The vision of a group of white, elderly men, educated almost exclusively at private schools and Oxford or Cambridge University, deciding on essential social values in areas such as gay rights, abortion, euthanasia and health care rationing will inevitably attract growing criticism.

The judiciary stresses that its composition is a reflection of the make-up of the legal profession and therefore something which will change naturally as younger lawyers drawn from more diverse backgrounds "trickle-up" through the ranks. Critics of this analysis point to structural and cultural barriers which keep non-traditional candidates out of the system and argue that more fundamental and conscious changes will be needed to the appointments process if a greater diversity in the composition of the judiciary is to be achieved.

THE REFORM OF THE JUDICIAL
APPOINTMENTS PROCESS

During recent years, the Lord Chancellor's Department has sought to address these criticisms of the system by introducing greater transparency into the appointments process, through the use of job advertisements, published selection criteria, formal interviews and the active encouragement of women and ethnic minority lawyers to apply for judicial office.[72] Despite these efforts, the reform lobby is growing stronger and proposals for the establishment of a judicial appointments commission now attract widespread support.[73] When the Labour government came to power in 1997, one of the first acts of the new Lord Chancellor, Lord Irvine, was to set up a consultation process on the creation of a judicial commission and to commission comparative research on the systems in North America and Europe.[74] Before the process was completed, however, he decided that the Lord Chancellor's Department was already overburdened with a program of reform in the areas of Legal Aid and the Civil Justice Process and could not initiate any further changes. But although the proposal for a commission was set aside, Lord Irvine made clear that he did not reject the idea outright. A year later he conceded that the implementation of the Human Rights Act in 2000 would inevitably lead to greater scrutiny of judges' backgrounds and he indicated that he might now be ready to consult over the possibility of setting up a commission.[75] Whether or not the Lord Chancellor moves ahead with a commission in the short-term, the pressure for reform of the system is bound to intensify and it can only be a matter of time before some significant change is introduced in response to the new role which the judiciary is being asked to fulfil.[76]

CONCLUSION

Over a period of thirty years the debate on a British bill of rights has moved from being a marginalized concern of a few civil liberties campaigners to a popular reform attracting a broad consensus of support amongst politicians, the public and the judiciary. As a product of that debate, in which resistance to constitutional change played such a strong role, the Human Rights Act is, in one respect, a very restrained provision which gives priority to the need to preserve parliamentary sovereignty and respect the existing constitutional arrangements. Yet it is also an unexpectedly radical piece of legislation. By placing a duty of compliance with Convention rights on all public bodies the Act lays the foundations for the creation of a rights-based culture throughout government and the court system of the UK. Whether or not this promise is fulfilled depends ultimately on the judiciary and its willingness to take up the new role envisaged for it by the Act. The increasing receptiveness of the courts to human rights arguments and the presence of a caucus of individuals amongst the senior judges who have expressed strong support for a human rights regime suggests that the judiciary is ready to take up that challenge. Equally, the increasing experience of the higher courts in scrutinizing administrative action and their growing familiarity with European legal concepts provide the building blocks on which a strong rights-based approach can be founded.

One consequence of this change will be that judges in the UK will increasingly come to see themselves as part of an international human rights community which includes, and extends beyond, the European Court of Human Rights. As the courts come to grapple with the task of setting human rights standards they will need to draw on decisions from comparable jurisdictions around the world. As the British judiciary joins the global community of human rights arbiters it will also come to be subject to the same public scrutiny which is being attracted by activist judges around the world. Its composition, selection criteria and method of appointment will be critically reviewed by a broader constituency than the legal establishment. In the light of the judges' expanding power some searching questions will find their way onto the political agenda: What changes are required to secure judicial independence and yet increase judicial accountability? Is the current judicial appointments process, with its secrecy and self-replication, still an acceptable way to select policy makers and guardians of our civil liberties? If not, what is to replace it? For those interested in the relationship between politics and law in Britain, the years ahead are likely to be a fascinating period of change.

NOTES

1 Anthony Lester, "Fundamental Rights: The UK Isolated," *Public Law* (Spring 1984), p. 50.
2 Quoted in Lester, "Fundamental Rights," p. 52. The Lord Chancellor broadly fulfils the functions of the Canadian Minister of Justice. His role is, however, more extensive and complex due to the fact that he occupies a unique constitutional position, simultaneously holding key positions in all three branches of government. As well as being a member of the cabinet, he is head of the judiciary and speaker in the House of Lords, the upper legislative chamber.

3 Quoted in Lester, "Fundamental Rights," p. 54.

4 The views of the Colonial Secretary, Jim Griffths quoted in Lester, "Fundamental Rights," p. 50.

5 Lester, "Fundamental Rights," pp. 60–61.

6 "Hooding" describes the practice of covering a suspect's head during interrogation and threatening to shoot him if he refuses to answer questions.

7 See Francesca Klug, Keir Starmer and Stuart Weir, *The Three Pillars of Liberty* (London: Routledge, 1996).

8 See Francesca Klug, Foreword to Institute for Public Policy Research, *A British Bill of Rights*, 2nd ed. (London: IPPR, 1996), p. viii.

9 John Wadham, "Bringing Rights Home: Labour's Plans to Incorporate the European Convention on Human Rights into UK Law," *Public Law* (Spring 1997), p. 76.

10 Klug, Starmer and Weir, *A British Bill of Rights*.

11 See Klug, Foreword to Institute for Public Policy Research, *A British Bill of Rights*, p. ii.

12 Klug, Starmer and Weir, *The Three Pillars of Liberty*.

13 Lord Lester is a senior barrister who has campaigned over many years on a wide variety of human rights issues. His peerage was granted in recognition of this work.

14 *Kaye v. Robertson* [1991] F.S.R. 62.

15 By the mid-1990s, the Law Society and the Bar Council had both publicly supported a bill of rights.

16 Klug, Starmer and Weir, *A British Bill of Rights*.

17 Liberty, *A People's Charter: Liberty's Bill of Rights* (London: Civil Liberties Trust, 1991).

18 Michael Zander, *A Bill of Rights?*, 4th ed. (London: Sweet & Maxwell, 1996), pp. 70–72.

19 Paradoxically, these were introduced by England, which extended the Convention to its dependent territories starting in Nigeria in 1959 when the Convention rights were included in the first Nigerian Constitution. (See Lester, "Fundamental Rights," p. 56.)

20 In Israel this takes the form of two Basic Laws, which set out many rights included in the European Convention on Human Rights.

21 Lord Hailsham, *Elective Dictatorship* (London: BBC Publications, 1976).

22 Richard Hodder-Williams, "Constitutional and Judicial Politics," in Andrew Adonis and Tim Hames (eds.), *A Conservative Revolution?* (Manchester: Manchester University Press, 1994), p. 49.

23 Ferdinand Mount, *The British Constitution Now: Recovery or Decline?* (London: Heinemann, 1994), p. 232.

24 Lord Chancellor's Department, "Rights Brought Home: The Human Rights Bill," Consultation Paper (October 1997), p. 5.

25 J.A.G. Griffith, *The Politics of the Judiciary* (London: Fontana, 1977).

26 Fabian tract no. 390, quoted in Zander, *A Bill of Rights?*, p. 3.

27 Lester, "Fundamental Rights," p. 64.

28 Confusingly, in England these common law powers are called "judicial review." This does not describe the process of reviewing the constutitionality of legislation as in North America but the scrutiny of administrative action to determine that it is not illegal, irrational or in breach of natural justice.

29 *Ex Parte Bennett* [1994] 1 A.C. 42, p. 62.

30 See Joshua Rozenberg, *A Trial of Strength* (London: Richard Cohen Books, 1997).

31 John Griffith, *The Politics of the Judiciary*, 5th ed. (London: Fontana, 1997), p. 341.

32 *The Guardian*, December 11, 1995.

33 Robert Stevens, "Judges, Politics, Politicians and the Confusing Role of the Judiciary," in Keith Hawkins (ed.), *The Human Face of Law* (Oxford: Clarendon Press, 1997).

34 Two MORI opinion polls in 1991 and 1995 found that 79 percent of the population supported a Bill of Rights.

35 Leslie Scarman, *English Law – The New Dimension*, The Hamlyn Lecture (London: Sweet & Maxwell, 1974).

36 Lester, "Fundamental Rights," p. 63.

37 Lord Bingham "European Convention on Human Rights: Time to Incorporate," *Law Quarterly Review*, Vol. 109 (July 1995), pp. 291–392.

38 Hansard House of Lords *Debates* June 5, 1996, column 1307.

39 Lord Chancellor's Department, "Rights Brought Home."

40 Both past and future legislation must be construed consistently with the Ordinance in so far as that is possible, but only past legislation is repealed where it cannot be so construed. The rationale underpinning this model is that it upholds the principle of parliamentary sovereignty which requires that an Act cannot bind future law-making. Thus, where a later Act is inconsistent with the provisions of the Ordinance it must ultimately take precedence. (See Yash Ghai, "Sentinels of Liberty or Sheep in Woolf's Clothing? Judicial Politics and the Hong Kong Bill of Rights," *The Modern Law Review*, Vol. 60, no. 4 (July 1997)). This model was favoured by Lord Lester in his last Bill introduced in 1995. See Anthony Lester, "The Mouse that Roared: The Human Rights Bill 1995," *Public Law* (Autumn 1995).

41 Lord Chancellor's Departement, "Rights Brought Home," p. 8.

42 Section 4, Human Rights Act.

43 Section 10, Human Rights Act. The process allows for the appropriate government minister to amend the legislation by order which will be subject to approval by Parliament.

44 Lord Chancellor's Department, "Rights Brought Home."

45 The right to derogate is allowed under Article 15 in times of war or other public emergency threatening the life of the nation.

46 Section 19, Human Rights Act.

47 See Klug, Foreword to the Institute for Public Policy Research, *A British Bill of Rights*, p. iv.

48 Section 6, Human Rights Act.

49 Lord Chancellor's Department, "Rights Brought Home," p. 7. A proposed amendment during the passage of the legislation, which attempted to exclude the Church from the category of a public body, failed.

50 Murray Hunt, "The 'Horizontal Effect' of the Human Rights Act," *Public Law* (Autumn 1998); Sir Stephen Sedley, "Human Rights Act Gains Royal Assent," JUSTICE Bulletin (Autumn 1998).

51 Lord Chancellor's Department, "Rights Brought Home," p. 7.

52 *R. v. Secretary of State for the Home Department Ex parte Brind and Others* [1991] 2 W.L.R. 588.

53 Unlike the Canadian Charter of Rights, the European Convention on Human Rights does not contain a general limitation clause. Instead, equivalent clauses are built into each of the rights, with the exception of freedom from slavery or servitude (Article 4(1)) and torture, inhuman or degrading treatment or punishment (Article 3) which are unqualified rights (see Appendix).

54 Stevens, "Judges, Politics, Politicians and the Confusing Role of the Judiciary."

55 Lord Chancellor's Department, *Modernising Justice* (December 1998), para. 1.22.

56 Lord Chancellor's Department, November 16, 1998.

57 Francesca Klug and Keir Starmer, "Incorporation Through the Back Door?", *Public Law* (Summer 1997).

58 Murray Hunt, *Using Human Rights Law in English Courts* (Oxford: Hart Publishing, 1997).

59 Klug and Starmer, "Incorporation Through the Back Door?"

60 Klug and Starmer, "Incorporation Through the Back Door?", p. 225.

61 See Anthony Smith, "The Human Rights Act 1998: The Constitutional Context," paper presented at a conference on The Human Rights Act and the Criminal Justice and Regulatory Process, University of Cambridge, January 1999.

62 Criminal Justice and Public Order Act 1994, Sections 34–37.

63 The European Court of Human Rights, when addressing the question of whether a breach of the Convention is "necessary in a democratic society," undertakes a two-stage process. First, it considers whether the breach falls within the category of interests listed under each right. For example, in the case of Article 8, the right to privacy, these cover national security, public safety, economic well-being, prevention of disorder or crime, the protection of health or morals, or the protection of the rights and freedom of

others (see appendix). These categories are so broad that few breaches are held to fall outside one or another of them. It is the second stage which is therefore the determining feature of most cases. For this, the court applies a "proportionality test" by considering whether the breach of rights was proportionate to the interest being pursued, or whether some less intrusive method could have been used to achieve the same results.

64 Lord Irvine interview in *The New Statesman*, December 6, 1996, p. 18.

65 Murray Hunt, "Human Rights: The Judge's Role," *Journal of the Judicial Studies Board*, issue 3 (1997), p. 7.

66 See Patrick Devlin, "Judges, Politics and Government," *Modern Law Review*, Vol. 41, no. 5 (September 1978), pp. 501–11.

67 Home Affairs Committee, *Judicial Appointments Procedures*, Vol. II (1996), para. 459.

68 Editorial, *Daily Telegraph*, November 29, 1998.

69 "The Secret Men of Justice," *The Guardian*, July 18, 1998, p. 1; "Just Who Are These People?", *The Sun*, August 6, 1998, p. 6.

70 The House of Lords was asked to determine whether the former President of Chile enjoyed sovereign immunity from prosecution in relation to charges of torture and kidnapping during his presidency (*R v. Bartle and the Commissioner of Police for the Metropolis and Others ex Parte Pinochet*) *The Times*, November 26, 1998.

71 The court's decision, which rejected Pinochet's claims to immunity, was set aside by the Lords in January 1999 when it emerged that Lord Hoffman, one of the judges in the case, had failed to declare his links to Amnesty International, one of the organizations which had given evidence against Pinochet. This was the first time that the House of Lords had overturned one of its own decisions and led to unprecedented media criticism of the Law Lords.

72 See Lord Chancellor's Department consultation paper "Developments in Judicial Appointments Procedures" (May 1994). Also see Lord Chancellors' speeches to the Association of Women Barristers, February 11, 1998.

73 A wide range of individuals and groups backed the proposal in evidence to the House of Commons Home Affairs Committee inquiry into the judicial appointments process in 1996.

74 Kate Malleson, *The Use of Judicial Appointments Commissions: A Review of the US and Canadian Models* and Cheryl Thomas, *Judicial Appointments in Continental Europe* (London: Lord Chancellor's Department Research Series no. 6, 1997).

75 "Judges Will Face Fiercer Scrutiny," *The Times*, December 14, 1998, p. 1.

76 The level of debate about the judicial appointments process in the UK appears to be much more intense than in Canada where, although there has been ongoing criticism of the system in the years since the Charter was passed, there is no immediate likelihood of structural change.

Rights and Freedoms from the European Convention on Human Rights Incorporated into the UK Human Rights Act.*

Article 2
Right to life

1. Everyone's right to life shall be protected by law. No one shall be deprived of his life intentionally save in the execution of a sentence of a court following his protocol of a crime for which this penalty is provided by law.

2. Deprivation of life shall not be regarded as inflicted in contravention of this Article when it results from the use of force which is no more than absolutely necessary:

   (a) in defence of any person from unlawful violence;
   (b) in order to effect a lawful arrest or to prevent the escape of a person lawfully detained;
   (c) in action lawfully taken for the purpose of quelling a riot or insurrection.

Article 3
Prohibition of torture

No one shall be subjected to torture or to inhuman or degrading treatment or punishment.

---

* The Act stipulates that "the Convention Rights" means the rights and fundamental freedom set out in –
  (a) Articles 2 to 12 and 14 of the Convention, and
  (b) Articles 1 to 3 of the First Protocol, as read with Articles 16 to 18
  of the Convention.

Article 4
Prohibition of slavery and forced labour

1. No one shall be held in slavery or servitude.

2. No one shall be required to perform forced or compulsory labour.

3. For the purpose of this Article the term "forced or compulsory labour" shall not include:

(a)   any work required to be done in the ordinary course of detention imposed according to the provisions of Article 5 of this Convention or during condtional release from such detention;

(b)   any service of a military character or, in case of conscientious objectors in countries where they are recognised, service exacted instead of compulsory military service;

(c)   any service exacted in case of an emergency or calamity threatening the life or well-being of the community;

(d)   any work or service which forms part of normal civic obligations.

Article 5
Right to liberty and security

1. Everyone has the right to liberty and security of person. No one shall be deprived of his liberty save in the following cases and in accordance with a procedure prescribed by law:

(a)   the lawful detention of a person after conviction by a competent court;

(b)   the lawful arrest or detention of a person for non- compliance with the lawful order of a court or in order to secure the fulfilment of any obligation prescribed by law;

(c)   the lawful arrest or detention of a person effected for the purpose of bringing him before the competent legal authority on reasonable suspicion of having committed an offence or when it is reasonably considered necessary to prevent his committing an offence or fleeing after having done so;

(d)   the detention of a minor by lawful order for the purpose of educational supervision or his lawful detention for the purpose of bringing him before the competent legal authority;

(e)   the lawful detention of persons for the prevention of the spreading of infectious diseases, of persons of unsound mind, alcoholics or drug addicts or vagrants;

(f)   the lawful arrest or detention of a person to prevent his effecting an unauthorised entry into the country or of a person against whom action is being taken with a view to deportation or extradition.

2. Everyone who is arrested shall be informed promptly, in a language which he understands, of the reasons for his arrest and of any charge against him.

3. Everyone arrested or detained in accordance with the provisions of paragraph 1(c) of this Article shall be brought promptly before a judge or other officer authorised by law to exercise judicial power and shall be entitled to trial within a reasonable time or to release pending trial. Release may be conditioned by guarantees to appear for trial.

4. Everyone who is deprived of his liberty by arrest or detention shall be entitled to take proceedings by which the lawfulness of his detention shall be decided speedily by a court and his release ordered if the detention is not lawful.

5. Everyone who has been the victim of arrest or detention in contravention of the provisions of this Article shall have an enforceable right to compensation.

Article 6
Right to a fair trial

1. In the determination of his civil rights and obligations or of any criminal charge against him, everyone is entitled to a fair and public hearing within a reasonable time by an independent and impartial tribunal established by law. Judgment shall be pronounced publicly but the press and public may be excluded from all or part of the trial in the interests of morals, public order or national security in a democratic society, where the interests of juveniles or the protection of the private life of the parties so require, or to the extent strictly necessary in the opinion of the court in special circumstances where publicity would prejudice the interests of justice.

2. Everyone charged with a criminal offence shall be presumed innocent until proved guilty according to law.

3. Everyone charged with a criminal offence has the following minimum rights:
- (a)   to be informed promptly, in a language which he understands and in detail, of the nature and cause of the accusation against him;
- (b)   to have adequate time and facilities for the preparation of his defence;
- (c)   to defend himself in person or through legal assistance of his own choosing or, if he has not sufficient means to pay for legal assistance, to be given it free when the interests of justice so require;
- (d)   to examine or have examined witnesses against him and to obtain the attendance and examination of witnesses on his behalf under the same conditions as witnesses against him;
- (e)   to have the free assistance of an interpreter if he cannot understand or speak the language used in court.

Article 7
No punishment without law

1. No one shall be held guilty of any criminal offence on account of any act or omission which did not constitute a criminal offence under national or international law at the time when it was committed. Nor shall a heavier

penalty be imposed than the one that was applicable at the time the criminal offence was committed.

2. This Article shall not prejudice the trial and punishment of any person for any act or omission which, at the time when it was committed, was criminal according to the general principles of law recognised by civilised nations.

Article 8
Right to respect for private and family life

1. Everyone has the right to respect for his private and family life, his home and his correspondence.

2. There shall be no interference by a public authority with the exercise of this right except such as is in accordance with the law and is necessary in a democratic society in the interests of national security, public safety or the economic well-being of the country, for the prevention of disorder or crime, for the protection of health or morals, or for the protection of the rights and freedoms of others.

Article 9
Freedom of thought, conscience and religion

1. Everyone has the right to freedom of thought, conscience and religion; this right includes freedom to change his religion or belief and freedom, either alone or in community with others and in public or private, to manifest his religion or belief, in worship, teaching, practice and observance.

2. Freedom to manifest one's religion or beliefs shall be subject only to such limitations as are prescribed by law and are necessary in a democratic society in the interests of public safety, for the protection of public order, health or morals, or for the protection of the rights and freedoms of others.

Article 10
Freedom of expression

1. Everyone has the right to freedom of expression. This right shall include freedom to hold opinions and to receive and impart information and ideas without interference by public authority and regardless of frontiers. This Article shall not prevent States from requiring the licensing of broadcasting, television or cinema enterprises.

2. The exercise of these freedoms, since it carries with it duties and responsibilities, may be subject to such formalities, conditions, restrictions or penalties as are prescribed by law and are necessary in a democratic society, in the interests of national security, territorial integrity or public safety, for the prevention of disorder or crime, for the protection of health or morals, for the protection of the reputation or rights of others, for preventing the disclosure of information received in confidence, or for maintaining the authority and impartiality of the judiciary.

Article 11
Freedom of assembly and association

1. Everyone has the right to freedom of peaceful assembly and to freedom of association with others, including the right to form and to join trade unions for the protection of his interests.

2. No restrictions shall be placed on the exercise of these rights other than such as are prescribed by law and are necessary in a democratic society in the interests of national security or public safety, for the prevention of disorder or crime, for the protection of health or morals or for the protection of the rights and freedoms of others. This Article shall not prevent the imposition of lawful restrictions on the exercise of these rights by members of the armed forces, of the police or of the administration of the State.

Article 12
Right to marry

Men and women of marriageable age have the right to marry and to found a family, according to the national laws governing the exercise of this right.

Article 14
Prohibition of discrimination

The enjoyment of the rights and freedoms set forth in this Convention shall be secured without discrimination on any ground such as sex, race, colour, language, religion, political or other opinion, national or social origin, association with a national minority, property, birth or other status.

Article 16
Restrictions on political activity of aliens

Nothing in Articles 10, 11 and 14 shall be regarded as preventing the High Contracting Parties from imposing restrictions on the political activity of aliens.

Article 17
Prohibition of abuse of rights

Nothing in this Convention may be interpreted as implying for any State, group or person any right to engage in any activity or perform any act aimed at the destruction of any of the rights and freedoms set forth herein or at their limitation to a greater extent than is provided for in the Convention.

Article 18
Limitation on use of restrictions on rights

The restrictions permitted under this Convention to the said rights and free-doms shall not be applied for any purpose other than those for which they have been prescribed.

PART II
THE FIRST PROTOCOL

Article 1
Protection of property

Every natural or legal person is entitled to the peaceful enjoyment of his possessions. No one shall be deprived of his possessions except in the public interest and subject to the conditions provided for by law and by the general principles of international law.

The preceding provisions shall not, however, in any way impair the right of a State to enforce such laws as it deems necessary to control the use of property in accordance with the general interest or to secure the payment of taxes or other contributions or penalties.

Article 2
Right to education

No person shall be denied the right to education. In the exercise of any functions which it assumes in relation to education and to teaching, the State shall respect the right of parents to ensure such education and teaching in conformity with their own religious and philosophical convictions.

Articles 3
Right to free elections

The High Contracting Parties undertake to hold free elections at reasonable intervals by secret ballot, under conditions which ensure the free expression of the opinion of the people in the choice of the legislature.

Are Judges Too Powerful?
Debate and Dialogue

Courts, Legislatures and Executives in the Post-Charter Era

HON. BEVERLEY McLACHLIN

In 1982, on a cold, windy day on Parliament Hill, the Queen signed the *Canadian Charter of Rights and Freedoms* into law. It marked a momentous step in Canadian constitutional history. Some, including many in England, viewed the step with grave apprehension. Today, it seems much less singular. Now the British have passed their own written Bill of Rights. In Africa, in Asia, in Europe – everywhere – people seem to have or to be getting constitutional bills of rights. New Zealand has a Charter. Australia does not, but its High Court is nevertheless prepared to strike down laws on the basis of unwritten constitutional conventions. People vehemently defend their own particular charter versions. The British, for example, make much of the fact that their Bill of Rights does not automatically invalidate offending legislation, instead giving Parliament one year to amend the law. But whatever the mechanism for ensuring compliance of the law with the basic charter principles, in the end it is a safe guess that substantial compliance there will be.

All over the world, people are subjecting their parliaments to a higher constraint, that of the written constitution. This may be the short answer to the debate that fills so many Canadian newspaper columns about whether we should or should not have a charter. It is increasingly difficult to imagine any modern democracy without a charter that sets out agreed-upon principles governing the conduct of parliament. Constitutional, rights-based democracy is swiftly becoming the international norm, if it has not already so become. It seems fair to suppose that sooner or later Canada, whose Parliament and legislatures were from their inception subject to the constraints of the *British North*

America Act, would have entrenched in a constitutional form the fundamental principles upon which our democracy and legal order are based, just as so many other countries have done or are poised to do.

This is the background against which we must set the Canadian Charter – a world that increasingly accepts that legislatures may properly be limited by the need to conform to certain basic norms – norms of democracy, norms of individual liberties like free expression and association, norms governing the legal process by which the state can deprive people of their liberty and security, and norms of equal treatment. No longer is democracy synonymous with naked populism. The world increasingly accepts that while the will of the people as expressed through their elected representatives must be paramount, that will should always respect the fundamental norms upon which the very notion of democracy and a civil society repose, and upon which the legitimacy of the legislative assemblies themselves is founded.

In one sense, the reordering of democracy necessitated by the entrenchment of constitutional rights norms is merely an evolutionary adjustment of the Canadian democratic landscape. Anyone who supposes that, prior to the Charter, Parliament and the legislatures were not constrained by basic constitutional principles, including fundamental democratic rights, has not studied our history closely enough. And anyone who supposes that the courts pre-Charter did not hear and decide on challenges to legislative powers is equally mistaken. From the beginning of Canadian democracy, courts have had the task of deciding whether laws challenged as going beyond the powers of the legislature that enacted them were valid or not. Moreover, even without a written bill of rights, courts required legislatures to conform to the basic principles of democratic government and equality. They did this through interpretation and in some cases – and this surprises some people – through striking laws down. Let me cite an example of each.

The first example is interpretative. It shows how, 50 years ago, the courts used the process of interpretation to recognize equality rights in Canada. Canada, of course, was founded amid the patriarchal notions prevalent in the mid-nineteenth century. Professions, governance – indeed, everything outside domestic work and a little teaching and nursing – was strictly reserved for men. When Emily Murphy was sworn in as a police magistrate in 1916 in Alberta, she was met on her second case with a challenge to her jurisdiction. The challenge went this way: Only "persons" are entitled to sit as judges. "Persons" means men. You are not a man. Therefore you cannot sit as a judge. Or to put it in the quaint but precise terms of Edwardian legalese: "Women are persons for pains and punishments, but not for privileges. Sitting as a judge is a privilege. Therefore, you, a woman, cannot sit as a judge."

To us this argument sounds ridiculous. But in the early 1900s it was not. Courts in England and in various parts of Canada had repeatedly ruled that laws enabling persons to do certain things – be they to practice law or medicine or sit as judges – applied only to men. Outside the criminal law, which applied regardless of sex, the word "persons," interpreted legally, meant "men." So the lawyer who challenged Emily Murphy's jurisdiction to sit as a police magistrate was on sound legal ground. But Emily Murphy refused to accept the legal status quo. She believed the law to be fundamentally unjust and decided to seek its change. She brought a case before the Supreme Court of Alberta and obtained a ruling, revolutionary at the time, that "persons" in the *Judges' Act* included women.

But that was not the end of the story. The federal government did not accept the view of the Supreme Court of Alberta that "persons" included women. It continued to deny women the right to sit in the Senate of Canada on the ground that women were not "persons" within the meaning of those provisions of the *British North America Act* dealing with the constitution of the Senate. Emily Murphy and four cohorts in Alberta sued again, this time for an order that "persons" included women. The government fought them all the way. They pursued their claim to the Supreme Court of Canada, which ruled against them. So they raised more money and took their case all the way to the Judicial Committee of the Privy Council in London, which was then Canada's court of last resort. There, finally, in a decision that has come to be known as the "Persons Case," they prevailed.

The Privy Council, in a landmark ruling that affected the law not only in Canada but in Britain and throughout the Commonwealth, held that contrary to previous law, "persons" should be read to include women. Viscount Sankey proclaimed that the Constitution of Canada was "...a living tree, capable of growth and expansion within its natural limits. The object of the *Act* was to grant a *Constitution* to Canada... Their Lordships do not conceive it to be the duty of this Board – it is certainly not their desire – to cut down the provisions of the *Act* by a narrow and technical construction, but rather to give it a large and liberal interpretation..."

In the course of interpreting the Constitution this way, two important things occurred: The law was altered, indeed fundamentally reversed; and women were accorded vast new rights they had not enjoyed before. Many people didn't like the ruling, and many people, we can safely speculate, muttered darkly about judicial activism. Sound like the Charter? Indeed, yes. Of course, at the time, it would have been open to Parliament to pass a new law saying expressly that women could not sit as senators. But reading the history books, one gets the sense that parliamentarians were not keen to remove from women what the Privy Council had found to be a fundamental right: the right to participate in the governance of the nation.

The second example illustrates how pre-Charter courts could and did require legislatures to conform to the fundamental principles of justice by striking down offending legislation. I refer to the 1938 *Alberta Reference*. The times were hard, people were desperate, and extreme ideas held great appeal. One of the strongest majoritarian governments Canada had ever known, the Aberhart government in Alberta, determined that for the good of the people, it must restrict the press' criticism of the government's economic policies. So it passed an act, modestly entitled "*An Act to Ensure the Publication of Accurate News and Information*," requiring critical comment to be submitted to the government for advance inspection.

Canada then possessed no bill of rights or charter. It had only the *British North America Act*, setting forth the division of powers between the federal and provincial governments. Nowhere did that *Act* mention free speech. Yet the Supreme Court of Canada struck the bill down. Although the result was ultimately based on the fact that the entire scheme was beyond the legislative competence of the provinces, the Court commented on the impact of this particular *Act*. It held that there was an implied guarantee in the Canadian Constitution that protected free expression about the conduct of government. Free speech was one of the pillars upon which the very notion of democracy itself existed. Free speech, said Chief Justice Duff, was "the breath of life for parliamentary institutions." As such, the Legislature of Alberta was bound by it, even though it did not formally appear in the *British North America Act*.

These are but two examples. There are many others. In the area of criminal law and evidence, for example, pre-Charter courts modified and adapted the common law and interpreted legislation in a way that ensured that the fundamental liberties of the individual were maintained. Thus, Charter rights did not spring, full-grown from the head of Zeus. Canadians had rights long before the Charter and the courts served as the guardians of those rights. The Charter accepted this tradition and entrenched the role of judges as interpreters and guardians of the rights it guaranteed. Once we came to realize as a community that some rights were fundamental, there was really no alternative. As former Supreme Court Justice Bertha Wilson writes in this volume, "You cannot entrench rights in the Constitution without some agency to monitor compliance. The judiciary was the obvious choice."

So in one sense, the Charter is old news. Yet in another, it has changed things, indeed, changed them profoundly. On a micro level, it has forced us to update our laws of criminal evidence and procedure. It has given impetus to the move to require governments to treat their citizens equally, without discrimination, regardless of factors like race, religion, sex or age. It has forced examination of electoral practices, like manipulative riding boundaries and bans on polling. And it has required us to consider again precisely where we should draw the line between the individual's right of free expression and the need to protect the community from harmful expression.

On the macro level, change has been equally important. I accept the frequently-made charge that the Charter has changed the way Canadians think and act about their rights. The Charter has made Canadians realize on a profoundly personal level what perhaps they had formally recognized only in a detached, intellectual sense: that their rights belong to them, that these rights are a precious part of their personal inheritance, and that they must exercise them and vigilantly protect them if they are to keep them healthy and strong.

If this is a culture of rights, then I welcome it. The debate we see every day on the editorial pages of our newspapers about the ambit of our rights and where lines should be drawn between conflicting rights and between the rights of the individual and the interest of the community, can only strengthen our society and our sense of being partners in this Canadian venture. It is the mark of a civil society, of a healthy mature democracy, that such things are debated in the newspapers and on the talk shows of our country, and not swept under the rug or, worse yet, fought out in back alleys and trenches.

The second general way the Charter has changed Canadian society is that it has increased the profile of the judicial branch of government. Before we had a Charter, judges were marking boundaries between rights, changing the law to reflect settled and emergent conceptions of rights, and occasionally even striking down laws that violated fundamental rights. However, the Charter, by putting the people's rights up front and centre, has accelerated the process. It is easier to challenge a law on the ground that it violates a fundamental right when you have in your hand a document that specifically proclaims your entitlement to that right. Compared to the task faced by Emily Murphy and her cohorts, for example, it is easier to change a legal interpretation that produces inequality, like the traditional interpretations of the word "persons," when you possess a document that commits the government to equal treatment. Moreover, people's new awareness of their rights has led individuals and interest groups – and they are to be found on both sides of virtually every issue – to come together and mobilize to protect their conception of a particular right. So the Charter has increased the challenges to laws on the basis of rights and thus incidentally increased the profile of courts called upon to resolve these issues.

This brings us to the current debate over whether the formal realignment in powers that the Charter has brought about has left too much power in the hands of judges. Depending on how the commentator views the issue, it is put in different terms. Some common variants include:

- "Judges have used the Charter to effect a giant power-grab."
- "Unelected judges are running the country."
- And simply, "Judges are too activist."

The idea of an overt power-grab is easily dismissed. There is no evidence that judges, individually or collectively, particularly wanted the Charter or that, once it arrived, they decided to use it to entrench their power at the expense of Parliament and the elected legislatures. Equally easily dismissed is the idea that unelected judges are running the country. True, judges are unelected, and I believe should remain unelected, having considered the conflicts of interest and related problems an elected-judge system presents. But that does not mean they cannot properly act as referees between conflicting rights and interests and as interpreters of the Constitution and the law. Nor does it mean that they are running the country.

Anyone seriously putting forth such a charge must confront the existence of Section 1 of the Charter, which permits the legislatures to trench on guaranteed rights to the extent that such a course can be shown to be justified in a free and democratic society. Should s. 1 fail to confirm a law, Section 33 is also available to permit the elected representatives of the community to override the courts' assessment of what the rights of the individual require.

At this point the proponents of the theory that the judges are running the country shift to pragmatic arguments. It's too hard to justify infringements under s. 1 or to use s. 33 to override judicial decisions, they argue. There is something in this. It is true that, as a practical matter, it is not easy for legislatures to say to the people, or even a small unpopular sub-group of the people, "Notwithstanding your rights, we are going to violate them." But that, I believe, is as it should be. Individual rights have substance and they should not lightly be cast aside. But the fact remains that, in some circumstances, Parliament and the legislatures can override judicial decisions on the Charter if the considered sentiments of the community make it politically feasible to do so. We must therefore reject the arguments that the judges of Canada have used the Charter to effect a power-grab and are running the country.

This leaves the charge of judicial activism. Judges, it is said, are too eager to overturn laws, too ready to strike statutes down, too apt to "rewrite" laws enacted by Parliament and the legislatures. I note at the outset that there is not much hard evidence that judges are inappropriately activist, whatever that may mean. A recent study by Professor Patrick Monahan of Osgoode Hall Law School concludes on the basis of considerable statistical analysis that the Supreme Court of Canada, far from being activist, as many have charged, is rather inclined to be judicially conservative and deferential to the elected arms of government. The same study suggests that it is very hard to find instances of the Court "rewriting" laws. Given the absence of any contrary studies of similar depth, this should at least give the critics pause.

Beyond this, it seems to me that if we are to talk sensibly about judicial activism, we must define our terms. Judicial activism means almost as many things to its critics as did the parts of the elephant to the blind men in the old parable.

Some people equate judicial activism with any judicial decision that changes the law. The theory here is that it is the job of judges to apply the law as it is found to exist, never to change or update it. This theory betrays a misapprehension of what judges have always done under both the common law and the civil law of this country. The venerable tradition of developing the law through an accumulation of precedent lies at the heart of our legal system, and is the lifeblood of a socially responsive body of law. New circumstances are brought before the courts. In applying the law, be it a previous case or a provision of the Charter, judges examine the law and the circumstances to see whether the old law should apply or whether it now seems unjust to do so. If a careful analysis reveals that the old law no longer reflects what is considered to be fair and appropriate, it is modified. This involves changing the law. But if changing the law is judicial activism, then judicial activism is neither new nor undesirable.

Ah, the critic says, but judicial activism is not merely changing the law, but changing the law too much. There is some truth in this. Radical changes of the law can be considered "activist" by definition. However, this does not get us any closer to answering the question of whether the Charter has made judges activist. We are left with many difficulties. The first problem is whether the fact that a change is radical necessarily means it is bad. Was it necessarily bad that the Privy Council in 1929 ruled that the word "persons" included women, thereby opening public life and the professions to women? The change was radical, but most would argue, desirable and long overdue.

The second difficulty lies in defining "radical." One person's "sensible incremental development" is another's "radical alteration of the law." Judicial activism in this sense thus often reduces itself to a debate about whether one likes or does not like a particular judicial decision. This does not bring us much closer to answering the question of whether the Charter has made judges inappropriately activist.

This concept of judicial activism is closely related to what I call the "political mirror" model of judicial activism. On this view, a decision is "activist" if it does not accord with one's political or legal viewpoint. This has led to the situation where both conservatives and liberals accuse the courts under the Charter of being too activist. Conservatives assail liberal, rights-affirming decisions as "activist." Liberals, on the other hand, assail as "activist" those decisions in which, rather than setting aside the law, the courts ignore or read down Charter provisions. Thus, as Professor Lorraine Eisenstat Weinrib writes in this volume, "…[I]t is the deferential, conservative justices who have been impermissibly activist. They have consistently ignored the values of the Charter text, its political history and its stated institutional roles." With the fire coming from both quarters, what, one might be forgiven for asking, is a judge to do?

Another version of judicial activism equates it with result-oriented, agenda-driven judging. I am the first to say that if it could be shown that Canadian judges were engaging in this kind of judging it would be bad. Judges must be impartial. They must not be biased. Their job is to study the law and the facts, listen to all the arguments pro and con, and after due deliberation, rule as their intellect, informed conscience, and training dictate. The spectre of agenda-driven judging is, to the best of my knowledge, just that – a spectre. If established, it would be a terrible thing and could not be tolerated. But it is not established.

It seems to me that people too often confuse agenda-driven judging, which would be bad, with judicial consistency, which is good. In the course of their work, judges may have developed fairly firm views about what a particular Charter provision means or where lines should be drawn between conflicting rights and interests. It is the task of the judge, at the beginning of each new case, to suspend those views and reconsider them in light of the submissions of the parties in that particular case. Yet if the judge, after considering all the submissions, arrives at a conclusion similar to that which he or she arrived at before, that is no cause for alarm. Indeed, it suggests a rational, carefully considered approach to the task of judging.

I am left with the feeling that the vague term "judicial activism," to the extent that it is used as more than merely a proxy for decisions the critic does not like, has to do with the fear that judges will depart from the settled law – that they will take advantage of the fact that no one, except for Parliament or the legislatures under s. 33, can override them, to foist unwarranted and unjustified laws on the people. The fear is well-known to jurists and not confined to rights litigation. Long before charters of rights were dreamed of, the English spoke ominously of "palm tree" justice, evoking the image of a colonial magistrate, seated under his judicial palm tree, meting out whatever decisions happened to seem right to him in the particular cases at hand.

The opposite of palm tree justice, or what we may call judicial activism in the Charter era, is justice rooted in legal principle and appropriate respect for the constitutional role of Parliament and the legislatures. The law has developed rules and ways of proceeding to assist judges in avoiding the evils of unprincipled, inappropriately interventionist judging. The first rule is that judges must ensure that their decisions are grounded in a thorough understanding of the Charter provisions at issue and the jurisprudence interpreting it. Where previous authority exists, changes should follow incrementally – absent the rare case of where manifest error is demonstrated, such as, for example, in the *Persons Case*. While the language of the Charter is open-textured and leaves room for judicial discretion in certain areas, it provides more guidance to those who study its language and values than is often realized. To quote Professor Weinrib again: "The Charter itself provides significant guidance for judicial interpretation."

It is still very early days for the Canadian Charter. But already we have a significant body of jurisprudence fleshing out its guarantees. Future decisions will build on this. The first time a Charter pronouncement is made that seems to change the law, it may strike many as "activist." But as a body of principle develops, the foundation of court decisions on the words of the Charter and the stable nature of the jurisprudence will become more apparent.

The second rule judges should follow is that they should be appropriately respecful of the role of Parliament and the legislatures and the difficulty of their task. While always important, this rule assumes particular significance in cases where the Charter or law at issue permits two or more interpretations or authorizes the judge to exercise discretion. "Appropriate respect" presupposes an understanding of the role of the legislative branch of government as the elected representative of the people to enact laws that reflect the will and interests of all the people.

To state this role is to acknowledge the difficulty of its execution. In a society as diverse and complex as ours, enacting laws is rarely a simple process of codifying the will of the people. It is rather a delicate task of accommodating conflicting interests and rights. Compromise is the watchword of modern governance. Judicial decision-making, on the other hand, is necessarily a blunt instrument, incapable of achieving the balances necessary for a workable law acceptable to society as a whole. On this point see Professor Rainer Knopff's essay in this book.

This is not to say that, where an individual's constitutional rights are at stake, the courts must always accept the compromises the legislators work out. Where laws unjustifiably violate constitutional rights, it is the clear duty of the courts to so declare, with the result that the offending law is to that extent null and void under Section 52 of the Charter. Slavish deference would reduce Charter rights to meaningless words on a scrap of paper. It is to say, however, that judging should be grounded in principle and an appropriate respect for the different roles of the elected representatives of the people and the courts.

Thus far in our Charter's short history, the courts have repeatedly countenanced respect for the choices of Parliament and the legislatures. They have repeatedly affirmed that it is not the court's role to strike the policy compromises that are essential to effective modern legislation. The role of the courts is the much more modest but nevertheless vital task of hearing constitutional claims brought by individuals, identifying unconstitutional legislative acts where such can be demonstrated, and applying the Charter we have all agreed upon.

We Didn't Volunteer

HON. BERTHA WILSON

There has been a lively discourse recently in the public press among academics and political analysts about the phenomenon they describe as "judicial activism." Some commend it; others condemn it. But it is clear that strong views are held on either side. I have been invited as a retired member of the Supreme Court of Canada to declare myself.

I am in complete agreement with those who see decision-making under the Charter as involving a mix of law and policy. I disagree, however, with those who see this as something new, who believe that judges in the evolution of the common law over many centuries paid no heed to policy considerations. I think former Supreme Court judge Emmett Hall was absolutely right when he said that "the common law grew and became a civilizing force in our society only because it considered social, political and economic facts." Of course, the doctrine of precedent ensured that judges could only make law in easy stages: They could not engage in radical departures from long-standing legal principles, but they certainly could review the applicability of these principles to new fact situations and changing social conditions. Chief Justice Laskin illustrated how this might occur in the case of an employee legally picketing against her employer on the sidewalk outside a shopping centre. The shopping centre owner ordered her to leave and when she refused laid a charge of trespass against her. The majority of the court applied the ordinary law of trespass to this situation but Chief Justice Laskin, in dissent, expressed the view that this was not the usual private property type of case. A modern shopping centre was of necessity open to the public because of the commercial nature of what went on there. He said: "It seems to me that the present case involves a search for an appropriate legal framework for new social facts (a shopping centre) which show up the inaptness of an old doctrine [trespass] developed upon a completely different social foundation."

Bora Laskin's outstanding contribution to Canadian jurisprudence flowed from his recognition that many existing precedents which emanated from the Privy Council were predicated on social and economic assumptions whose underpinnings had disappeared. His goal, once appeals to the Privy Council were abolished, was to develop a distinctively Canadian jurisprudence rooted in Canadian experience. His lone dissent in the *Murdoch* case, in which he invoked the equitable doctrine of unjust enrichment to find Mrs. Murdoch entitled to a share in the farm after she and her husband separated, is a striking example of his judicial creativity. It changed the whole direction of Canadian family law.

Professor Louis Jaffee said of Bora Laskin that he was a great judge "because when the occasion cried out for new law he dared to make it." He was undoubtably an "activist." He saw the law as a living organism dependent upon a continuing process of renewal and he adapted it to the uniquely Canadian way of life.

In 1982, Canada enacted its Charter of Rights and Freedoms, thus entrenching certain rights in the constitution. Those rights were not to be absolute, however: They were to be subject to "such reasonable limits prescribed by law as can be demonstrably justified in a free and democratic society."

The rights the Charter guarantees are expressed in very broad general terms such as "liberty," "security" and "equality" and the courts under the Charter are required to interpret them in a wide variety of fact situations. Security of the person, for example, may mean one thing in the context of overcrowding in prisons and something else in the context of the release of pollutants into the food chain. The Supreme Court of Canada held that a "contextual" approach to interpretation was appropriate – the kind of approach adopted by Justice Laskin in the shopping centre case. It also held that the "purposive" approach to interpretation applied at common law in relation to ordinary statutes should be applied to the interpretation of Charter rights as well. In other words, the rights guaranteed in the Charter should be interpreted in accordance with the general purpose of having rights, which is to secure for individuals and minority groups protection against the exercise of excessive power by the majority.

The court's role is of necessity anti-majoritarian. Governments in a democracy are elected by popular vote and are accountable to the electorate. They will, in general, enact legislation which furthers the interests of the majority. Judges, in interpreting and applying the Charter, therefore have to ask themselves which groups in society are typically shut out of the political process – the poor, the powerless, racial minorities, accused criminals. The courts have to make sure that the rights of these groups are not sacrificed in the pursuit of majority goals.

The role of the courts under the Charter is not an easy one and judges may legitimately differ as to its nature and scope. I think the time has come, however, to give the lie to some political commentators who still maintain that the advent of the Charter was a colossal "power grab" by the courts. On the contrary, we should keep in mind that by a widely accepted constitutional process Canadians decided to charge the courts with the onerous responsibility of reviewing legislative and executive action for compliance with the constitution, and they did so with full knowledge of the American experience and the criticism of the role of the courts in that society by some of its most eminent judges. Mr. Justice Learned Hand, for example, warned against the possibility of the judiciary dividing along ideological lines on controversial social issues. He thought that such division was inevitable in a court possessed of the power to strike down legislation that diverged from its notion of what was tolerable in terms of government restrictions on individual rights, and he was particularly concerned about the impact of such division on the credibility of the courts.

Nevertheless you cannot entrench rights in the constitution without some agency to monitor compliance. Because of its independence, relative impartiality, and security of tenure the judiciary was the obvious choice. Governments had available to them the notwithstanding clause if they felt that their policy-making role was being unduly frustrated. It is said, however, that they might be reluctant to resort to that clause lest they give the impression of being anti-Charter and anti-human rights.

Some judges who decry judicial activism say the answer lies in a policy of judicial deference to legislatures when exercising their review function. They should bear in mind that they were not elected to judicial office. What right have they to frustrate the will of the people's duly elected representatives? None, I would say, except for the fact that in enacting the Charter these same duly elected representatives conferred not just that right but that duty upon them. I wonder whether a policy of deference to the legislature comports easily with a duty of judicial review designed to protect the entrenched rights of citizens. I have difficulty reconciling the two.

Professor Hogg, Professor Slattery and others have advanced a view of the Charter and of the roles of the different "players" under it which they believe avoids the problem of unelected judges invalidating legislation passed by the people's duly elected representatives. They say it is a mistake to focus exclusively on the review function of the judiciary because that is not the whole story. Rather, the central feature of the Charter is that all branches of government – the legislatures, the executive and the judiciary – have an equal responsibility to carry out the Charter's mandate, and we should concentrate on their reciprocal roles. If we do this, we see that a sort of "dialogue" is going on. First, the legislatures have to examine any legislation they are contemplating passing in order to ensure that they have discharged their responsibility of Charter compliance. Then, if that legislation, once passed, is called into question, the courts must ask themselves: Did the legislature discharge its responsibility to comply with the Charter when it passed this legislation? If the answer is yes, there is no problem. If the answer is no, then the courts are obliged to strike down the legislation, though in so doing they must identify its vitiating aspects as clearly as possible so that the legislature will be in a position to correct them. The matter then goes back to the legislature for the appropriate remedial action. The courts' assessment of the legislation's constitutionality is not the last word; it is merely one step in the process.

No one, and in my view certainly not the judges, would dispute the existence of a primary obligation on legislatures to measure their own proposed legislation against the Charter before they enact it. They are well aware what a costly process it is for a citizen or group to launch a Charter challenge and I would assume that legislators would seek the advice of their own counsel before proceeding. It would be thoroughly irresponsible of governments and a dereliction of their obligation of Charter compliance to fail to do so. Because speedy action may in some cases be necessary – for example, in the case of police – the obligation on the executive may be less stringent than that on the legislature, but it is still required to exercise some judgment as to whether or not its proposed conduct is constitutional. It is to be hoped that police training will reflect any relevant court decisions.

There have been times, of course, when governments have been unable for political reasons to respond to judicial decisions. The *Morgentaler* case comes to mind. Though in such cases the decision of the court does become final this is no fault of the courts. The same would be true if the purpose of the impugned legislation was itself held to be unconstitutional and the law therefore could not be cured by amendment. The federal *Lord's Day Act*, the purpose of which was held to be to compel observance of the Christian sabbath, is an example. These situations do not arise very often, however. In the vast majority of cases, there is room for a legislative response to the court's judgment, even if that response is simply to repeal the impugned legislation. Whether these cases can be viewed as the result of a "dialogue" in the ordinary sense of that word seems doubtful. Still, the merit of the approach is that it puts the role of the courts into a larger Charter perspective. I certainly find the concept of judicial co-operation with legislatures in the protection of human rights much more palatable than the concept of judicial deference to legislatures, which seems to me to have the potential to weaken that protection considerably.

The United Kingdom has been considering the desirability of enacting human rights legislation for many years and in the year 2000 it is expected that the *Human Rights Act* which it passed in 1998 will be brought fully into force. (In the meantime, the Judicial Studies Board will have provided training for judges, magistrates and members of tribunals in the substance and effect of the *Act* at a cost of approximately six million pounds.) In effect, the *Act* mandates that, as far as possible, domestic legislation in the United Kingdom should be interpreted by the courts in a manner compatible with the international obligations the UK has assumed under the European Convention. However, UK courts will not have power to set aside provisions in domestic statutes which are incompatible with European Convention rights and which cannot by a process of interpretation be rendered compatible with such rights. In these circumstances, their authority under the *Act* is limited to making declarations of incompatibility, leaving it to the legislature to make the necessary repairs.

The enactment of the *Human Rights Act* was presumably a response to the view expressed by the House of Lords in a 1991 case that to permit the courts to review the exercise of broad statutory powers conferred in domestic legislation in light of the European Convention would be to incorporate the Convention into domestic legislation by the back door when Parliament had failed to admit it by the front door. As Lord Bridge of Harwick put it: "When confronted with a simple choice between two possible interpretations of some specific statutory provision, the presumption whereby the Courts prefer that which avoids a conflict between our domestic legislation and our international treaty obligations is a mere canon of construction which involves no importation of international law into the domestic field. But where Parliament has conferred on the executive an administrative discretion without indicating that it must be exercised within the Convention limits, to presume that it must be exercised within Convention limits would be to go far beyond the resolution of an ambiguity...and I cannot escape the conclusion that this would be a judicial usurpation of the legislative function."

Section 3 of the new United Kingdom legislation is of special interest to us in Canada because it attempts to address the difficult question of how far the interpretive process of the UK courts can legitimately go in trying to make their domestic legislation compatible with the UK's international obligations. Canadians are asking a similar question, namely: How far can Canadian courts go in trying to reconcile ordinary legislation or executive acts with our Charter of Rights and Freedoms? Section 3 does not say that the UK Courts must give preference to a "reasonable" interpretation that is compatible with international law. It requires only a "possible" interpretation that achieves compatibility as opposed to a "reasonable" one. However, if it is necessary to adopt an arbitrary or perverse interpretation in order to achieve compatibility, the courts should limit themselves to a declaration of incompatibility under section 4. The government will then have a choice between amending its legislation or doing nothing and leaving the claimant, armed with a favorable judgment from the UK domestic court, to seek redress from the European Court of Human Rights.

It will be interesting to watch evolving jurisprudence under the UK *Human Rights Act* to see to what extent, if any, it follows constitutional case law from other parts of the Commonwealth interpreting similar language or instead follows decisions of the European Court interpreting the intention of the framers of the Convention. Canada would appear to have avoided this problem by enacting its own constitutional Charter of Rights and Freedoms to set the standard against which its domestic legislation must be measured.

Those who are unhappy with the role of the courts under the Charter see it as undermining the sovereignty of Parliament as the foundation of our democracy. In fact, the notwithstanding clause, which has been described as the typical Canadian compromise, was intended to affirm parliamentary sovereignty. Governments are, however, reluctant to use it, fearing a backlash from the people, who are generally sympathetic to the concept of the Charter as a shield against big government.

The United Kingdom has decided to limit the role of the UK courts and repose the ultimate authority to determine the constitutionality of domestic UK legislation in the European Court of Human Rights. Complaints submitted by a dissatisfied UK complainant to the European Commission of Human Rights and found by it to be "admissible" on the ground that the complainant has exhausted all his or her domestic remedies and obtained no relief may be referred by it to the European Court of Human Rights. If the Court agrees with the domestic court's finding of incompatibility, and it seems highly likely that it would, it may award "just satisfaction to the injured party." This is, of course, quite incompatible with the concept of parliamentary

sovereignty which we inherited from the United Kingdom but completely consonant with the evolving concept of European unity.

I believe that Canada has achieved the best of all possible worlds.
Parliament as the sovereign power has itself conferred the power of
review on the courts, thereby recognizing and endorsing another vital
aspect of our democratic system, the independence of the judiciary
from the other two branches of government. It is up to the courts to
use that power in a responsible and sensitive manner.

The Activist Constitution

LORRAINE EISENSTAT WEINRIB

The critics of judicial activism in Canada target a mode of constitutional interpretation which, they say, illegitimately usurps the role of legislators. "Jurocracy" threatens democracy. Any court ruling that invalidates a statute or imposes a duty on the state to comply with the Charter of Rights and Freedoms suffices to raise the charge. But the greatest outrage registers against rulings that uproot laws preserving conservative social mores. While the critique lays claim to the high ground of democratic process, its detailed articulation reveals a thin and outdated idea of majority rule. The underlying commitment is to an unchanging and unchangeable political order, in which the state is minimal, human nature is fixed, and persistent identity-based inequality is untroubling.

As their starting point, the critics invoke the doctrine of separation of powers. Judges are to execute the judicial function, that is, to apply and interpret the laws passed by legislators, and to serve as simple servants to the text and the understandings it embodies. In particular, judges must confine themselves to well-established ideas of rights – fixed and finite reflections of human nature so fundamental as to enjoy long-standing and widespread support.

Judges may extend these traditional and accepted understandings to novel or unforeseen facts but may not innovate. More specifically, they must not make personal or ideological value judgments on contested and relativistic moral questions. In so doing, they impose their own values in the guise of constitutional adjudication, usurping the role of the people's representatives and flaunting the public will. This area of life is the exclusive preserve of those who make law in public, deliberative, representative and accountable legislative bodies.

In fact, this rejection of judicial subjectivism does not capture anything that is in dispute. No one reads the Charter as mandating judges to re-make the world in their own image. Those who recognize the legal legitimacy of the judicial role under the Charter reject this simplistic idea just as emphatically as do the critics.

The battle line falls elsewhere. Indeed, it falls at the intersection of the two axes of the critics' own position. They contend, on the one hand, that judges should confine themselves to well-established, unchangeable ideas of human nature and, on the other, that they interpret an authoritative legal instrument according to its text and political history. But what if the Charter's text and history themselves repudiate the notion that the political order consecrates well-established and fixed ideas of human nature?

The Canadian critics of judicial activism are social conservatives resisting a judiciary they perceive to be impermissibly liberal. Following their American counterparts, they preach fidelity to the constitutional text, its original understandings and its political history, and they portray their battle as one of constitutional principle and legitimacy, rather than political preference. This comparison is little more than wishful thinking.

Judicial work along the lines advocated – application of the Charter as a legal text consistent with its plain meaning and original understanding – is best exemplified in the cases the critics love to hate, that is, the most "activist" and "liberal" of the Supreme Court's judgments. This will surprise only those who presuppose that national constitutions are not only unchanged and unchangeable but indistinguishable one from the other. Lost in the ideological thicket is the fact that the Charter was designed to transform the Canadian legal system. This basic fact alone should alert us to the fragility of claims that the judges who find fault with pre-Charter laws are, for that reason, off on a frolic of their own.

In sharp and deliberate contrast to the US Bill of Rights, the Charter is unequivocal in departing from the values of a stable, hierarchical, paternalistic and patriarchal society. For example, it: guarantees freedom of conscience in addition to freedom of religion; does not entrench property rights; guarantees equality before and under the law, as well as equal protection and equal benefit of the law; prohibits state discrimination based on features of personal and communal identity; permits affirmative action for disadvantaged groups; and requires that interpretation respect gender equality as well as multiculturalism.

Unlike the United States, where judicial review was itself a contentious judicial creation, the Charter's final formulation drew a new and explicit baseline for the separation of powers. The courts would elaborate, on a case-by-case basis, a coherent understanding of the content of the various rights guarantees, as well as the stipulation of the exclusive, principled basis for justification of legal limitation upon those rights in a free and democratic society. The executive and the legislative arms of government would undertake the primary responsibility for fulfilling the entitlements created by the guarantees, subject to judicial oversight. In addition, legislatures would acquire the power to override some rights by simple majority vote for the duration of their electoral mandate, as long as the invocation of the override was expressly embodied in a statute that referred specifically to the rights suppressed.

The Charter thus transformed the values and institutional responsibilities at the core of Canadian constitutionalism. The critique of judicial activism provides no insight into the complex features of the new judicial role. It is meaningless to characterize judicial methodology, or even court decisions, as activist or restrained without detailed consideration of the history and theory informing the content of the right or freedom engaged, the purpose and terms of the legislation impugned, the mode of analysis adopted, and the arguments and evidence submitted by the parties and intervenors. To simply add up the results in these cases, as the critics of judicial activism like to do, is tabulated nonsense.

Contrary to the critics' complaint, it is the deferential, conservative justices who have been impermissibly activist. They have consistently ignored the values of the Charter text, its political history and its stated institutional roles. These justices evoke the ideologies of morality and family that the Charter text ultimately repudiated. They re-make the rules of Charter analysis at will in order to reach the results they desire. In the guise of interpretation, they not only impose their own personal values – those timeless ideas of human nature prized by the critics of judicial activism – they also take up an institutional role that the Charter does not vest in them. If the problem is illegitimate judicial creativity, they are the ones who consider the Charter a blank canvas on which to express their own fundamental values.

The critics would reply that the constitution is not "out there," that rights and their justified limits are in the eye of the beholder, and that interpretation is more a matter of what the judges read into the text than what they read out. Conservative interpretations are just as valid as liberal ones, and much to be preferred. Again, these claims play better in the US context where the text is old and (perceived as) static, the values not fully articulated, and the institutional roles undefined. Those who formulated Canada's Charter had the benefit of examining the operation of a variety of rights-protecting instruments which offered clear alternatives as to values and institutional roles. They also learned from professional and academic commentary on these systems.

To the extent that the critics' position depends on a backward-looking or indeterminate text, they are on weak ground. After numerous drafts more conducive to the critics' political preferences, the final version of the Charter firmly mandated elaboration of the content of the rights, and perhaps more importantly the justification of limits upon those rights, in the mode of international human rights instruments and post-war domestic constitutions. The Charter, in other words, was to provide a living constitution for a liberal democratic state, a constitution that honoured the equal human dignity of all members of Canadian society. The idea was specifically rejected that these guarantees embodied only the protections already enjoyed at law (which would have given the rights only their traditional, positive-law content) or that the rights were to cede to state action that embodied "a valid legislative objective" or was merely "reasonable" and "generally acceptable" in a democratic society. Language designed to carry forward, from the Canadian Bill of Rights, "moral and spiritual values," the "supremacy of the family," and property rights was also specifically rejected.

To be sure, no rights-protecting instrument dictates singular correct answers to the wide array of complex questions that can be put forward as alleged rights violations. Nonetheless, against the background of its drafting history, legal purposes and chosen models, the Charter provides a significant degree of guidance for judicial interpretation. At the very least, its text precludes the unthinking rush to deference that the critics advocate.

Since text, history, comparative models and interpretive canons undermine the critics' position, what of their claim to democratic legitimacy? So rigidified a view of the judicial role might suggest a vibrant democratic function. While there is some reference to representation, deliberative democracy and public engagement, there doesn't seem to be more in play than a very thin notion of representative, majority rule. No more than that, despite the fact that, as we near the end of the twentieth century, experience and theory have joined hands in making clear the failings, indeed the perils, for liberal democracy of unmitigated reliance on majoritarian processes.

For example, the critics recognize no democratic legitimacy in citizen involvement in the Charter's formulation. The Charter's value structure and institutional roles crystallized after weeks of nationally televised parliamentary hearings. Public interest groups came forward, representing the widest array of interests, bound together only by persistent, political powerlessness. They insisted that the only kind of Charter worth having was one that recognized the equal human dignity of all Canadians. Citing their own bitter experiences at the hand of Canadian governments, courts and legislatures, they called for an end to prejudice, disadvantage and disregard based on gender, race, ethnicity, physical and mental disability, aboriginal status, religion and so on. Their demand was a simple one: inclusion in the "we" of Canadian public life. The Charter text was redrafted to reflect their concerns. These hearings captured the imagination of ordinary Canadians, and across the country support for the Charter soared. In this broad-based, grassroots cry for better political representation and greater accountability, the critics see the emergence of a powerful, political machine of special interests.

The critics also disdain the continued commitment of citizens to their Charter rights. Groups that had appeared before the parliamentary hearings in 1980–1 and others of similar bent later lobbied governments for Charter compliance and/or took their claims to the courts. They also organized against proposed constitutional amendments that would have diminished the Charter's force. These efforts were largely the work of volunteers and public interest organizations operating on shoe-string budgets. The Charter critics condemned the emergence of a nefarious cabal of liberal lawyers, academics, politicians and judges – often with a bitterness that seems related to the fact that these liberal groups were more successful than their conservative counterparts.

The only element of the Charter that the critics admire is the legislative override clause, its one element that is not, in their eyes, anti-democratic. In this, too, political history and text take a back seat to ideology. The override emerged as the final compromise on the Charter, accepted by the premiers who opposed the Charter when they could not face the alternative – a national referendum on a Charter their constituents strongly supported. Both the models on which the politicians based the override clause and contemporary accounts of their bargain demonstrate that it offered an exception to the Charter's normative framework that was to be used rarely, perhaps only in emergency circumstances. In spite of this, today's critics of judicial activism seek to secure more from the bargain than their political counterparts were able to garner in 1981.

The critics regard the override as a simple and ordinary mechanism by which politicians can re-instate laws illegitimately deposed by unelected judges. They seek to neutralize the sting of the conditions attached to its exercise, conditions designed to generate focused and informed legislative debate and public engagement. What a defeat it therefore was for them when Premier Klein announced he would not use his electoral majority to suppress the equality rights successfully claimed in *Vriend*. He said that the Supreme Court had been right in requiring Alberta's human rights legislation to prohibit discrimination on the basis of sexual orientation, and he indicated that some of the mail he had received on the issue had turned his stomach – which suggests that even those who urge reliance on the override must now speak something close to the Charter's language. The premier urged Albertans to tolerance and respect for their fellow citizens' personal dignity. This denouement to the *Vriend* case embodies the critics' worst nightmare: the spectre of conservative politicians, their last, best hope, internalizing the Charter's core values.

Now we have the full picture. The Charter provides new rights, subject only to normatively justified limits, and an exceptional, qualified legislative override. The critics of judicial activism, in contrast, would prefer frozen or morality-based rights that reflect the so-called enduring truths of human nature, generally acceptable limits on those rights, and recourse to a legislative override released, not only from its built-in political sting, but also from the conventions that elected governments have built up against its use. Carefree resort to the override is the closest thing to what they really want – which is no Charter at all.

The critics' specious delineation of the fixed and fundamental values of our constitutional order, with judges in their service, resurrects the arguments of the conservative premiers who rejected the Charter until its popularity made them yield. Portrayed as a principled objection to judicial excess under the Charter, the position rejects the Charter in its entirety – its values, text, political history and institutional arrangements. The critics repudiate not merely the possibility of a living constitution but the reality of the formal constitutional change that actually put one in place in Canada. The only merit in their position lies in their acceptance of the principle that naked political preferences have no legitimate role to play in judicial interpretation of legal texts. The primary weakness of their position is the failure to apply this principle to their own naked preferences.

The allegiance to majoritarian democracy that underpins the critique tells us nothing about the new world of democracy ushered in by the Charter – a world in which we live our lives as free, equal, rights-holding citizens, not merely as occasional voters. It denies precisely what the Charter embraces: the post-war honouring of individual conscience and equal human dignity as intrinsic to the modern democratic state. The critique of judicial activism in Canada is not a serious engagement in the methodology of adjudication, the propriety of institutional roles, the distinction between law and politics or the study of comparative constitutionalism. It is the expression of deep anguish by the stakeholders of a world view in demise.

Courts Don't Make Good Compromises

RAINER KNOPFF

Charles Tupper, Nova Scotia's chief father of Confederation – and later Canada's shortest-serving prime minister (yes, even shorter than John Turner or Kim Campbell!) – was a hard-nosed politician. Like the Athenian youth Polemarchus, who appears early in Plato's *Republic*, Tupper subscribed to the ethic of rewarding friends and punishing enemies. As Christopher Moore puts it in his wonderful *1867: How the Fathers Made a Deal*, Tupper was a "bully [who] was constantly eager not merely to defeat but to humiliate his rivals." Tupper, it was aptly said, got his name from the French *tu perds*, "you lose."

By introducing it so early in the *Republic*, Plato indicated that the kind of belligerent partisanship that both Polemarchus and Tupper represented is endemic to political life. James Madison, writing much later, agreed. Faction, said Madison, is rooted in human nature. It stems from the fact that reason is connected to self-love, so that we become passionately attached to our own opinions and wish to see them triumph over the opinions of others. By faction, Madison obviously meant more than simple disagreement; he meant political zealotry. Political controversy, he suggested, is animated not by the philosophical yearning for truth and wisdom but by the lust for victory.

So powerful is the tendency toward zealous factionalism, Madison maintained, "that where no substantial occasion presents itself the most frivolous and fanciful distinctions have been sufficient to...excite [the] most violent conflicts." In other words, if politics involves the desire for victory, great victories are much better than small ones, and combatants are thus inclined to turn objectively minor disagreements into major conflicts. Tupperism – the inclination to exult in the phrase *tu perds* – leads to the exaggeration and inflation of public disagreements. One thinks here of the conflict between those Lilliputians who broke their eggs at the small end and those who, contrary to the Emperor's edict, continued to break them at the big end. Gulliver reports six rebellions and thousands of lives lost over this conflict between Big-Endians and Small-Endians.

If, as Madison believed, the tendency to political exaggeration or inflation is natural, the task of constitutionalism is not to eradicate it but to find ways to temper it, especially (though not exclusively) through institutional checks and balances. This is the standard by which I propose to evaluate the increasing power of the courts in Canada's system of government. Does judicial power dampen or fan the flames of rhetorical inflation in public life?

Consider the prominent controversies about gay rights and abortion. These are among our most perplexing social issues, and they are particularly susceptible to the kind of rhetorical inflation Madison was concerned about. The gay rights issue is (to use Mary Ann Glendon's colourful formulation) often made to "look like a battle between Yahoos and perverts." Abortion politics, as everyone knows, tends to similar extremism. Abortion and gay rights, moreover, are issues with respect to which the courts are playing a major policy-making role.

Judges are certainly aware of the intense emotions aroused by such issues, and they often appear to seek the path of moderation. A common moderating strategy is to insist that the state be neutral among intensely clashing moral views. According to Supreme Court Justice Wilson, for example, "the basic theory underlying the Charter [is] that the state will respect choices made by individuals and, to the greatest extent possible, will avoid subordinating these choices to any one conception of the good life." For Wilson, this meant leaving the decision to have an abortion, at least during the earlier stages of pregnancy, to the free choice of individual women. Women themselves must search their own hearts regarding the goodness or evil of abortion; the state should be non-judgmental.

The same non-judgmentalism underlies *Chamberlain*, a gay-rights decision of the British Columbia Supreme Court. In *Chamberlain*, Madame Justice Saunders invalidated the Surrey School Board's refusal to approve for use in kindergarten and grade one several books that portray same-sex relationships in a positive light. Invoking the interpretive authority of "Charter values," Justice Saunders insisted that the public school "be premised upon principles of tolerance and impartiality so that all persons within the school environment feel equally free to participate." This meant that the public school, as an instrument of the state, should not judge between "alternate family models." To the contrary, the school should send the non-judgmental message provided by the gay-positive books in question, namely, that alternative family models, including models with same-sex parents, "ought to be valued in the same way as other family models." By excluding these books from the curriculum, the board was being illegitimately judgmental; it could be appropriately neutral only by permitting teachers to use the books.

As Justice Saunders makes clear, the point of this neutrality is "toleration," understood as the equal approval of alternative lifestyles. Such toleration, she implies, will undercut hatred, and thus remove the cause of strife. Public neutrality, in other words, is an education in moderation and harmony.

Unfortunately, public neutrality on such intensely controversial issues is impossible. The state, as Harvard political scientist Michael Sandel has observed, cannot avoid taking sides. For example, when Stephen Douglas claimed in 1858 that each new American state should be free to vote slavery up or down, Abraham Lincoln rightly pointed out that this "pro-choice" position made sense only if slaves were not human persons. Douglas had taken sides on precisely the issue that divided slavers and abolitionists. His rhetoric of public neutrality camouflaged a far-from-neutral judgment.

Similarly, if the fetus is a person, abortion is murder, and no one can legitimately be neutral about murder. Only if the fetus is not a person does the pro-choice position on abortion make sense. Again, far from being neutral about the central issue – whether the fetus is a person – the pro-choice position implicitly, and quite judgmentally, gives victory to one side of the debate.

The same is true with respect to the Surrey case. A school curriculum that places same-sex relations on the same plane as heterosexual relations necessarily takes sides on the central issue of whether they deserve equal status. Traditionalist parents will rightly object that such a curriculum indoctrinates their children in beliefs contrary to those taught in the home. If the books are not placed on the curriculum, on the other hand, gays and lesbians can claim with equal justice that children are being indoctrinated in the abnormality or even deviance of same-sex relationships. The curriculum inescapably sends one or the other of these messages. It cannot avoid judging and discriminating.

Far from being the path of moderation, in other words, non-judgmental neutrality in intense moral conflicts really represents the victory of one of the extremes. The apparent neutrality is just a disguised way of saying *tu perds*.

Nor should this rhetorical disguise be expected to achieve the hoped-for approval of alternative lifestyles. Hatred, if Madison is right, cannot be expunged from human affairs. Toleration, understood as equal approval, is not a widespread possibility. At best people can learn to be tolerant in an older sense of that term, namely, putting up with what they hate rather than trying to eliminate it. But people are unlikely to learn this lesson from a public policy that treats hatred and toleration as polar opposites rather than as two sides of a single coin. We should not be surprised when, having been taught that toleration presupposes approval, people refuse to tolerate what they hate. Ironically, the non-judgmentalism intended to diminish intolerance may actually increase it.

It follows that moderation in controversial moral issues lies not in public neutrality, but in relatively messy compromise – the kind of compromise difficult to justify by the strict standards of judicial rationality, but precisely the kind attractive to representative assemblies.

The 1969 abortion law struck down in *Morgentaler* is a good example. This legislative compromise allowed for abortion if a therapeutic abortion committee (TAC) determined that continuation of the pregnancy threatened the life or health of the mother. Whether or not TACs were established at accredited hospitals, and how they defined "life and health," were questions left to local determination, so that the country had a *de facto* patchwork of local abortion regimes, ranging from no local access in some places to complete freedom of choice in others.

This patchwork law satisfied neither extreme in the abortion debate, and was predictably challenged in court by both extremes. Moreover, the law's local variation offended those who insist on legal coherence. From the standpoint of moderation and political accommodation, however, the 1969 law had the virtue of giving something to both sides and taking local opinion into account. No haughty *tu perds* here.

When the Supreme Court struck down this fragile compromise, it proved impossible to replace it, even though most of the justices were careful to leave room for new legislation. Unlike Justice Wilson, in other words, the rest of the Morgentaler majority insisted only on policy coherence, not on neutrality. They simply wanted a law that restricted abortion in procedurally cleaner and more equal ways. Of course, what they got – what we all got – was no law at all, which is to say, the complete victory of one of the extremes in the abortion debate. No one could reasonably claim that this result has calmed or moderated the debate. Far from it! Even a carefully moderated judgment fanned, rather than cooled, the flames of extremism.

But perhaps *Morgentaler* is the exception. Peter Hogg and Allison Thornton point to other cases in which legislatures, engaging in a more productive "dialogue" with courts, have enacted more moderate versions of invalidated legislation. When the Supreme Court struck down Quebec's signs law, for example, the province initially used the Charter's legislative override to resurrect the law. Five years later, however, Quebec allowed the override to lapse and amended the law along the lines indicated by the Court, namely, allowing the reasonable use of other languages while still giving French preferential status. Here, surely, we have an example of how courts can moderate an emotional policy controversy.

Or have we? Hogg and Thornton neglect the broader political context of this case. The Bourassa government had been poised to moderate the law in any case but had to scrap its plans in order to resist the policy imposition of "Ottawa's Court." The moderation of the law eventually came, but it was very likely delayed rather than facilitated by the Court's ruling.

A more important point is that, for the public outside Quebec, the Court's ruling vastly inflated the stakes in Quebec's language disputes. The language wars, to be sure, were not as trivial as the Lilliputian wars between the Big Endians and Small Endians, but neither was Quebec's restriction on English in commercial advertising a tyrannical violation of truly "fundamental rights." The law was arguably foolish and wrong-headed, but the state was not killing or jailing anyone because of their race, religion, or political views. Even those who couldn't read French could still recognize *Arrêt* signs and find Eaton's – or *Eaton* – and McDonald's. But for Canadians outside Quebec, the Supreme Court had said "fundamental rights" were being ignored, and that was enough. Enough, for example, to help kill the Meech Lake Accord. How, after all, can one possibly compromise with tyrants who trample on fundamental rights? Yes, a more moderate form of the language law eventually emerged from the "dialogue" between court and legislature, but in the meantime, a major constitutional accord was undermined. Even Meech sceptics – and I am one – should be troubled by this.

Finally, one may wonder about the utility of the term "dialogue" to describe what happens in such cases. As Ted Morton's contribution to this volume points out, it is a very strange "dialogue" when the major "input" of legislatures consists of following judicial instructions.

Coming back to gay rights and the Surrey School Board case: Given the impossibility of neutrality, what kind of messy compromise might emerge in the public school system? One view is to leave controversial issues about sexuality and the family out of the early grades and address them only later on. Another holds that this part of the curriculum, whenever it is introduced, should be optional, so that dissenting families could withdraw their children. A variation would require an "opt in" rather than an "opt out" for such classes. Others argue that equally credible representatives of all sides should be invited to address the issues in class. Still others advocate two streams of classes, one for "traditionalists," one for "progressives." None of these solutions is perfect or consistent, and none would be acceptable to either extreme. But they are precisely the kinds of questions being discussed in some school boards.

Far from contributing to such discussion, the decision in the Surrey case seems more likely to foreclose it and to harden what debate does take place. Indeed, a predictable – and surely ironic – consequence of the Surrey judgment is that some children will migrate out of the public schools into private schools.

One swallow does not a summer make, and the few examples that could be cited in this short essay cannot clinch my argument that courts are more apt to intensify than moderate the tendency to Tupperism in political life. Still, the issue might be further clarified by coming at it from the other direction – that is, by reflecting on the non-judicial mechanisms that moderated Tupperism in the case of Tupper himself.

Christopher Moore observes with amazement that Tupper refused to attend the 1864 Charlottetown conference unless leaders from the opposition benches accompanied him. Why? Because he could not be sure of ramming a Charlottetown agreement through his legislature. Given the less disciplined legislative context of the time, he felt compelled to share both the credit and the potential blame for the risky Confederation enterprise. If his hated partisan foes contributed to the making of the agreement, they would have no choice but to help sell it, rather than torpedo it, on the home front. In short, the institutional context in which Tupper worked gave him the incentive to get together with partisan foes to formulate controversial policy, a procedure that is almost bound to produce compromises, albeit often messy ones. As Moore recounts, the other delegations to the Charlottetown conference were similarly multi-partisan.

In the last 130 years, of course, the legislative process has changed dramatically. In our own era of hyper-disciplined parties, partisan opponents have less influence over the policy process. Indeed, the apparent decline of checks and balances in the legislature is one of the justifications for enhanced judicial power: Inter-institutional dialogue between legislatures and courts supposedly can substitute for intra-institutional dialogue within legislatures. But this amounts to saying that the increasingly unaccountable power of legislatures should be balanced by the even more unaccountable power of judges – that good policy (i.e., moderate policy) will come from a (one-sided) "dialogue" of the unaccountable.

Forgive me if I resist this conclusion. I'd much rather look carefully to see if the legislative policy process is really as unaccountable – and undeliberative – as it is made out to be (which is exactly the kind of work that Queen's University's Janet Hiebert has contributed to this volume). And if it turns out that the legislative process really is so terribly unaccountable, then I'd rather look for ways of reforming it than turn power over to judges. As a system of checks and balances, a "dialogue of the unaccountable" holds little attraction, especially if, as I think, it will not often achieve the central purpose of any good system of checks and balances: political moderation and compromise.

The Charter and Legitimization of Judicial Activism[1]

SÉBASTIEN LEBEL-GRENIER

Popular wisdom suggests that a bad compromise is better than a good verdict. It holds that a verdict is the fruit of conflict, while a compromise is born of the reconciliation of competing interests. The choice is between bridging social divisions and laying them bare. This remark summarizes the scope of the argument presented here.

It is probably unnecessary to recall that the adoption of the Canadian Charter of Rights and Freedoms profoundly changed the face of law and politics in Canada. Yet it seems that the deep-rooted causes of this phenomenon have not been sufficiently debated whether in learned journals or in the mass media.

From the start, it is important to remember the motives that created momentum in favour of the adoption of the Charter. One of these prime motives, purely political in nature, was to inspire in Canadians a feeling of belonging that was supposed to rally them around a symbol which, it was hoped, would eventually embody their identity. One hundred years after Canada was united by the railway, and taking into account the internal political troubles that prevailed at the start of the 1980s, it seemed urgent to accomplish this task. It appears today that this objective was met, especially outside Quebec. However, as a result of this very success, we unwittingly grew closer to our American neighbours from an identity standpoint. The fact that this symbolic union was carried out against the express will of Quebec is not sufficient to account for the lesser impact of the Charter in this province. The odds are that Quebec's distinct characteristics shielded it from the

Canadian identity dilemma, while the Charter's invalidation of certain legislative provisions that had been popular in Quebec led to mistrust of this document.

The second major motive was to reinforce the dominance of liberalism in the Canadian political system. For reasons probably not without foundation, but that were essentially specific to his own experience, Prime Minister Trudeau wanted to establish a mechanism that would make it possible for individuals to oppose the State. Seen from this perspective, the State was not a forum at the disposal of the individual but rather a separate seat of power which, detached from the citizenry, had to be subjected to the possibility of *ex post facto* control by the citizenry. In many ways, Trudeau was probably not wrong, but in selecting this means to meet his concerns, he gave the courts a free hand. These two motives for the establishment of the Charter could only mean increased judicial activism. Today, we must wonder about the democratic legitimacy of this phenomenon.

Judges, probably more than most social actors, are aware of the principle of the separation of powers. Having inherited a political system based on the British model, the separation between the executive and legislative powers is already somewhat weak in Canada. However, the distinction remained relatively airtight between these powers and the judiciary. Yet it seems that the Charter is now pushing us toward integration, or at least toward a disquieting convergence, of the legislative and executive powers on the one hand and the judiciary on the other. This reality has been expressed by the phrase "government by judges."

This convergence essentially operates along two axes, both of which lack legitimacy. First and foremost, the courts are now asked to rule on the wisdom of legislative measures that conflict with the rights embedded in the Charter. Judges are very much aware of the problems that this new obligation may create given its similarity to the process of determining legislative objectives. This is why the courts claim their actions are based on a purely formal type of control. It remains, however, that such control is carried out in an expressly political, philosophical and social context. Whether they want it or not, the courts play the role of social arbiter, a role that should be played by legislative actors in accordance with the theory of the separation of powers.

On the other hand, until now the courts were generally wary of directly subverting the role of the lawmaker by imposing explicit legal standards under the Charter. They preferred to limit their action to a more or less formal control of legislative content. This voluntary self-restraint is absent when one reads the *Vriend* decision rendered by the Supreme Court in 1998. In this case, the Court found that the protection against discrimination contained in the Alberta *Individual's Rights Protection Act* was constitutionally invalid because of its incompatibility with the protection against discrimination provided by the Charter. Rather than simply stating that it was invalid, and thereby eliminating the protection against discrimination offered by the Alberta statute, the Court enacted a judicial amendment of the clause to make it compatible. It therefore directly imposed a new legal standard. Despite the fact that we may, *a priori*, agree with the result in this particular case and that relatively convincing arguments can be made to defend this decision, it marks a departure by the Court from its customary position of respecting the separation of powers.

The courts did not demand that the Charter be adopted. It was imposed on them by Canadian political actors. This leads me to the second axis of convergence between the legislative, executive and judicial powers, which involves the devolution by the first two of their responsibilities to the third, especially regarding social policy. With alarming frequency, governments, whether provincial or federal, now invoke the possibility of a challenge under the terms of the Charter to proposed or requested social measures as grounds for refusing to act. Moreover, other delicate political choices are often submitted to the arbitration of the courts by means of the reference procedure. Through such maneuvering, governments avoid backlash for adopting unpopular measures or for their inaction on issues which do have popular support but which, for one reason or another, they do not want to address. By acting in such a manner, for reasons that are essentially political in nature, governments abandon to the judiciary their primary role as social arbiters.

In fact, the adoption of the Charter has increased an antidemocratic tendency. Despite the fact that the Supreme Court has stressed many times that the Canadian courts must interpret the Charter in such a way as to ensure that it does not become an "instrument of exclusion" and that they should assist "discrete and insular minorities," it remains that in practice the courts are an inappropriate forum for responding to such considerations. They are not representative of the social realities to which they claim to respond and often address them with a certain lack of understanding mingled with good faith. Moreover, and this is more serious, Charter justice is often not accessible to those who need it either because of a lack of information and education or insufficient means. The latter problem has increased with federal government cutbacks to the assistance funds formerly available to support challenges to government measures. In fact, Supreme Court precedents dealing with the Charter have often led to the protection of interests *a priori* incompatible with those it claims to be of principal concern. This is the case for the denial of protection for the right to strike, recognition of extensive rights to protect the accused at the expense of the victims of criminal acts (in cases of rape for instance), invalidation of progressive policies such as those aimed at limiting the use of tobacco, protection of commercial speech, and so on.

The extension of the role of the courts brought about by the introduction of the Charter has not been accompanied by an effort to legitimize the judiciary. Apart from the fact that judges are not very representative of society, they are ultimately appointed by the Prime Minister of Canada in the case of higher courts and by the provincial premiers in the case of the lower courts. Once appointed, they are, in practice, sheltered from any control. An essential principle of administrative law is that it is just as important for justice to appear to have been rendered as for it to have actually been rendered. In this regard, our appointment system seems to be unsatisfactory to say the least. This raises legitimacy concerns.

Although this exceeds the limited framework of this text, it is useful to list certain other consequences of the introduction of the Charter that are probably even more harmful than those mentioned above:

- In redefining social and political discourse in terms of inalienable rights, it has rendered incommensurable certain positions that should have been dealt with through social arbitration.
- In downplaying obligations, the corollary of rights, it has made the mediation of social relations more difficult.
- In stressing individual rights, it has undermined the feeling of community belonging and accelerated the atomization caused by an inordinate adoption of liberal measures.

Obviously, the Charter is not the devil's work, nor is it the source of all social evils. On the contrary, it is the foundation of important advances. However, it has had, on the whole, a deleterious influence in that its consequence has been to inspire a false feeling of security for citizens who believe that it can offset the growing lack of representation in our political system. It is a fundamental error to believe that challenging government policies under the Charter can replace the function of social arbitration by government. On the contrary, this practice contributes to a democratic deficit despite all the statements of good intentions.

In the final analysis, the Charter that was supposed to confirm the distinct character of the Canadian identity forces upon us a liberal conceptual framework which brings us closer to the political discourse that prevails in the United States. It is doubtful whether this solution is appropriate within a Canadian context characterized more by the dialectic between group belonging and autonomy than the dichotomy between individual and society.

NOTES

1   Originally published in French.

The Provincial Court Judges Case and Extended Judicial Control[1]

PIERRE PATENAUDE

The other contributors to this book examine the impact of the adoption of the Canadian Charter of Rights and Freedoms, some to emphasize the extension of judicial authority, others to insist that the framers of the 1982 Constitution forced this new role on the judges.

But recently, the Supreme Court of Canada unilaterally extended its constitutional power of control considerably. In a decision concerning the judges of the Provincial Court, the majority, through a judicial activism that cannot be excused by the claim that it was forced upon them by the framers of the Constitution ("We didn't volunteer"), has opened the door to the constitutionalization of vague political principles of British Common Law. The consequences are predictable.

The late Jean-Charles Bonenfant wrote in 1976: "Good government by judges still remains government by judges with all the hazards this may entail....I fear that...in a political, social, economic and ethnic system as complicated as that of our country, the regulation of essential problems may well be abandoned to the dialectical game of a few learned and honest people. Honest people who do not get along only give a different meaning to words. There is sometimes nothing more between a majority decision and a dissent than a faulty syllogism. Yet, this difference in logic...may determine the future of our country."[2]

Far be it from us to challenge the principle of the supremacy of the Constitution and its corollary, the judicial control over the constitutional validity of laws. However such judicial control must be circumscribed. It only remains legitimate when it operates within parameters set by the Constitution. The judiciary should not extend it unilaterally.

Restraint by the judiciary should therefore be the rule, especially when its jurisdiction leads it to limit the actions of those who were elected by the people.

The case of implied constitutional guarantees discussed in the provincial court judges case[3] splendidly illustrates Bonenfant's observation and brings to the fore the necessity of thinking twice before increasing judicial control over the democratic process.

Some people have argued that the *Constitution Act, 1867* contains certain tacit guarantees of fundamental rights that are supposed to limit parliamentary sovereignty. For instance, Mr. Justice Abbott wrote the following: "The right of free expression of opinion and of criticism...are essential to the working of a parliamentary democracy such as ours...This right cannot be abrogated by a Provincial Legislature...Parliament itself could not abrogate this right of discussion and debate."[4]

In the same vein, we read the following extracts in a decision by the Quebec Court of Appeal regarding the education rights of Jehovah's Witnesses[5]: "It would seem useful to remember that the right to give one's children the religious education of one's choice, as well as freedom of conscience, antedate positive law....If these rights find their source in positive law they can be taken away. But if, as they do, they find their existence in the very nature of man, then they cannot be taken away ..."[6]

According to these judges, certain fundamental rights that are not specifically entrenched in the *Constitution Act, 1867*, restrict the omnipotence of Parliament. Yet it would seem, according to others, that this theory of implied rights is without foundation. In Canada, only formal constitutional texts can restrain parliamentary sovereignty. Professor Hogg summarizes the opinion of the majority regarding the existence of implied constitutional guarantees that limit the power of lawmakers:

A difficulty with this line of reasoning is that the central feature of the constitution of the United Kingdom, and of its Parliament, was in 1867, and still is, parliamentary sovereignty. In the United Kingdom the tradition of respect for civil liberties is not reflected in the law of the constitution. Any of the civil liberties, including free speech, can be abolished by the Parliament at any time. Thus, when the B.N.A. Act established parliamentary institutions on the model of the United Kingdom, the plausible assumption would be, as the courts have so often emphasized, that the Canadian institutions would enjoy powers of the same order as those of the Parliament at Westminster....It is the theory of exhaustive distribution, not the implied bill of rights, which is more faithful to both the history and the text of the B.N.A. Act.[7]

Similarly, in a case prior to the adoption of the Canadian Charter of Rights and Freedoms, it was argued before the Supreme Court that the freedoms of speech, assembly and association, the freedom of the press and the freedom of religion had been inherited from the United Kingdom and included in the Canadian Constitution by virtue of the Preamble of the Constitution Act, 1867. On behalf of the majority, Mr. Justice Beetz replied as follows: "None of the liberties mentioned were granted by the Constitution to the point of being beyond the reach of all legislation."

Nevertheless, in the reference regarding provincial court judges, Chief Justice Lamer concluded that said preamble could be used to limit the sovereignty of Canadian legislatures and that therefore the elected representatives of the people could not unilaterally reduce the salary of judges. Yet the lawmakers of Alberta, Manitoba and Prince Edward Island had reduced the salary of their magistrates, in the same way as they had done for their civil servants, as part of their budget cuts.

These laws were found to be unconstitutional and Chief Justice Lamer took advantage of this decision to revisit the question of implied protections:

The preamble articulates the political theory which the Act embodies....It recognizes and affirms the basic principles which are the very source of the substantive provisions of the Constitution Act, 1867...the preamble is not only a key to construing the express provisions of the Constitution Act, 1867, but also invites the use of those organizing principles to fill out gaps in the express terms of the constitutional scheme.[8]

....The preamble's recognition of the democratic nature of Parliamentary governance has been used by some members of the Court to fashion an implied bill of rights, in the absence of any express indication to this effect in the constitutional text. This has been done, in my opinion, out of a recognition that political institutions are fundamental to the "basic structure of our Constitution" and for that reason governments cannot undermine the mechanisms of political accountability which give those institutions definition, direction and legitimacy.

These examples – the doctrines of full faith and credit and paramountcy, the remedial innovation of suspended declarations of invalidity, the recognition of the constitutional status of the privileges of provincial legislatures, the vesting of the power to regulate political speech within federal jurisdiction, and the inferral of implied limits on legislative sovereignty with respect to political speech – illustrate the special legal effect of the preamble. The preamble identifies the organizing principles of the Constitution Act, 1867, and invites the courts to turn those principles into the premises of a constitutional argument that culminates in the filling of gaps in the express terms of the constitutional text.

The same approach applies to the protection of judicial independence...the preamble of the Constitution Act, 1867, and in particular, its reference to "a Constitution similar in Principles to that of the United Kingdom," was "textual recognition" of the principle of judicial independence.[9]

On the opposite side, Mr. Justice La Forest, who was in favour of a more classical approach, wrote in his dissent:

Even if it is accepted that judicial independence had become a "constitutional" principle in Britain by 1867, it is important to understand the precise meaning of that term in British law. Unlike Canada, Great Britain does not have a written constitution. Under accepted British legal theory, Parliament is supreme. By this I mean that there are no limitations upon its legislative competence. As Dicey explains, Parliament has "under the English constitution, the right to make or unmake any law whatever; and, further, that no person or body is recognized by the law of England as having a right to override or set aside the legislation of Parliament" (A.V. Dicey, Introduction to the Study of the Law of the Constitution (10th ed. 1959), at pp. 39–40). This principle has been modified somewhat in recent decades to take into account the effect of Great Britain's membership in the European Community, but ultimately, the British Parliament remains supreme....[10]

The idea that there were enforceable limits on the power of the British Parliament to interfere with the judiciary at the time of Confederation, then, is an historical fallacy. By expressing a desire to have a Constitution "similar in Principle to that of the United Kingdom," the framers of the Constitution Act, 1867 did not give courts the power to strike down legislation violating the principle of judicial independence.[11]

Implying protection for judicial independence from the preambular commitment to a British-style constitution, therefore, entirely misapprehends the fundamental nature of that constitution.[12]

This brings us back to the central point: to the extent that courts in Canada have the power to enforce the principle of judicial independence, this power derives from the structure of Canadian, and not British, constitutionalism. Our Constitution expressly contemplates both the power of judicial review (in s. 52 of the Constitution Act, 1982) and guarantees of judicial independence (in ss. 96–100 of the Constitution Act, 1867 and s. 11(d) of the Charter). While these provisions have been interpreted to provide guarantees of independence that are not immediately manifest in their language, this has been accomplished through the usual mechanisms of constitutional interpretation, not through recourse to the preamble. The legitimacy of this interpretive exercise stems from its grounding in an expression of democratic will, not from a dubious theory of an implicit constitutional structure. The express provisions of the Constitution are not, as the Chief Justice contends, "elaborations of the underlying, unwritten, and organizing principles found in the preamble to the Constitution Act, 1867" (para. 107). On the contrary, they are the Constitution. To assert otherwise is to subvert the democratic foundation of judicial review.

In other words, the approach adopted by the Chief Justice, in my view, misapprehends the nature of the Constitution Act, 1867.[13]

The opinion of the Chief Justice is surprising in several respects. The principle of the sovereignty of Parliament is the cornerstone of the British constitutional structure. Therefore, if the Preamble of the Canadian Constitution embodies the great unwritten principles of the British Constitution, if according to the very words of the Chief Justice "by its reference to a constitution similar in principle to that of the United Kingdom," the Preamble indicates that the judicial and institutional organization of Canada must be similar to the constitutional system from which the Canadian Constitution emanates,[14] it is first and foremost the principle of parliamentary sovereignty that it attaches to the structure of our state. The only limitations are the formal clauses of the written Constitution, such as those that govern the division of legislative powers (Sections 91–92 of the Constitution Act, 1867), those that ensure the protection of fundamental rights (Constitution Act, 1982) or the maintenance of the formal constitutional structure against a unilateral modification (the amending formula)!

This opinion is also surprising for other reasons. First of all, if it is true, as stated by the Chief Justice, that "there are many important reasons for the preference for a written constitution over an unwritten one, not the least of which is the promotion of legal certainty"[15] how is it possible to reconcile this need for certainty with the incorporation in the major constitutional order of vague Common Law principles that govern the operation of the British political structure? Is not the fact of inviting "courts to transform these principles into a constitutional theory designed to bridge the gaps between explicit provisions of a constitutional text" the equivalent of introducing great uncertainty? How, in restricting the sovereignty of the legislative power through implied limitations, is this legal certainty so dear to the former Chief Justice achieved?

Finally, several of the examples selected by the Chief Justice seem inappropriate. He writes at length about the constitutionalization of the legislative privileges of the provincial legislatures[16] but fails to add that the legislatures remain sovereign when modifying these privileges and could even abolish them. To support his argument, he states that the principle of the rule of law is fundamental to the Constitution of Canada,[17] which is true. However, it may be remembered that in Great Britain this last principle could never be used to restrict parliamentary sovereignty!

It is possible that the reflections of the Chief Justice on the role of the Preamble are only opinions that are not binding on the courts (*obiter dicta*). After all, did he not write before his lengthy argument: "These appeals were all argued on the basis of s. 11(d), the Charter's guarantee of judicial independence and impartiality. From its express terms, s. 11(d) is a right of limited application – it only applies to persons accused of offences. Despite s. 11(d)'s limited scope, there is no doubt that the appeals can and should be resolved on the basis of that provision. To a large extent, the Court is the prisoner of the case which the parties and interveners have presented to us."[18]

The future will tell us what the courts will do with this opinion by Chief Justice Lamer!

Whatever the status of so-called "implied guarantees," depending on whether the musings of Chief Justice Lamer or those of Justice La Forest are vindicated, restrictions to parliamentary power will differ to a great extent. The logic of one will win over that of the other and the status of the legislative power will depend on it.

What we know for sure is that the separation of powers exists to act as a counterbalance. Furthermore, the constitutional amending formula is rigid to ensure that major changes cannot be made to the Constitution unilaterally. But when the judiciary unilaterally expands its constitutional jurisdiction, there is no mechanism that can put on the brake and stymie its ambitions!

The triumph of judicial control, carried out by an unelected institution, clearly represents a step backwards for democratic sovereignty. It is legitimate when the Constitution is itself marked by the seal of legitimacy (this may create some problems in Quebec!). But the judges, as they exercise this power, must show some self-restraint and curb democracy only when a formal and explicit clause of the Constitution forces them to do so.

NOTES

1 Originally published in French.
2 Jean-Charles Bonenfant, "La cour suprême et le partage des compétences" *Alberta Law Review* Vol. 21 (1976), p. 32.
3 *Reference re Remuneration of Judges of the Provincial Court of Prince Edward Island* [1997] 3 S.C.R. 3 [hereinafter *Reference re Remuneration of Judges*].

4 *Switzman v. Elbling* [1957] S.C.R. at pp. 326 and 328.

5 *Chabot v. Comm. de Lamorandière* [1957] B.R. 707.

6 *Chabot v. Comm. de Lamorandière* [1957] B.R. at pp. 716 and 722.

7 Peter Hogg, *Constitutional Law of Canada* (Toronto: Carswell, 1977), p. 430.

8 *Reference re Remuneration of Judges* [1997] 3 S.C.R. 3 p. 69.

9 *Reference re Remuneration of Judges* [1997] 3 S.C.R. 3 at pp. 75–76.

10 *Reference re Remuneration of Judges* [1997] 3 S.C.R. 3 at p. 178.

11 *Reference re Remuneration of Judges* [1997] 3 S.C.R. 3 at p. 179.

12 *Reference re Remuneration of Judges* [1997] 3 S.C.R. 3 at p. 183.

13 *Reference re Remuneration of Judges* [1997] 3 S.C.R. 3 at pp. 183–184.

14 *Reference re Remuneration of Judges* [1997] 3 S.C.R. 3 at p. 70.

15 *Reference re Remuneration of Judges* [1997] 3 S.C.R. 3 at p. 68.

16 *Reference re Remuneration of Judges* [1997] 3 S.C.R. 3 at p. 72.

17 *Reference re Remuneration of Judges* [1997] 3 S.C.R. 3 at p. 71.

18 *Reference re Remuneration of Judges* [1997] 3 S.C.R. 3 at p. 63.

The Charter Dialogue between Courts and Legislatures

PETER W. HOGG AND
ALLISON A. THORNTON

Judicial review is the term used to describe the action of courts in striking down laws. Lawyers and political scientists, especially those employed at universities, love to debate the question of whether judicial review is legitimate. In Canada, the question arises because our Charter of Rights vests judges, who are neither elected to their offices nor accountable for their actions, with the power to strike down laws that have been made by the duly elected representatives of the people. Is this a legitimate function in a democratic society? Is the Charter of Rights itself legitimate, inasmuch as it provides the authority for a much expanded role for judicial review?

The conventional answer to these questions is that judicial review is legitimate in a democratic society because of our commitment to the rule of law. All of the institutions in our society must abide by the rule of law, and judicial review simply requires obedience by the legislative bodies to the law of the Constitution. When, for example, the Supreme Court of Canada strikes down a prohibition on the advertising of cigarettes (as it did in the *RJR-MacDonald* case, 1995), it is simply forcing the Parliament of Canada to abide by the Charter's guarantee of freedom of expression. Similarly, when the Court adds sexual orientation to the list of prohibited grounds of discrimination in Alberta's human rights legislation (as it did in the *Vriend* case, 1998), it is simply forcing the Legislature of Alberta to observe the Charter's guarantee of equality.

The difficulty with this conventional answer is that the Charter of Rights is for the most part couched in such broad, vague language that in practice judges have a great deal of discretion in applying its provisions to laws that come before them. The process of applying the Charter inevitably involves "interpreting" its provisions into the likeness favoured by the judges. This problem has been captured in a famous American aphorism: "We are under a Constitution, but the Constitution is what the judges say it is!"

In this chapter, we argue that, in considering the legitimacy of judicial review, it is helpful to think of such review as part of a "dialogue" between judges and legislatures. At first blush, this concept of dialogue may not seem particularly apt. Given that the Supreme Court of Canada's decisions must be obeyed by the legislatures, one may ask whether a dialogue between judicial and legislative institutions is really possible. Can a legislature "speak" when its laws are subject to the constitutional views of the highest Court? The answer, we suggest, is "Yes, it can," certainly in the vast majority of cases where a judicial decision is open to reversal, modification or avoidance by the competent legislative body. Thus a judgment can spark a public debate in which Charter values are more prominent than they would have been otherwise. The legislative body is then in a position to decide on a course of action – the re-enactment of the old law, the enactment of a different law, or the abandonment of the project – that is informed by both the judgment and the public debate that followed it.

Dialogue will not work, of course, if the effect of a judicial decision is to prevent the legislative body whose law has been struck down from pursuing its legislative objective. But this is seldom the case. The first reason why a legislative body is rarely disabled by a judicial decision is the existence in the Charter of Rights of the override power of s. 33, under which a legislature can simply insert a "notwithstanding" clause into a statute and thereby liberate the statute from most of the provisions of the Charter, including the guarantees of freedom of expression (s. 2(b)) and equality (s. 15). Section 33 was added to the Charter of Rights late in the drafting process at the behest of provincial premiers who feared the impact of judicial review on their legislative agendas, and it is the most powerful tool legislatures can use to overcome a Charter decision they do not accept.

When the Supreme Court of Canada struck down a Quebec law forbidding the use of English in commercial signs on the ground that the law violated the guarantee of freedom of expression (*Ford*, 1988), Quebec answered by enacting a law that continued to ban the use of English on all outdoor signs. The new law violated the Charter's guarantee of freedom of expression as much as the previous one had, but the province protected it from challenge by inserting a s. 33

notwithstanding clause into it. The Quebec National Assembly recognized that it was restricting the freedom of expression of its anglophone citizens, but concluded that the enhancement of the French language in the province was important enough to justify overriding the Charter value.

More recently, when the Supreme Court of Canada held that Alberta's human rights legislation violated the guarantee of equality by not providing protection for discrimination on the ground of sexual orientation (*Vriend*, 1998), there was much debate in the province about re-enacting the law in its old form under the protection of a s. 33 notwithstanding clause. In the end, the Alberta government decided to live with the decision of the Court. But because using the notwithstanding clause to override the decision had been an option, it is clear that this outcome was not forced on the government, but rather was its own choice based on, among other things, what the Court had said about the equality guarantee in the Charter of Rights.

Both these cases are examples of the dialogue that s. 33 permits. Admittedly, because of the political climate of resistance to the use of the clause, "notwithstanding" is a tough word for a legislature to use. But making tough political decisions is part of a legislature's job. In the dialogue between courts and legislatures, "notwithstanding" is therefore at least a possible legislative response to most judicial decisions.

The second element of the Charter of Rights that facilitates dialogue is Section 1, which provides that the guaranteed rights are subject to "such reasonable limits prescribed by law as can be demonstrably justified in a free and democratic society." In other words, Parliament or a legislature is free to enact a law that infringes on one of the guaranteed rights, provided the law is a "reasonable limit" on the right.

Since 1982, the Supreme Court has established rules for determining whether a law is such a reasonable limit. The rules can be boiled down to: (1) The law must pursue an objective that is sufficiently important to justify limiting a Charter right, and (2) it must limit the right no more than is necessary to accomplish the objective. In practice, the Court usually holds that the first requirement is satisfied – that is, the objective of the law is sufficiently important to justify limiting a Charter right – and in most cases the area of controversy concerns the second requirement, whether the law limits the right by a means that is the least restrictive of the right.

When a law is struck down because it impairs a Charter right more than is necessary to accomplish the legislative objective, then it is obviously open to the legislature to fashion a new law that accomplishes the same objective with provisions that are more respectful of the

Charter right. Moreover, since the reviewing court that struck down the original law will have explained why the law did not satisfy the s. 1 justification tests, the court's explanation will often suggest to the legislative body exactly how a new law can be drafted that will pursue the desired ends by Charter-justified means.

In the Quebec language case, for example, the Supreme Court acknowledged that protection of the French language was a legislative objective that was sufficiently important to justify limiting freedom of expression. However, the Court also held that a complete ban on the use of other languages in commercial signs was too drastic a means of accomplishing the objective, and it suggested that the province could make the use of French mandatory without banning other languages, and could even require that the French wording be predominant on the sign. Such a law, the Court implied, would be justified under s. 1.

As we have explained, the province was not initially inclined to follow this suggestion and simply re-enacted the outright ban under the protection of the notwithstanding clause. However, five years later, when language passions had died down a bit, the province did enact a law of the sort the Supreme Court had suggested, requiring that French be used on commercial signs and be predominant, but permitting the use of other languages.

Many other examples could be given of laws which have been modified and re-enacted following a Charter decision. The point is that s. 1 allows dialogue to take place between the courts and the legislatures. Section 1 dialogue facilitates compromise between legislative goals and the courts' judgment on what the Charter requires.

Several of the rights guaranteed by the Charter are expressed in qualified terms. For example, s. 8 guarantees the right to be secure from "unreasonable" search or seizure. Section 9 guarantees the right not to be "arbitrarily" imprisoned. Section 12 guarantees against "cruel and unusual" punishment. When these rights are violated, the offending law can always be corrected by substituting a law that is not unreasonable, arbitrary, or cruel and unusual.

For example, the enforcement provisions of the *Competition Act* have been struck down on the grounds that they authorized unreasonable searches and seizures contrary to s. 8 of the Charter (*Hunter*, 1984). So have the comparable provisions of the Income Tax Act (*Kruger*, 1984). But in both cases the Supreme Court also laid down guidelines as to how s. 8 could be complied with. What was required was the safeguard of a warrant issued by a judge before government officials could search for evidence. Parliament immediately followed this advice and amended both acts so that they now authorize searches and seizures only on the basis of a warrant issued by a judge. The legislative objective is still achieved, but in a way that is more respectful of the privacy of the individual.

Once again, many other examples could be given, but the essential point is that the very language of the qualified rights encourages a continuing dialogue between the courts and the legislatures.

The proof of the pudding is in the eating, and our research has indicated that most of the decisions of the Supreme Court of Canada in which laws have been struck down for breach of a Charter right have in fact been followed by the enactment of a new law. In a study published in 1997 in the *Osgoode Hall Law Journal*, we found that there had been 66 cases in which a law had been struck down by the Supreme Court of Canada for breach of the *Charter of Rights and Freedoms*. Only 13 of these had prompted no legislative response at all, and these 13 included both recent cases, in which there may have been little time to react, and cases in which corrective action was under discussion. In seven of the 66 cases, the legislature simply repealed the law that had been found to violate the Charter. In the other 46 cases, a new law was enacted to accomplish the same general objective as the law struck down.

A critique of the Charter of Rights based on its supposed usurpation of democratic legitimacy simply cannot be sustained. To be sure, the Supreme Court of Canada is a non-elected, unaccountable group of middle-aged lawyers. To be sure, from time to time the Court strikes down statutes enacted by elected, accountable, representative legislative bodies. But the decisions of the Court almost always leave room for a legislative response, and they usually receive a legislative response. In the end, if the democratic will is there, a legislative way will be found to achieve the objective, albeit with some new safeguards to protect individual rights. Judicial review is not "a veto over the politics of the nation," but rather the beginning of a dialogue on how best to reconcile the individualistic values of the Charter with the accomplishment of social and economic policies enacted for the benefit of the community as a whole.

Dialogue or Monologue?

F.L. MORTON

In this volume, as in an earlier article in the *Osgoode Hall Law Journal*,[1] Peter Hogg and Allison Thornton argue that the alleged illegitimacy of the courts' new power under the Charter is much ado about nothing. According to their theory, the Charter encourages a "dialogue" between courts and legislatures. Courts scrutinize legislative means not ends. If courts do try to block an important legislative objective, governments have the option of the final say via the use of the section 33 override power (the "notwithstanding clause"). The result is a democratic process enriched by a new rights dialogue between independent judges and accountable legislators.

I will briefly address three of the principal problems that I see in Hogg and Thornton's "dialogue" defence of the Supreme Court's activist exercise of Charter review.

To begin with, their definition of "dialogue" is self-serving. Obeying orders is not exactly what most of us consider a dialogue. If I go to a restaurant, order a sandwich, and the waiter brings me the sandwich I ordered, I would not count this as a "dialogue." Yet this is how the concept is used in Hogg and Thornton's 1997 study. They count as dialogue *any* legislative response to the judicial nullification of a statute. If a government repeals the offending legislation or amends it according to specifications laid out by the Court, this is "dialogue." No wonder they found a two-thirds incidence of dialogue!

This lax operationalization of the concept of dialogue also obscures important differences between types of legislative response. When Parliament added a new search warrant requirement to the *Anti-Combines Act* after *Hunter v. Southam* it simply did what the Court told it to do. After *Daviault*, by contrast, Parliament created a new offence that explicitly rejected the Court's ruling that self-induced intoxication can be used as a *mens rea* defence against assault charges. Similarly, Quebec's 1988 use of section 33 to avoid compliance with the Court's ruling in the "French-only" public signs case is clearly not on a par with the same government's decision in 1993 to comply with the Court's ruling. Yet, in the 1997 study, these very different responses are all counted equally as "dialogue."

Hogg and Thornton anticipate this response and declare that even if one excludes cases in which governments simply followed judicial directions, "there would still be a significant majority of cases in which the competent legislative body has responded to a Charter decision by changing the outcome in a substantive way" (p. 98). It would have been more reassuring to have an actual number to attach to the phrase "significant majority." It is also hard to reconcile this assertion with their earlier claim that, "In most cases, relatively minor amendments were all that was required in order to respect the Charter" (p. 81). Were most of the 46 legislative responses "minor" or "substantive"? Did governments deliver the sandwich the judges had ordered or did they change the menu?

Another essential element of the dialogue theory is the means/ends distinction. By this account, Charter review only impinges on the "how," not the "what," of government policy. Under the "reasonable limitations" provisions of section 1 of the Charter, as operationalized by the now famous *Oakes* test, judges review government policy to ensure that legislators have chosen the "least restrictive means" of achieving their policy objectives. When judges believe a policy fails the "least restrictive means" test, it remains open to the responsible government to re-draft the legislation to achieve its original goal with more carefully tailored means.

As Rainer Knopff and I have argued elsewhere, the means/ends distinction sounds fine in theory but breaks down in practice. In the first place, politics is as much about means as ends. Everyone wants equal employment opportunities for women and racial minorities, but not everyone favours preferential treatment or quotas as the way to achieve this goal. No respectable person is willing to defend child pornography, but many will argue that restrictions on it must be balanced with our respect for freedom of expression and privacy.

A second difficulty is that apparent disagreement about means sometimes turns out to be disagreement about ends. Everything depends on the purpose(s) a judge attributes to the statute. The broader the purpose(s), the easier it is to find that the legislation passes the "least restrictive means" test. In fact, any half-clever judge can use procedural objections as a pretense to strike down legislation that he opposes for more substantive reasons. As examples, I would point to the very cases used by Hogg and Thornton: those involving voluntary religious instruction in Ontario schools and the federal prisoner-voting cases. In both instances, courts initially struck down policies for failing the "least restrictive means" test. In both instances, the responsible governments re-drafted the legislation to restrict its impact on religious freedom and voting rights, respectively. And in both instances, the courts again ruled that the new legislation was still "too restrictive" of the rights at stake. In cases such as these, the means/ends distinction becomes a charade for substantive disagreement about public policy.

Perhaps the best example of this instrumental use of procedural objections comes from the Chief Justice of Canada. In the 1988 *Morgentaler* case, Justice Lamer joined Justice Dickson in an opinion striking down the abortion provisions of the Criminal Code because the procedures required to attain a legal abortion were too restrictive and ambiguous. However, speaking on the tenth anniversary of the *Morgentaler* decision in 1998, Mr. Lamer told law students at the University of Toronto that in fact he voted to strike down the abortion law for a very different reason: because a majority of Canadians were against making it a criminal offence. Does this mean that his 1988 procedural objections were simply after-the-fact rationalizations to justify striking down a law that he opposed for other reasons?

Hogg and Thornton assume that if a government is unhappy with a judicial nullification of one of its policies, then it has the means at its disposal to reverse it – either by enacting revised legislation or, more emphatically, by re-instating the old law through the use of the section 33 notwithstanding clause. "If there is a democratic will, there will be a legislative way," they declare. If a government fails to use the tools at its disposal, that's the government's fault, not the court's.

This account fails to recognize the staying power of a new, judicially-created policy status quo, especially when the issue cuts across the normal lines of partisan cleavage and divides a government caucus. I develop this argument by adapting Thomas Flanagan's recent analysis of the Mulroney government's response to the Court's 1988 *Morgentaler* ruling.

Contrary to Chief Justice Lamer's beliefs, in 1988 the majority of Canadians were not opposed to the abortion policy that he voted to strike down. Under that policy, abortion was deemed wrong in theory but available in practice. (Dr. Morgentaler and his lawyers could not produce a single witness who had actually been prevented from getting an abortion.) This compromise accurately reflected Canadians' conflicting opinions on the abortion issue. In 1988, 24 per cent said that abortion should be legal under any circumstances; 14 per cent that it should be illegal under any circumstances; and 60 per cent that it should be legal only under certain circumstances.

A recently published study of abortion politics in Canada and the US found that from the late 1960s through the early 1990s "the contours of public opinion toward abortion have been generally unchanged. What exists is a situation where two intense minorities have polarized views of abortion policy that do not represent the feelings of a majority of Americans or Canadians. In both countries, the majority stands to the right of the strongest pro-choice position but left of the absolutist pro-life position."

This pattern of support was replicated in House of Commons voting on the Mulroney government's efforts to enact a new abortion policy after the *Morgentaler* ruling. The new policy was designed to meet the procedural problems identified in the written judgment of Justices Dickson and Lamer. (The government mistakenly believed these were the "real" reasons for Justice Lamer's vote.) It left abortion in the Criminal Code, but would have significantly widened access to it. In its final form, the new policy would have abolished the requirement of committee approval, broadened the definition of health to include "mental and psychological" health, and lifted the "hospitals only" restriction.

The government's "compromise" approach was opposed by both pro-choice and pro-life factions within Parliament, albeit for opposite reasons. Two pro-choice amendments – which basically affirmed the new judicially-created policy status quo of "no abortion law" – were easily defeated in the House by votes of 191–29 and 198–20. A strong pro-life amendment, which would have created a more restrictive policy than the one struck down by the Court, received much more support but was narrowly defeated, by a vote of 118–105. A paradoxical coalition of pro-choice and pro-life MPs then combined to defeat the government's own compromise proposal by a vote of 147–76.

The following session, the government introduced a new compromise abortion policy – Bill C-43. To avoid a repeat of the earlier disaster, Prime Minister Mulroney invoked party discipline for his 40 cabinet ministers and warned pro-life MPs that this would be his last attempt. The House then approved the bill by a vote of 140–131. However, it was subsequently defeated by a tie vote (43–43) in the Senate. As in the House of Commons the year before, the pro-choice and pro-life minorities combined to vote against the policy compromise, but in the Senate there were no Cabinet ministers to save it. The new judicially-created policy status quo of "no law" thus continued by default, not because it commanded majority support in either Parliament or the public.

The defeat of Bill C-43 illustrates a common dynamic between public opinion and Supreme Court decisions on contemporary rights issues. Contrary to the rhetoric of majority rule and minority rights, on most contemporary rights issues there is an unstable and unorganized majority or plurality opinion, bracketed by two opposing activist minorities. In terms of political process, the effect of a Supreme Court Charter ruling declaring a policy unconstitutional is to transfer the considerable advantages of the policy status quo from one group of minority activists to the other. The ruling shifts the burden of mobilizing a new majority coalition (within voters, within a government caucus and within a legislature) from the winning minority to the losing minority.

This transfer is a significant new advantage for the winning minority. Just as, prior to the *Morgentaler* decision, it was impossible for pro-choice activists to persuade either the Trudeau or Mulroney governments to amend Parliament's compromise abortion law of 1969, so, after the ruling, it has been impossible for pro-life activists to interest the Chrétien government in amending the new judicially-created policy status quo of no abortion law. The reasons are the same: The issue is not a priority for the government, the opposition parties or the majority of voters.

Indeed, the priority for most governments on such "moral issues" is to avoid them as much as possible. Such issues cross-cut normal partisan cleavages and thus fracture party solidarity, from the cabinet to the caucus to the rank and file membership. Nor do they win any new supporters among the (essentially disinterested) majority. To act risks losing support from the activist policy minority you abandon without securing the support of the activists you help. (After all, you only did what was "just.") On such issues, political self-interest favours government inaction over action.

A similar pattern occurred in Alberta after the Supreme Court's *Vriend* ruling in April, 1998. The Klein government – and the Conservative Party of Alberta – were deeply divided on whether to add sexual orientation to the *Alberta Human Rights Act.* Two previous task forces had recommended against it, but with minority reports. Gay rights groups had lobbied aggressively for the reform. Social conservatives – a force to be reckoned with in Alberta politics – were just as strongly opposed. For the majority of Albertans, it was an issue of secondary importance.

When the Supreme Court "read in" sexual orientation to the *Alberta Human Rights Act*, there was a strong public outcry – especially among the rural wing of the Alberta Tories – to invoke section 33. After a week of public debate, the Cabinet was as divided as before. In the end, Premier Klein declared that his personal preference was not to invoke section 33 and a majority of the caucus fell into line.

Describing the Alberta government's decision to "live with" the *Vriend* ruling, Hogg and Thornton write: "But because 'notwithstanding' was an option, it is clear that this outcome was not forced on the Government, but was the Government's own choice." They are only half right in this assertion. They ignore that the Court's decision decisively changed the government's options. Its preferred choice was not to act at all – to simply leave the status quo in place. The Court destroyed this option and – with the clever use of the "reading in" technique – created a new policy status quo.

Before the ruling, the government could safely ignore the issue – upsetting only a small coalition of activists, few of whom were Tory supporters in any case. After the ruling, the government had to choose between accepting the judicially-created policy status quo or invoking the notwithstanding clause – a decision it knew would be strongly criticized in the national media and which risked creating a backlash among otherwise passive government supporters. The judicial ruling significantly raises the political costs of saying "no" to the winning minority. The same reasoning that caused the Klein government to refuse to alter the old policy status quo now caused it to accept the new judicially-created policy status quo. In both instances, the safest thing to do was to do nothing.

Hogg and Thornton write that judicial nullification of a statute "rarely raises an absolute barrier to the wishes of democratic institutions" (p. 81). The observation is right, but the conclusion they draw from it wrong. Nullification does not have to raise an absolute barrier. Depending on the circumstances, a small barrier may suffice to permanently alter public policy.

To conclude, Hogg and Thornton's theory must be qualified to account for different circumstances. A government's ability to respond to judicial nullification of a policy depends on a variety of factors. When the policy is central to the government's program, it should have little difficulty mustering the political will to respond effectively. Examples of this pattern of dialogue would include the Quebec government's use of the override in response to *Ford* and the Devine government's overruling of the Saskatchewan Court of Appeal's rejection of its back-to-work legislation.

By contrast, when the issue cuts across partisan allegiances and divides the government caucus, and when public opinion is fragmented between a relatively indifferent middle bracketed by two opposing groups of policy activists, the judicial creation of a new policy status quo may suffice to tip the balance in favour of one minority interest over another. Both *Morgentaler* and *Vriend* illustrate this pattern of response. Some, of course, will applaud these practical results. Others, such as my colleague Rainer Knopff, would see them as further examples of how courts are "more apt to intensify than moderate the tendency to Tupperism in political life."

In sum, what Professor Hogg and Ms. Thornton describe as a dialogue is usually a monologue, with judges doing most of the talking and legislatures most of the listening. They suggest that the failure of a government to respond effectively to judicial activism is a matter of personal courage, or the lack thereof, on the part of government leaders. The fault, if there is any, rests with individuals. By contrast, I believe that legislative paralysis is institutional in character – that, in certain circumstances, legislative non-response in the face of judicial activism is the "normal" response. When the issue in play is cross-cutting and divides a government caucus, the political incentive structure invites government leaders to abdicate responsibility to the courts – and this may be even more true in a parliamentary as opposed to a presidential system. If I am correct, the Canadian tradition of responsible government is in for a rough ride in our brave new world of Charter democracy.

NOTE

1 "The Charter Dialogue Between Courts and Legislatures: Or Perhaps the Charter of Rights Isn't such a Bad Thing After All," Vol. 35, no. 1, pp. 75–124. Page references in the text are to this earlier article.

Reform's Judicial Agenda

PETER H. RUSSELL

In an era of increasing judicial power, when judges are playing a much greater role in shaping the laws and policies of the country, it is both logical and reasonable for a democratic society to become more concerned about how judges are appointed and how they discharge their expanded responsibilities. The Charter of Rights and Freedoms has certainly ushered in such an era in Canada. The public and the media have come to pay much more attention to the judiciary – who the judges are and what they do – than ever before. But until the Reform Party came along, Canada's political parties, in their national platforms, had virtually ignored these growing concerns about judicial power.

There are very good reasons, of course, for politicians to exercise restraint in taking up concerns about the judiciary. Judicial independence is a hallmark of a liberal democracy. The job of judges is to adjudicate disputes about citizens' and governments' legal rights and duties, without fear or favour, on the basis of their knowledge of the law and their assessment of the submissions of the parties appearing before them. In its constitution and laws, our democracy has established rights that protect minorities and individuals, regardless of their popularity. Making judges as directly accountable to the public as politicians are would completely undermine judicial independence. Those who call for the election of judges would replace liberal democracy with mob rule.

But it is wrong to treat judicial independence as an absolute principle. In a democracy that has given a very large role in its governance to the judiciary, there must be some lines of accountability for the judicial system. For instance, though electing judges defeats the very point of having a judiciary, the process through which judges are appointed should be as transparent as possible and as free as possible from hidden political manipulation. And it is entirely appropriate for legislatures to review judicial decisions vetoing or modifying laws they have enacted. This is especially so when our Constitution, through the override clause in the Charter of Rights and Freedoms, empowers legislative bodies to decide if they wish to retain legislation notwithstanding that the courts have found it in violation of constitutional rights.

It is to the credit of Preston Manning, Leader of the Opposition, that the proposal he has put forward with respect to the Supreme Court of Canada addresses both these points. It is also to the credit of the Reform Party which he leads that its official platform now contains a whole section on "Justice Reform." Mr. Manning and his party deserve an "A" for effort for raising important issues of judicial reform that have been neglected by the old-line parties. However, when we look at the substance of their proposals, their grades fall. While the Leader deserves a decent "B+" for his offering, his party earns a clear failure for the centrepiece of its proposal.

Mr. Manning proposes the establishment of a "judicial review" committee of the House of Commons. The committee would have two functions: 1) to conduct hearings on the qualifications and judicial philosophy of persons proposed by the prime minister for appointment to the Supreme Court of Canada, and 2) to review Supreme Court decisions that appear to violate the purpose of legislation or "the original intent" of the Charter of Rights and to recommend whether Parliament should use the notwithstanding clause in the Charter. Let me deal with the second of these functions first, as it is the very novel part of Mr. Manning's proposal.

Already, without a judicial review committee, Parliament frequently reacts to Supreme Court decisions by enacting new laws. Indeed, the article by Peter Hogg and Allison Thornton in this volume shows how this is the normal response to Supreme Court findings that legislation fails to meet Charter standards. A parliamentary committee such as Mr. Manning proposes would guarantee that this "dialogue" between the legislature and the judiciary takes place whenever the country's highest court finds national legislation has violated constitutional rights in a manner that is unreasonable and unjustifiable in a free and democratic society. Systematic parliamentary review of judicial review would increase both government's and opposition's accountability for the positions they take on rights issues.

But why not also have a parliamentary committee look at proposed new laws *before* they are enacted to see if they meet Charter standards? Why should Parliament wait until the horse is out of the barn to consider the Charter implications of legislation? Often when the courts are considering Charter challenges to legislation there is no indication that Parliament considered the law's impact on Charter rights nor that the government offered a justification for possibly encroaching on Charter rights. Queen's University's Janet Hiebert has offered a strong argument for such scrutiny of legislation by a parliamentary committee before laws are passed. This would ensure that the first step in the dialogue between legislatures and courts about the balance to be struck between Charter rights and other important considerations of public policy is taken deliberately and responsibly. Evidence that Parliament had carefully considered the Charter implications of legislation would give the courts stronger grounds for being deferential to legislators' judgment.

If politicians had to participate in the work of a judicial review committee, that might also reduce their inclination to engage in judge-bashing, the practice of vigorously objecting to the bottom-line result of judicial decisions without giving any consideration to the reasons given by the judges in support of their decision. Judge-bashers are wont to assert that in reaching their perverse decision judges have simply imposed their personal opinions on the country. An abysmal example occurred in the very article in which Mr. Manning put forward his judicial review proposal. He slammed the Supreme Court's decision on the doctrine of Aboriginal title in *Delgamuukw,* hysterically misconstruing it as leading "to a claim by $3\frac{1}{2}$ per cent of the population of BC over virtually all the land and resources of that province." Members of a judicial review committee might be expected to actually take the time to read judges' decisions and consider them with the same degree of respect they expect from the judiciary.

The other part of Mr. Manning's proposal – having a parliamentary committee conduct hearings on persons the prime minister proposes to appoint to the Supreme Court – though not a new idea, is an idea whose time has surely come. Today, Supreme Court justiceships rank among the most important positions in Canadian government. The influence a justice will have in shaping the rights of citizens and the power of government certainly ranks in importance with the impact of any cabinet minister. But unlike most ministers, Supreme Court justices typically hold office for a great many years. A mature democracy should be prepared to have its elected representatives ask those about to take on such a momentous responsibility how they propose to approach the job. As Mr. Manning puts it, paraphrasing Edmund Burke: "Before we allow these people to do as they please, we ought first to inquire what it may please them to do."

Many Canadians reject importing American-style confirmation hearings into Canada because of the unsavory scenes they remember from the US Senate Judiciary Committee hearings on the Clarence Thomas nomination. But the Thomas hearing was an aberration. Normally, hearings involve an instructive give-and-take on the theory and practice of adjudication, especially in the context of interpreting a country's constitution. Such a hearing can have a sobering effect on both sides of the dialogue. I well remember how Robert Bork, when called upon in this democratic forum to explain his "original intent" approach to constitutional interpretation, found he had to admit that there were important cases where it could not or should not apply. The open, public scrutiny of the ideas and experience of candidates for high judicial office that occurs in the United States strikes me as much more adult and democratic than the rumour-mongering and gossip carried on in the Canadian media for weeks before the prime minister unveils his choice. Do Canadians really prefer to be "blind-sided"?

The other frequently voiced objection to confirmation hearings for Supreme Court nominees is that many very well qualified candidates would refuse to subject themselves to such a process. The answer to this is surely very simple – good riddance. A person who is so adverse to public scrutiny, no matter how well qualified he or she may be in a technical professional sense, is not qualified for service on the Supreme Court of Canada. Supreme Court justices, given the importance of their work and the interest the public takes in it, will be under constant public scrutiny. Confirmation hearings will rightly eliminate anyone who cannot take the political heat. In days gone by, when it was not easy to attract top-notch jurists to the Court, this objection had some weight. But those days are long gone. Today there is no dearth of outstanding lawyers and judges willing to submit to public scrutiny as a condition of donning a Supreme Court justice's robes.

The Reform Party's justice reform proposals are much more radical and much less sensible than their leader's. The party proposes that provincial legislatures "rather than the Prime Minister" be responsible for nominations to the Supreme Court and all other courts to which the federal government appoints judges. This would mean that provincial and territorial politicians would select the judges for all of the provincial and territorial courts of appeal, the highest trial courts of the provinces and territories, the Federal Court of Canada, the Tax Court of Canada and the Court Martial Appeal Court. This is a crazy idea.

Recruiting and selecting the best-qualified persons for the highest trial and appeal courts across this country is not an appropriate task for legislative assemblies. It is a task best performed by well-structured nominating committees made up of representatives of government, bench and bar, and the general public. A number of provinces have such committees in place for nominations to provincial courts. At the federal level, the Mulroney government in 1988 took the first step in this direction when it set up a system of advisory committees in each province and territory. The members of these committees are the provincial or territorial Chief Justice or a judge designated by the Chief Justice, two representatives of the legal profession, and two persons who are expected to be non-lawyers – one appointed by the federal Minister of Justice and the other by the provincial or territorial Attorney General. These committees do not function as nominating committees. They are screening committees who advise the federal government on whether or not persons under consideration for judicial appointment are qualified. The Chrétien government refined the system a little, introducing regional committees in the larger provinces and inviting the committees to distinguish "highly qualified" candidates from those who are merely "qualified."It is through a reformed system of nominating committees that the Reform party should seek to strengthen the provincial role in selecting judges for Canada's highest trial and appeal courts.

The judiciary advisory committees still have many inadequacies. They do not function as true nominating committees. As a result the selection process is still too much under the unfettered control of the federal justice minister and the prime minister. Nor is the system an accountable one. Very little is known about it; the committees do not report on their work to the legislature; and the membership of the committees could be larger and more representative. The Reform party would do the country much more of a service if it concentrated on reforming this system rather than advocating its ill-considered alternative.

Still, I conclude by commending the party and its leader for entering into an area where the established parties have been either too timid or too complacent to tread. In the final account, however, I fear that until we Canadians produce a Parliament that requires a more accountable government, the federal government will pay little attention to producing more accountable arrangements for the appointment of judges.

Editors note: Since this paper refers to specific policies of the Reform party, the original text has not been updated to reflect the dissolution of Reform and the establishment of the Canadian Alliance.

A "B" for Prof. Russell

E. PRESTON MANNING

Peter Russell's article concerning the Reform party's desire for democratic control over judicial power is a thoughtful analysis which recognizes the importance of the issue. Overall, he certainly deserves a "B," with prospects for improvement through further interaction with legislators and others concerned about the problem.

We welcome his support for the "judicial review committee" proposed in our "New Canada Act." And he raises an important point as to the need for a committee of the House to review proposed legislation before it is enacted for Charter compliance.

At present, section 4.1 of the *Department of Justice Act* gives the Minister of Justice responsibility to examine all regulations and all government bills "to ascertain whether any of the provisions thereof are inconsistent with the purposes and provisions of the *Canadian Charter of Rights and Freedoms*" and to report any inconsistency to the House "at the first convenient opportunity."

The idea of examining all legislation in advance is therefore not new. The problem is that the system clearly is not working. Legislation that has been cleared by the Minister of Justice is frequently found wanting by the courts. Has she been receiving bad legal advice? We do not know because the Department's advice is given to the minister confidentially and not to Members of Parliament.

Perhaps independent experts should give the judicial review committee assessments of legislation when a question of possible infringement of Charter rights arises. Indeed, the committee should make such assessments public so that everyone – voters and Supreme Court judges – can recognize the balance which elected and accountable

MPs strike between competing rights, and how they understand the Charter of Rights' great qualifier: "subject to such reasonable limits prescribed by law as can be justified in a free and democratic society."

I am not sure that such prior review of legislation will do much to rein in judges, however. The child pornography legislation followed public hearings and a great deal of consultation and parliamentary debate, including the presentation of private members' bills. And yet Justice Shaw did not deign to examine or comment on the parliamentary record when declaring unconstitutional the criminal sanctions against possession of child pornography.

I find Prof. Russell's strictures on provincial nomination of judges unconvincing. Calling the idea "crazy" is simply not a substitute for rational analysis. He concedes that there are serious problems with the current system of appointing judges and calls for the system to be "as transparent as possible and as free as possible from political manipulation." At the Supreme Court level, he favors our proposal to have public hearings before federal legislators, but for some unspecified reason he considers this "not an appropriate task" for provincial legislators. Why? Provincial legislators would seem to be just as qualified as MPs to consider the qualifications of persons who wish to sit on the bench.

The essential point is that the public have confidence in the process for nominating judges. Prof. Russell suggests tinkering with the membership of judicial nomination committees, but there is precious little evidence that nominating committees have been effective in raising the standards of the bench. After all, Justice Flahiff – recently convicted of money-laundering – was nominated through this process. Certainly, no committee providing a list of "qualified" candidates after a secret process can ever provide the transparency that nomination by a legislature would entail.

In a democracy, policy must be made by persons who are elected by and accountable to the people. Yet, increasingly the courts are arrogating this role to themselves. What are the people to think of the Supreme Court's use of the Charter in criminal matters when:

- Thousands of accused avoid a trial because the Court adopted a mechanical and artificial approach to determining the appropriate time for a case to come to trial;
- The "rape shield" protection of witnesses in sexual assault trials is struck down;
- Convicted sexual offenders are allowed to loiter near a school ground, playground, public park or bathing area;
- The defence of self-induced intoxication is allowed in a sexual assault case;

- The police officer who was investigating a heinous murder of an old man is said to have a flagrant disregard for Charter rights simply because, after knocking and receiving no answer, he entered a trailer and found the accused, Feeney, covered with his victim's blood. Five Supreme Court judges chastised the officer and declared that the bloody shirt could not be used in evidence.

Our criminal courts no longer examine the evidence to determine whether the accused is guilty. Instead, they examine every action of the officer under a microscope, in case there is the slightest breach of the rights of the accused so the evidence can be excluded. The Feeney case illustrates the way our trials are not a search for truth.

In future, Prof. Russell might address another significant problem in the relation between legislators and the judiciary. That is the preference shown by Liberal justice ministers to leave the law open to judicial interpretation. In the child pornography matter, Anne McLellan whipped her caucus into line to wait for the appeal courts rather than allowing them to follow their own consciences and defend the will of Parliament, which unanimously passed the law banning the possession of child pornography only six years ago.

Allan Rock when he introduced amendments to the *Human Rights Act* was pressed by Reform for a definition of "sexual orientation" to ensure that paedophiles could not argue they were protected. He refused to clearly exclude paedophilia, leaving it to the courts to determine the meaning in a subsequent case. To me, this is a clear abdication of his responsibility as a minister to ensure that legislation clearly expresses the will of Parliament.

With such weak justice ministers, it is not surprising that the Supreme Court has become the favoured venue for deciding major social policies, rather than the legislatures and Parliament. Activist Supreme Court decisions on social policy include:

- deciding how to organize minority language instruction
- striking down abortion laws
- deciding how BC should spend scarce health-care dollars
- reading-in "sexual orientation" to the human rights legislation of the province of Alberta, even though its legislature had explicitly refused to do so
- stripping the legislatures of their authority to set the salaries of judges they appoint.

Is it any wonder people are asking who is in charge and to whom judges are accountable? Prof. Russell might in future wish to offer a fuller discussion of the effect of these activist decisions on our democracy. The fundamental question is: At the end of the day, who makes law in Canada? The men and women from all walks of life whom we elect to Parliament and the provincial legislatures or the appointed and unaccountable judges?

I conclude by commending Prof. Russell for his thoughtful contribution to the debate. Like him, I believe that we need a more accountable government before significant reform will occur. On that subject, I invite his continued consideration of the proposals for democratic reform we have put forward in the "New Canada Act" to make government more accountable to the House of Commons and to empower Members of Parliament to vote as they see fit rather than as the whips instruct. Prof. Russell's participation in that debate would be most welcome.

PROF. RUSSELL REPLIES

Mr. Manning is mistaken in thinking my approach to reforming the federal judicial appointing system is simply "tinkering with the membership of judicial nominating committees." My point is that at the federal level we do not yet have nominating committees. The judicial advisory committees that are now in place function basically as screening committees. They advise the Minister of Justice whether persons whose names are sent to them are "not qualified," "qualified" or "highly qualified." Unlike nominating committees, they do not: advertize positions, carry out intensive background inquiries, interview the most promising candidates or submit to the minister a short list of the most outstanding candidates (a list from which the minister must select the person to be appointed). Nominating committees with these responsibilities function in several provinces, including Ontario – for judges who are provincially appointed. Contrary to Mr. Manning's suggestion, there is plenty of evidence that they have been effective in raising the standards of the provincially appointed bench.

So what I am calling for – and what the Canadian Bar Association and the Canadian Law Teachers have called for in the past – is that the federal government adopt a true nominating committee system for the judicial appointments which under our Constitution are its responsibility.

Why do I think it would be a "crazy idea" to have these nominating committees at the federal level made up entirely of provincial legislators? First, because I believe they should have a federal/provincial structure. Though it is true that the main courts to which the federal government makes appointments are the highest trial and appeal courts of the provinces and territories, I have always thought of these courts as national courts. They play a major role in administering and interpreting all of our laws – federal and provincial. Both levels of government should have a role in staffing the nominating committees that recruit and select persons for these courts.

An even more fundamental objection to the Reform party proposal is that a nominating committee made up solely of legislators would lack the requisite mix of experience and knowledge. In assessing the qualifications of candidates for judicial office, nominating committees need the wisdom of experienced judges and of respected and knowledgeable representatives of the legal profession. They also should have lay members representative of the community served by the courts. I have no objection to provincial legislatures (and the federal parliament) naming people to these committees, and indeed would prefer that to having the federal and provincial governments select the lay members (as is the case now with the federal screening committees). And if members of legislatures are willing to make the the very considerable commitment of time that the work of a true nominating committee entails, then I see no objection to their serving on such committees, though only as part of the committees' membership.

With or without the participation of legislators, however, I think it would not be a good idea for committees dealing with the selection of judges below the Supreme Court to interview candidates in public sessions. This would exclude too many outstanding candidates who would be unwilling to submit themselves to such a public process and, in the case of rejection, risk serious damage to their professional standing. On the other hand, at the Supreme Court level, given the enormous importance of the Court's decisions to the country and the prestige attached to even being considered for such a position, I think the risk of losing the odd blushing violet is well worth taking.

I am pleased to learn that Reform does not favour the election of judges. However, I do not accept Mr. Manning's assertion that in a democracy it is only elected persons who can legitimately make policy. In the common law tradition, judges have always made law. They made and continue to develop the common law, including the defences available to an accused person. They have never had the last word, however, as legislatures by statute can modify or reject their articulations of common law – which is exactly what Parliament did in response to the Supreme Court's decision on the defence of self-induced intoxication. I agree with Parliament's action in this case, but not with Mr. Manning's suggestion that the Supreme Court has no business developing the common law.

The common law is by no means the only area in which courts traditionally have had a major influence in shaping public policy. In interpreting the general terms of statutes and applying them to particular circumstances which inevitably were unforeseen by the legislature, courts have an inescapable influence on policy. Similarly, in interpreting the broad terms of our Constitution – phrases like "peace, order and good government" and "property and civil rights," which delineate the boundary between federal and provincial jurisdiction – our courts have had a major influence on the real, living Constitution. And this influence was bound to grow when Canada added a charter of fundamental rights and freedoms to our Constitution. Phrases such as "freedom of expression," "the right to life, liberty and security of the person" or of limits on rights that "can be demonstrably justified in a free and democratic society" are not self-interpreting. In applying them, case by case, the courts flesh out their meaning – and in so doing play a major role in making "the policy of rights."

Fortunately, our Canadian democracy had the good sense not to give the judiciary the last word in making this policy of rights. On most Charter rights, our legislators can reject or modify the judicial policy product for five years at a time, and if what the courts have produced is overwhelmingly unpopular they can reverse them permanently by amending the Constitution.

Making the policy of rights should be seen as a joint responsibility of courts and legislatures. For instance, with respect to the Supreme Court's interpretation of the right of an accused person "to be tried within a reasonable time," instead of simply attacking the Court for adopting "a mechanical and artificial approach" Mr. Manning should direct his party research office to develop, as possible *Criminal Code* amendments, better guidelines than the Court's for balancing all the factors that ought to be taken into account in determining whether the delay in bringing an accused to trial is unreasonable. I am willing to wager that such an exercise will persuade him to be less scathing about the Supreme Court's effort.

Finally, I would also wager that spending just one day in a trial court anywhere in this country would induce Mr. Manning to withdraw the quite extraordinary statement that "Our criminal courts no longer examine the evidence to determine whether the accused is guilty."

Judicial Authority, Issues and Controversies

Merit Selection and Democratization of Appointments to the Supreme Court of Canada

JACOB S. ZIEGEL

INTRODUCTION

The long simmering debate over the appropriate method of appointing judges to the Supreme Court of Canada in the Charter era has flared up again over the past year. It is safe to assume that the debate will continue to attract the attention of Supreme Court watchers until a more satisfactory method of appointment is adopted than the present.

The current resurgence of interest is illustrated, among others, by the following events. In Alberta and elsewhere in Canada, right wing politicians have long been critical of the activist role of the Supreme Court.[1] The criticism mounted last year with the Supreme Court's decision in the *Vriend* case[2] declaring Alberta's Human Rights Code to be in violation of the equality provision in the Charter because it discriminated against gays and lesbians.[3] Critics urged the Klein government to use the override provision in the Charter to reverse the Supreme Court's judgement, although the province eventually decided against it. Then, much more recently, Justice McClung's unprecedented public outburst over Justice L'Heureux-Dubé's criticisms of his judgement in the *Ewanchuk* case[4] sparked a vigorous media debate on gender issues in the Supreme Court and Justice L'Heureux-Dubé's gender philosophy.[5]

Not surprisingly, these events have encouraged editorialists and politicians to renew their calls for greater transparency in the appointment of Supreme Court judges.[6] Members of the Supreme Court have also been drawn into the debate. Last September, shortly after announcing his retirement from the Court, Justice Gérard V. La Forest indicated his support for some sort of confirmation procedure for appointments of Supreme Court judges.[7] On the other hand, in a similar but more recent interview following the announcement of his retirement, Justice Peter Cory expressed strong opposition to any confirmation procedure that included questioning of nominees for appointment about issues likely to come before the Court.[8] In a subsequent address to law students, Justice Frank Iacobucci also expressed his hostility to a public confirmation procedure.[9]

Meanwhile, reacting to common knowledge in the Toronto legal community that supporters of John Laskin and Rosie Abella, both members of the Ontario Court of Appeal, had actively lobbied for their favoured candidate to succeed Justice John Sopinka on the Supreme Court, Chief Justice Lamer publicly rebuked both factions for engaging in conduct that, in his view, was bound to tarnish the Court's good image in the public eye.[10]

Events of this genre are not peculiar to Canada. Similar debates about the role of the country's highest court and desirable changes in the method of appointments are taking place in Australia, England and New Zealand, and in the Council of Europe with respect to the European Court of Human Rights. At the same time, a vast literature has been spawned in the US about the confirmation procedure for appointments to the US Supreme Court following the Senate's rejection of Robert Bork's nomination in 1988 and the approval of Clarence Thomas by a narrow margin in 1991.

What is surprising about the Canadian scene is that since the rejection by Canadian voters of the Charlottetown Accord, both the Conservative and Liberal governments have evinced no interest in revising the selection method for appointments to the Supreme Court. In the case of the current administration, this may suggest either that Prime Minister Chrétien is quite happy with the existing system or that he feels that any changes must take place in the framework of generally agreed upon constitutional changes – changes, as he has often made clear, that are unlikely to take place in the foreseeable future. Another article, therefore, on appointments to the Supreme Court may seem futile. I do not share this pessimism and this article proceeds from the premise that greater accountability and transparency in the appointments is much overdue although some constitutional hurdles may have to be overcome in order to bring about the necessary changes.[11]

Two alternative or cumulative recommendations are presented below to address the shortcomings of the existing system of appointments:

- The establishment of a nominating committee that would present the prime minister with a short list of candidates to fill vacancies as they arise;
- The introduction of a parliamentary confirmation procedure for candidates presented by the prime minister for appointment to the Supreme Court.

Before describing these recommendations, I first consider the role of the Supreme Court, the existing appointment procedure, and the methods in place in other countries for appointments to the highest courts.

THE SUPREME COURT'S ADJUDICATIVE ROLES

An appropriate starting point for the discussion is an appreciation of the overarching role played by the Supreme Court in Canada's legal firmament.[12] The Court's position as the final arbiter of the meaning and interpretation of the Charter of Rights and Freedoms is its most visible and intrusive role since 1982, but it is only one of several roles. Since the abolition of appeals to the Privy Council in 1949, the Court has also become the court of last resort in appeals concerning the division of powers between the federal and provincial governments and on all other constitutional questions arising under the Constitution Act, including being expected to advise the country on the meta-legal rules applying in a post-secessionist Canada!

Thirdly, unlike many other constitutional courts in the Western hemisphere, the Supreme Court discharges the very heavy burden of supervising Canada's criminal justice system and other public law areas, as well as having the last word on judicially crafted doctrines and principles in the private law area applicable at both the provincial and federal levels. It is common to speak of the Supreme Court's role in the non-constitutional arena as being interstitial in character since its decisions can be changed by legislation. This is true in theory but it does not reflect the actual practice since to a large extent the federal and provincial legislatures have been content to let the courts apply and develop private law principles with little interference, especially those applying outside Quebec. Significantly, the Supreme Court's value-laden Charter role has also encouraged it to adjudicate much more boldly on non-Charter issues than it did before 1982.[13]

Still, it is the Court's decisions on the Charter that have engendered the most debate and, it is safe to assume, will continue to do so in the future. It is easy to see why. In a couple of dozen sections the Charter entrenches those democratic, legal and egalitarian values regarded as fundamental in regulating relations in a modern liberal state between a government and its citizens. Unavoidably, since the values themselves are open-ended and relative, so are the Charter provisions. It is left to the nine members of the Court to give them meaning and content, and equally to determine when the rights-oriented norms can be departed from under section 1 of the Charter because of compelling societal needs. Apparently some Canadian judges still believe that this "interpretive" task is no different from the roles played by the Supreme Court before 1982,[14] but clearly this is not so. In giving content to the Charter provisions, judges are bound to bring into play their own political philosophies and life experiences and thus to support or disappoint the various interests appearing before them.

This consequence of the entrenchment of a bill of rights is well understood in the US and accounts for the close scrutiny and sometimes fierce debates surrounding new appointments to the US Supreme Court. As Justice Felix Frankfurter wrote in 1930, "It is because the [US] Supreme Court wields the power that it wields, that appointment to the Court is a matter of general public concern and not merely a question for the profession. In truth, the Supreme Court *is* the Constitution."[15] These words are equally apt in describing the role of the Canadian Supreme Court.[16]

EXISTING SYSTEM OF APPOINTMENTS TO THE SUPREME COURT

Anomalously for a federal system and subject to what is said hereafter, the Supreme Court is not entrenched in the Canadian constitution. In fact, the Supreme Court was not mentioned by name before the adoption of the *Constitution Act 1982*. Rather, the *Constitution Act 1867* merely *empowered* the federal Parliament to establish a general court of appeal for Canada[17] and that power was only exercised eight years later with the establishment of the Supreme Court in 1875.[18]

This casual approach to the need for an indigenous final court of appeal for Canada was not accidental. On the contrary, it very much reflected the belief of the Fathers of Confederation that the Privy Council in London should remain the court of final resort on questions of Canadian law, not only on questions of constitutional law and in other public law areas but in matters of private law as well. Although sentiments began to change after the First World War, it was not until 1949 that appeals to the Privy Council were fully abolished[19] and that the Supreme Court truly became master in its own home.

During the intervening 74 years the Supreme Court was not only eclipsed by the much greater prestige and senior position occupied by the Privy Council, but it suffered the further indignity that if the litigants so elected appeals from provincial appellate decisions could be taken direct to the Privy Council, and in practice often were.[20] Worse still, successive federal governments also treated the Supreme Court as a mere adjunct of the executive arm and not as a separate branch of government. Appointments to the Court were tarnished by patronage, just as they were at the provincial level in appointments to the provincial superior courts, and the Court's judgements were of indifferent quality. In Peter Russell's trenchant description, the Court was "a thoroughly second rate institution and treated as such by the federal government."[21]

Abolition of appeals to the Privy Council was one important step in the post-World War II transformation of the Supreme Court but others were equally important in improving the efficiency and quality of the Court's work and in elevating its constitutional status as Canada's pre-eminent court. These factors included the abolition as of right of appeals to the Court in civil cases (1974) and the abolition of oral hearings in leave applications except at the Court's option (1990). The most important event of course was the adoption of the Charter in 1982 because it dramatically changed the character of much of the Court's work and therefore also forced the federal government to take its appointive role much more seriously. To this list of transformative factors should be added the introduction of law clerks during Chief Justice Laskin's tenure of office. The law clerks (usually the top graduating students in their year) not only greatly assist the Supreme Court judges in handling their heavy case load but play an equally important role in keeping the judges abreast of legal scholarship in the various branches of the law and of current trends in legal and political philosophy,[22] and thus in assisting the members of the Court in discharging their policy-making functions.[23]

Most observers would agree that the cumulative impact of these changes has been greatly to improve the quality of appointments to the Supreme Court and of the judgements rendered by the Court, certainly as compared with the prewar standards and probably also as compared with the period between 1949 and 1982. However, this is not meant to imply that the actual process of appointments has become any more transparent and that further changes are not needed to improve the quality of appointees still further.

The Supreme Court Act simply provides[24] that the nine members of the Court, including the Chief Justice, are to be appointed by the Governor in Council, that three of them must come from Quebec, and that an appointee must either be a judge of a superior provincial court or be a barrister or advocate of at least 10 years standing at the bar of a province. By convention, Ontario is entitled to be represented by three judges, the Maritime provinces by one, and the Prairie provinces and British Columbia by two.[25] Everything else about the appointing process is left to the discretion of the appointing Cabinet, and it remains shrouded in vagueness, and unsubstantiated rumour and gossip. Obviously the Minister of Justice is involved and so, we are told, is the Prime Minister's Office, since by convention the Prime Minister makes the actual decision. If that is the case, does the Cabinet do more than simply rubber stamp the Prime Minister's choice? What role does the Chief Justice of Canada play? To what extent does the Minister of Justice confer with the attorney general or attorneys general of the province or region from which the candidate is to be appointed? What is the role of lobbyists for special interests or on behalf of specific candidates? In the Charter era, how much attention does the federal government pay to the constitutional philosophy of prospective appointees? There are no sure answers to any of these questions.

According to the Canadian Bar Association's *Report on the Appointment of Judges*,[26] federal Ministers of Justice follow the same selection procedure as they do in appointments to the Federal Court of Canada, the federal Tax Court, and provincial superior courts. This is not very reassuring because the process in respect of those courts is just as unstructured and lacking in transparency as it is at the Supreme Court level. Worse still, political patronage and personal friendships still play a prominent role in appointments to the lower courts.[27] In one respect, however, appointments to provincial superior courts offer better safeguards than appointments to the Supreme Court. This is because of the system of advisory committees established by the Mulroney administration in 1988 to screen applicants for provincial judicial appointments and continued by the Chrétien government. We also have a more or less firm commitment from the Chrétien government not to make an appointment unless the candidate has received at least the passing grade of "recommended" from the Committee.[28] Admittedly, as discussed further below, the threshold of acceptability is low and the screening system is a poor substitute for one in which the advisory committees actually present the appointing authority with a short list of the best qualified candidates. However, it is at least a beginning on the journey to a more accountable and transparent system of appointments. This and other alternatives to achieving this goal are considered in the following sections of this article.

COMPARATIVE METHODS OF APPOINTMENT TO THE HIGHEST COURTS

Broadly speaking, there are three methods in use today in Western Europe, North America and other common law jurisdictions for the selection of members of the highest constitutional court. These are selection by the executive, selection by the legislature or a legislative committee acting alone or in conjunction with other government agencies, and selection through a career judiciary. It needs to be emphasized that there is no rigid division between the three methods because of the many variations within each of the methods and the extent to which they borrow from one another. To obtain a complete taxonomy of the range of alternatives, one would have to add as a minimum the use of judicial nominating commissions[29] preceding the actual appointment of or voting on candidates, as well as the existence of confirmation procedures after the selecting agency has named its nominee for judicial office. Although only the executive appointive method has ever been used in Canada, it is still useful to reflect on the non-appointive methods of selection to act as a corrective to a sense of superior virtue one may have about the Canadian model.

The legislative model is used in some fashion in such countries as Germany, Austria, Switzerland and Italy. In Germany, for example, the members of the Federal Constitutional Court (*Bundesverfassungsgericht* [BVG]) are appointed by the members of the lower house (*Bundestag*) and upper house (*Bundesrat*) of the German Parliament, with each house voting for one of the two eight-judge senates into which the Constitutional Court is divided.[30] The *Bundesrat* is made up of representatives of the German states (*Länder*), thereby supplying the federal component in elections to the Constitutional Court. The *Bundesrat* also participates actively in the selection of judges for the five other specialized final courts of appeal with which Germany's federal structure is endowed.[31] An important difference between the judges in the Constitutional Court and the other appeal courts is that only six of the judges of the Constitutional Court are required to be drawn from the career judiciary. Even more significant is the fact that the legislative role in the selection of judges for the Constitutional Court reflects a widespread sentiment in civil law systems that constitutional law is "political law" and that the members of the Court should therefore be appointed by the elected representatives of the German people and representatives of the *Länder*.[32]

An elective system also applies to the members of the International Court of Justice (ICJ), who are elected by combined majorities of the

United Nations General Assembly and the Security Council, and to the members of the European Court of Human Rights (ECHR). The latter are elected by the member states of the General Assembly of the Council of Europe from short lists of candidates presented by the member countries.[33] However, it is not so much a democratic impulse that drives the elective method in the ICJ and ECHR as the fact that the United Nations and the Council of Europe are not governments and lack an effective executive authority.

A much more authentic Jacksonian spirit of democracy inspired the American states in the 19th century to adopt a populist system of election of judges. That system has now been heavily diluted in about half the states and in the District of Columbia through the use of judicial nominating boards, often, but misleadingly, referred to as the Missouri plan after the state which first introduced the system in 1940.[34] Under the Missouri plan, when a vacancy arises in a court the board presents the Governor with a list of three candidates from which he or she must choose one and appoint the candidate until the next general election for judges but not for less than one year. After this probationary period, the appointee must be approved by the electorate for a full 12 year term in the appellate court, or a lesser term in the trial court. The tradition is for the judge to run unopposed on a separate non-partisan judicial ballot at the time of the general election.[35]

With rare exceptions, Canadian lawyers find any entanglement with an elective system repugnant, at least where the electorate is made up of ordinary voters. They find it demeaning to the candidate running for judicial office and likely only to attract second rate talent. They also see it as basically incompatible with the concept of judicial independence if the candidate has to submit herself to re-election at various intervals. These are serious weaknesses to be sure. But a sceptic is entitled to ask whether the results are worse, or significantly worse, than the partisan system of federal judicial appointments that still obtains in some of the provincial superior courts and to some extent in the Federal Court of Canada. In any event, no Canadian scholar and no investigative committee has ever recommended adoption of a US-style electoral system for Canadian judges.[36] It is true to say, however, that over the past twenty years Canadian discussions and organizational changes in judicial appointments have been much influenced by the use of judicial nominating boards of the type associated with the Missouri plan. The adoption of this model, as we shall see, has also been recommended in connection with appointments to the Supreme Court of Canada.

ORIGINS AND EVOLUTION OF
THE EXECUTIVE APPOINTIVE
SYSTEM IN CANADA

The Canadian system of judicial appointments, at all levels, is derived from the English model and, so far as federal appointments to the Section 96 courts are concerned, is enshrined in the Canadian constitution. Historically, the system arose in England because the monarch was regarded as the fountain of justice. The courts were the King's courts and the judges were the King's judges. So it was natural that all the superior court judges should be appointed by the reigning monarch or his designate and that the appointive system should be retained even after the introduction of responsible government and universal suffrage. Patronage considerations undoubtedly influenced the appointment of judges in earlier centuries but the problem was never as serious in England as it became in Canada after Confederation. This was (and largely remains so) because of the much smaller number of full-time judges in England and Wales and because of the rigid division until recently of the legal profession into barristers and solicitors.[37]

Another difference between Canada and England is the unique role of the Lord Chancellor under the British constitution as head of the judiciary, presiding officer in the House of Lords, and a member of the Cabinet. In his judicial capacity, the Lord Chancellor is responsible for appointments to most of the superior courts and, since the last century, for appointments to most of the lower courts as well. Because of his unique position the Lord Chancellor was able to develop a high degree of independence from the other branches of government in making the appointments. He has been greatly aided in this task since the last part of the 19th century by the introduction of a permanent secretariat attached to the Lord Chancellor's Office.[38]

Nevertheless, complaints about the lack of transparency in the Lord Chancellor's appointments, the predominance of white male upper class Oxbridge appointees and the under-representation of women and visible minorities at all levels of the judiciary have led to increasing demands for reform. Observers predict that the pressure for broader changes is bound to mount with the incorporation into British domestic law of the European Convention on Human Rights.[39] Some changes were introduced by the Conservatives during Margaret Thatcher's prime ministership. In a 1995 pre-election manifesto, the Labour party committed itself to introducing a system of advisory committees for appointments to the bench.[40] The system is not yet in place and it is not clear whether it will ever be applied to the House of Lords in its judicial capacity. Nevertheless, Lord Irvine, the new Lord Chancellor, has recently reaffirmed the Blair government's commitment to continue with the reform of the appointive system, including the establishment of the advisory committees.

CANADIAN DEVELOPMENTS: THE CASE FOR A NOMINATING SYSTEM FOR APPOINTMENTS TO THE SUPREME COURT

Canada has never had a Lord Chancellor's Office, we have many more judges, and federal ministers of justice are generally ambitious politicians. It is therefore not surprising that since Confederation federal governments of whatever political hue, and regardless of pre-election promises, have never been able to resist using judicial offices for rewarding party supporters, personal friends and professional associates.

The mounting criticisms of the abuses of the appointive power led postwar Canadian governments to make modest changes[41] – first, through the use of the Canadian Bar Association's National Committee on the Judiciary to act as a screening device for prospective appointees, then, starting with Otto Lang in 1968, with the hiring of a special assistant to the Minister of Justice to compile dossiers on candidates for office, and, most recently, with the introduction of provincially-based but federally-sponsored advisory committees with no powers actually to nominate candidates for judicial office.

Those who have followed this evolution are near unanimous in their criticisms that the federal government has not gone far enough and that the advisory committee system introduced in 1988 is only a palliative which does not ensure appointment of the best qualified candidates. Moreover, the advisory committees do not play even a screening role with respect to the promotion of existing judges and there is no committee to advise the federal government on appointments to the Supreme Court.[42] The critics argue that the correct model for the federal government to follow is the merit-based system of nominations for appointments of provincial court judges in force in British Columbia, Manitoba, Ontario and Quebec,[43] and strongly endorsed in the 1985 reports of the committees on judicial appointments of the Canadian Association of Law Teachers (CALT) and the Canadian Bar Association (CBA).[44]

Both the CBA and CALT reports recommended that the same system of committee nominations (although differently constituted) should be adopted for appointments to the Supreme Court as were recommended for appointments to the provincial superior trial and appellate courts.[45] More recently, Professor Martin Friedland has made the same recommendation in his important report to the Canadian Judicial Council.[46] During its term of office the Mulroney administration showed no disposition to surrender its valuable patronage power in deference to these recommendations and unhappily the Chrétien government seems as firmly committed to the status quo as its predecessors.[47] That being the case, it seems unrealistic to expect Prime Minister Chrétien to establish a nomination procedure for appointments to the Supreme Court of Canada.

In defence of the present government's position, it might be argued that since it is generally agreed that Supreme Court appointments are now substantially free of party biases the need for an independent nomination procedure has disappeared. It could also be urged that the present informal system of consultation in the filling of vacancies provides much greater flexibility than would be available in the conversion to a formalized nomination mechanism.

There may be some merit to the second argument, but there is little merit to the first. If major controversies have been avoided over the appointment of Supreme Court judges since the adoption of the Charter (still only a short 19 years ago), this is largely because successive Prime Ministers – Trudeau, Mulroney, Chrétien – have shared similar constitutional philosophies and because the full impact of the Charter has not yet sunk in. If an Alliance-type government were to be elected in the future, it is entirely predictable, based on recent US experience,[48] that without the restraining force of an independent nomination procedure or confirmation process appointments would become much more polarized, as the appointees would be selected on the basis of their conservative political and social philosophies. The same would be true, of course, if Canadians were to elect a government with a strong left wing agenda.

Another argument often put forward to avoid the establishment of an independent nomination procedure is that the federal government is responsible to Parliament for its actions and should only be held accountable in that forum for its judicial appointments. The reasoning, in my view, is specious. There appears to be a long-standing tradition in the British Parliament that specific judicial appointments should not be debated because it might impair the independence of the judiciary. The tradition may not be as well entrenched in Canada but even if questions were permitted in the House of Commons it would do little good. The opposition would always be faced with a *fait accompli*.

The excuse of parliamentary accountability would only be meaningful if there were an opportunity to debate appointments *before* they were made or, better still, if nominations had to be confirmed by Parliament before they could take effect, as is true of federal judicial appointments in the US. The desirability of such a confirmation procedure in Canada and whether it should be adopted in place of, or in addition to, an independent nomination procedure is discussed below. For the moment it is sufficient to say that since there are already strong precedents in Canada for the establishment of judicial nomination committees, this should be a first step in assuring Canadians of a more objectively-based, better structured and more transparent system for selecting Supreme Court judges than exists at present.

If a Commonwealth precedent were needed to support a judicial nomination committee at the highest constitutional level, it will be found in the new South African constitution. This provides for the appointment of a Judicial Services Commission (JSC) of 23 members, whose mandate is to provide the South African President with a short list of nominees for appointment to the Constitutional Court, the Supreme Court of South Africa, and members of the South African High Court.[49] The Commission has now been in operation for five years and appears to be functioning well. One of the distinctive features of the JSC is that it conducts public interviews of prospective nominees before presenting its list to the President.

MODUS OPERANDI OF THE NOMINATING COMMITTEE

The 1985 recommendations of the CALT and CBA committees provide a useful starting point for defining the structure and operation procedures of a Supreme Court nominating committee. In commenting on these recommendations, Lorraine Weinrib of the University of Toronto Law School has justly complained that they are too meagre and contain very little information about the nominating committee's terms of reference and how the committee is expected to go about its work.[50] The following notes are designed to respond to her questions and to offer further non-exhaustive suggestions on the *modus operandi* of a nominating committee.

1. Size of the Committee. The CALT committee envisaged a nominating committee of seven members composed of the following:

- the Chief Justice of Canada
- a nominee of the Canadian Judicial Council
- a nominee of the Minister of Justice
- a nominee of the attorney general(s) of the province or provinces from which the candidate is likely to be selected

- two members of the Bar
- a member of the public to be nominated by the other members of the committee.

The size of the committee, as well as its composition, should be reconsidered. Given the committee's important role and the range of constituencies it must accommodate, a larger size than seven is called for. The question is how much larger. The Ontario provincial advisory committee has 13 members, a majority of whom are non-lawyers. The South African Judicial Services Commission has 23 members, 10 of whom are drawn from the South African Parliament and the provincial legislatures. On the other hand, Professor Friedland recommends a body of nine,[51] a suitable number because of the importance of balancing representativeness with the need for collegiality and effectiveness.[52] In light of these considerations, the committee should be structured as follows, though my suggestions are not written in stone:

- one nominee of the federal Minister of Justice
- two nominees of provincial governments
- two nominees of the Canadian Bar Association and provincial law societies
- one nominee of the aboriginal communities
- two members of the public to be appointed by the Governor General
- one chair of the committee, also to be appointed by the Governor General.

2. *Other Compositional Issues.* The following issues also arise in determining the composition of the committee. The first is whether the Chief Justice of Canada should be directly represented. The office is included in the CALT list; judges are also strongly represented in the South African commission. On the other hand, the inclusion of judges is generally not favoured in American state nomination committees. I believe the American position is the right one. Undoubtedly, the incumbent Chief Justice of Canada should always be consulted but, in my view, it would be a mistake for him or her to be a member of the committee. If the Chief Justice were a member the other members might feel obliged to defer to his views. If they failed to do so the incumbent might feel slighted.

A second issue is whether members of Parliament should be included. The German and South African models strongly argue for their inclusion, particularly if there is to be no confirmation procedure for the nominee ultimately chosen by the federal government. If a confirmation procedure is put in place this seems to dispense with the need for parliamentary representation.

The role of provincial representation raises a separate set of issues. Finding the right formula for provincial input in the selection of members of the Supreme Court has been a dominant theme in constitutional discussions between the federal and provincial governments, starting with the Victoria Charter (1971) and ending with the Charlottetown Accord (1992). The trouble with all the proposals was that they focused on the provincial role in the selection of the judges to the exclusion of other democratic inputs, and were therefore seriously flawed.[53] If this is conceded there is no justification for giving the provincial representatives a majority voice on the committee.[54] This reasoning gains further strength from the fact that division of powers issues and other questions peculiarly of provincial concern now only occupy a modest part of the Supreme Court's agenda.

A related issue is whether the provincial representatives for a particular appointment should be selected by the province or provinces from which the judge is likely to be drawn. I have argued elsewhere that it is a mistake in the Charter era to attach so much importance to balanced regional representation to the exclusion of other factors. Nevertheless, given Canada's size, its dispersed population and the strength of the tradition favouring regional representation, a compromise might be struck by giving one seat on the nomination committee to the province or provinces from which the new appointee is expected to be drawn and allowing the other provinces to select the second provincial representative. Quebec's status on the committee would also need to be considered. It is not clear whether Quebec's legislatively prescribed three seats on the Court is now constitutionally entrenched,[55] but, regardless, no one would question the province's entitlement to be represented on the committee when a Quebec vacancy arises on the Court. However, for the reasons I have given in respect of appointments from the other provinces, Quebec's role should not be to the exclusion of other provincial representation.

3. Scope of the Committee's Jurisdiction and Appointment of the Chief Justice. A question requiring some consideration is whether appointment of the Chief Justice should also fall within the committee's jurisdiction. If the position falls vacant and is to be filled by a person not already on the court then clearly the committee should be involved. However, the Canadian tradition is to appoint the Chief Justice from existing members of the Court.

Should this make a difference in determining the Committee's role? The US position is that the chief justiceship of the Supreme Court is a separate position requiring separate nomination and therefore confirmation by the Senate. Leaving aside the constitutional requirements, American scholars believe that the Chief Justice wields so much influence and power on the Court that his designation requires special consideration, even if legally he is only *primus inter pares*, first among equals. The current members of the Canadian Supreme Court seem to take a less exalted view of the Canadian chief justiceship and seem to treat it more as a prestigious administrative position than anything else.[56] Whatever be the correct assessment of the Canadian position, Professor Friedland reports a growing sentiment among Canadian judges at the puisne and appellate levels that the selection of the Chief Justice should not be a unilateral decision by the Prime Minister and that the office should only be held for a limited term. He supports both these sentiments and also recommends a separate selection procedure for chief justices.[57] It would be anomalous if a separate selection procedure were to be adopted for provincial chief justices and not for the Chief Justice of Canada. It is surely also correct to say that most Canadians attach considerable symbolic significance to the office of Chief Justice of Canada and that they see the incumbent as being much more than a presiding administrator of the Supreme Court.

4. *Committee's modus operandi.* To address now some of Professor Weinrib's more specific concerns, she is right to stress the importance of compiling a full dossier on every candidate. This means that the committee must have adequate, skilled and sensitive support staff, including an executive director of appropriate seniority.[58] The committee should be required to solicit suggestions for nominations from all segments of the legal community and to advertise the vacancy. A personal interview with candidates appearing on a short list should be equally essential, although whether the interviews should be held in public is more debatable. As already mentioned, in South Africa the hearings are held in public. In my view, the Canadian position should turn on whether the candidate favoured by the federal government must also run the gauntlet of a parliamentary confirmation procedure. If a confirmation procedure is rejected as unnecessary (a critical issue that is addressed below), then public hearings by the nominating committee are indispensable to give its proceedings the needed transparency and to permit representations from interest groups and members of the public.

5. *Selection criteria among candidates.* Professor Weinrib seems strongly of the view that the committee needs to be armed with a statutorily prescribed list of criteria to assist it in its search for the ideal candidate. This is not self-evident, first, because persons with the presumed sophistication required of members of the committee should not need instruction about the requisite attributes of a successful member of the Supreme Court and, second, because even Supreme Court judges differ in their ranking of the necessary qualities. There is surely also widespread agreement that Supreme Court judges should not be clones of each other but should have varied backgrounds and experiences, and should represent a spectrum of philosophical positions on the most pressing constitutional issues with which the appointees are likely to be faced in the course of their judicial careers.

Subject to these caveats, my wish list for the essential attributes of a Supreme Court judge would include the following: complete personal integrity; robust health; industriousness and good work habits; a sense of collegiality with other members of the Court to enable the court to discharge its very heavy work load efficiently and without unnecessary friction;[59] an excellent intellect and fine writing skills to match it; a deep understanding of the Canadian constitution and the Charter, and of the role of law in general in contemporary Canadian society; and not least, keen discernment in being able to project the consequences of a judgement on to a broader canvass.[60]

Professor Weinrib has suggested that a candidate's strong track record in a career requiring demonstration of these virtues would greatly assist the nominating committee in its search, and apparently believes that prior appellate service would be a particularly valuable source of information. Not everyone would agree, certainly not Justice Frankfurter, who was no mean judge of what makes for a successful Supreme Court judge. In an oft cited passage, he wrote that "One is entitled to say without qualification that the correlation between prior judicial experience and fitness for the Supreme Court is zero."[61] In fairness to Professor Weinrib it needs to be explained, however, that she is not simply relying on the presence of prior judicial service but on the *quality* of that service. This raises an entirely new dimension for consideration.

6. *Disposition of the Committee's recommendations.* Both the CALT and CBA reports envisaged the committee presenting the federal government with a short list of recommended candidates from which the federal government would be obliged to pick the appointee or give reasons for its refusal to do so. Professor Friedland has ingeniously suggested that the federal

government should be free to go outside the list but would then have to justify its decision in some kind of confirmation procedure.[62]

THE CASE FOR A
CONFIRMATION PROCEDURE

Professor Friedland's bold suggestion brings us face to face with what is currently the most contentious issue in Canadian discussions of appropriate selection procedures for the Supreme Court. This is whether a confirmation procedure is needed and whether it is also required where a nominating committee system has been installed.

Neither the CBA nor the CALT committee recommended the introduction of confirmation procedures for appointments to the Supreme Court, or to any other court whose judges were appointed by the federal government. They did not feel it was needed given the existence of a credible nomination procedure. I was a member of the CALT committee and I concurred with my colleagues' views. I have changed my mind since then, at least so far as the Supreme Court is concerned.

The most important reason for my change of position is this. It is precisely because of the intensely political role (I use the word political in a positive and not pejorative sense) played by the Supreme Court judges in applying and interpreting the Charter as well as the rest of the constitution that it is critical to inject a democratic and balancing note in the appointing process. Canadians should be able to learn about, see, and evaluate the candidate before his or her appointment becomes a *fait accompli*. If the federal government has chosen well, with or without the help of a nomination committee, it will have little to fear. The candidate is likely to earn quick approval from the confirming body.

If the candidate is controversial, underqualified or otherwise unacceptable to a significant constituency, all the more reason why his or her merits should be publicly debated while there is still time for it. If candidates for the office of Prime Minister are expected to expose themselves to close public scrutiny, why should we require less of a nominee for the Supreme Court, who is likely to remain in office long after the appointing Prime Minister has disappeared from the public scene and who, in many respects, wields as much power as the Prime Minister and with less accountability?

There is also another reason that justifies the introduction of a separate confirmation procedure. Assuming the confirming body is made up of parliamentarians, it will help to educate our elected representatives on the impact of the Charter on traditional concepts of responsible government and give them a better appreciation of where the line should be drawn between their role and the Charter's role. Members of Parliament and senators (and likewise their provincial counterparts) have been slow to react to the steady erosion of Parliament's authority, implicit though it may be in the very existence of the Charter. As noted at the beginning of this article, the mood of acquiescence is changing and Canadians are beginning to appreciate the important roles of personalities and judicial philosophies in the interpretation and application of the Charter norms. The "inconvenience" of a confirmation procedure will be readily forgiven if it provides a regular opportunity for reviewing the work of the Supreme Court and in raising our collective awareness of its norms propounding role.

The notion of a confirmation procedure is no longer radical. It appeared in the report of the Ontario Advisory Committee on the Constitution in 1978 and in Bill C-60 introduced by the federal government in the same year. Both provided for confirmation of Supreme Court nominees by a revised upper chamber. In the case of Bill C-60, upper chamber approval would have been necessary even though the nominee would have been selected by the co-operative efforts of the Attorney General of Canada and the attorney general of the appointee's province. The Charlottetown Accord saw a confirmation role for the revised Senate in the appointment of members of senior government agencies and boards. It would surely be anomalous if the public were given a greater opportunity to comment on the potential head of the CBC, the CRTC or the Canadian Transportation Agency than is available to them to assess the qualities and suitability of a future member of the Supreme Court or a candidate for the chief justiceship of Canada.

As we have seen, Justice La Forest accepted the legitimacy of confirmation hearings after he retired from the Supreme Court a year ago, whereas Justices Cory and Iacobucci have taken a very different position.[63] We know that other members of the Supreme Court share their misgivings, so they deserve closer analysis. The objections appear to fall under two main headings, though it may be that the second is only a subset of the first.

The first objection is that the existing system works well, so why knock it?[64] The defence of the status quo is coupled with a warning not to be beguiled by foreign models (more particularly the US confirmation procedure) which may work well in their own environment but are alien to Canadian soil. This reasoning is quite unpersuasive and ignores the historical reasons for the adoption of the confirmation procedure in the US constitution.

The American Founding Fathers were divided over which arm of government should have the power to appoint the members of the US Supreme Court; some favoured the President, others the Senate. A compromise was reached by conferring the nomination power on the President but requiring the President's nominations to be confirmed by the Senate.[65] The delegates to the Constitutional Convention of 1789 appreciated that giving the President an untrammelled power of appointment would give rise to abuses or lead to an unrepresentative Court. History has amply confirmed their intuition. Between 1789 and 1992, the Senate refused to confirm 28 of the 142 Supreme Court nominees, or nearly one out of five nominees, whose names were submitted by the President.[66] We may be sure that an even larger number of prospective nominees were never forwarded to the Senate because the President and his advisors anticipated rejection of their choices.

In short, even allowing for political partisanship in the Senate, the US confirmation requirements have on the whole met the Founding Fathers' expectations in eliminating clearly unqualified candidates and in ensuring that the nominees enjoyed broad political acceptance. If US confirmation hearings have erred, it is on the side of accommodating the President's choice even where the candidate was not of the first quality, an almost inevitable result where the President's party also dominates the Senate.

Had Canada had an equivalent screening device for appointments to the Supreme Court, the well documented abuses of the appointment power that occurred during the first 75 years of the Court's history[67] might well have been avoided. In what sense then, has Canada been well served by a paternalistic executive power of appointment not subject to public scrutiny? It is true that the quality of appointments has been much better over the past 20 years or so. Even so, there is little room for complacency. There have undoubtedly been weak appointments and a surprising number of Supreme Court judges have taken early retirement for reasons other than ill health.[68] We are also entitled to ask how much *better* the appointments might have been if there had been an independent nominating procedure or if the government's selections had been subject to a confirmation requirement. The warning against the danger of importing foreign innovations must also be viewed with much scepticism, given the fact that Canada has borrowed many legal concepts from the US during its relatively short history, including, not unimportantly, the concept of an entrenched bill of rights!

But what about Justice Cory's complaint that prospective appointees to the Supreme Court should not have to run the gauntlet of public questioning by politicians? The concern is that parliamentarians may be more interested in embarrassing the candidate or in scoring political points than in engaging in serious debate on the meaning of the Charter or the role of Supreme Court judges as guardians of Charter values. Justice Cory has also argued that it is unfair to expect candidates to justify decisions they may have rendered many years earlier as lower court judges and highly improper to ask them to explain their positions on current legal controversies or to predict how they would decide those issues as members of the Supreme Court.

No doubt the horror stories the critics have in mind are the confirmation hearings of Robert H. Bork and Clarence Thomas before the US Senate. However, they overlook the fact that public questioning of candidates is a relatively recent innovation in proceedings by the Senate Judiciary Committee[69] and that there were exceptional features about the Bork and Thomas cases.[70] The more recent nominees that have appeared before the Judiciary Committee have been approved without difficulty and they have not complained about unfair treatment. The nominees have reserved the right not to answer questions concerning their position on future cases that could come before the Supreme Court, and that right is generally conceded.[71] If it was deemed appropriate or necessary in the Canadian context, rules could also be adopted to delimit the scope of a nominee's examination before the parliamentary committee.

We can also learn from overseas experience. The public hearings before the South African Judicial Service Commission show that they can be conducted with decorum and that the chair can be relied on to prevent improper questioning. According to a perceptive British observer, "The original fear that good candidates would not put themselves forward does not appear to have materialized."[72] Again, to quote the reactions of the Deputy President of the Constitutional Court to his appearance before the JSC:

Speaking as a person who is sitting on this seat now, I must say I would have preferred not to have been interviewed at all, but I realize that the interviewing process is useful and I think it is essential and correct and I am fully in support of having open hearings.[73]

Several other objections to a Canadian confirmation procedure involving the use of parliamentary committees also deserve to be noted. One is that the Senate cannot be expected to supply the federal component in confirmation hearings because its members do not speak for the provinces. Equally the Senate cannot remedy the

Table 1
Federal Election Results 1974–2000

Election Year	Party Forming Government	Total Seats	Number of Government Seats	Seats Required for Two-Thirds Super Majority	Government Super-Majority?
1974	Liberal	264	141	176	No
1979	PC	282	136	188	No
1980	Liberal	282	146	188	No
1984	PC	282	211	188	Yes
1988	PC	295	169	197	No
1993	Liberal	295	177	197	No
1997	Liberal	301	155	197	No
2000	Liberal	301	173	197	No

democratic deficit in the appointment of Supreme Court judges since its members are unelected. Both these points seem to militate against the Senate playing a role in the appointive process of members of the Supreme Court. Nevertheless, the Senate is an integral part of Parliament and it may seem anomalous that it should be denied any role in a confirmation procedure when it continues to play an active role in the enactment of legislation. A case can therefore be made for giving the Senate *some* representation on a confirmation committee, say up to one-half the total membership of the committee, even before the long-delayed reform of the Senate is finally agreed upon.

There are also difficulties in expecting a House of Commons confirmation committee to remain free of partisan bias. The members of the House of Commons are of course elected, but they are also expected to follow party discipline. In the case of a majority government, this means that the committee's approving vote would be a foregone conclusion[74] unless somehow the government could be persuaded to give its members a free vote. The same difficulty would arise if a full House of Commons vote were required to approve the committee's recommendation with respect to the government's nominee for the Supreme Court.

One solution to these obstacles would be to require supermajority voting in the committee and/or the full House of Commons.[75] Table 1, which is based on the results of recent parliamentary elections, shows that a two-thirds majority voting requirement would have given the opposition parties an effective voice in voting for confirmation in six of the seven parliamentary elections held between 1974 and 2000.

Nevertheless, the requirement of a supermajority vote runs very much against the grain of our parliamentary tradition and even if voluntarily adopted by the present administration would not be binding on future governments unless the requirement were constitutionally entrenched.

A SUPREME COURT NOMINATING COMMITTEE OR A CONFIRMATION PROCEDURE, OR BOTH?

If it is concluded that an independent parliamentary confirmation procedure cannot be secured without a constitutional amendment (an issue that is considered below), then the establishment of a separate nomination committee as previously described is the best alternative to ensure a broader input into the selection of future Supreme Court judges. The question that needs to be considered is whether such a nomination procedure is desirable *in addition* to a parliamentary confirmation process.

At first blush, the answer would seem to be no. Since the nominating council would represent a range of constituencies it would have little incentive, and little opportunity, to make clearly partisan nominations. One of the basic objectives of a confirmation procedure – to prevent abuse of the executive's appointive powers – would therefore already be met. It is true the government would still select the actual candidate for appointment from the short list of candidates prepared by the nominating council, but the scope of that discretion would be heavily circumscribed. We are also entitled to assume that all the candidates on the short list will be highly qualified professionally and meet all the basic requirements for appointment to the Supreme Court.

However, there is another side to the coin. I have argued earlier that the involvement of Parliament in appointments to the Supreme Court should not be limited to curbing abuses by the executive but should serve a higher function in encouraging members of Parliament to take a closer interest in the work of the Court and in gaining a better appreciation of the interaction of the legislative and judicial roles under the Canadian constitution. It is also conceivable, though perhaps not very likely, that the parliamentary committee will conclude that the nominated candidate, while professionally very meritorious, will tilt the philosophical balance unacceptably on the Court.

It may be safely assumed that the federal government would strenuously resist the imposition of two layers of control over its appointive powers, and that if forced to choose between the establishment of a nomination council and a parliamentary confirmation procedure, it will opt for the latter. The government could be expected to argue that it is as capable of nominating very highly qualified candidates as is a nomination council and that, unlike the council, it is responsible for its actions to Canadian voters. The government would also protest that it is unacceptable in a democratic society that its role should be reduced to providing a courier service between the council and Parliament. One could question the soundness of several of these assertions but it is difficult to deny that historically and constitutionally the federal government has played a key role in the appointment of federal judges at all levels. The issue, therefore, is not whether the federal government should play a role but *how large* that role should be. Given my own preference for an open parliamentary confirmation requirement, if forced to choose between a confirmation procedure and an unelected nomination council, I would concede the government's prerogative to select the nominees whose names are to be brought before the parliamentary committee. A confirmation requirement is the more important reform, and is consistent with the approach adopted over the past 30 years or more in discussions dealing with the entrenchment of the Supreme Court.

CONSTITUTIONAL POSITION

I have assumed so far, as do most other observers discussing desirable changes in the appointment procedure for Supreme Court judges, that there are no constitutional obstacles. Unfortunately the position is not straightforward and it requires some discussion.

As previously discussed, the Supreme Court is not entrenched in the Constitution Act. Rather, the Court owes its existence to an ordinary Act of Parliament adopted pursuant to s.101 of the *Constitution Act, 1867* empowering the federal Parliament, from time to time, to provide for the Constitution, Maintenance and Organization of a General Court of Appeal for Canada. The *Supreme Court Act* entrusts the appointive power in respect of members of the Court to the Governor General in Council but, since it is only an ordinary enactment, there would appear at first sight to be no hurdles to introducing new and more democratic methods for appointing the judges along the lines discussed in this article.[76]

The difficulties arise because of the changes adopted in the *Constitution Act, 1982*. Section 41 of that Act requires the unanimous consent of the federal Parliament and all the provincial legislatures for five classes of amendments, including, in s.41 (d), "the composition of the Supreme Court of Canada." In addition, section 42 lists "the Supreme Court of Canada" as one of the six classes of amendment subject to a less stringent ratification procedure (the federal government and two-thirds of the provinces representing 50 percent of the population), but "subject to paragraph 41 (d)." This raises an important question, so far as changes in the status of the Supreme Court are concerned, about the proper relationship between sections 42 and 41.

Scholars are divided in their views about the meaning of these provisions. Some scholars, such as Professor Cheffins and the late Professor Lederman,[77] believe some meaning must be given to the provisions in sections 41 and 42 and that they cannot be ignored. Other scholars, such as Peter Hogg and Peter Russell,[78] take the position that the provisions are ineffective for the following reason. Sections 41 and 42 only apply to amendments to "the Constitution of Canada." That term is defined in section 52(2) of the Constitution Act 1982, and the list of instruments enumerated there does not include the Supreme Court of Canada. Whatever their individual views, the scholars are agreed that the references to the Supreme Court of Canada in sections 41 and 42 have created "an intolerably confusing situation."[79] While a reference to the Supreme Court would ordinarily be desirable to clarify the meaning of these provisions, the difficulty in this case is that the judgement of the members of the Court may appear to be clouded by views they have previously expressed for or against the need for changes in the existing system of appointments to the court.

There is no reason, however, why the federal government cannot proceed with at least one of the changes recommended in this article – the creation of a Supreme Court appointments nominating committee – without waiting for the results of such a reference. As previously noted, advisory committees already exist to screen applicants for appointments to the other federal courts and the superior provincial courts. It has not been suggested that this violates the federal government's responsibility under section 96 of the *Constitution Act, 1867* to appoint the judges of these courts. What remains unsettled is whether the federal government could agree constitutionally to appoint only a person whose name appears on a short list prepared by a nominating committee – as recommended here – because that would encroach substantially on the federal government's appointive responsibilities.

In sum, while a confirmation procedure before Parliament is the more desirable reform, the establishment of an advisory committee may be a more practical and attainable measure in light of the constitutional uncertainties involving changes to the Supreme Court.

CONCLUSION

In addressing future appointments to the Supreme Court of Canada, there are two key questions. The first is whether we are satisfied with the existing system of appointments which vests complete and unaccountable discretion in the executive even though the judges of the Supreme Court are the ultimate arbiters of the Canadian constitution and collectively exercise a power as great as that of the federal Cabinet. If this question is answered no, the second question is what changes we deem desirable to bring transparency and accountability to the selection procedure and to ensure that only the best qualified candidates are appointed.

There may be honest differences of opinion about the answer to the second question, but there should be little doubt about the answer to the first. Over the past 15 years there has been a near unanimous chorus of opinion among scholars reinforced by many publicly-sponsored reports that the existing system of appointments is incompatible with a modern federal democratic constitution governed by the rule of law and incorporating one of the most powerful bills of rights in the Western hemisphere. What ought to give cause for concern is that none of these reasoned arguments have had any apparent impact on successive federal governments whose spokespersons continue to insist that there is no need for change and that the federal government is and has been doing an impeccable job. One's best hope is that there will be a rising tide of opinion in favour of change within the major political parties[80] and that more members of the Supreme Court will join Justice La Forest[81] in recognizing the anomaly of owing their appointments to the unrevealed and undebated preferences and partialities of one or more unaccountable members of the federal Cabinet.

NOTES

- I am grateful to David Bronskill, University of Toronto, LL.B. II, and Sarit Shmulevitz, University of Toronto, LL.B. III, for research assistance, and especially indebted to my colleague and good friend Professor Peter Russell for his advice and perceptive observations in the preparation of this article. However, I alone am responsible for the views expressed in it. I have also made use of my earlier article "Appointments to the Supreme Court of Canada," *Constitutional Forum*, Vol. 5, no. 1 (Fall 1994), p. 10.

1 For criticisms outside Alberta, see for example, *Bar and Bench Daily News Digest*, August 27, 1998, "'Godzilla' Judges Overpowering Cabinets: Crosbie," referring to a "scathing critique" of recent Supreme Court of Canada

judgements by former Justice Minister John Crosbie in an address to the annual meeting of the Canadian Bar Association in St. John's, Newfoundland. Justice Minister Anne McLellan replied vigorously to Crosbie's criticism at the same meeting.

2 *Vriend v. Alberta* [1998] 1 S.C.R. 493.

3 See Brian Laghi, "Debate on Gay Rights Polarizes Albertans," *Globe and Mail*, April 2, 1998, p. A5 (as quoted in *Bar and Bench Daily News Digest* VIII, Issue 64).

4 *R. v. Ewanchuk* (1999) 169 D.L.R. (4th) 193 (S.C.C.).

5 See *National Post*, February 27, 1999, p. A2 (text of JA McClung's letter), and Barbara Amiel, "Feminists, Fascists, and Other Radicals," *National Post*, March 6, 1999, p. B7. To her great credit, in an address to Ottawa University law students Justice Beverley McLachlin strongly encouraged debate about the role and rulings of Canadian courts as a "healthy process" while warning against the debate slipping into personal attacks against the judiciary. See Erin Anderssen, "Debates on Courts Healthy: Judge," *Globe and Mail*, March 27, 1999, p. A5.

6 See, for example, Editorial, *Globe and Mail*, March 5, 1999, p. A14. The Reform Party has also adopted a policy statement requiring all federally appointed judges, including appointments to the Supreme Court, to be nominated by the provincial governments and to be ratified by a Triple-E Senate. See the Reform party's "Bluebook." See also: Preston Manning, "Parliament, not Judges, Must Make the Laws of the Land," *Globe and Mail*, June 16, 1998, p. A23; Editorial, "A Supreme Challenge for Reformers," *Globe and Mail*, June 17, 1998, p. A24; See also Peter H. Russell's first of two articles in this volume and Preston Manning's article in this volume.

7 *Hill Times*, September 2, 1998.

8 Kirk Makin, "Top-Court Judge Defends Bench," *Globe and Mail*, March 3, 1999, p. A5.

9 Erin Anderssen, "Top-Court Judge Rejects Proposal to Quiz Nominees," *Globe and Mail*, March 25, 1999, p. A8.

10 Kirk Makin, "Lamer Blasts Unseemly Lobbying for Positions on Supreme Court," *Globe and Mail*, February 5, 1999, p. A2.

11 On the constitutional issues, see p. 18.

12 Compare A. Wayne MacKay and Richard W. Bauman, "The Supreme Court of Canada: Reform Implications for an Emerging National Institution," in Clare F. Beckton and A. Wayne MacKay (eds.), *The Courts and the Charter*, Royal Commission on the Economic Union and Development Prospects for Canada (Toronto: University of Toronto Press, 1985), Vol. 58, p. 37.

13 Examples of the Supreme Court's willingness to rewrite important private law doctrines include:
   • adoption of the constructive trust as a discretionary remedial device;
   • expansion of the scope of fiduciary duties and remedies for breach thereof;

- admissibility of punitive damages for breach of contract;
- repudiation of long standing precedents in the conflict of laws area in favour of more "modern" rules, including the finding of an implicit "full faith and credit" doctrine in the Canadian constitution requiring the recognition and enforcement of judgements by the courts of sister provinces.

14 See, for example, Justice Cory, note 9.

15 Paul A. Freund, "Appointment of Justices: Some Historical Perspectives," *Harvard Law Review*, Vol. 101, no. 6 (April 1988), pp. 1146, 1153.

16 And indeed, Justice Cory's disclaimer notwithstanding, this is almost universally accepted in Canada, and recognized by the Supreme Court's own law clerks. See Lorne Sossin, "The Sounds of Silence: Law Clerks, Policy Making and the Supreme Court of Canada," *University of British Columbia Law Review*, Vol. 30, no. 2 (1996), pp. 279–82, 307. Sossin claims that the largest impact of the law clerks has been on the institutional culture of the Supreme Court as a policy-making institution.

17 Section 101 of the *Constitution Act, 1867*.

18 See now Supreme Court Act, R.S.C. 1985, c. S-26, as amended.

19 Appeals in criminal matters had previously been abolished in 1933.

20 In the constitutional area, 77 out of 159 appeals to the Privy Council from Canada were taken direct to the Privy Council. P.H. Russell, *The Judiciary in Canada: The Third Branch of Government* (Toronto: McGraw-Hill Ryerson, 1987), p. 336.

21 Russell, *The Judiciary in Canada*, p. 337.

22 On the law clerks' various roles, see Sossin, "The Sounds of Silence."

23 There is no doubt that law clerks assist the judges in the writing of judgements (Sossin, "The Sounds of Silence," pp. 296–98), but in my experience, based on discussion with former law clerks, there is disagreement about the importance of that role. Mr. Sossin argues that Supreme Court policy decisions are typically the result of a process in which many different actors invariably have a role, and he insists that "*no clerk ever considered the decision to be his or her own*" (Sossin, "The Sounds of Silence," pp. 297–98; italics in original). Far more reaching claims have been made about the influence of law clerks in the preparation of judgements in the US Supreme Court. See Tony Mauro, "The Hidden Power Behind the Supreme Court, Justices Give Pivotal Role to Novice Lawyers," *USA Today*, March 13, 1998 (reviewing Edward Lazarus, *Closed Chambers* (1998)).

24 Supreme Court Act, sections 4–6.

25 Some observers believe that there is now an implicit understanding that British Columbia is entitled to its own representative. I express no view one way or the other.

26 *Report of the Canadian Bar Association on The Appointment of Judges in Canada* (Ottawa: Canadian Bar Foundation, 1985), p. 11.

27 Peter H. Russell and Jacob S. Ziegel, "Federal Judicial Appointments: An Appraisal of the First Mulroney Government's Appointments and the New Judicial Advisory Committees," *University of Toronto Law Journal*, Vol. 41, no. 1 (Winter 1991), p. 4.

28 While he was Minister of Justice, Allan Rock committed himself, except in the case of affirmative action appointments, not to appoint a candidate unless he or she was rated "highly recommended." Under the original scheme, the advisory committees were required to report whether a candidate was qualified or not qualified. These categories were changed in 1991 to recommended, highly recommended, or not recommended.

29 In this paper, I use the terms judicial nomination committees, judicial appointment committees, judicial appointments advisory committees and similar expressions interchangeably and in a non-technical sense.

30 See Henry J. Abraham, *The Judicial Process*, 6th ed. (Oxford: Oxford University Press, 1993), pp. 294–95. The lower house makes its selection through a special committee of 12 electors established on the basis of proportional representation in the *Bundestag*. A two-thirds majority is required for the election of the judges by each house.

31 Carl Baar, "Comparative Perspectives on Judicial Selection Processes," in *Appointing Judges: Philosophy, Politics and Practice* (Toronto: Ontario Law Reform Commission, 1991), pp. 143, 152.

32 Donald P. Kommers, *The Constitutional Jurisprudence of the Federal Republic of Germany*, 2nd ed. (Durham, NC: Duke University Press, 1997), esp. pp. 3–4.

33 See H.C. Kruger, "Selecting Judges for the New European Court of Human Rights," *Human Rights Law Journal*, Vol. 17, nos. 11–12 (December 1996), p. 401.

34 See Abraham, *The Judicial Process*, pp. 35–38. The designation is misleading because there are two major types of plans, the other, introduced in 1934, being the California plan. There are also great variations among the plans adopted in the several states.

35 The judges are usually re-elected but re-election cannot be taken for granted if the electorate becomes aroused because of controversial judicial policies. In 1986, Chief Justice Bird and two of her colleagues on the California Supreme Court were "decisively" rejected by the voters in a retention election for just this reason. Abraham, *The Judicial Process*, p. 36.

36 However, at least one Canadian scholar greatly admires the German system for the selection of members of the German Constitutional Court and regards it as combining the best elements of a merit-based and democratically accountable system of appointment. See David M. Beatty, *Talking Heads and the Supremes* (Toronto: Carswell, 1990), pp. 10, 265–66.

37 It is less so now because of the changes introduced by former Lord Chancellor, Lord Mackay, during Margaret Thatcher's last term of office,

permitting solicitors specializing in litigation to appear in the High Court under carefully controlled conditions and also permitting solicitors to be appointed to lower courts.

38 Robert Stevens, *The Independence of the Judiciary: The View from the Lord Chancellor's Office* (Oxford: Clarendon Press, 1992).

39 The Blair government has committed itself to giving the British courts a limited power to find British legislation and executive acts incompatible with the Convention but the power to act on such findings would be left up to a special committee of Parliament.

40 Kate Malleson, "Assessing the Strengths and Weaknesses of a Judicial Appointments Commission," *Amicus Curiae* (May 1998), p. 13.

41 For the details, see Russell and Ziegel, "Federal Judicial Appointments," pp. 26–33.

42 Martin Friedland, *A Place Apart: Judicial Independence and Accountability in Canada, A Report for the Judicial Council of Canada* (Ottawa: Canadian Judicial Council, 1995), pp. 255–58.

43 An Alberta committee also recommended the establishment of an Ontario style nominating committee in May 1988. See Alberta, Judicial Selection Process Review Committee, *Report and Recommendations* (Edmonton: Alberta Justice Communications, May 1998).

44 The committees reported within a few months of each other in the late spring and summer of 1985. Although their recommendations were strikingly similar, the committees were differently structured and worked quite independently of each other. The writer was a founding member of the CALT committee and later its chair.

45 For the details see Christopher Kendall, "Criticism and Reform: A Survey of Canadian Literature on the Appointment of Judges" in Ontario Law Reform Commission, *Appointing Judges: Philosophy, Politics and Practice*, p. 211.

46 Friedland, *A Place Apart*, pp. 256–57.

47 When Professor Russell and this author discussed the matter by telephone in 1995 with Allan Rock, then Minister of Justice, he made it clear that a change in the system of judicial appointments was "not in the cards." See also Friedland, *A Place Apart*, p. 241.

48 Presidents Nixon, Reagan and Bush were all committed to a right-wing political agenda and to appointing US Supreme Court and lower federal court judges who shared their political philosophy and could be relied on to roll back the legacy of the Warren Court of the 1960s and 1970s. It was this attitude that prompted President Nixon to nominate Clement F. Haynsworth, Jr. and G. Harold Carswell to the Supreme Court, President Reagan to nominate Robert Bork, and President Bush to nominate Clarence Thomas.

As is well known, the first three candidates were rejected by the Senate and the fourth, Clarence Thomas, was only confirmed by a narrow majority after long and painful public hearings. See Henry J. Abraham, *Justices and Presidents: A Political History of Appointments to the Supreme Court*, 3rd ed. (Oxford: Oxford University Press 1992), pp. 14–18, 356–59. It is important to note, however, that partisan nominations reflecting the political philosophy and personal predilections of the incumbent president are not confined to right-wing Presidents but have come to be accepted as part of a US president's prerogative. For example, President Roosevelt was just as committed to appointing, and did appoint, judges supporting his New Deal reforms. Subsequent Democratic presidents followed the same pattern (Abraham, chaps. 9 and 13). In the US, the objection is not to presidents nominating candidates whose political philosophy is compatible with the president's, but to presidents using the nominating power to appoint unqualified or underqualified candidates or candidates whose constitutional philosophy offends the dominant ethos. In Canada, this aspect of the federal government's appointing powers has so far attracted little attention.

49 See Constitution of the Republic of South Africa, 1996, sections 173–76, the *South African Judicial Services Commission Act* 1994, and Kate Malleson, "Assessing the Performance of the Judicial Service Commission," *South African Law Journal*, Vol. 116, no. 1 (March 1999), p. 36. (I am very grateful to Dr. Malleson for providing me with a copy of her article as well as other much valuable information.)

50 Lorraine E. Weinrib, "Appointing Judges to the Supreme Court of Canada in the Charter Era: A Study in Institutional Function and Design," in *Appointing Judges: Philosophy, Politics and Practice*, pp. 136–37.

51 Friedland, *A Place Apart*, p. 256.

52 On the other hand, Professors Bauman and MacKay prefer a nominating committee of 13 ("The Supreme Court of Canada," p. 80).

53 Ziegel, "Appointments to the Supreme Court of Canada," p. 12.

54 There is even less justification, in my view, for the Reform party's suggestion (see note 6), that only the provinces should be entitled to nominate candidates for the Supreme Court. I share Professor Russell's position that the proposal has little to commend it. The Reform party's terse policy statement on the issue does not explain how the ten provinces (and territorial governments?) would go about exercising their powers, which would likely present a logistical nightmare. Arguably, the provinces and territorial governments could delegate their powers to a standing committee on nominations to the Supreme Court but it is unlikely that the provinces would agree to this. Further difficulties arise because of Quebec's statutory entitlement to three judges and the well-established convention that Ontario should be represented by three judges and the other regions by one each.

Substantively, a still more serious objection to the Reform party's proposal is that it suffers from a democratic deficit unless somehow each province is expected to strike a sub-provincial nominating committee representing diverse constituencies, which would create new problems of its own. Apparently, the Reform party proposal envisages a Triple-E Senate providing the democratic input through the confirmation requirement included in the proposal. This feature is also troubling, first, because there is no prospect of the Canadian constitution being amended in the foreseeable future to accommodate an elected Senate and, second, because if the change did take place there would be no justification for a purely provincially-based nominating committee. A reformed Senate would be expected to reflect provincial attitudes and interests.

On balance, therefore, I believe the judicial nominating procedure envisaged in the CALT and CBA recommendations is greatly to be preferred to the Reform party's proposal.

Professors MacKay and Bauman, "The Supreme Court of Canada," p. 81, recommend that all members of the nominating committee must be approved by the federal government and by at least four provinces. While not as objectionable as the Reform party proposal, this requirement could unduly complicate filling the slots on the committee and lead to potential gridlock if the two levels of government could not agree.

55 See the discussion, pp. 18–19.

56 Ian Greene, Carl Baar, Peter McCormick, George Szablowski, and Martin Thomas, *Final Appeal: Decision-Making in Canadian Courts of Appeal* (Toronto: Lorimer, 1998), p. 103. Four of the Supreme Court judges who responded to the question saw the Chief Justice primarily as an administrator who attended to the scheduling of cases, composition of panels, and budgetary issues. Two of the judges saw the ceremonial aspects of the job as important features. Only one saw the Chief Justice as the Court's intellectual leader; another saw him/her as chief spokesperson for all Canadian judges.

57 Friedland, *A Place Apart*, pp. 229–31.

58 The Commissioner for Judicial Affairs, who holds the status of a deputy minister, would seem a logical person to fill this position.

59 It goes without saying that a sense of collegiality as described in the text does not mean intellectual conformity. However, a strong and independent personality is not incompatible with courtesy to and cooperation with other members of the court.

60 In the Greene *et al.* study, *Final Appeal,* none of the Supreme Court of Canada respondents felt they could comment on what factors currently play a role in Supreme Court appointments. In their opinion, however, the factors that *ought* to be considered are a sense of fairness and good judgement (2 respondents), demonstrated legal ability (2), being representative of Canadian society in general (2), good interpersonal skills (1), and good work habits (1).

The attributes listed in the text and mentioned by the Supreme Court respondents differ in important respects from the preferred attributes of a distinguished US Supreme Court watcher. His *de minimis* qualifications are: "One, demonstrated judicial temperament. Two, professional expertise and competence. Three, absolute personal as well as professional integrity. Four, an able, agile, lucid mind. Five, appropriate professional background or training. Six, the ability to communicate clearly, both orally and in writing, especially the latter." Abraham, *Justices and Presidents*, p. 4.

61 Frankfurter, "The Supreme Court in the Mirror of Justice," *University of Pennsylvania Law Review*, Vol. 105, no. 6 (1957), p. 781, cited in Abraham, *Justice and Presidents*.

62 Friedland, *A Place Apart.*

63 *Hill Times*, September 2, 1998; Makin, "Top-Court Judge Defends Bench"; Anderssen, "Top-Court Judge Rejects Proposal to Quiz Nominees."

64 This is the gist of Justice Iacobucci's position (see Anderssen, "Top Court Judge Rejects Proposal to Quiz Nominees"). It is also echoed in spades in a subsequent quote attributed to Justice Minister Anne McLellan: "I think the way we appoint Supreme Court judges in this country has served this country very well. I am very satisfied." Janice Tibbets, "PM Shows Little Interest in New Supreme Court Process," *National Post*, May 3, 1999, p. A7.

65 Charles L. Black, "A Note on Senatorial Consideration of Supreme Court Nominees," *Yale Law Journal*, Vol. 79 (1970), p. 657; Henry J. Abraham, *Justices and Presidents*, pp. 24–25.

66 Abraham, *Justices and Presidents*, p. 39.

67 Russell, *The Judiciary in Canada*, p. 337: "prime ministers and justice ministers in making appointments were highly susceptible to pressure from their federal and provincial political friends."

68 I am not of course suggesting that there is anything wrong with a judge electing to retire 10 or 15 years after the judge's appointment and before the mandatory retirement age of 75. There is cause for concern, however, where a Supreme Court judge decides to retire before having served for at least 10 years or before reaching 65. This paper does not deal with the important question of whether all Supreme Court appointments should be for a limited chronological term, as is true for example of appointments to the German Constitutional Court and various international tribunals. In any event, this would require an amendment to the Canadian constitution, even assuming a strong consensus exists in favour of such a change.

69 Questioning of nominees was only introduced in 1939 with the confirmation hearings on Felix Frankfurter. See Freund, "Appointment of Justices: Some Historical Perspectives," p. 1153.

70 For two contrasting views on the Bork nomination see Nina Totenberg, "The Confirmation Process and the Public: To Know or Not to Know," *Harvard Law Review*, Vol. 101, no. 6 (April 1988), p. 1227; and Patrick B. McGuigan and Dawn M. Weyrich, *Ninth Justice: the Fight for Bork* (Durham, MD: Free Congress Research and Education Foundation, 1990). For

Bork's own account, see Robert Bork, *The Tempting of America: The Political Seduction of the Law* (London: Collier Macmillan, 1990). According to Professor Ross, "The more unsavoury aspects of recent confirmation struggles, particularly the distortions of Robert Bork's record, were the fault of individuals and organizations rather than the confirmation process itself. What is needed is self restraint rather than a more closed process, and perhaps, a re-examination of the proper role of a Supreme Court that is so powerful that appointments to it inspire such widespread concern." William G. Ross, "The Supreme Court Appointment Process: A Search for a Synthesis," *Albany Law Review,* Vol. 57 (Summer 1994), pp. 993, 998–99.

It is fair to note that not all American observers are enthusiastic about recent developments in US Senate confirmation proceedings. In particular, the Twentieth Century Task Force expressed its concern in 1988 on the politicization of confirmation hearings and a majority of its members favoured non-public examination of nominees for appointment. See *Judicial Roulette: Report of The Twentieth Century Fund Task Force on Judicial Selection* (New York: Priority Press Publications, 1988), pp. 8, 10. However, there were strong dissents on both recommendations and current public opinion seems strongly to support the continuance of public confirmation hearings and public examination of nominees. See Ross, "The Supreme Court Appointment Process."

71 For example, at her confirmation hearing before the Senate Judiciary Committee, Justice Bader Ginsburg included the following reservation in her opening statement: "I come to this proceeding to be judged as a judge, not as an advocate. Because I am and hope to continue to be a judge, it would be wrong for me to say or to preview in this legislative chamber how I would cast my vote on questions the Supreme Court may be called upon to decide." Ross, "The Supreme Court Appointment Process," note 56.

72 Malleson, "Assessing the Performance of the Judicial Service Commission," p. 42.

73 Malleson, "Assessing the Performance of the Judicial Service Commission," p. 42.

74 The same would be true of a joint Senate-House of Commons confirmation committee where the government also enjoys majority representation in the Senate. However, in recent years majority representation in the Senate has not been common in the early years of a new government and some years may elapse before the incoming government can appoint enough new senators to achieve a majority.

75 I am indebted to my colleague David Beatty for making this suggestion.

76 The position is therefore very different from the constitutionally entrenched provision in section 96 of the Constitution Act, 1867 entitling only the Governor General to appoint the judges of the Superior, District and County Courts in each province except for the judges of the Probate

Courts in Nova Scotia and New Brunswick. There is a great deal of jurisprudence interpreting section 96 but none, to the best of my knowledge, discussing whether and to what extent the federal government can delegate or dilute its appointive powers by establishing advisory or nominating committees or providing for a parliamentary confirmation role. There has been some discussion of the issues in the Australian context because of the Commonwealth government's exclusive grant of constitutional powers in section 72(i) of the Commonwealth Act to appoint the members of the High Court of Australia. See Tony Blackshield and George Williams, *Australian Constitutional Law and Theory: Commentary and Materials*, 2nd ed. (Sydney: The Federation Press, 1998), pp. 465–69, and J.A. Thompson, "Appointing Australian High Court Justices: Some Constitutional Conundrums," in HP Lee and G. Winterton (eds.), *Australian Constitutional Perspectives* (Sydney: Law Book Co., 1992), pp. 251, 266–69.

77 R.I. Cheffins, "The Constitution Act, 1982 and the Amending Formula: Political and Legal Implication," *Supreme Court Law Review*, Vol. 4 (1982), p. 42; W.R. Lederman, "Constitutional Procedure and the Reform of the Supreme Court of Canada," *Cahiers de droit*, Vol. 26, no. 1 (March 1985), p. 195.

78 Russell, *The Judiciary in Canada*, pp. 67–68. See also MacKay and Bauman, "The Supreme Court of Canada," pp. 49–50, who however, express no views about the proper resolution of the conflict.

79 Canadian Bar Association, Committee on the Supreme Court of Canada, *Report of the Canadian Bar Association Committee On The Supreme Court of Canada* (Ottawa: The Association, 1987), p. 14.

80 As there already is within the Reform party. See note 6 and accompanying text.

81 See note 7 and accompanying text.

Wrestling with Rights: Judges, Parliament and the Making of Social Policy

JANET L. HIEBERT

INTRODUCTION

When the Canadian Charter of Rights and Freedoms became part of the Canadian legal and political landscape in 1982 it changed fundamentally the role and responsibilities of Canadian courts. With the scope of their constitutional judicial role no longer confined to arbitrating jurisdictional conflicts between two orders of government, judges have seen a fundamental change in their responsibilities. This change has signalled an end to the historic reluctance to enter into a sphere previously considered explicitly political and, as such, the exclusive prerogative of Parliament. Although the constitution gives courts little choice but to review state actions for their consistency with protected rights, the judiciary has demonstrated little inclination to minimize the policy implications of this task by either interpreting rights narrowly or declining judicial leave to review issues involving political or moral questions. Since the Charter's introduction, the judiciary has passed judgement on the constitutionality of a breathtakingly broad range of political and social issues from the testing of cruise missiles in Canadian airspace to euthanasia.

Most observers assume that the principal effect of the Charter is on courts. But what should not be overlooked is how a judicially reviewable bill of rights affects governing. Governments at all levels are constrained in their ability to pursue legislative priorities, even where legislation is considered to represent a compelling public interest. These constraints do not arise solely from judicial rulings. Other factors are: interest groups, who raise Charter concerns when trying to influence legislative decisions; government lawyers, who play a pivotal role in analyzing policy and evaluating whether government bills are consistent with the Charter; and political concerns about the social and economic consequences of having legislation invalidated by courts. In short, the Charter has changed the political environment and climate of legislating and is influencing legislative choices at all stages of the policy process.

How the Charter affects governing is the subject of this paper. The paper has seven components. The first section discusses expectations in the literature about how representative institutions might respond to the Charter, particularly in situations where rights issues arise. Section two, "Internal Scrutiny of Proposed Legislation," examines the federal government's internal processes for evaluating legislation from a Charter perspective. Sections three to five analyze the Charter's effects on legislative decision-making in three policy areas: restrictions on the advertising of tobacco products, the rules for the conduct of sexual assault trials and access to victims' private records in sexual assault cases. All three policies reveal important insights into how Parliament views its responsibilities to interpret the Charter and how it has chosen to respond to judicial rulings that reflect a different interpretation of rights as they apply to complex social conflicts. Section six, "Assessing Political Responses to Charter Conflicts," revisits the issue of how representative institutions are responding to the Charter and comments on tensions that arise between the judiciary and Parliament. The final section recommends a process to augment Parliament's role and effectiveness in evaluating legislation in light of Charter considerations.

THE CHARTER'S EFFECT ON LEGISLATIVE DECISION MAKING

How the Charter affects political decision making is significant for a number of reasons. First, legislation often represents a final and authoritative decision about how to balance rights, values, interests and other policy perspectives. Despite the constraints imposed on Parliament by judicial decisions, for many issues Parliament retains a hegemonic position to define the scope and parameters of legislation. Thus, the extent to which public and political officials internalize Charter values (as measured by, for example, the influence of rights on how policy is conceptualized and formulated) is a vital indicator of the Charter's effects on governing.

Second, the Charter may diminish political resolve to define pressing social problems and exercise judgement about how best to reconcile these with constitutional standards. The desire to avoid difficult decisions, by waiting for courts to resolve them, may be tempting. Analysis of how Parliament and government are interpreting legislative priorities within the constitutional framework shaped by the Charter will shed light on how the Charter is affecting political responsibility.

Third, a deeper understanding of the Charter's effect on political decision making may alter public perceptions of the proper roles and prerogatives of the different institutions of governance. The criteria against which legislation is assessed are both open-ended and subject to philosophical disagreements. Disagreements between judicial and elected officials on how best to resolve rights conflicts lead some to question whether judicial opinions should always determine the relative priority of conflicting rights and values. The Canadian Constitution anticipates conflicts between courts and Parliament and provides a mechanism for resolving these: the legislative override (notwithstanding clause) in section 33. This controversial clause allows Parliament to set aside a judicial finding under the Charter, with some important exceptions.[1] Yet public and political opinion is unsettled about whether the use of the override is appropriate and, if so, under what circumstances. This scepticism may be well-founded if Parliament does not pay due regard to the values of the Charter when developing legislation. If, however, legislative decisions are based on careful and sensitive consideration of how best to balance conflicting rights and values, and these decisions are, nevertheless, invalidated by the judiciary, the override might have greater acceptance.

Theoretical Debates about the Charter's Likely Influence

Two divergent views have emerged about the Charter's likely influence on political will to pursue policies that attract rights-based criticism. One view, which is pessimistic about the purported advantages of a Charter, considers the Charter as offering a convenient refuge for politicians to avoid or delay difficult political and moral decisions.[2] Elected representatives can insulate themselves from criticism, and political parties can avoid risking party cohesion, by ignoring controversial issues and claiming that fundamental issues of rights should first be resolved by courts before political decisions are taken. Conflicts involving rights are treated as legal questions rather than political ones with the concomitant assumption that judges, instead of elected representatives, should resolve them. Thus, the expectation is for political inaction in which Parliament not only avoids issues but does not exert influence on how the Charter should be interpreted and applied to social conflicts.

If this assessment were accurate, it would mean that there has been an abrogation of political responsibility to make policy decisions in the public interest. Reasonable people may have different views on how to resolve competing claims around rights and of the proper uses of state power in their resolution. This is because many social conflicts are political in the sense that they invoke differing philosophical assumptions about which values are important, what priorities should be attached to conflicting rights, and what the role of the state should be in defining and responding to pressing social and cultural concerns. This likelihood of philosophical differences in resolving contentious issues suggests why answers to rights conflicts should not be assumed to be uniquely and intrinsically legal, and why a political regime should not vest exclusive authority in courts for reconciling them. As Peter Russell suggests, this abrogation of political responsibility weakens the fabric of democratic decision-making: "[W]e should not lose sight of the possibility that excessive reliance on litigation and the judicial process for settling contentious policy issues can weaken the sinews of our democracy. The danger here is not so much that non-elected judges will impose their will on a democratic majority, but that questions of social and political justice will be transformed into technical legal questions and the great bulk of the citizenry who are not judges and lawyers will abdicate their responsibility for working out reasonable and mutually acceptable resolutions of the issues which divide them."[3]

A more optimistic view of how judicial review will affect parliamentary responsibilities suggests that Parliament will not be treated or consider itself as an inferior partner in constitutional interpretations. Instead, Parliament will become part of a dialogue on how the Charter should be interpreted. This dialogue model suggests that the Charter need not frustrate legislative agendas. The Supreme Court rarely rules that a legislative objective itself is inconsistent with the Charter and therefore cannot be pursued. Instead, judicial concerns tend to focus on the reasonableness of how legislative objectives are implemented. This provides Parliament the opportunity, which it frequently takes, to revise legislation to respond to judicial concerns. Thus, Parliament is not impeded from pursuing its legislative initiatives; it simply has to give more sensitivity and thought to how it proposes to accomplish them. This view, then, suggests that the Charter will facilitate healthy dialogue about "how best to reconcile the individualistic values of the *Charter* with the accomplishment of social and economic policies for the benefit of the community as a whole."[4]

Elsewhere, I have expressed an optimistic view of the Charter's potential to facilitate conversation between Parliament and courts, with reservations. Parliament can incur difficulty when attempting to introduce legislative measures that are similar to those which have been struck down as unconstitutional. Not all policies are necessarily suitable to "fine tuning" because it may not always be possible to identify alternative policy means that will be effective and practical and, at the same time, impose a less intrusive infringement on a protected right.[5] Furthermore, the political costs of introducing legislation similar to that struck down cannot be discounted. Supreme Court decisions attract strong allies who find in these judgements powerful ammunition in the actual words of the country's highest judges. Not only do these judgements provide the pretext for critics of legislative initiatives to engage in armchair judging, but their opposition to legislative initiatives is expressed in the moral language of rights. It makes little difference whether the Court has ruled that previous legislation is only faulty in part, that the legislative means, as opposed to objective, are problematic. The very fact that the Court has ruled that legislation violates the Charter provides critics strong rhetorical force when opposing similar, albeit revised, legislative initiatives. Moreover, the nature of the rights infringement seems to matter little in the willingness of critics to use the language of rights to claim moral and legal primacy for their view.

Thus, the dialogue model may not always capture the relationship between courts and Parliament. As will be discussed in section three, for example, the tobacco example only appears at first blush to demonstrate how the Charter is working to facilitate dialogue to improve the quality of legislation by making it more sensitive to considerations of rights. It will be argued that in fact the Charter's influence was not this benign. The "right" at issue in this case was not only peripheral to the kind of fundamental values that underlie a bill of rights but the judicial suggestion about how to improve the legislation was related to technical or plumbing matters about which the Court had little expertise. Nevertheless this suggestion served as a significant constraint on legislative options and led to less comprehensive legislation than had originally been enacted.

At the same time, the government's treatment of the tobacco case is difficult to characterize as inaction because of its willingness to pursue legislation that would almost certainly lead to a Charter challenge. Yet this too must be qualified. Despite its commitment to the goal of discouraging tobacco consumption, the government was not willing to pursue more comprehensive and effective measures because of fear that these would be invalidated. Some might view this as government immobility and a reneging on political responsibility to pursue the public interest.

Other cases offer evidence of a more assertive government response. As discussed in sections four and five, Parliament saw itself as an important contributor in a dialogue about the rules of consent and access to victims' private records in sexual assault trials. In these cases, Parliament consciously attempted to change the legal paradigm in which conflicting rights are assessed. Thus, neither view fully captures how the Charter is affecting the policy process: if the government has sometimes accepted a secondary role in Charter interpretation, at other times it has fought hard to be recognized as an equal partner in a Charter dialogue with the judiciary.

INTERNAL SCRUTINY OF PROPOSED LEGISLATION

Before turning to these examples of the political reaction to adverse court rulings, there is an earlier stage of the policy-making process to consider: the internal scrutiny of proposed legislation by Justice officials and Cabinet. An impetus for the government to assess the Charter implications of proposed legislation before its introduction to Parliament is the requirement that the Justice Minister certify that government bills have been assessed in light of the Charter and when inconsistent with its purposes and provisions, report this fact to Parliament.[6] To date, no report has been made. As will be argued below, this is not explained by a disregard for the Charter but rather by the development of a bureaucratic and political culture which frowns upon introducing legislation that would require such a report.

The nature of this internal process of Charter analysis, and its effects on policy decisions, are difficult to assess. Those in the Department of Justice whose job it is to identify Charter concerns and give advice are reluctant to speak frankly about the specific policies which raise Charter difficulties, the exact nature of the advice given, and the response of other departments and political officials to that advice. The secretive nature of this exercise is protected by confidentiality requirements of lawyers working within the Department of Justice to those receiving their advice (referred to as their clients), by a lack of public access to the relevant paper trails and by cabinet secrecy.

Despite the secretive nature of this process, interviews with a number of former and current Justice lawyers who are willing to speak generally and anonymously, occasional policy statements or background papers released by the Department, and testimony of Justice lawyers who appear before parliamentary committees, allow for the following observations and assessment of the process.

Evaluating Bills in the Department of Justice

The Charter has increased the influence of the Department of Justice in shaping legislation. The Department established the Human Rights

Law Section in 1982 to review existing legislation for the purposes of identifying Charter conflicts and bringing statutes into conformity with the Charter and to provide ongoing advice on Charter issues. The latter task involves analyzing the legal implications of policy proposals and systematically assessing whether government bills comply with the Charter.

The Department has responsibility for drafting all government bills. However, before this takes place the sponsoring Minister must submit to Cabinet a memorandum setting forth the objectives and implications of the proposal, including any Charter concerns. The awareness that Charter difficulties will be noted, along with their implications for the viability of the policy in terms of judicial review, places pressure on departments to work with Justice officials to address Charter concerns before the memorandum is submitted.

Justice lawyers are acutely conscious of the need to distinguish legal advice on the Charter from policy advice; it is recognized that the responsibility for allocating priorities in social policy conflicts remains political in nature. From their perspective, if legal opinion is replaced by policy advice about whether a proposed course of action has merit, Justice lawyers will have overstepped their responsibility and undermined their credibility to provide legal advice on Charter issues. Yet this distinction between advice and opinion can become blurred because Charter advice may be inextricably connected to evaluating the justification of legislation. For example, to conclude that a bill imposes a restriction on a right that is not reasonable, and therefore may not survive the Charter, can be interpreted as another way of saying that the bill is not justified because its objectives are not important enough to warrant such a grave restriction on protected rights.

With this delicate balance in mind, of the need to distinguish legal advice from policy opinion, the Department has adopted an approach for reviewing bills based on a risk assessment of the degree of difficulty for justifying legislation under the Charter. Risk assessments are undertaken on a continuum from minimal, significant, substantial, serious to unacceptable risks, the latter representing almost certainty that courts would invalidate the legislative action. At times, Justice officials have been asked to put their assessment into numerical terms: to evaluate, for example, whether legislation has a 60 percent chance of surviving as opposed to a lesser chance, or to indicate where the degree of risk is situated on a scale of one to ten. However, they are reluctant to offer advice in these quantitative terms; while it can be difficult to distinguish between significant, substantial or serious risks, assessments continue to be framed in qualitative terms.

The approach to the evaluation of bills has been greatly influenced by Supreme Court jurisprudence. The Charter's structure and, in particular its inclusion of a general limitation clause in section 1, has encouraged the Court to adopt a two-stage approach to judicial review: i) does the rights claim have constitutional protection and is it infringed and, if so, ii) is the restriction reasonable? The Charter states explicitly in section 1 that rights can be subject to "such reasonable limits prescribed by law as can be demonstrably justified in a free and democratic society." It is largely with reference to this second stage that risk assessments occur, particularly for those rights and freedoms which do not contain any internal reference to reasonableness.

The Human Rights section has sought to convince other departments to seek Charter advice as early as possible in the process of developing policy. Justice lawyers believe that when Charter assessments are done early it is easier to identify ways of accomplishing legislative objectives in a manner that is both more likely to survive a Charter challenge and to minimize disruption in attaining the policy goal. Another perceived advantage of thinking about Charter implications early in the policy process is to anticipate possible Charter challenges and consciously develop a legislative record for addressing judicial concerns. This record may include research on policy objectives, consultations with interested groups, social science data, the experiences of other jurisdictions with similar legislative initiatives, and testimony before parliamentary committees by experts and interest groups. Another form of anticipating judicial review is the increased use of legislative preambles, stating the objectives and assumptions underlying the legislation, of which more will be said later.

This sensitivity to the Charter does not mean that policies are forsaken because they incur serious Charter risks. The threshold for accepting that a policy complies with the Charter, and therefore does not require a report to Parliament, is whether or not a credible Charter argument can be made. When less risky ways to accomplish policy objectives cannot be identified, Cabinet ultimately will be required to render a political judgement about whether to proceed. However, the context in which this judgement is made gives rise to obvious tension between the Justice Minister's statutory obligation to report to Parliament, if a bill is inconsistent with the Charter, and an emerging political culture that assumes that no report should be made. Thus, the prevailing assumption is that government should not pursue legislation that is considered to be so patently inconsistent with the Charter that it would require the Justice Minister to report to Parliament; before reaching this stage, the bill should be either amended or withdrawn. This political presumption against a report to Parliament creates strong incentives to find ways of pursuing legislative objectives in a manner that incurs lower Charter risks. It puts pressure on the

Minister of Justice, who also serves as the Attorney General, to convince his or her colleagues of the need to amend policies so that a credible Charter argument can be made. If the government is intent on pursuing a course of action for which the Justice Minister concludes that no credible Charter argument can be made, the Minister will likely feel compelled to resign. To date, these conflicts have been resolved to the satisfaction of the Justice Minister, at least to the extent that no Minister has yet concluded that it is necessary to report to Parliament or resigned for this reason.

While the Minister has considerable influence in Cabinet, he or she must be prudent in deciding when and how this influence will be exercised. Other ministers will have a strong commitment to their departments' policies and may not be easily convinced about the need or value of modifying or withdrawing proposals. Consequently, the Minister of Justice must save these ultimate recourses, a warning of the need for a report to Parliament or the even stronger threat of resignation, for those rare circumstances when other forms of influence and pressure are not successful and where the Minister believes emphatically that a credible Charter argument cannot be made. Exactly how often these conflicts occur or how they are resolved are confidential; however, informed sources indicate that occasional "wing-ding" fights have occurred in the Cabinet room.

Some might understandably interpret the lack of reports to Parliament with scepticism about the influence and rigour of Charter advice and scrutiny.[8] Although the secretive and confidential nature of the process for evaluating proposed legislation makes it difficult to assess whether scepticism is appropriate or misplaced, a fuller explanation for the absence of reports to Parliament likely has the following three elements.

First, the Charter has helped to facilitate a political culture within the bureaucracy and government that is reluctant to be, or appear to be, indifferent or insensitive toward the Charter. One manifestation of this culture is the view that the integrity of the Charter, as a statement of fundamental constitutional values, would be undermined if the government purposively pursued a course of action considered by its own Justice Minister to be unreasonable under the Charter. From a pragmatic standpoint, legislation requiring a report to Parliament would be in an extremely precarious position, vulnerable both to political embarrassment and successful Charter challenge. Opposition parties would have a field day criticizing the government for pursuing a course of action that its own Justice Minister believes to be patently unconstitutional. Furthermore, litigants would readily argue that the legislation should not be upheld because even the government recognizes that it violates the constitution in a manner that cannot be considered reasonable or justifiable. It is difficult to imagine that the Supreme Court would be prepared to uphold legislation as a justifiable infringement of the Charter, when the Justice Minister has admitted such profound inconsistency.

This political culture of not reporting has interesting implications for government if it wishes to pursue legislation that is clearly inconsistent with the Charter or leading Supreme Court precedents. It suggests that the only political option for introducing legislation that is patently inconsistent with Charter jurisprudence is to enact the legislative override. While the override overcomes the difficulty of courts overturning legislation, it is as susceptible to political difficulty as is a report to Parliament.

A second reason for the absence of reports is that the threshold for avoiding one is not mandated by the *Justice Act* but has evolved from practice. Ultimately, judgement about whether a credible Charter argument can be made has political and subjective elements and may vary depending on the philosophical views and interpretation of the Charter by the particular Justice Minister of the day. However, this threshold is broad enough that it is unlikely that many bills for which there is substantial Cabinet and political support cannot be subsumed under this criterion. The Charter itself, and how it has been interpreted, have contributed to the breadth of this threshold. Questions of what values are consistent with a free and democratic society, which is the normative framework for evaluating limits on rights, are not exclusively legal and will invoke differences of opinion amongst reasonable people.[9] The Supreme Court itself has declared that these are not universal standards but that the Charter's structure (its inclusion of limitation and override clauses) provides a unique context for evaluating the justification of legislative policies that differentiates assessments of reasonableness in Canada from other jurisdictions.[10] Furthermore, issues relating to a policy's reasonableness, evaluated against a changing and evolving jurisprudence around interpretations of proportionality criteria, are also subject to differences of opinion, both within the Supreme Court and amongst political and public officials.

A third reason for the lack of reports is the tension between the role the Justice Minister serves as Attorney General, and his or her partisan role as a member of Cabinet, which may be sufficient to dissuade the Minister from reporting to Parliament in very close calls which involve substantial Charter risk. The breadth of the threshold, and the real possibility that reasonable and tolerant people will differ in their conclusions about whether legislation is justified, may reinforce this reluctance.

In summary, the Charter's effects on how policies are assessed and analyzed before they are introduced to Parliament may not be visible. However, its influence has been both systemic and systematic and has changed the political environment in which policies are conceptualized, drafted and defended in public debate. Bureaucratic scrutiny and the Justice Minister's obligation to report to Parliament ensure that the Charter receives significant consideration before legislation is put forward.

But this is only the first stage in the policy-making process where the Charter has a marked impact. As discussed in the following three sections, when courts nullify legislation, Parliament must decide what response is appropriate. The responses chosen in the cases under examination offer further evidence of the way in which the government has tried to exercise some influence over Charter interpretation.

THE CHARTER'S EFFECTS ON LEGISLATIVE RESPONSE TO JUDICIAL DECISIONS: RESTRICTIONS ON TOBACCO ADVERTISING AND SPONSORSHIP

In 1995 the Supreme Court in *RJR-MacDonald Inc.*[11] struck down legislation with the ambitious objective of discouraging tobacco consumption, particularly amongst impressionable and young people, by prohibiting the advertisement and promotion of tobacco products and by requiring that manufacturers of tobacco products display health warnings on packaging. The Court ruled that the legislation violates freedom of expression. The Court did not disapprove of the legislative objective but by a five to four majority ruled that the legislative means were not reasonable. Parliament subsequently enacted new legislation, in an attempt to respond to the Court's concerns, which itself is being challenged under the Charter by tobacco companies.

Supreme Court Decision in RJR-MacDonald Inc.

The majority decision, written by Justice McLachlin with Lamer CJ, Iacobucci, Sopinka and Major concurring, stated that no matter how important Parliament's objective may seem, if the government cannot demonstrate that the means by which its goal will be achieved are reasonable and proportionate to the infringement of rights, the law should fail.[12] The legislation was not rational because no causal connection, based on direct evidence, logic or reason, exists between the legislative objective of decreasing tobacco consumption and the legislative means of prohibiting tobacco trademarks on advertisements for other products.[13] The majority ruled that the Court should not accept the "mere intuition" of Parliament because the Charter's requirement that legislation be demonstrably justified and reasonable should be based on "rational inference from evidence or established truths."[14] The majority was also critical of the use in the legislation of a ban on all advertising and promotion, particularly in light of the government's failure to introduce evidence about the utility of less intrusive measures despite its knowing of relevant studies. This failure to introduce evidence to support its ban on advertising led to the majority's conjecture "that the results of the studies must undercut the government's claim that a less invasive ban would not have produced an equally salutary result."[15]

As will be argued shortly, the majority's assessment of the legislation had a substantial influence on the subsequent legislative response. The majority speculated that a ban on lifestyle advertising would be an effective way of achieving the objective of deterring tobacco consumption and yet satisfy judicial concerns of minimal impairment. Although neither argument nor evidence were put forward to sustain this opinion, the majority, nevertheless, pronounced that as a matter of "common sense" lifestyle advertising will likely discourage those who might otherwise cease tobacco use from doing so. Thus, the message the majority sent to Parliament was that it could pass legislation restricting tobacco lifestyle advertising and be reasonably assured that this would pass judicial scrutiny in the future.

Both the majority's inferences about why the government had not introduced evidence to support the ban on advertising and the suggestion of an alternative choice of policy means provoked criticism from Justice La Forest, who wrote the dissenting opinion, with L'Heureux-Dubé, Gonthier and Cory concurring. The minority thought it unwise for judicial conjecture about the contents of documents unavailable to judges to "displace the overwhelming evidence that the prohibition was a reasonable one." Parliament has a reasonable basis, after 20 years of research and legislative experimentation, to believe that all tobacco advertising stimulates tobacco consumption.[16] The minority characterized tobacco legislation as the archetypal case in which the Court should be prepared to give Parliament substantial latitude in choosing the legislative means it considers the most appropriate for addressing the social problem. It was critical of the majority's speculation that Parliament should have considered restrictions on lifestyle advertising, stating that it is not appropriate for the Court to substitute its own judgement for Parliament's, particularly on a matter for which the Court lacks expertise: "[I]t would be highly artificial for this Court to decide, on a purely abstract basis, that a partial prohibition on advertising would be as effective as a full prohibition. In my view, this is precisely the type of 'line drawing' that this Court has identified as being within the institutional competence of legislatures and not courts."[17]

Assessing the Judicial Decision

Two aspects of the Court's approach to judicial review warrant comment because of their implications for how the Court evaluated Parliament's legislative initiative: 1) the exceedingly broad definition of freedom of expression and 2) the manner in which the Court assessed the reasonableness of how Parliament's initiative was translated into legislation. By elevating tobacco advertising to the level of constitutionally protected speech the Court has transformed a purely political issue, involving conflicting economic and political interests, into a constitutional debate over fundamental rights. Once it concluded that speech is violated, the Court was drawn into the middle of a complex and multi-faceted policy debate.

Yet it can be argued that the conflict over tobacco advertising is not about rights at all. At issue is a policy disagreement between tobacco companies' economic interests to maximize profits and maintain market share and the government's objective to dissuade young and impressionable people from becoming smokers. Citizens may have different views on the logic or effectiveness of controlling tobacco advertising. However, democratic principles of representative government generally assume that these kinds of policy disagreements should be resolved in the representative branch of government. Apart from the necessity that courts arbitrate jurisdictional disagreements between different levels of government in federal states, political conflicts should only be subject to judicial review when state action has implications for fundamental rights. The Charter, like other bills of rights, was intended to protect citizens and other human members of the polity. Thus, the Court's elevation of a corporate economic interest to the same status as individuals' constitutional rights, and its protection of that interest, are ill-conceived.

In this case, the Court was not required by the Charter to extend protected speech to corporate activities. Instead, it could have adopted a more limited definition of speech by excluding trivial claims unrelated to the healthy functioning of a democratic polity, however broadly interpreted. Under this approach, the Court would have inquired whether and how tobacco advertising relates to the kinds of values the Court elsewhere has said underlie freedom of expression: (1) seeking and attaining the truth; (2) encouraging participation in social and political decision making; and (3) cultivating diversity in forms of individual self-fulfillment in a tolerant and welcoming environment for speakers and listeners.[18]

This decision in favour of such a broad definition of speech was discretionary, as opposed to being mandated by the Charter, and is now firmly entrenched in jurisprudence. In the Court's opinion, any activity that conveys or attempts to convey a meaning has expressive content and *prima facie* falls within the scope of the guarantee.[19]

The Court may not like the idea of relying on definitional limits for speech. Nevertheless, it is important to realize that the Court has in the past, and will in the future, rely to some degree on such limits. Before the Court ever addressed whether the Charter protects commercial expression, it did in fact adopt definitional limits to exclude the right to strike from the scope of the Charter's protection for freedom of association.[20] It is difficult to appreciate how the Court can coherently rule that one form of economic activity (striking by labour unions) is beyond the Charter's protection, while another form (corporate advertising) is protected. Furthermore, the Court has indicated that it will exclude violent activities from the scope of the Charter's protection of speech.[21] This is logical because it would greatly trivialize the significance of constitutional rights were murder or physical violence to be treated as protected speech, subject only to reasonable limits.

But even accepting the decision to classify commercial advertising as protected speech, it can still be argued that the Court could have minimized the extent to which it was interfering with Parliament's choice of policy means. For example, it could have followed the minority's suggestion that substantial deference was owed to Parliament on the question of how best to tackle this ambitious and complex legislative objective. This would have been consistent with past rulings where the Court has warned against taking "a restrictive approach to social science evidence" that requires "legislatures to choose the least ambitious means to protect vulnerable groups."[22] It has also indicated that when the rights claim is peripheral to the values intended to be protected the standard for justifying limitations is lower. Thus, where a rights claim is only "tenuously connected to the values" underlying a protected right, restrictions on that right are easier to justify, as in the case of restrictions on hate literature.[23] In this vein, restrictions on commercial speech have been easier to justify than infringements on other rights.[24]

For those who do not desire judicial deference, comfort might be found in the majority's warning: "To carry judicial deference to the point of accepting Parliament's view simply on the basis that the problem is serious and the solution difficult, would be to diminish the role of the courts in the constitutional process and to weaken the structure of rights upon which our constitution and our nation is founded."[25]

However, this statement would be more appropriate in another context: where, for example, the legislative infringement on speech undermines the robust and healthy functioning of a liberal democratic polity or restricts artistic and cultural expressions that reflect diverse and contrary views. The statement ignores the difference between the need for the Court to be vigilant when protecting fundamental rights as distinct from reviewing an economic policy disagreement where the language of rights has been invoked strategically, but inappropriately, to dress up a corporate policy interest that does not reflect any reasonable moral or normative claim on society. The value advanced by tobacco advertising is far removed from what is essential to preserve the constitutional foundations that the majority worries about. Its failure to distinguish between different kinds of speech, and the appropriate level of judicial scrutiny attendant on these, is shallow. Moreover, it risks trivializing the significance of constitutionally protected rights and undermines public acceptance of judicial intervention when fundamental rights are jeopardized by state actions.

It is important to emphasize the consequences of this judicial approach. Stated simply, the more broadly that courts interpret rights, the more often judges will be required to don the hat of the policy analyst and assess the reasonableness of the means chosen to pursue social policy. When the judiciary acts in this manner, it is engaging in policy analysis pure and simple. And yet judges lack a policy background and access to resources that allow for informed evaluations of complex policy options. No matter how eminent judges are, no matter how principled in interpreting the Charter, policy analysis is not where their training and expertise lie. In this case, an informed assessment of Parliament's chosen means to discourage tobacco consumption would require review of issues related to marketing strategies, behavioural research and health studies. Such issues are well beyond judges' area of expertise. They are of a nature for which legal training provides virtually no guidance but are peculiarly apposite to Parliament, with its access to the necessary resources and comparative knowledge to develop policy.

A related concern is the Court's method for assessing the reasonableness of the legislative means. The Court's speculative discussion of whether the legislation comports with judicially-created proportionality criteria demonstrates their ill fit to complex social problems. It is particularly difficult to measure the effects of tobacco advertising on consumption. To even suggest that this measurement is attainable suggests false confidence that society possesses the requisite knowledge and appropriate methodology to predict how to change human behaviour with regard to an addictive habit. Moreover, policy developers must anticipate the many ways in which tobacco companies will attempt to undermine this objective because of their fundamental and vested interest in encouraging tobacco consumption.

Thus, it is worrisome to see the strategies for pursuing this complex social policy evaluated against judicial interpretations of whether the means chosen were significantly more restrictive than some other hypothetical possibility. By structuring the conflict in this way, those who opposed the legislative initiative were at a distinct advantage. Inconclusive social science data and behavioural/health studies make it difficult to challenge, empirically, tobacco companies' twin claims: that less restrictive measures are required to satisfy reasonableness criteria and that because no clear causal linkage can be established between advertising and tobacco consumption, this must mean that restrictions on advertising are not rational.

Had the Court adopted a more precise definition of expression, or engaged in a more purposive or thoughtful discussion of what is important about free speech and what kinds of state actions impede it, the Court might never have ruled that the legislation conflicted with the Charter. It would also not have been placed in the position of having to review the fine-tuning of such a complex social policy. In short, the Court's decision, in this case, seems ill-founded.

In light of the marginal nature of the speech claim in this issue, and the difficulties inherent in judicial review of Parliament's choice of policy means, a forceful response from Parliament might have been anticipated. However, this was not to be the case.

Influence of Decision on Subsequent Legislation

Less than a year after the Court's decision, the federal Liberal government introduced new legislation (Bill C-71) with similar purposes but using different legislative means.[26] What is significant about the new legislation was the centrality of the majority's emphasis on restricting lifestyle advertising. Then Health Minister David Dingwall made it clear that policy developers had moved "painstakingly" to examine the Supreme Court's decision "line by line" and sought two independent consultations to ensure that the new legislation would be constitutionally valid.[27] In developing the legislation, the department took guidance from the Court's decision by incorporating the majority's suggestion for a ban on lifestyle advertising.[28] A senior official with the Department of Health confirmed the influence of this dimension of the Court's ruling on the design of the legislation: "We have taken those parameters and that is how we've crafted the bill, so that any promotion that appeals to youth or is associated with youth or has a lifestyle connotation is an area that is restricted. We feel we have taken a lot of care to reflect the guidance provided by the Supreme Court."[29]

It seems extraordinary that the judiciary's speculative comment would have such influence on the design of legislation that addresses a complex social problem that baffles the policy experts and can hardly be said to fall within the Court's competence. From a pragmatic perspective, it is understandable why the government would have been tempted by this suggestion, particularly with its attendant message that this would likely be considered a constitutionally valid way of discouraging tobacco consumption. The government would obviously be anxious to avoid suffering another judicial setback. Nevertheless, the prudence of framing this policy around the majority's "common sense" observation may be questionable. Disagreements expressed during parliamentary committee hearings about whether lifestyle advertising affects consumption suggest uncertainty about how effective this legislative strategy will be. They also raise doubts about whether the legislation will be immune from successful Charter challenge on the same grounds that were used to defeat the previous legislation.

Tobacco companies have focused much of their considerable criticism of the legislation on its targeting of lifestyle advertising as a principal measure for discouraging tobacco consumption. They argue that there is no existing empirical or scientific data to suggest that lifestyle advertising will induce individuals to smoke[30] and therefore the legislation amounts to little more than cosmetic measures to give the appearance that the government is doing something effective. Other critics who feel threatened by the legislation have argued that since there is no evidence of any causal linkage between tobacco consumption and advertising tobacco logos on products or events, the legislative means are not rationally connected to the objective.[31]

Tobacco companies have challenged the legislation as unconstitutional. Since the government has framed much of its legislative strategy for the new tobacco bill around the window of opportunity established by the majority, it will be interesting to see how the Court evaluates the legislation. The Court may find it difficult, politically, to rule this approach unreasonable. However, the composition of the Court has changed since the earlier legislation was struck down and at least four different judges will be on the bench when the case is next reviewed.[32] Since the new legislation raises issues very similar to those in the previous case, it invites the following question: *Apart from the Court's "ownership" of the recommended suggestion to restrict lifestyle advertising, is there a coherent reason to assume that the new legislation comes any closer to satisfying the majority's requirement that it be based on "rational, reasoned defensibility"[33] as opposed to the "mere intuition" which it earlier ruled to be inadequate?*

Twists and Turns in the Legislative Saga

As a federal election neared, and speculation increased that sporting events like the Grand Prix might not be staged because of restrictions on tobacco sponsorship, the federal government announced intended amendments to exempt the racing car industry. The announcement came shortly after Canada's three major tobacco manufacturers warned in newspaper advertisements that if the legislation was passed it would "inevitably lead to the cancellation of many events" and would cost thousands of jobs and millions of lost tourism dollars.[34]

The proposed amendment to exempt the racing industry from sponsorship restrictions drew criticism from the Reform and NDP parties, which wanted much tougher and comprehensive legislation to restrict tobacco advertising. It also exposed the legislation to even greater vulnerability in terms of satisfying the Court's interpretation of the Charter. Even with the announced exemption, Canada's three major tobacco companies, Imperial Tobacco Ltd., RJR MacDonald Inc. and Rothmans, Benson & Hedges Inc., filed a court challenge arguing that the legislation was unconstitutional. Ironically, they tried to turn the exemption to their advantage, arguing that the government could hardly claim that the legislation was reasonable under the Charter since it "has shown willingness to modify restrictions on rights guaranteed by the Charter supposedly enacted by the House of Commons and by the Senate for health reasons to further its own political purposes."[35] The increased vulnerability of the legislation, if exemptions were made for political purposes, was also noted in parliament by the Reform party: "If the government exempts auto racing in the Tobacco Act, other groups will be sprinting to the courts. [Minister Rock] knows that. What possible defence will this government offer at that time in court for exempting one event but not others?"[36]

The amendments (Bill C-42) were enacted more than a year after the original announcement was made.[37] The legislation created a five-year exemption for all events and activities that had received tobacco sponsorship before April 25, 1997 when Bill C-71 became law, likely in order to escape the vulnerability of exempting only racing. The government tried to put the best face forward on these changes, claiming that the amendments strengthened the legislation because after five years all sponsorship would be banned, which would give groups "more time to adjust and to find alternate sponsors."[38] However, a more probable explanation is that during the course of evaluating the proposed amendments, the Department of Justice warned of the high Charter risks that would be incurred if exemptions were based solely on discretionary political decisions: exemptions for only some events would be difficult to justify under the Charter as would be the argument that the legislation is rational and complies with the minimal impairment criterion.

Summary

The Charter had a significant influence on all aspects and stages of developing this policy. The legislative initiative to restrict tobacco advertising was developed with careful reference to the Supreme Court's decision. Even in the face of political pressure which resulted in the government's overtly political attempt to weaken its own legislation, these attempts were almost certainly constrained by considerations of how to make the new policy more viable in the face of an inevitable Charter challenge.

The willingness to persevere with this legislative initiative, after having similar legislation struck down, does not demonstrate inaction in the face of a rights conflict. Nevertheless, the government was not aggressive in pursuing its legislative initiative. It did not question the wisdom of the Court's characterization of tobacco advertising as protected speech. It accepted, and built its response around, the judicial view that fundamental rights were at stake without pressing the alternative view that these rights are really economic interests far removed from the kind of values intended to be protected under the Charter. Furthermore, the government accepted the judiciary's suggestion about how to frame subsequent legislation, even though this suggestion had little to do with judicial expertise. This suggests that the desire to implement some aspect of the legislative initiative that would survive judicial scrutiny, at the cost of weaker legislation, was politically preferable to facing yet another Charter defeat. It was also preferred to overtly challenging the judicial decision by enacting more comprehensive measures that would almost certainly have required the controversial enactment of the legislative override – an option discussed and dismissed by Cabinet.[39]

RULES RELATING TO SEXUAL ASSAULT TRIALS

Profound judicial and political differences exist over whether legal rules for sexual assault trials and access to victims' private records discriminate against women. At issue is whether equality rights of women should be considered relevant when assessing the requirements of a fair sexual assault trial. Parliament's response to these conflicts is an important indicator of how the Charter is affecting governing. Parliament has twice passed legislation that reflects an interpretation of rights that differs in important ways from the majority Supreme Court view. This suggests that Parliament's behaviour under the Charter is not characterized by inaction but reveals its intent to change legal norms about how the Charter relates to sexual assault trials. These differences appear in the legislative responses to a trilogy of Supreme Court decisions, *R. v. Seaboyer, R. v. O'Connor,* and *R. v. Carosella.*[40] The first legislative enactment, pertaining to assumptions around consent, is discussed in this section; the second piece of legislation, relating to access to victims' private records, is considered in the next section.

R. v. Seaboyer

The *R. v. Seaboyer* decision initiated the parliamentary/judicial conflict over the rules of sexual assault trials. A majority of the Court ruled unconstitutional sections of the Criminal Code, known as rape shield provisions, which prevented women's sexual histories from generally being introduced as evidence by defence lawyers. Parliament had considered this legislation necessary because judge-made rules had been highly prejudicial towards women. Judges had routinely allowed evidence of women's sexual histories, with inferences frequently made that consent in earlier circumstances in all likelihood meant that consent had been given in the incident at trial or that the woman was not a credible or truthful witness.

In 1991 the Court, in a 7–2 decision, struck down the legislation for violating the principles of fundamental justice (section 7) and presumption of innocence (section 11(d)). The Court did not question the importance of the legislation but thought its effects were too restrictive because of the potential to exclude evidence "of critical relevance to the defence."[41] The majority judgement, written by Justice McLachlin with Lamer CJ, La Forest, Stevenson, Iacobucci, Sopinka and Cory concurring, concluded that a woman's sexual history could be relevant.[42] Rather than being denied this evidence, because of legislation, the judiciary should use discretion to distinguish between necessary and irrelevant evidence.[43]

The dissenting judgement of L'Heureux-Dubé, in which Gonthier concurred, contained a sharp rebuke of those judges, particularly at the trial level, who have succumbed to biases in the law that reflect unfair, stereotypical myths about women and rape. This skepticism of judicial impartiality led to the suggestion that Parliament was justified when trying to legislate a different paradigm for sexual assault trials:

Parliament exhibited a marked, and justifiedly so, distrust of the ability of the courts to promote and achieve a non-discriminatory application of the law in this area. In view of the history of government attempts, the harm done when discretion is posited in trial judges and the demonstrated inability of the judiciary to change its discriminatory ways, Parliament was justified in so choosing. My attempt to illustrate the tenacity of these discriminatory beliefs and their acceptance at all levels of society clearly demonstrates that discretion in judges is antithetical to the goals of Parliament.[44]

The majority's decision generated widespread concern from women's groups who believed that it would discourage sexual assault victims from proceeding with criminal charges. The decision reinvigorated criticism that assumptions in the law with respect to sexual assault trials treat female sexual assault victims unfairly.[45]

Legislative Response: Bill C-49

The federal government and Parliament were not prepared to accept the ruling as the final word on the rules governing sexual assault proceedings. After extensive consultation with women's groups, the Justice Minister was persuaded to undertake substantial changes to the Criminal Code in Bill C-49, to address the issue of consent in particular. The legislation, which received all party support, amended the Criminal Code[46] to define consent and to make it clear that relevant inferences cannot be drawn from a woman's conduct or from her previous sexual history.[47] The legislation also made it more difficult for the accused to use mistaken belief as a legal defence. Previous legislation had allowed an accused to be acquitted if he could persuade the judge or jury that he honestly believed the victim had consented. However, the new legislation requires that the accused take reasonable steps to ascertain that the complainant was consenting and it explicitly stipulates that mistaken belief about consent is not accepted where it arises from intoxication, recklessness or willful blindness.

In response to the Court's rejection of the blanket exemption on evidence of a woman's sexual past, the legislation provides judicial guidelines for determining admissibility; for example, it stipulates that evidence that a complainant has engaged in previous sexual activity is not admissible to support an inference that she is more likely to have consented to the sexual activity in question or is less worthy of belief. The legislation further stipulates that evidence of a woman's sexual history can only be included where it is clearly relevant to the issue at trial and where its probative value is not substantially outweighed by its prejudicial effects.

The legislation was controversial and reactions to it revealed profoundly different views about how to ensure a fair trial without debasing sexual assault victims. Critics of the legislation, in particular defence counsel, argued that men can honestly but mistakenly believe that a woman has agreed to the sexual act in question and therefore the preclusion of this defence would undermine the right to a fair trial. Critics also disagreed with Parliament's definition of consent, which they characterized as a "grotesquely distorted view of relations between men and women" reflecting an unrealistic vision of sexual relations more suited to contract law than "the way such things happen in the real world." These assumptions were rejected, vigorously, by a number of women's groups who argued that if men are in any way uncertain about whether consent was granted, they should take reasonable steps to ensure that their partner has consented and, if still uncertain, abstain. They also rejected the view that the legislation should be guided by "realistic vision[s] of sexual relations" which, in their opinion, perpetuate the view that women's words, when it comes to sexual relations, cannot be taken at face value.[48]

The bill was studied extensively by a parliamentary committee established for that purpose in which Charter concerns were a prominent component of political debate. Parliament addressed and responded to Charter concerns in a manner that was neither dismissive of rights-based criticisms nor intimidated by suggestions that the judiciary was the more appropriate venue for resolving conflicts over the rules of sexual assault trials.

What was most significant about political handling of this issue was the government's attempt to give a different emphasis to the conflicting rights than appeared in the Court's decision. Parliament agreed with the government's characterization of the Charter issues as involving more than the right of the accused to a fair trial and presumption of innocence; also relevant are the equality rights of women in section 15 and their security of person rights in section 7. This more complex interpretation of how the Charter should apply to this conflict clearly distinguishes the political from judicial judgement. For the majority of the Court in *Seaboyer*, only one rights-holder has a Charter interest in this issue: the accused.

This willingness to articulate a different view of how the Charter applies to sexual assault trials is significant for what it reveals about how elected representatives are interpreting their responsibilities under the Charter. Parliament has consciously and deliberately sought to change assumptions underlying sexual assault trials. In so doing, Parliament has made abundantly clear that elected representatives are not prepared to defer to judges on all interpretations of the Charter. Its alternative assessment was made explicit in a legislative preamble for all to read – in particular, judges. The intent of the preamble was twofold: to serve as an education device for courts on how to broach sexual assault trials and to provide a statement of parliamentary intent in anticipation of a subsequent constitutional challenge to the legislation.

The preamble indicates Parliament's grave concern about sexual violence and abuse in Canadian society and its sense that judicial decisions should be made within the context of conflicting rights: those of the accused to a fair trial and the equality and security of women. It suggests that notwithstanding the Supreme Court's concerns about the exclusionary rule, Parliament is of the belief "that evidence of the complainant's sexual history is rarely relevant and that its admission should be subject to particular scrutiny, bearing in mind the inherently prejudicial character of such evidence." One does not have to strain too hard to interpret this statement as Parliament's belief that the Supreme Court has not interpreted this conflict in an appropriate manner because insufficient regard was given to the equality rights of women. A political interpretation of the preamble's message to the judiciary is the following:

Dear Judges: Parliament believes that the relevant Charter rights to consider in sexual assault trials are not confined to the right of the accused to a fair trial. Equality and security of women's persons also must be duly considered. In drafting these legislative amendments, Parliament has been neither insensitive, unprincipled nor in denial of its responsibilities under the Charter or of the rule of law. With all due respect, this, in Parliament's thoughtful opinion, is a more appropriate and fair way of reconciling the conflicting rights and interests at issue in sexual assault proceedings.

One can think of a preamble as representing a stage in a conversation between elected and judicial officials on how the Charter should be interpreted and applied to the particular case at hand. What is attractive about the use of the legislative preamble is that it makes explicit the concerns and intents animating legislative decisions and leaves less room for courts to ascribe objectives to Parliament. This is a more honest and forthright way of attempting to justify a legislative objective than relying on government lawyers to speculate, after the fact, about the reasons behind a legislative decision. At this early stage in Charter jurisprudence it is difficult to assess what influence preambles will have in convincing judges about the reasonableness of Parliament's legislation. However, the intent to educate trial court judges and change their legal assumptions (at least in the context of sexual assault cases) does not appear to be as effective as Parliament may have wished.

Parliament's Intent to Define Consent Upheld

Parliament's tough rules, which made it difficult for an accused to suggest that he was mistaken about whether consent was granted, were at issue in *R. v. Ewanchuk*.[49] In this case, the accused initiated several sexual advances toward a woman, despite her repeated statements of "no." He was acquitted at trial of sexual assault in which his defence was that consent had been implied. In 1999, the Court unanimously upheld the appeal of his acquittal and used its discretion to enter a conviction against him.

The Court ruled that in sexual assault cases, where an accused argues mistaken understanding, the judge must be convinced that the accused "honestly believed *that the complainant had communicated consent.*" Any other belief, however honestly held, is not a defence. Furthermore, for this claim to be accepted, the accused's mistaken belief "cannot be reckless, willfully blind or tainted by an awareness of any of the factors" enumerated in Bill C-49. At any point, if the woman has expressed a lack of agreement to engage in sexual activity, "it is incumbent upon the accused to point to some evidence from which he could honestly believe consent to have been re-established *before* he resumed his advances."[50]

Justice L'Heureux-Dubé, who accepted the principal judgement, written by Justice Major, felt compelled to speak out against what she considered to be prejudicial and discriminatory statements by the Court of Appeal. In supplementary comments, she indicated her concern with the statement of Justice McClung that the complainant did not present herself to the accused "in a bonnet and crinolines." This statement, in her view, should not be condoned: "[These comments] help reinforce the myth that under such circumstances, either the complainant is less worthy of belief, she invited the sexual assault, or her sexual experience signals probable consent to further sexual activity. Based on those attributed assumptions, the implication is that if the complainant articulates her lack of consent by saying 'no,' she really does not mean it and even if she does, her refusal cannot be taken as seriously as if she were a girl of 'good' moral character."[51]

L'Heureux-Dubé stated that the Court of Appeal's treatment of this case does not dispel the concerns she expressed in *Seaboyer* about why Parliament was justified in attempting to halt judicial reliance on myths and stereotypes in sexual assault complaints: "Complainants should be able to rely on a system free from myths and stereotypes, and on a judiciary whose impartiality is not compromised by these biased assumptions. The Code was amended in 1983 and in 1992 to eradicate reliance on those assumptions; they should not be permitted to resurface through the stereotypes reflected in the reasons of the majority of the Court of Appeal. It is part of the role of this Court to denounce this kind of language, unfortunately still used today, which not only perpetuates archaic myths and stereotypes about the nature of sexual assaults but also ignores the law."[52]

ACCESS TO VICTIMS' PRIVATE RECORDS

Within a few years of Bill C-49's passage, women's groups and those who work with rape crisis centers became alerted to a new trend in sexual assault cases: defence counsel seeking and receiving access to a wide range of women's private medical and therapeutic records. Women's groups attribute this to defence counsels' determination to discourage women from pressing sexual assault charges by finding alternative ways to introduce prejudicial assumptions about women's credibility or by intimidating victims to withdraw their charges.[53]

In 1995 the Supreme Court in *R. v. O'Connor* ruled on whether defence lawyers in sexual assault cases can get a judicial order to compel those who have access to a woman's confidential records (counsellors and doctors who have treated alleged victims of sexual assault) to produce these for defence purposes. The jurisprudence had been unsettled on this issue. The Supreme Court ruled that these records are relevant, but split five to four on what the law should be governing the release of records.

The Supreme Court Ruling

The Court was profoundly divided, not just in the sense of the vote, but on whether judicial interpretation of legal rules discriminates against women and on the relevance of equality considerations in the context of sexual assault cases. The question of access to women's private records arose in the trial of a bishop of the Roman Catholic Church who was charged with rape and indecent assault relating to incidents alleged to have taken place between 1964 and 1967 when he was the principal of a native residential school. The presiding judge issued an order requiring disclosure of the complainants' entire medical, counselling and school records in response to the defence counsel's argument that this was necessary to test the complainants' credibility. This court order was made without any inquiry into the relevance of the records or consideration of how to balance a complainant's privacy right with the right of an accused to a fair trial.

When the Supreme Court reviewed this issue, a core assumption in the majority's ruling, written by Lamer CJ and Sopinka with Cory, Iacobucci and Major concurring, is that access to therapeutic records should not be difficult because these may often be relevant and necessary for full answer and defence in a fair trial. The majority established a low threshold for demonstrating relevance; the accused should not be placed in a "Catch-22" situation of having to make submissions to the judge without precisely knowing what is contained in the records.[54] The majority ruled that information contained in third party records might be relevant in sexual assault cases in the following circumstances:[55]

i)   they may contain information concerning the unfolding of events underlying the criminal complaint;
ii) they may reveal the use of a therapy which influenced the complainant's memory of alleged events;
iii) they may contain information that bears on the complainant's credibility, including testimonial factors such as the quality of their perception of events at the time of the offence, and their memory after the alleged event.

Once likely relevance has been established, the trial judge must determine whether these records should be available to the accused. This requires that the judge weigh "the salutary and deleterious effects of a production order" and determine whether a decision not to provide the accused with access "would constitute a reasonable limit on the ability of the accused to make full answer and defence." In the majority's view, decisions about access to women's private records involve a "balancing process" that must recognize the competing claims of a constitutional right to privacy with the right to full answer and defence. However, the right to privacy should not result in the "possibility of occasioning a miscarriage of justice" by unduly restricting an accused's ability to access relevant information.[56]

The dissenting opinion differs significantly in a number of important respects. The minority established a substantially higher threshold for demonstrating likely relevance, attached far greater importance to privacy, claimed that equality should be considered when determining whether defence counsel should gain access to women's records, and suggested that judges keep in mind "the extent to which production of records of this nature would frustrate society's interest in encouraging the reporting of sexual offences."[57] This opinion, written by L'Heureux-Dubé with McLachlin, La Forest and Gonthier concurring, characterized the assumption that private therapeutic or counselling records are necessary to a full answer and defence as "highly questionable"[58] and suggested that access to these records is more likely "to derail than to advance the truth-seeking process."[59] Both privacy and equality rights justify "a presumption against ordering" production of women's records.[60] Equality is relevant because sexual assault overwhelmingly affects women, children and the disabled.[61]

The minority noted that courts should be aware of the "pernicious role" that past evidential rules in the Criminal Code and the common law have played in the legal system and cautioned judges to be careful "not to permit such practices to reappear under the guise of extensive and unwarranted inquiries into the past histories and private lives of complainants of sexual assault."[62] A legal system should not devalue the evidence of complainants of sexual assault by "*presuming* their uncreditworthiness"[63] and judges should be sensitive to the difference that vulnerability and gender may make in the application of criminal justice rules.[64]

Another significant departure from the majority's reasoning was the minority's reconciliation of conflicting rights in this conflict. As important as is the right to full answer and defence, it must "co-exist with other constitutional rights, rather than trample them."[65] In the minority's view, the notion of balancing conflicting rights is the wrong imagery for sexual assault trials because access to women's records is rarely necessary for a fair trial and restrictions on access might actually enhance privacy and equality.[66]

Public and Political Responses to Majority Decision

The majority's decision alarmed women's groups who believed that it established too low a threshold for obtaining access to private records. Critics argued that the ruling reinforced "destructive myths" associated with sexual assault, for example that women who report rape, as opposed to other crimes, are likely to be "liars, discreditable, or easily duped."[67] Some predicted that women would be forced to choose between reporting sexual assaults and seeking therapy to deal with its traumatic effects,[68] while others suggested sexual assault centres would do whatever is necessary to ensure a women's confidentiality, including the shredding of documents and no longer taking detailed notes at counselling sessions.[69] Commentators also speculated that the Court's decision would hurt sexual assault centres unable to afford the expenditures of time and money involved in challenging subpoenas for records and attending court, which would reduce the support available for victims.[70]

Following the decision, the federal government introduced Bill C-46 in reaction to what it considered too low a threshold in the majority opinion for gaining access to private medical records. In a press release, the Department of Justice suggested that the "public's confidence in the criminal justice system is weakened when complainants' records are disclosed without regard to their Charter rights to privacy and equality."[71]

Bill C-46: Choosing the Minority Judicial View

Bill C-46 establishes a different two-stage process for obtaining access to records and imposes criteria considerably more difficult to satisfy than those set out in the majority *O'Connor* judgement. Underlying the legislation is the assumption that women's private records are neither as relevant, nor should access be as frequently granted, as suggested by the majority. The legislation does not contradict the majority's conclusion that the Charter requires that records be produced where the accused establishes their likely relevance to an issue at trial. However, the legislation seeks to influence how judges decide whether relevance has been established. It does so by stipulating, in the first stage, that certain grounds used in the past by defence counsel to obtain access to women's records are not, on their own, sufficient for establishing relevance.[72] The legislation also differs from the majority decision by imposing additional criteria the judge must assess before ordering that records be produced:

(a) the extent to which the record is necessary for the accused to make a full answer and defence;
(b) the probative value of the record;
(c) the nature and extent of the reasonable expectation of privacy with respect to the record;
(d) whether production of the record is based on a discriminatory belief or bias;
(e) the potential prejudice to the personal dignity and right to privacy of any person to whom the record relates;

(f) society's interest in encouraging the reporting of sexual offences;
(g) society's interest in encouraging the obtaining of treatment by complainants of sexual offences; and
(h) the effect of the determination on the integrity of the trial process.

What is significant about the legislation is how closely it resembles the minority view that in addition to the accused's right to make a full answer and defence, equality and privacy rights are also necessary considerations in an order to produce medical records. The factors that judges are expected to take into account are almost identical to those cited in the dissenting judgement, of which the majority accepted the first five (a-e) but not the last three (f-h). The majority rejected explicitly the idea that privacy should be considered during the inquiry for production stage, suggesting that this would unduly restrict an accused's access to information which may be required for a full answer and defence,[73] and did not agree that equality was relevant at either the inquiry for production stage or the release of records to defence counsel.[74]

The legislation also differs from the majority decision in two other ways. In the second stage of the process (sharing materials with the defence) it stipulates that equality should also be considered. Furthermore, it imposes difference disclosure requirements on the Crown. The majority ruled that whenever a woman's records are in the hands of the Crown, the woman ceases to have a privacy interest in them and the Crown is required to disclose these to the defence.[75] However, the legislation forbids the production of a record relating to a complainant or witness unless that individual has expressly waived his or her privacy rights.

Interest Group Submissions

Bill C-46 was subject to considerable comment by interest groups who appeared before the House of Commons Committee on Justice and Legal Affairs. Debate about the bill was reminiscent of the debate five years earlier on Bill C-49, with opinion sharply divided on whether the legislation was constitutionally valid. As before, reconciliation of competing views was hindered by profound differences in philosophical and conceptual understandings of the law and how legal sexual assault rules affect women.

Rights claims were a prominent feature of commentaries both critical and supportive of the legislation. Criminal defence lawyers viewed the accused as having the only relevant Charter consideration and argued that the right to a fair trial is unduly restricted by other legislative considerations that establish "artificial hurdles" for determining whether records are likely relevant to a full defence. In their view, the legislation changes the standard for the production of records from one of presumptive production, emphasized by the majority in *O'Connor*, to presumptive exclusion. Consequently, the legislation "[would] have the effect of depriving accused persons of relevant information"[76] and would create a "significant potential for miscarriage of justice" that would be "a disgrace to the administration of justice."[77] Criminal lawyers were particularly troubled by the legislation's removal of unlimited judicial discretion to determine which third party records can be called forward. They argued that the legislation would not withstand Charter scrutiny because it improperly reflects a hierarchy of rights, in which the protection of the accused is accorded a lower priority than complainants' privacy rights.[78]

Women's groups and service providers, particularly those representing rape crisis centers, also invoked Charter rights in their arguments in support of the legislation. But the rights central to this issue, from their perspective, were equality, privacy and security. They rejected the claim that the legislation would compromise the right of an accused to receive a fair trial because private records will be rarely, if ever, relevant. "Bill C-46 will not deprive any accused person of a fair trial. It will deprive them of the benefit of a selective interpretation of the Charter, which persistently disregards some of the Charter's provisions and some citizens' equal right to equal protection and benefit of criminal law and constitutional law. In particular, Bill C-46 will correct for the constitutional blind spot now consistently revealed by a very bare majority of the Supreme Court."[79]

Although many women's groups do not accept the relevance of private records, they nevertheless support the legislation for addressing what they consider to be inappropriate judicial rules and approve of Parliament's intent to introduce equality, privacy and security rights into judicial determinations.[80]

Preamble

The legislation received support from all parties and was prefaced with a preamble stating Parliament's intent. The preamble reveals Parliament's view that court orders for access to private records should consider a number of Charter rights: equality, dignity and privacy, as well as a fair trial. While the production of private medical records may be necessary "for an accused to make a full answer and defence," it may also breach rights to privacy and equality; hence these judicial determinations "should be subject to careful scrutiny." The preamble does not explicitly rank these conflicting rights (no doubt because of the Court's explicit aversion to promote a hierarchy of conflicting Charter rights).[81] Nevertheless, it contains an implicit message to the judiciary: courts, in the past, have not given due regard to other relevant Charter rights and the purpose of this legislation is to establish a more balanced set of rules to govern requests for access to private records.

Parliament's use of a preamble, and the messages to the judiciary it conveyed, prompted varied reactions from interest groups. Those supportive of the legislation approved of the preamble and its message that access to private records should be assessed in terms of the adverse effects for equality and privacy rights. Any reservations about the clause from women's groups concerned its placement in the legislation. Rather than stating in a preamble Parliament's intent and theoretical assumptions about how the law should operate, many would have preferred to see these important statements in the actual text of the Criminal Code. Their concerns were that the educative and theoretical messages would too easily be forgotten by the judiciary when interpreting and applying the legislation.[82]

The very fact that this issue of access to private medical records in sexual assault cases has become a serious concern reinforces skepticism about the educative value of preambles. As discussed earlier, the preamble in the rape shield legislation, Bill C-49, had similarly stressed the importance of equality and women's security in sexual assault proceedings. However, this earlier preamble does not seem to have had an influence on the judiciary, which has steadily compelled the production of private medical records allowing defence counsel to impeach the complainant's character. Despite the preamble, judicial practices have allowed, indirectly, what the legislation explicitly prohibited. As one commentator notes, judicial history after the *Seaboyer* decision demonstrates "when the preamble does not form part of the text itself, part of the law is lost, never to be referred to by any trial judge in this country."[83]

Not all participants in the debate support the preamble. Those who were critical of the legislation were, not surprisingly, also critical of the preamble. They disputed the legitimacy of Parliament's desire to interpret the Charter differently from the Court and were particularly offended by this bold pronouncement of intent which they considered to be beyond Parliament's competence: only courts can validly interpret the Charter.[84] Defence lawyers considered the preamble to be an affront to the judiciary because of its implicit suggestion that "the judiciary cannot be trusted to examine third-party records" or to "reach a proper determination." In their view, it is "a sad day" when legislation with this message to courts is passed.[85]

Additional Incentive to Pass Legislation: R. v. Carosella

Two days after the introduction of Bill C-46, the Supreme Court in *R. v. Carosella* handed down a decision which provided additional incentive to pass the legislation.[86] The issue in this case was how to proceed in sexual assault trials when a claim has been made for access to private records which have been destroyed; under these circumstances is the right of an accused to make a full answer and defence breached and should the proceedings against him be stayed?

Once again, the Supreme Court split five to four on how to assess the relevance and necessity of access to private records for a fair sexual assault trial. The decision revealed even stronger philosophical disagreements than in *O'Connor*, with the same judges represented on the majority and minority sides.

The majority stated that disclosure is a component of the right to make full answer and defence. Consequently, if the destroyed materials satisfy the *O'Connor* threshold test for disclosure or production, the section 7 right of the accused is breached.[87] The majority established new guidelines to determine what remedy is appropriate in sexual assault cases where the standard for relevance is met but the records have been destroyed. Either one of the following two factors justifies a stay of the criminal charges:[88]

1) no alternative remedy exists to overcome the prejudice to the accused's ability to make full answer and defence, and
2) if irreparable prejudice to the integrity of the judicial system were to arise with the continuation of the prosecution.

In this case, the majority concluded that both conditions were satisfied and suggested that confidence in the system would be undermined if the Court condoned conduct designed to defeat the processes of the Court, particularly by a sexual assault centre or similar organization "that not only receives public money but whose activities are scrutinized by the provincial government."[89]

The dissenting judges disagreed that there is a right to disclosure as part of section 7, suggesting that while the production of every relevant piece of evidence might be an ideal goal from the perspective of the accused, this goal should not be elevated to a right, the non-observance of which leads instantaneously to an unfair trial. Where evidence is unavailable, it is not enough to speculate that there is the potential for harm. For missing evidence to violate the Charter "there must be a real likelihood of prejudice to the right to full answer and defence, in that the evidence if available would have been more likely than not to assist the accused."[90] The dissenting judges also thought that had the trial judge conducted a proper inquiry into the need for these documents, the "likely relevant" test of *O'Connor* would not have been satisfied. Defence counsel's request for production of these notes "amounted to no more than a fishing expedition in the hopes of uncovering a prior inconsistent statement."[91]

Judicial Review of Bills C-49 and C-46

The Court has now reviewed both Bills C-49 and C-46. It is difficult to explain what accounts for changes to judicial opinion; in this context, changes to the norms for sexual assault trials. Nevertheless, the Court's rulings are consistent with Parliament's attempt to articulate a different assessment of how the Charter affects sexual assault trials. The *Ewanchuck* decision did not deal specifically with the Charter. Nevertheless, the Court's treatment of consent reflects Parliament's concerns in Bill C-49 that the defence of mistaken understanding not be used easily or interpreted broadly. The part of Bill C-49 that was subject to Charter challenge occurred in a later case, *R v. Darrach*, in which a unanimous Court upheld the provisions that restricted the use of previous sexual activity as evidence. These legislative provisions represented Parliament's attempt to respond to the Court's concerns in *Seaboyer* that earlier legislation was too restrictive in banning evidence relating to a woman's sexual history. In evaluating Bill C-49, the Court ruled that the provisions relating to consent do not represent a "blanket exclusion"but only prohibit the use of evidence of past sexual activity when it is offered to support two specific, illegitimate inferences: that a complainant is more likely to have consented to the alleged assault and that she is less credible as a witness by virtue of her prior sexual experience.[92]

Earlier, in *R. v. Mills,* a 7–1 majority upheld the constitutionality of C-46 (which addressed the use of personal and therapeutic records in trials of sexual offences). In *Mills* the trial judge had concluded that the legislation so alters the balance struck by the majority in *O'Connor,* between privacy rights and the rights of an accused to a fair trial, that it should be struck down. The Supreme Court disagreed. In reviewing the legislation, the Court had to confront whether it was willing to accept the obvious will of Parliament which was contrary to its own majority judgement. The Court ruled that the mere fact that the legislation did not "mirror" the majority *O'Connor* ruling does not mean that Parliament's response is unconstitutional.[93] The Court acknowledged that the judiciary does "not hold a monopoly on the protection and promotion of rights and freedoms." A range of reasonable standards may exist. When it ruled in *O'Connor* the Court was operating "in a legislative vacuum" and created what it considered to be the "preferred common law rule." However, this rule should not be considered a "rigid constitutional template." The Court invoked the dialogue metaphor to discuss the relationship between courts and parliament on this issue. The Court suggested a "great value" in this dialogic relationship is that each of the branches "is made somewhat accountable to the other."[94]

ASSESSING POLITICAL RESPONSES TO CHARTER CONFLICTS

The Charter has changed the political environment and climate of legislating and in the process has tested political resolve to pursue controversial and complex initiatives that attract substantial rights-based concerns.

The policies examined here demonstrate the Charter's substantial influence on legislative choices at all stages of the policy process; from initial conception, parliamentary debate, and beyond, to the political decision of how to respond to judicial decisions that legislation is unconstitutional. When assessed in light of two contrary expectations of the Charter's effects on political will, it is apparent that neither view fully captures how the Charter is affecting the policy process.

Firstly, political response has not been characterized by inaction in the face of Charter conflict. In the case of tobacco legislation, the government revised its initiative and passed new legislation in an attempt to pursue its objective through means it hoped would receive judicial approval. But Parliament could have been more assertive in pursuing its preferred course of action. Despite the marginal nature of the speech claim, it did not challenge the Court's assessment of the issue as involving a fundamental conflict around free speech and it adopted less comprehensive measures than those struck down.

Legislative initiatives addressing the rules for sexual assault trials and access to private records provide stronger indication that Parliament is not reneging on the responsibility to pursue what it believes to be important social policy when rights conflicts arise. Parliamentary views on sexual assault issues indicate not only that elected representatives have a different assessment of how the law should operate, but that Parliament believes it has a legitimate role to play in interpreting the

Charter. Parliament's passage of legislation that differs significantly from judicial views is not explained by a denial of the rule of law or dismissal of the priority of constitutional values and obligations. It is also not explained by ignorance of the Charter or the triumph of partisan, electoral or other self-serving interests over rights-based principles. Rather, these legislative initiatives are based on a deliberate and conscious intent to change the prevailing normative and legal assumptions for sexual assault trials and to alert the judiciary to an alternative interpretation of the Charter which situates trial fairness in a broader context of respect for other Charter rights (privacy and equality).

These policy debates, at first blush, may give the impression that the Charter has had a largely salutary effect on the political process, by focussing greater attention on the rights dimensions of policies. However, the optimistic view that the Charter is promoting dialogue about how to improve legislation, to ensure that policy is achieved in a rights-conscious and sensitive manner, is too simplistic a portrayal of the Charter's effects on policy or the options available to Parliament. The policies examined here suggest at least three caveats to this optimistic interpretation.

The first caveat is that a dialogue between Parliament and the judiciary may not be the appropriate means of resolving all policy conflicts involving rights-based claims. The tobacco legislation raises the question of whether this issue should have even been dealt with under the Charter and subject to its constraints. What is troubling in this case is that at no stage of the debate did it seem to matter that the "fundamental" Charter right at stake – tobacco advertising – was not a right in any philosophical sense but a right created by judicial decree. The government did not contest the claim that tobacco advertising deserved constitutional protection (in fact it conceded that speech had been infringed). Nor did it discuss publicly whether its objective warranted more comprehensive legislation which, given the Court's prior ruling, would inevitably have led to discussion of whether the enactment of the legislative override was justified.

When the judiciary pronounces not on human rights but on exaggerated or misappropriated rights claims it intervenes into policy conflict rightfully resolved elsewhere. This decision and the political reluctance to challenge the use of rights discourse in this context had important consequences. Most obviously, it allowed this conflict to be reviewed in the judicial arena rather than in the realm of representative politics and, in so doing, changed the manner in which the relevant issues were identified and assessed, by whom, and according to what criteria. Instead of Parliament assessing the legislation in terms of workability and practicality, judges reviewed it but from an entirely different perspective: whether the objective was rationally connected to the means and whether its effects impaired rights as little as some other, hypothetical strategy.

It is understandable why a government may not welcome the possibility of another judicial setback and consequently will devise legislation to satisfy a specific judicial suggestion. But when a renewed legislative initiative is designed to correspond to a judicial suggestion about complex policy options it is entirely possible that more appropriate guidance, which draws upon previous trials and errors, comparative experiences and informed best estimates, will be forsaken. A consequence may be impractical or less effective legislation that casts doubt on the purported benefits of constitutional dialogue.

A second caveat is that the Charter conflict between Parliament and the judiciary may be far more profound than can be remedied by simply improving or revising legislation. The issue of access to victims' private records reveals philosophical differences within the judiciary and between the Supreme Court majority and Parliament about how the Charter speaks to this conflict and how conflicting rights should be reconciled. Parliament may be engaged in dialogue with the Court but it is not around the issue of whether and how the legislation can be improved to satisfy Charter requirements of reasonableness. Instead the purpose is to convince a majority of the Court and trial judges that Parliament's is a more balanced and fair reading of how the Charter applies to sexual assault trials. The Supreme Court's decisions to uphold Bills C-49 and C-46 indicate that Parliament may have some influence on Charter interpretation. Nevertheless, the possibility of future disagreements over principles, and not just legislative means, suggests that the Canadian polity needs to give more thought to how these more fundamental institutional disagreements should be resolved.

A third caveat is that even if Parliament can satisfy judicial concerns when revising legislative initiatives, its will can be undermined by backdoor legal means. This has occurred, with judicial approval and in the name of the Charter, in the form of defence counsel gaining access to women's private records to attack sexual assault complainants' credibility despite the explicit stipulation in legislation that such evidence is inappropriate and may not be lawful, according to the Criminal Code.

AUGMENTING PARLIAMENT'S ROLE: ESTABLISHING A CHARTER COMMITTEE

Despite these caveats, the idea that the Charter should be the subject of institutional dialogue is a desirable ideal. Constitutional dialogue or conversation requires listening and responding to the other party's concerns (I prefer to think of it as conversation because less structure or formality is implied). Legislation should be crafted with careful consideration not to impair rights unduly. If legislation is challenged, and Parliament is committed to its policy objective, it should try to respond to the Court's concerns where possible. On the other hand, conversations do not necessarily imply or produce agreement. There may be times when judicial suggestions are not appropriate or where fundamental disagreement arises on the basic interpretation or application of the Charter. Addressing these differences is where the Charter presents the most difficult and challenging dilemmas for governing.

The inevitability of institutional disagreements has serious implications for policy. If Parliament is to be a significant partner in a constitutional conversation, its processes for Charter evaluation of legislation need to be reassessed. Elsewhere, I have argued that Canada should establish a parliamentary committee with specific responsibility to evaluate bills from a Charter perspective.[95] Although in each chamber a committee may look at the rights dimension of a bill as part of its larger mandate, Parliament would benefit from adopting a more conscious and systematic approach to Charter scrutiny by vesting this task in a specific committee. This would allow for specialization and the cultivation of greater expertise of members (who should not be drawn exclusively from those parliamentarians with legal training). The committee's role would include not only discussion of the significance of possible rights claims but the justification for legislative decisions.

A Charter committee would benefit from receiving a statement from the Justice Minister which explains the conclusions reached in the government's internal assessment: for example, the degree of risk and the particular Charter concerns identified.

It is important to distinguish the purpose of parliamentary scrutiny from the kind of Charter analysis that takes place within the executive. Clearly, a system of executive-based rights scrutiny is welcome. For public officials in departments and agencies and ministers who bear ultimate accountability, it provides necessary advice about specific legal difficulties that can be anticipated and enables ministers to revisit policy objectives, assess alternative means, and ultimately make more responsible decisions about whether to recommend that legislation be introduced. But since this information is generally confidential, and the evaluation of bills is ultimately a parliamentary responsibility, parliamentarians need adequate resources and skills to conduct their own assessments of legislation from a Charter perspective.

The purpose of a parliamentary Charter committee would be different from bureaucratic scrutiny. Its role would not be to establish a rival or parallel procedure for undertaking risk assessments as the basis for making policy decisions. Rather its purpose would be to ensure that legislative decisions, which have implications for fundamental rights, are made only after more public deliberation. In short, its role would be to provide a foundation for Parliament's collective and principled judgement about whether polices are important and responsible in light of the Charter and consistent with the values of a free and democratic society.

The object of a Charter committee is not to present a roadblock to legislative options whenever Charter concerns are raised. The claim for a right is often a shorthand or abbreviated form of a more complex argument about the importance of certain kinds of normative considerations and how these should be factored into policy deliberations. Definitions and understandings of rights are neither universal nor uncontested. Rights claims should be seen as part of a complex political process in which political actors must evaluate their strength alongside the importance of a legislative objective. The issue is not whether a freestanding right should dictate particular outcomes or direct the resolution of social or political conflicts in a singular manner. Rather, the relevant considerations are whether legislation is warranted, given the seriousness of the rights infringement and the importance of the policy objective and, if so, how the legislative objective(s) can be pursued in a manner that respects rights as much as is reasonably and practically possible.

Since this committee would be an important reflection of Parliament's undertaking to interpret and apply constitutional principles to legislative decisions, it should be viewed as one of the more important and coveted responsibilities for parliamentarians. Although parliamentary committees typically have weak influence, and members are prone to partisan pressures, a Charter committee would likely be in a stronger position to exert influence and enjoy some degree of independence from partisan constraints. The important role this committee would assume when assessing proposed legislation in light of the Charter would likely draw judicial notice, particularly if its concerns or queries were not addressed by the government. This is not to suggest that a government should be obliged to heed a Charter committee's concerns, but when in disagreement, it should be expected to defend its viewpoint.

If Parliament allows courts to settle contentious issues, without first making its position known by passing legislation that has carefully considered how to pursue the objective in a rights-conscious manner, it will have forfeited the opportunity to influence judicial decisions. If Parliament is seemingly cavalier about Charter obligations, the judiciary will have little incentive to defer to Parliament's legislative intent. Consequently, legislation may be struck down. After that, if Parliament disagrees with a legal interpretation that produces a different outcome in social conflicts, it will have to introduce new legislation, which may incur increased policy, political and fiscal costs. Alternatively, it will have to rely on the blunt and controversial response of enacting the legislative override.

Another reason for establishing a parliamentary Charter committee is to make legislative decisions that restrict rights more accountable and transparent. This is important from a democratic standpoint because the inevitable discussion and debate will put pressure on governments to justify and, where warranted, amend bills. But it is also important as part of the conversation with courts which will arise when legislation is challenged under the Charter. The availability of a public record of debate that focuses directly on Charter issues, the considerations that have influenced legislative decisions, and the policy arguments about justification, will be invaluable for judicial assessments of the reasonableness of impugned legislative decisions.

This suggestion for a parliamentary Charter committee differs in an important respect from a recommendation by the Reform party to establish a judicial review committee that would systematically review Supreme Court decisions that find federal laws in contravention of the Charter. In the Reform proposal, a parliamentary committee would consider whether to refine legislation to address the court's objections or to use the notwithstanding clause to retain the law, unchanged. From my perspective, this emphasis on responding to Charter concerns only after legislation has been struck down is misplaced. Parliamentary scrutiny should occur before legislation is drafted. As Peter Russell questions, "Why should Parliament wait until the horse is out of the barn to consider the Charter implications of legislation?"[96]

Former Reform party leader Preston Manning does not seem inclined to consider parliamentary scrutiny before legislation is enacted. In his view, prior review of legislation will not likely do much "to rein in judges."[97] I'm not convinced he is correct. A clearly documented parliamentary record, in which both the committee and government address specific Charter concerns and explain the reasons and rationale for the legislative objective, will be difficult for judges to discount. Judges will have to be extremely confident in their objections to legislation before ignoring a clear and transparent record of Parliament's intents and concerns. Courts have never before had to consider, systematically, Parliament's thought processes where rights are implicated. While snippets of parliamentary records have been introduced by government lawyers when litigating Charter conflicts, the lack of any systematic and routine parliamentary assessment and government explanation, at the time of policy development, have made these records easy to ignore as mere anecdotal evidence of witnesses who have appeared before various parliamentary committees.

More importantly, from a democratic perspective, Manning's criticism misses the point. Quite independent of whether courts will be influenced by the committee's scrutiny of legislation, Parliament owes it to itself and to Canadians to take a more active and independent role to interpret and apply the Charter to social policy and to exercise its collective judgement about whether legislation is constitutionally justified. Charter scrutiny should be proactive and not simply reactive.

If a Charter committee is effective, it will facilitate meaningful debate about the implications of legislation for the Charter and prompt the government to justify and, where warranted, amend its legislation. From more careful parliamentary scrutiny will come more reasonable legislation. From a more conscious and transparent parliamentary Charter debate, the reasonableness of legislative decisions will also become more apparent. For both reasons, courts will have less cause to set aside legislation.

Still, institutional disagreements will not end simply because Parliament has taken its responsibilities under the Charter more seriously. This raises the question of how Parliament should proceed in the wake of a negative judicial ruling. Some might suggest that if an effective Charter committee is in place it will already have contributed to the creation of legislation that Parliament considers defensible under the Charter. So if the Court disagrees, what is the point of further deliberation? If Parliament is committed to its legislation, why not simply resolve the disagreement by enacting the override?

From my perspective, it may be premature to respond to a negative ruling with immediate consideration of the override. Before taking that step, careful consideration needs to paid to why the Court was troubled with the legislation.

Courts have the prerogative to disagree with parliamentary decisions, no matter how careful or thoughtful these were. Judges may flatly disagree with Parliament's contention that its objective is important enough to restrict rights or they may fault the legislation on how it was conceptualized and designed. While judges' opinions are not necessarily the definitive word about how best to resolve contentious rights conflicts, their concerns should be given careful attention. Often legislation can be revised without compromising the legislative objective. If not, it is essential that Parliament give careful consideration both to whether the right in question is too fundamental to be overridden and to whether the objective is important enough that it justifies being given primacy in the social conflict.

Although I do not disagree philosophically with the override, it is not obvious to me that a Charter committee itself should initiate suggestion of its use. If parliamentarians are concerned about the implications of a judicial ruling, they can make suggestions about the appropriate course of action in the normal channels of parliamentary debate. A concern I have with a Charter committee suggesting the override is that this risks transforming what should be an option of final resort into an option of first response to a negative judicial decision. Although the Reform proposal does not preclude modifications to legislation, the very fact that consideration of the override would be in the Committee's terms of reference might increase incentives to use this heavy-handed approach.

If the government decides to use the override in response to a negative judicial ruling, the Charter committee would be an ideal venue for careful study of whether its use is appropriate. The Charter committee should conduct hearings that would facilitate public and political deliberation about the seriousness of the potential rights deprivation. This would reflect the assumption that reliance on the override should be extraordinary, rather than ordinary, and used only on rare occasions when further conversation (or redrafting) is pointless because Parliament is convinced about the justification for its policy and believes that judicial concerns are misplaced.

The override should not be used to simply vent frustration with a judicial decision. I also have difficulty with the idea that Parliament might override equality or what I consider to be other "core" rights essential to ensure the fair treatment and dignity of all citizens (though this argument will have to be developed and explored elsewhere). It also follows, from the emphasis placed on the advantages of conversation, that the override should never be used pre-emptively, before a ruling from the highest court, because this would deny the polity the benefit of hearing judges' contribution to constitutional deliberations.

The attention that would accrue to parliamentary conversation about the override is important and should place those who advocate its use in the position of having to respond to critics' concerns that the action is unjust or based on unfounded or unjustified prejudices. The significance of this conversation, which places an onus on those who support using the override to justify their position, cannot be overstated. The demand for reasons and principles, publicly expressed, that justify the restriction of a protected right makes it much harder to hide behind prejudices or traditional preferences that may no longer be valid policy considerations. The controversy generated from a discussion about using the override should compel parliamentarians to search their conscience and satisfy their convictions that the use of the override is justified in what should be a free vote, independent of partisan constraints, and perhaps sustained by a larger than normal parliamentary majority.

CONCLUSIONS

Too often political and academic commentators assume that the Charter's guidance for policy conflicts is a matter for judges alone to determine. A bill of rights represents more than a codified set of principles that judges interpret and apply when state actions are challenged. It represents a normative and symbolic statement of those rights and values that a society believes ought to be respected in, and by, the polity. Although judicial review is an important element in ensuring that rights are duly protected, it is wrong to assume that Parliament does not also have an important role to play when assessing government or private bills and determining, normatively and philosophically, whether and how the Charter should constrain legislative decisions.

Ideally, as political thought matures on how the Charter affects governing, parliamentarians will develop more rigorous methods for assuming responsibility to assess whether legislation is constitutionally justified. The government needs to recognize that whatever executive scrutiny has taken place, Parliament still has a legitimate role to perform when evaluating bills from a Charter perspective. It can facilitate this by supporting the creation of a Charter committee and by providing committee members with a summary or analysis of the government's Charter concerns and how the Charter has influenced the development and design of proposed legislation.

A systematic and proactive approach to the Charter will signal to judges that Parliament has been mindful of the Charter and has exercised its informed judgement about how the Charter should be interpreted and applied to social policy. This message will be conveyed via the parliamentary record of debate and by continued uses of preambles and will afford judges a more full and complete appreciation of the purposes of legislation and the reasons for choosing particular policy means.

As Parliament's approach to the Charter matures, this may influence how the Supreme Court approaches its task of judicial review. The acknowledgement earlier in the paper of a lack of judicial expertise in evaluating complex policy objectives should not be construed as a claim that judicial review of legislative decisions is inherently inappropriate or undesirable. When fundamental rights are affected by legislation, judicial review performs the salutary role of requiring governments to justify their choices in light of the seriousness and severity of the rights infringement. Under these circumstances this judicial role may present some tension for democratic principles of representative government, but is desirable and defensible in light of other aspects of democracy that emphasize the equal treatment and fair participation of all in society. However, an important distinction needs to be made between evaluating rights and scrutinizing the minute details and fine tuning of complex legislative choices.

The record that would accompany a Charter committee, revealing the full extent to which Charter considerations did or did not influence the objective and the choice of policy means, would certainly be an advantage for the Court. If confident that Parliament has been sensitive towards the Charter, the Court may be more willing to respect parliamentary decisions about how to achieve complex social policy objectives. On the other hand, if the record is superficial and does not reflect careful thought, or has raised serious concerns that have not been adequately addressed by the government, the Court may be understandably reluctant to defer to legislative decisions.

Parliament may not always arrive at the same conclusions as courts about what priority should be given to rights claims or how conflicting rights and values should be reconciled. But institutional disagreements should not be thought of as a disadvantage to democratic politics. The Charter introduces a dynamic force into the policy process that requires more attention be paid to whether and how policies undermine important rights. Judicial review, and the prospects of nullifying legislation that does not comply with the judiciary's interpretation of the Charter, enhance the pressure to comply with constitutional values. Yet this increased focus on rights need not result in frequent or destabilizing conflicts. This is the genius of the Charter's contribution to the Canadian polity.

Parliament can rely on the override to resolve serious political/judicial differences. However, Parliament's power to override judicial decisions is not simply the retention of the principle of parliamentary supremacy, unadulterated, as it existed prior to the Charter. This residual element of Parliament's supremacy does not diminish Parliament's obligation to give effect to the Charter's values in the course of developing and passing legislation. Changes to the Canadian political landscape due to the Charter have been too significant to allow for this power to be invoked easily or uncritically. Although Parliament has the power to ensure the primacy of its decision, this power should be exercised only after careful consideration of why its views on an issue deserve to be paramount. Effective processes to facilitate meaningful public and political debate about the merits of Parliament's judgement will provide protection against misuse of this important power.

NOTES

* I would like to acknowledge financial assistance from the Social Science and Humanities Research Council which allowed for the policy research and interviews undertaken.

1 Section 33 (1) provides that "Parliament or the legislature of a province may expressly declare in an Act of Parliament or of the legislature, as the case may be, that the Act or a provision thereof shall operate notwithstanding a provision included in section 2 or sections 7 to 15 of this Charter."

2 Michael Mandel, *The Charter of Rights and the Legalization of Politics in Canada* (Toronto: Wall & Thompson, 1989).

3 Peter H. Russell, "The Political Purposes of the Canadian Charter of Rights and Freedoms," *The Canadian Bar Review,* Vol. 61, no. 1 (March 1983), p. 52.

4 Peter W. Hogg and Allison A. Bushell, "The Charter Dialogue Between Courts and Legislatures (Or Perhaps the Charter of Rights Isn't Such a Bad Thing After All)," *Osgoode Hall Law Journal*, Vol. 35, no. 1 (Spring 1997), pp. 104–05.

5 Janet L. Hiebert, "Parliament, Courts and Rights: Sharing the Responsibility for Interpreting the Charter," in Alain Gagnon and James Bickerton (eds.), *Canadian Politics*, 3d ed. (Toronto: Broadview Press, forthcoming 1999); "Why Must a Bill of Rights be a Contest of Political and Judicial Wills? The Canadian Alternative," *Public Law Review*, Vol. 9 (March 1999).

6 This requirement arises in section 4. 1 of the Department of Justice Act and is a similar obligation to the reporting requirement still in force in section 3 of the 1960 Canadian Bill of Rights. Department of Justice Act, R.S.C. 1985, c. J-2, s.4; SOR/85–781.

7 This review process culminated in omnibus legislation, which amended a wide range of statutes.

8 This opinion is implied by David Kinley, *The European Convention on Human Rights: Compliance Without Incorporation* (Aldershot, UK: Dartmouth, 1993), pp. 103–05.

9 For a more developed argument, see Janet L. Hiebert, *Limiting Rights: The Dilemma of Judicial Review* (Montreal: McGill-Queen's University Press, 1996).

10 *R. v. Keegstra* [1990] 3 S.C.R. 697 at p. 743.

11 *RJR-MacDonald Inc. v. Canada (Attorney General)* [1995] 3 S.C.R. 199.

12 *RJR-MacDonald Inc.* [1995] at p. 329.

13 In the majority's view it is "hard to imagine how the presence of a tobacco logo on a cigarette lighter...would increase consumption; yet, such use is banned." *RJR-MacDonald Inc.* [1995] at p. 342.

14 *RJR-MacDonald Inc.* [1995] at p. 329.

15 *RJR-MacDonald Inc.* [1995] at pp. 344–45.

16 *RJR-MacDonald Inc.* [1995] at pp. 310–11.

17 *RJR-MacDonald Inc.* [1995] at p. 312.

18 *Ford. v. Quebec (Attorney General)* [1998] 2 S.C.R. 712 at pp. 765–67.

19 *Irwin Toy Ltd. v. Quebec (Attorney General)*, [1989] 1 S.C.R. 927 at p. 968.

20 *Reference re Public Service Employee Relations Act (Alta.)* [1987] 1 S.C.R. 313; *Government of Saskatchewan v. Retail Wholesale and Department Store Union, Locals 544, 496,635 & 955* [1987] 1 S.C.R. 460; *R. v. Public Service Alliance of Canada* [1987] 1 S.C.R. 424. Two reasons were given. One is that the Charter is not principally concerned with economic interests, which is how striking was characterized. Second, the Court indicated that if it upheld a right to strike it would subsequently be required to intervene in economic disputes between governments and their public sector unions, when deciding whether labour legislation is reasonable under section 1. This, in the Court's opinion, was a task for which it was ill-equipped based on judicial expertise and competence.

21 *Irwin Toy Ltd* [1989] at p. 970.

22 *R. v. Butler* [1992] 1 S.C.R. 452 at p. 505.

23 *R. v. Keegstra* at [1990] pp. 761–63.

24 *Rocket v. Royal College of Dental Surgeons of Ontario* [1990] 2 S.C.R. 232 at p. 247.

25 *RJR-MacDonald Inc.* [1995] at pp. 332–33.

26 Tobacco Act S.C. 1997, c. 13. The legislation prohibits sales of tobacco products to persons under 18 years of age; requires health messages on packages of tobacco products that are attributable to health authorities and detailed information about tobacco products and their emissions; prohibits the advertising of tobacco products, except product information and brand preference advertising in publications with primarily adult readership; prohibits the distribution and promotion of tobacco products if any of their brand elements appear on a non-tobacco product that is associated with youth or lifestyle; and restricts sponsorship promotions that contain tobacco brand elements to 10 percent of the display surface and to those publications with primarily adult readerships or events or places where young persons are not permitted by law.

27 David Dingwall, House of Commons *Debates*, December 5, 1996, p. 7115.

28 Dingwall, House of Commons *Debates*.

29 Judy Ferguson, Director General, Health Policy and Information, *Proceedings of the House of Commons Standing Committee on Health*, December 6, 1996.

30 Robert Parker, Chair and Chief Executive Officer of the Canadian Tobacco Manufacturers' Council, *Proceedings of the Senate Committee on Legal and Constitutional Affairs*, April 3, 1997.

31 Rick Dearden, Legal Counsel, Molstar Sports Entertainment, *Proceedings of the Senate Committee on Legal and Constitutional Affairs*, April 3, 1997.

32 Four different judges are on the bench (at the time of writing). They are Justices Binnie, Bastarache, Arbour and Lebel.

33 *RJR-MacDonald* [1995] at p. 328.

34 Barrie McKenna, "Dingwall Softening on Tobacco Bill," *The Globe and Mail*, February 4, 1997, pp. A1-A2.

35 Laura Eggertson, "Tobacco Companies Fighting Back," *The Globe and Mail*, April 22, 1997, pp. A1-A2.

36 Maurice Vellacott, House of Commons *Debates*, December 5, 1997, p. 2805.

37 An Act to Amend the Tobacco Act, S.C. 1998, c. 38.

38 Information bulletin, Health Canada, June 1998.

39 Former health minister David Dingwall says the Cabinet discussed, but dismissed, his suggestion that the override be used following the *RJR-MacDonald* decision. He also suggests that while he expects the new legislation to pass judicial scrutiny, if it is nullified he thinks Parliament should use the override. Interview with author, Ottawa, April 17, 1999.

40 *R. v. Seaboyer* [1991] 2 S.C.R. 577; *R. v. O'Connor* [1995] 4 S.C.R. 411; *R. v. Carosella* [1997] 1 S.C.R. 80.

41 *R. v. Seaboyer* [1991] at p. 616.

42 *R. v. Seaboyer* [1991] at pp. 612–16.

43 She outlined judicial guidelines for determining when evidence of a woman's sexual past should be included at trial. *R.v. Seaboyer* [1991] at pp. 634–36.

44 *R. v. Seaboyer* [1991] at p. 707.

45 See for example Julian V. Roberts and Renate M. Mohr, *Confronting Sexual Assault: A Decade of Legal and Social Change* (Toronto: University of Toronto Press, 1994).

46 An Act to Amend the Criminal Code (Sexual Assault) S.C. 1992, C. 38, s.2.

47 Consent is defined as voluntary agreement to engage in sexual activity and cannot be inferred as having been granted in a number of situations. For example, consent cannot be assumed to have been granted where the agreement was expressed by someone other than the complainant, where the complainant is incapable of consenting to the activity, or where the complainant had initially consented to engage in sexual activity but

subsequently expressed a lack of agreement to continue to engage in sexual activity.

48 For discussion of groups' reaction to and comments on Bill C-49, see Janet Hiebert, "Debating Policy: The Effects of Rights Talk," in F. Leslie Seidle (ed.), *Equity & Community: The Charter, Interest Advocacy and Representation* (Montreal: The Institute for Research on Public Policy, 1993), pp. 41–56.

49 *R. v. Ewanchuk* [1999] 1 S.C.R. 330.

50 *R. v. Ewanchuk* [1999] at p. 361 [emphasis in original].

51 *R. v. Ewanchuk* [1999] at pp. 372–73.

52 *R. v. Ewanchuk* [1999] at p. 376.

53 Susan Bazilli, Legal Director, Metro Action Committee on Public Violence Against Women and Children (METRAC) Minutes of Evidence, *Standing Committee on Justice and Legal Affairs*, March 11, 1997. One MP reported to Parliament that he had heard of a workshop for defence counsel, which provided tips when seeking medical, psychiatric, hospital and immigration records as part of a strategy "to whack the complainant hard at the preliminary inquiry" to encourage complainants to have the charges withdrawn to avoid a grueling and embarrassing treatment in court. Gordon Kirkby (Parliamentary Secretary to Minister of Justice and Attorney General of Canada, Liberal), House of Commons *Debates*, February 4, 1997, p. 7650.

54 *R. v. O'Connor* [1995] at p. 439.

55 *R. v. O'Connor* [1995] at pp. 439–41.

56 *R. v. O'Connor* [1995] at pp. 433–34.

57 *R. v. O'Connor* [1995] at p. 504.

58 *R. v. O'Connor* [1995] at p. 499.

59 *R. v. O'Connor* [1995] at p. 481.

60 *R. v. O'Connor* [1995] at pp. 482–84.

61 *R. v. O'Connor* [1995] at p. 488.

62 *R. v. O'Connor* [1995].

63 *R. v. O'Connor* [1995] [emphasis in original].

64 *R. v. O'Connor* [1995] at p. 489.

65 *R. v. O'Connor* [1995] at p. 491.

66 *R. v. O'Connor* [1995].

67 Margaret MacGee, Chair, National Council of Women of Canada, *Standing Committee on Justice and Legal Affairs* March 12, 1997.

68 K. Makin, "Court Rules Against Rape Victims," *The Globe and Mail*, December 15, 1995, p. A1.

69 As cited in Andrea Neufeld, "A.(L.L.) v. B.(A.): A Case Comment on the Production of Sexual Assault Counselling Records," *Saskatchewan Law Review*, Vol. 59, no. 2 (1995), p. 354.

70 Kane, *Standing Committee on Justice and Legal Affairs*, March 4, 1997.

71 Backgrounder, Press Release, "An Act to Amend the Criminal Code"

(Production of Records in Sexual Offence Proceedings), Department of Justice, June 12, 1996.
72 These grounds are stipulated in section. 278.3(4).
73 *R. v. O'Connor* [1995] at pp. 433–34.
74 *R. v. O'Connor* [1995] at p. 442.
75 *R. v. O'Connor* [1995] at pp. 429–30.
76 Marvin Bloos, Chair, Canadian Council of Criminal Defence Lawyers, *Proceedings of the Standing Committee on Justice and Legal Affairs*, March 13, 1997.
77 Bruce Durno, President, Criminal Lawyers' Association, *Proceedings of the Standing Committee on Justice and Legal Affairs*, March 13, 1997.
78 Bloos, March 13, 1997.
79 Sheila MacIntyre, National Legal Committee, Women's Legal Education and Action Fund, *Proceedings of the Standing Committee on Justice and Legal Affairs*, March 6, 1997.
80 A proposed amendment to the legislation, which did not pass, would have required the accused to prove that access to confidential records was "probably essential" instead of "likely relevant," the term used in the bill.
81 *Dagenais v. Canadian Broadcasting Corp.* [1994] 3 S.C.R. 835 at p. 877.
82 A number of witnesses argued that this would be beneficial to counteract these sexist myths and prejudices which are still clearly present in our judicial system. See for example, Regroupement québécois des centres d'aide et de lutte contre les agressions à caractère sexuel, the Ontario action group to combat violence against women, LEAF, and METRAC.
83 Jennifer Scott, Director of Litigation, Women's Legal Education and Action Fund, *Proceedings of the Standing Committee on Justice and Legal Affairs*, March 6, 1997.
84 Irwin Koziebrocki, Treasurer, Criminal Lawyers' Association, *Proceedings of the Standing Committee on Justice and Legal Affairs*, March 13, 1997.
85 Durno, *Proceedings of the Standing Committee on Justice and Legal Affairs*, March 13, 1997.
86 *R. v. Carosella* [1997] 1 S.C. R. 80.
87 *R. v. Carosella* [1997] at p. 107.
88 *R. v. Carosella* [1997] at pp. 113–14.
89 *R. v. Carosella* [1997] at p. 114.
90 *R. v. Carosella* [1997] at pp. 120–22, 137–38.
91 *R. v. Carosella* [1997] at pp. 142, 146–47.
92 *R. v. Darrach* Supreme Court of Canada, October 12 2000 (unreported at time of writing).
93 *R. v. Mills* [1999] 3 S.C.R. 688 at p. 745.
94 *R. v. Mills* [1999] at pp. 711–712, 748–749.
95 "A Hybrid Approach to Rights Protection: An Argument in Favour of Supplementing Canadian Judicial Review with Australia's Model of Parliamen-

tary Scrutiny," *Federal Law Review,* Vol. 26, no. 1 (1998); "Legislative Scrutiny: An Alternative Approach for Rights Protection," in Joseph Fletcher (ed.), *Ideas in Action: Essays on Politics and Law in Honour of Peter Russell* (Toronto: University of Toronto Press, forthcoming 1999).

96 Peter H. Russell, "Reform's Judicial Agenda," *Policy Options,* Vol. 20, no. 2 (April 1999), p. 13. This article is also reproduced in this collection.

97 E. Preston Manning, "A 'B' for Prof. Russell," *Policy Options,* Vol. 20, no. 2 (April 1999), p. 15. This article is also reproduced in this collection.

Interest Group Litigation and Canadian Democracy

GREGORY HEIN

INTEREST GROUPS IN COURT

The Debate

Anyone who wants to understand judicial politics in Canada has to consider the efforts of organized interests. Groups are at the centre of most policy debates, trying to persuade an audience of elected officials, bureaucrats, editorialists and ordinary citizens to accept rival positions. The stakes are higher when they enter the courtroom. Organizations shoulder the burden of representing thousands of individuals, hundreds of unions scattered across the country, or entire industries. Some use impressive resources to mobilize the law, deploying teams of lawyers and expert witnesses. Advocates who want to reform society urge courts to make the bold decisions that infuriate critics of judicial activism. Instead of asking conventional legal questions, they often present novel arguments that stretch the boundaries of law.

Canadians can no longer ignore interest group litigation because it affects the style and substance of our political life. Though a specialized activity practiced by lawyers and discussed by legal scholars, it has become an important strategy for interests trying to shape public policy. Stories about court challenges are reported in the media every week and interest groups participate in most of the cases: civil libertarians guard free expression with vigilance, even if their efforts help men who produce and consume child pornography;[1] disabled people refuse to accept laws that ignore their needs;[2] feminists take on defence lawyers who attack Criminal Code measures designed to counter sexual assault;[3] pro-choice activists and pro-life groups return to court to argue about the presence or absence of fetal rights;[4] gays and lesbians pursue an ambitious campaign to stop discrimination based on sexual orientation;[5] First Nations assert Aboriginal treaty rights;[6] hunters enter the courtroom to oppose measures that restrict the use of guns;[7] groups that promote law and order denounce judges for paying too much attention to the rights of the criminally accused and too little attention to the victims of violent crimes.[8] Unions enter the judicial system to help workers[9] and corporations challenge regulations that frustrate their ability to maximize profits.[10] Their adversaries also litigate. Environmentalists and economic nationalists try to enforce laws that discipline the free market.[11]

Canadians who find these efforts unsettling identify several concerns. Organizations raise difficult moral, economic and political questions, but courts are not designed to sustain public discussions on complex issues. The most controversial claims pit courts against legislatures by asking judges to reject choices made by elected officials. Political life is pulled into our judicial system by groups that generate a steady stream of cases, but without confirmation hearings we know little about the men and women elevated to the Supreme Court. We know even less about superior court judges who also exercise broad powers. These fears are expressed by those who think that litigation can undermine the struggle for a better society and by those who insist that democracy is threatened by organizations that encourage judicial activism.

The debate in the 1980s was initiated by critical legal scholars and neo-Marxists who refused to believe that courts would be transformed into brash agencies of social change. Their assessment was scathing.[12] The Charter cannot create a forum of principle elevated above the fray of politics, they argued, because courts are not immune from the public pressures, economic realities and ideological contests that affect legislatures. Citizens have new guarantees, but they are grandiose declarations that will not alter the allocation of power and the distribution of wealth. What did these sceptics predict? The barriers impeding access to legal remedies would not wither away. Working people would fail to win dramatic victories because too many judges are guided by values that favour corporate interests. Feminists so determined to win in court would soon discover grave dangers – their resources would be depleted and their adversaries would use the Constitution to attack the welfare state. After discovering the limits of litigation, activists trying to build a just society would see that Parliament is the real engine of reform.

The debate in the 1990s has been dominated by scholars and politicians on the right.[13] According to their account, activists on the left have been wildly successful because so many judges are "removed from reality."[14] These interests flood the courts because they cannot win the support of legislative majorities: most voters find their demands radical and dogmatic. We are told that gays and lesbians want to impose values that will undermine the traditional family. Aboriginal peoples are determined to establish title over huge tracts of land and secure access to lucrative resources just by presenting flimsy oral histories. Feminists promote an interpretation of equality that leads to "reverse discrimination." Civil libertarians, by guarding the rights of alleged criminals, make it more difficult for police and prosecutors to secure law and order. For critics on the right, these "special interests" belong to a coalition which could be called the "court party."[15] They bring the claims that fuel the growth of judicial power. Instead of trying to build public support for their ideas, these activists urge the Supreme Court to expand social services and benefits, alter the meaning of Aboriginal treaties written centuries ago, bolster regulatory regimes or repair legislative omissions. This use of litigation diminishes Canadian democracy, we are told, because it allows members of the court party to circumvent the legislative process.

This study offers an alternative argument by marshalling a large body of empirical data. The account advanced by conservative critics is incomplete and misleading. While warning us about "zealous" activists who invite judicial activism, they never tell us that courts are filled with a broad range of interests that express a wide array of values. Litigants talk to judges about child custody, labour disputes, income tax policy, advertising laws, medical procedures that cause harm, and the dangers of hazardous substances. This diversity exists because successive generations of Canadians have asked courts and governments to create new opportunities to participate in the judicial system and the legislative arena. We will see that critics on the right are correct when they argue that social activists are eager to pursue legal strategies. However, their interpretation ignores the economic interests that also appreciate the benefits of litigation. Corporations exert a surprising degree of pressure by asking judges to scrutinize the work of elected officials.

At the heart of this argument is an important analytical distinction designed to help us understand the strategic choices that groups make. The propensity to litigate is elevated by *stable characteristics*. Interests will be more inclined to mount court challenges when they have impressive legal resources, collective identities energized by rights, and normative visions that demand judicial activism. Strategic choices are also affected by *changing circumstances* that can make litigation seem attractive or even essential. Interests take advantage of interpretive opportunities, counter immediate threats that can be addressed by judges, and move policy battles into the courtroom when their political resources have been eroded.

The evidence below suggests that Aboriginal peoples, Charter Canadians, civil libertarians, and new left activists have the greatest potential to influence public policy through litigation because they are pulled and pushed into the courtroom by both stable characteristics and changing circumstances. These interests can be called *judicial democrats* because a provocative idea is embedded in their legal arguments and political appeals – judicial review can enhance democracy. Finding deficiencies that weaken our system of government, they believe that the courts should listen to groups that lack political power, protect vulnerable minorities and guard fundamental values, from basic civil liberties forged by the common law tradition to ecological principles that have emerged in the past century.

This study also reveals that corporations do not have the stable characteristics that elevate the propensity to litigate. However, they do confront the changing circumstances that make legal action a compelling strategic manoeuvre. Businesses enter the courtroom to counter hostile actions, to block investigating government agencies and when their political resources have been depleted.

The Study

In vibrant liberal democracies, we find a dizzying array of interests that take different shapes: incorporated companies, unions with compulsory membership, unconventional organizations that belong to social movements, associations that represent entire industrial sectors, societies of professionals, and legal advocacy groups that have been designed to fight court battles. Theoretical perspectives devise classifications to order this universe of activity, often by emphasizing a single variable. We also find shifting boundaries in our discourse because political players define their aspirations and rename their opponents. After considering the academic literature and the current debate over judicial activism, nine categories were identified that are both coherent and salient. Examples appear in Table 1.

- Aboriginal peoples have a unique claim to land and resources as the first inhabitants of the continent now called North America. They are nations struggling to win recognition of land, treaty and self-government rights.
- Civil libertarians are determined to stop the state from undermining traditional guarantees that many individuals prize. Students, journalists, writers, church activists and defence lawyers challenge

Table 1
Categories of Organized Interests

ABORIGINAL PEOPLES	Assembly of First Nations
	Assembly of Manitoba Chiefs
	Congress of Aboriginal Peoples
	Dene Nation
	Native Council of Canada
	Union of New Brunswick Indians
CIVIL LIBERTARIANS	Amnesty International
	Canadian Civil Liberties Association
	Canadian Council of Churches
	Canadian Federation of Students
	Centre for Investigative Journalism
	Criminal Lawyers Association
CORPORATE INTERESTS	Canadian Bankers Association
	Canadian Manufacturers Association
	Canadian Telecommunications Alliance
	Merck Frosst Canada
	Thomson Newspapers
	R.J.R. MacDonald
LABOUR INTERESTS	Canadian Labour Congress
	International Longshoremen's and Warehousemen's Union
	National Federation of Nurses' Union
	Public Service Alliance of Canada
	Union des employés de service
	United Fishermen and Allied Workers Union
PROFESSIONALS	Association provinciale des assureurs-vie du Québec
	Association québécoise des pharmaciens propriétaires
	Canadian Association of University Teachers
	Canadian Bar Association
	Canadian Institute of Chartered Accountants
	Canadian Medical Association
SOCIAL CONSERVATIVES	Alliance for Life
	Evangelical Fellowship of Canada
	Human Life International
	Inter-Faith Coalition on Marriage and the Family
	National Firearms Association
	REAL Women

Table 1 (*continued*)

VICTIMS	Canadian Cancer Society
	Canadian Council on Smoking and Health
	Canadian HIV/AIDS Legal Network
	Canadian Resource Centre for Victims of Crime
	Centre Ontario Hemophilia Society
	Westray Families
CHARTER CANADIANS	Canadian Council of Refugees
	Canadian Disability Rights Council
	Canadian Jewish Congress
	Fédération des francophones hors Québec
	Native Women's Association of Canada
	Women's Legal Education and Action Fund
NEW LEFT ACTIVISTS	Canadian Peace Alliance
	Council of Canadians
	Equality for Gays and Lesbians Everywhere
	National Anti-Poverty Association
	Sierra Legal Defence Fund
	Société pour vaincre la pollution

laws that violate freedom of expression, freedom of religion and rights that protect the criminally accused.
- Corporate interests are businesses that compete in a range of sectors: financial, retail, manufacturing, construction, pharmaceutical, agricultural, communications and natural resources. Their advocacy groups demand low levels of taxation, flexible regulatory regimes and trade liberalization.
- Labour interests are organized into unions and advocacy groups that represent miners, loggers, civil servants, teachers, nurses, police officers, auto-makers and technicians. Eager to improve the lives of workers, they defend the welfare state and oppose trade policies that produce unemployment.
- Professionals have the credentials to practice as lawyers, judges, accountants, academics, pharmacists, doctors, architects and engineers. Most work in the private sector as entrepreneurs, but some are employed by large public institutions. They pursue collective action to promote their interests and to protect the integrity of their respective professions.
- Social conservatives want to preserve traditional values sustained for centuries by church and family. They oppose open access to abortion services, homosexuals who demand "special rights," gun

regulations that punish citizens without reducing crime, feminists who want to marginalize fathers, and a popular culture that encourages promiscuity.

- Groups that represent victims want to help individuals hurt by cancer, AIDS, drug addiction, smoking, intoxicated drivers, violent crimes, mining tragedies, silicone breast implants, the transmission of infected blood and sexual abuse in schools.
- Charter Canadians believe that state intervention is required to solve pressing social problems.[16] They derive inspiration and impressive legal resources from the 1982 Constitution. Groups representing ethnic, religious and linguistic minorities, women and the disabled can base their claims on guarantees designed to protect their interests.
- New left activists also believe that state intervention is needed to address grave social problems, but they do not enjoy constitutional rights that were explicitly designed to protect their interests. Environmentalists, gays and lesbians, anti-poverty advocates and economic nationalists can invoke the Charter to stop military tests, fight discrimination, preserve wild spaces and stop governments from dismantling the welfare state, but they have to hope that judges will use their discretion to extend the scope of existing guarantees.

To understand the legal strategies that these groups pursue, every decision appearing in the Federal Court Reports (1,259) and the Supreme Court Reports (1,329) from 1988 to 1998 was reviewed.[17] My Court Challenges Database records relevant facts about each case, including the legal status of litigants.[18] Organizations appear as *parties* when they have a direct stake in a case. If groups are allowed to participate as *intervenors*, they can present oral arguments and written submissions to address issues raised in a dispute. To understand the purpose of litigation, six possible targets were identified.

- Groups can achieve their objectives by confronting *private parties.* They counter individuals, unions, professional associations and corporations.
- Litigants also take aim at *bureaucratic officials* who exercise limited statutory powers. Some work for line departments, but most have positions on boards, tribunals, commissions and inquiries.
- Organizations can bring claims against *cabinet ministers* to block unfavourable decisions or to make governments act. By seeking writs of mandamus, they can ask courts to enforce mandatory duties.
- The stakes are higher when groups mobilize the law to overturn the *statutes and regulations* that are introduced by governments.
- To improve their chances of winning future contests, litigants can try to shape *judicial interpretations.* The primary goal of this strategy is to

direct judges when they define the meaning, purpose and scope of common law rules, ordinary statutes and constitutional guarantees.

- Groups also enter the courtroom to defend favourable policies when their adversaries launch *hostile actions*.

Some cases were excluded from the analysis. Challenges against Crown corporations, universities and hospitals were removed because they are relatively independent agencies that rarely exercise coercive authority. Minor actions against cabinet ministers were also taken out. For example, businesses fight tax assessments or sue departments for breach of contract without addressing larger issues.

Several limitations should be noted. Because most intervenors appear before the Supreme Court, groups that favour this form of participation might be overrepresented. Interests that mobilize federal administrative law might also be overrepresented because the Federal Court has exclusive jurisdiction. We cannot look for regional variations that might exist because provincial superior courts are not examined. For the same reason, it will be impossible to compare patterns in English Canada and Quebec.

Interest Group Litigation before the Charter

Courts played an important role before the Charter was entrenched by protecting property, hearing administrative actions, enforcing the criminal law and resolving disputes between both levels of government. Certain interests appreciated the potential value of litigation. Businesses filled the judicial system to advance pecuniary and proprietary claims. They also attempted to influence public policy. This became very apparent during the 1930s, when corporations invoked the division of powers to obstruct the growth of the welfare state.[19] They succeeded when the Judicial Committee of the Privy Council promoted provincial autonomy and economic liberties by invalidating federal laws.[20]

Courts were also asked to defend civil liberties, even in the nineteenth century. Most cases were initiated by individuals facing charges or governments fighting jurisdictional battles, but organizations supported some challenges at a distance.[21] Francophones and Roman Catholics in Manitoba asserted constitutional rights that guarantee the use of French in public institutions and funding for denominational schools.[22] After winning the right to vote, suffragettes turned their attention to a provision in the Constitution that was interpreted to exclude women from the Senate. In a case that is still celebrated by feminists, they persuaded the Judicial Committee of the Privy Council that the term "qualified persons" encompassed both sexes.[23] This campaign was backed by the National Council of Women and a number of smaller groups. In the 1950s, prominent members of the legal community began helping religious minorities and communists who were deemed to be "subversives."[24] By the 1970s, feminists were hoping that courts would use the Canadian Bill of Rights to eliminate discrimination. At the same time, environmentalists were exploring various claims to punish corporations and governments for failing to respect new pollution laws.

These efforts were exceptional. For more than a century, few organizations entered the courtroom to affect public policy. It was possible to have a complete understanding of Canadian politics without ever thinking about interest group litigation. The labour movement concentrated on the party system because courts did little to help workers; relying on the assumptions of classical liberalism, judges allowed market forces to settle most issues.[25] Activists who wanted to solve social problems pressured legislators and devised novel strategies in order to change public attitudes, but few imagined that litigation could be turned into an instrument of reform.[26] While achieving some of their objectives in court, corporations lobbied cabinet ministers and senior officials because they appreciated the importance of elite accommodation and the power of bureaucracies.[27]

Interest Group Litigation after the Charter

This study reveals that a transformation has occurred. Interest group litigation is now an established form of collective action. Organizations present 819 claims between 1988 and 1998. They appear as parties or intervenors in 30 percent of the disputes considered by the Federal Court and the Supreme Court.[28] Figure 1 records the frequency of participation.

Groups from every category pursue legal strategies. This single finding is remarkable – we now find the same mix of political players trying to influence courts and governments. But if there has been an important change, we also find elements of continuity. Court dockets are still laden with corporations. They bring 468 legal actions, far more than the other interests. Companies engage in civil litigation against private parties, and challenge regulations governing banking, federal elections, international trade, environmental protection and the pharmaceutical industry. Groups representing professionals participate in 32 cases. They try to win higher salaries as employees and as experts they talk to judges about a range of issues, including the principles that guide child custody disputes and criminal investigations. Very few of

Figure 1
Organized Interests in Court, 1988–1998

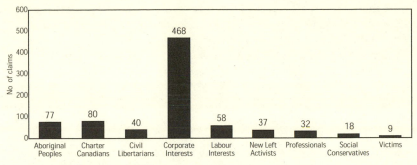

Source: Court Challenges Database.

their challenges try to alter major public policies. The unions and advocacy groups that represent labour interests bring 58 claims. They back members alleging gender discrimination, fight for higher salaries, counter measures that undermine collective bargaining, try to scape criminal contempt charges and assert the right to strike.

The big change is that courts now hear from interests that struggled for decades to win access. For more than a century, courts and governments in Canada maintained barriers that discouraged or even prevented litigation. The Indian Act was amended in 1927 to stop Aboriginal peoples from bringing legal claims. Although this restriction was lifted in 1951, the Supreme Court did not begin to recognize and protect Aboriginal rights until 1973, when it considered a case brought by the Nisga'a.[29] Steep obstacles were preserved by the common law. Rules on standing, proof, evidence and costs reflected a clear preference. Judges wanted to sift through intrinsic evidence to settle discrete legal questions raised by two parties engaged in a live controversy. Applicants who could demonstrate a direct stake in a dispute were allowed to exercise their private rights. Citizens who organized to address public problems were usually sent away.[30]

Some interests were also hampered by weak legal resources. Environmentalists discovered that few regulatory laws established the causes of action and the precise mandatory duties that make litigation more effective. Governments resisted these measures because they believed that legal campaigns would diminish their autonomy and disrupt political life. Groups could base their claims on the Canadian Bill of Rights after 1960. A minor provision in the Indian Act was found to be inconsistent with the guarantee of equality a decade later.[31] This ruling encouraged feminists and civil libertarians who were eager to help victims of discrimination, but it turned out to be an aberration.

Subsequent decisions returned to a narrow interpretation of equality.[32] Litigants also confronted a wall of judicial deference. In the end, most members of the Supreme Court refused to believe that the doctrine of legislative supremacy could be constrained by an ordinary federal statute that lacked constitutional status.

Figure 1 reveals that litigation is now an important strategy for groups that once confronted these obstacles:

- Aboriginal peoples launch 77 claims between 1988–98. First Nations take on the federal government when it fails to act in their best interests; they secure title to land by asserting Aboriginal rights and challenge laws that fail to respect treaty rights.
- Charter Canadians are just as active: 80 legal arguments are presented to oppose measures restricting abortion services, to chastise provincial governments for breaching language rights, to reveal racism in the criminal justice system, and to overturn election laws that discriminate against the mentally ill.
- Civil libertarians participate in 40 cases that attack policies impairing democratic rights, fundamental freedoms and guarantees that protect the criminally accused.
- New left activists bring 37 claims. They enter the courtroom in order to protect delicate ecosystems, help poor people facing arrest, overturn policies that exclude homosexuals, and counter measures that limit demonstrations.
- Social conservatives bring fewer claims, only 18. The most controversial claims try to persuade courts to recognize fetal rights. Unlike their American allies and their Canadian adversaries, social conservatives have not formed any legal advocacy groups; these are specialized organizations designed to fight legal campaigns.[33] In the early 1990s, the Canadian Rights Coalition was established to take on doctors who dared to perform abortions, but it soon disappeared.
- Organizations that represent victims bring even fewer court challenges, only nine. They usually participate outside the courtroom. Most legal claims are brought by individuals who allege negligence or breach of trust to win compensation. Class actions are also orchestrated to counter threats that harm hundreds of victims.[34]

[We find this diverse range of interests pursuing litigation because governments and courts have created new opportunities to participate.] The Charter was entrenched by federal politicians who wanted to strengthen the national community and weaken regional identities.[35] Though guided by this strategic calculation, they also sensed that a shift was occurring. A growing number of citizens were willing to accept or even embrace the idea of constitutional guarantees because their attitudes and expectations had been affected by the international rights movement and the work of the United Nations and by social movements in Canada and the United States that were mobilizing to promote free expression, equality, and reproductive rights. Since the patriation round in 1982, governments have introduced funding programs and statutory rights to make administrative regimes, the regulatory process and the judicial system more accessible.

The Supreme Court has also introduced changes that have encouraged interest group litigation. The law of standing has been liberalized in stages.[36] The old common law rule favoured property owners and corporations trying to protect private rights and filtered out citizens who wanted to address public problems. Under the new rule, applicants who ask a serious legal question and demonstrate a "genuine interest" can win access if certain conditions are satisfied. The Supreme Court has also relaxed the requirements for intervening. Groups with a record of advocacy displaying expertise in a particular area usually receive permission to appear as friends of the court.[37]

The Legal Status of Participants

Looking at evidence from the Court Challenges Database, we can find out how organizations participate. A clear pattern emerges. Corporations, professionals, unions, Aboriginal peoples, and victims usually participate as parties because they tend to seek "private" benefits for partners, shareholders, or members. Figure 2 reveals that litigants with this legal status present 81 percent of their claims. Standing is not a barrier because it is easy to demonstrate a direct stake in a dispute. These interests do intervene when they are represented by advocacy groups that want to influence public policy.

We find the very opposite in Figure 3. Charter Canadians, civil libertarians, new left activists, and social conservatives usually participate as intervenors because they tend to seek "public" benefits. Litigants with this legal status present 78 percent of their claims. Most appear before the Supreme Court. Groups that take this route have to accept several constraints. Intervenors cannot file motions, submit evidence, call witnesses, cross-examine or appeal decisions. These limitations do not discourage public interests because they appreciate the advantages of this form of intervention. Not confined to a specific set of facts, intervenors are free to develop bold claims that dissect complicated social problems. Instead of wasting time and money participating as parties, intervenors can be selective. They can monitor thousands of cases moving up the levels of our judicial system. By appearing before the

Figure 2
The Legal Status of Interests Seeking Private Benefits

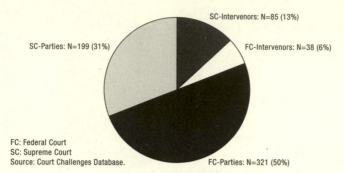

SC-Intervenors: N=85 (13%)

SC-Parties: N=199 (31%)

FC-Intervenors: N=38 (6%)

FC: Federal Court
SC: Supreme Court
Source: Court Challenges Database.

FC-Parties: N=321 (50%)

Supreme Court, interests seeking diffuse public benefits can build precedents, shape public policy and counter hostile actions – without exhausting their resources.

LEGAL ACTION AS A POLITICAL STRATEGY

Interest Group Litigation and State Intervention

The central purpose of litigation is to influence the state. There are three variations. Groups from every category choose litigation to *direct state intervention.* They challenge bureaucracies, boards, tribunals, commissions and inquiries that make decisions about such areas as telecommunications, energy policy, workplace discrimination, labour relations, international trade, transportation rates and agricultural marketing. Interests also try to prod governments that ignore mandatory duties and constitutional obligations. For example, businesses demand that federal officials enforce tariffs and rules protecting copyright.[38]

Litigants also try to *bolster state intervention.* Charter Canadians pursue this strategy more than other interests. Groups asserting minority language education rights make governments create new institutional arrangements that courts have to supervise.[39] Advocates who represent the disabled try to expand health-care services.[40] Feminists determined to eliminate "systemic discrimination" invite judges to re-write social policy by extending unemployment benefits and to alter the distribution of wealth by amending income tax provisions.[41] New left activists also rely on this strategy. Environmentalists try to improve regulatory laws by asking courts to offer a broad interpretation of the

Figure 3
The Legal Status of Interests Seeking Public Benefits

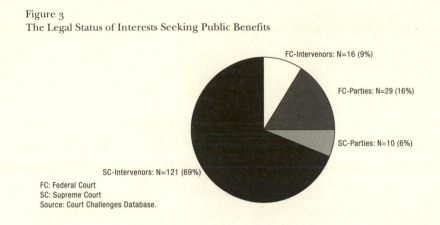

FC-Intervenors: N=16 (9%)

FC-Parties: N=29 (16%)

SC-Parties: N=10 (6%)

SC-Intervenors: N=121 (69%)

FC: Federal Court
SC: Supreme Court
Source: Court Challenges Database.

duties that bind the Crown.[42] Gays and lesbians choose litigation to win benefits and fill in legislative omissions.[43]

Some litigants do the opposite. They try to *block state intervention.* First Nations resist the application of laws that inhibit practices central to their culture and commercial activities that promote economic autonomy.[44] Civil libertarians invoke traditional guarantees that constrain the exercise of state authority. To promote the free exchange of ideas, they challenge provisions that limit forms of expression labelled hate speech, pornography and libel.[45] Social conservatives object to laws that erode traditional values. Some argue that gun-control restrictions are intrusive and ineffective. Others are determined to stop governments from granting homosexuals the rights and benefits that heterosexuals now enjoy. The relationship between professionals and the state is mediated by bodies that set standards for admission and enforce rules of conduct. Members who feel too constrained challenge measures that restrict their entrepreneurial activities.[46] Corporations are affected by the constraints and costs of state intervention more than other interests. They mobilize the Constitution to attack environmental regulations that produce "inefficiencies," bans that limit advertising and marketing regimes that control interprovincial trade.[47]

Confronting Private Parties and Bureaucratic Officials

The debate over judicial activism gives us a distorted picture of interest group litigation because it focuses on the contentious cases that pit courts against legislatures. This study reveals that organizations achieve some of their objectives without asking judges to review the work of elected officials. Half of the actions initiated by corporations are civil claims against private parties. They are driven by one of the great engines of capitalism – the desire to accumulate profits. Businesses enter the courtroom to stop trademark, copyright and patent infringement. They also seek damages for negligence and breach of contract. It is important to acknowledge this body of litigation to understand why companies enter the courtroom, but these cases rarely affect public policy.

Groups from every category target bureaucratic officials exercising statutory powers. Some of these claims are ignored because they lack the drama of constitutional challenges. However, organized interests know that bureaucracies, boards, tribunals, commissions and inquiries make thousands of decisions that implicate major public policies. Aboriginal peoples and new left activists take on federal administrators responsible for environmental assessments. Charter Canadians confront the adjudicators who hear immigration claims. Social conservatives attack human rights tribunals for extending too much protection to homosexuals. Groups that represent victims defend inquiries investigating negligent practices. Labour litigants pursue this strategy more than other interests. According to the Court Challenges Database, 38 percent of their campaigns are directed at bureaucratic officials who consider such issues as the certification of bargaining units, the role of conciliation boards, transportation rates, the re-classification of workers, telecommunications policy and gender discrimination.[48]

Shaping the Interpretive Process

Courts define the meaning, purpose and scope of common law rules, ordinary statutes and constitutional guarantees. Organizations aware of this central fact know that precedents are building blocks. Over time they can persuade judges to jettison old standards, reject threatening arguments advanced by adversaries and improve their chances of winning future contests. For instance, corporate interests try to influence the interpretation of laws that govern the banking industry.[49] To help poor people, new left activists insist that governments have a constitutional obligation to provide legal aid.[50] Professionals eager to offer their expertise talk to judges about child custody provisions in the Divorce Act, the requirements for establishing title to land and the principles that discipline criminal investigations.[51] Social conservatives ask courts to protect the fetus by redefining negligence.[52]

Charter Canadians and civil libertarians pursue this strategy more than other interests. A full quarter of their claims target judicial interpretations. Feminists try to influence the defence of consent, the law of limitations and the rules governing disclosure in sexual assault proceedings.[53] Ethnic minorities enter the courtroom to talk about racism in the criminal justice system.[54] Civil libertarians intervene when journalists are denied access to evidence, when broadcasters are compelled to surrender video footage, when judges contemplate publication bans, and when libel claims discourage free debate.[55] Organizations representing criminal defence lawyers try to affect search and seizure procedures and the requirements for proving aggravated assault.[56] This strategy can be very effective, but success creates a burden because interests have to fight an endless number of battles to secure and maintain an advantage.

Challenging Elected Officials

Claims that challenge elected officials are more captivating because the stakes are higher. When litigants target Cabinet decisions and public policies they ask appointed judges to reject choices made by politicians who have won the support of citizens in general elections. The consequences can be unsettling, even for Canadians who admire the Charter and recognize the legitimacy of judicial review. Decisions can rearrange legislative agendas that reflect public concerns, strain regulatory regimes already burdened by onerous responsibilities, alter spending priorities when governments are striving to trim deficits and spark violent reactions that divide communities. The evidence presented in Table 2 cuts to the very heart of the debate over judicial activism. It demonstrates which interests exert pressure on the federal state by challenging laws and political executives.

Professionals oppose mandatory retirement, social conservatives attack laws that fail to protect the fetus, and unions question measures that restrict collective bargaining and the right to strike, but these are the exceptions.[57] They bring only 10 percent of the claims that target elected officials and most cases try to knock down minor provisions. Groups supporting victims never pursue this strategy.

Far more pressure is generated by the interests that worry critics on the right. Aboriginal peoples, Charter Canadians, civil libertarians and new left activists bring 52 percent of the claims that attack Cabinet decisions and public policies. To win, these litigants have to persuade judges to accept a controversial role – to be full partners in the legislative process who use their skills to solve pressing problems and exercise their authority to improve society. Aboriginal peoples and new left activists question laws passed by both levels of government, but they often target cabinet ministers. First Nations, alleging a breach of trust, demand the enforcement of a broad fiduciary duty that requires the federal government to act in their best interests.[58] Invoking Aboriginal

230   Gregory Hein

Table 2
Targeting Elected Officials, 1988–1998

Organized Interests	Cabinet Ministers		Statues and Regulations		Total	
	No. of claims	(%)	No. of claims	(%)	No. of claims	(%)
Corporate Interests	48	42	45	34	93	38
Aboriginal Peoples	33	29	18	14	51	21
Charter Canadians	10	9	19	14	29	12
New Left Activists	15	13	9	7	24	10
Civil Libertarians	2	2	20	15	22	9
Labour Interests	3	3	9	7	12	5
Social Conservatives	1	1	6	5	7	3
Professionals	1	1	5	4	6	2
Victims	0	0	0	0	0	0
Totals	113	100	131	100	244	100

Source: Court Challenges Database.

rights, they hope to establish title to huge tracts of land worth billions of dollars and try to expand existing treaties to secure better access to natural resources.[59] Environmentalists try to stop massive projects that are championed by provinces hungry for new sources of revenue.[60] Cabinet ministers responsible for telecommunications and social assistance are confronted by anti-poverty activists.[61]

Charter Canadians and civil libertarians also pursue this strategy, but they tend to target statutes and regulations. Feminists try to remove measures restricting access to abortion services.[62] Religious minorities oppose immigration procedures that violate the right to counsel and military policies that discriminate against Jewish officers.[63] Groups representing the disabled try to knock down Criminal Code provisions that discriminate against the mentally ill.[64] Civil libertarians ask courts to scrutinize reapportionment plans, rules that deny prisoners the right to vote, and laws that bar the publication of opinion polls.[65] To help the criminally accused, they ask courts to overturn provisions that undermine the right to be presumed innocent and the right to bail.[66]

These interests do not belong to a unified coalition. Charter Canadians complain that civil libertarians ignore the dangers of pornography and hate speech. Feminists denounce First Nations for failing to recognize the distinct rights of Aboriginal women and environmentalists express frustration when Aboriginal bands challenge laws that regulate the development of natural resources. Still, common concerns often bridge these divisions. Outside the courtroom, activists linked by a national network orchestrate campaigns to oppose privatization, trade liberalization, deregulation and the devolution of responsibilities to the provinces. During constitutional negotiations, they rally against proposals that would jeopardize existing guarantees and the federal spending power.

These interests also work together in court. Charter Canadians and civil libertarians intervene when criminal defendants encounter racism.[67] Feminists who ask courts to rewrite federal tax laws and disabled activists who demand the extension of health-care services receive support from groups that try to help poor people.[68] Charter Canadians eager to fight discrimination enter the courtroom with gays and lesbians to attack laws that favour heterosexuals and exclude homosexuals.[69] Environmentalists form alliances with Aboriginal peoples and economic nationalists to protect delicate ecosystems and defend regulatory regimes that discipline the free market.[70]

The big surprise is that corporate interests are so active in targeting elected officials. Table 2 reveals that they present 38 percent of the claims that challenge laws and Cabinet decisions. Requesting writs of mandamus, businesses try to enforce rules governing international trade. Invoking the federal division of powers, they attack laws that address competition, new drugs, environmental protection and tax policy.[71] The Charter is also mobilized by corporate litigants. Companies insist that marketing regimes controlling interprovincial trade violate mobility rights and the guarantee of equality.[72] Media corporations challenge laws that restrict their ability to collect and disseminate information.[73] The owners of Thomson Newspapers, for example, won a dramatic victory in 1998, when they persuaded the Supreme Court to nullify a measure that barred the publication of opinion polls at the end of election campaigns.[74] Some of the most controversial cases seek to protect commercial expression by knocking down social policies. Corporations, for instance, have challenged provisions that prevent advertising aimed at children and the advertising of tobacco products and liquor.[75]

Propensity to Litigate

This study demonstrates that hundreds of businesses enter the judicial system to advance their interests and that a significant proportion ask courts to confront governments. However, the evidence does not suggest that corporations have a strong propensity to litigate. To understand strategic preferences, we have to consider the entire universe of associations – those that choose legal action and those that

Table 3
Propensity to Litigate

Organized Interests	Population	No. of claims	Ratio
Corporations	180,000	468	1:385
Aboriginal Peoples, Charter Canadians Civil Libertarians, New Left Activists	1,600	234	1:7

Source: Court Challenges Database.

stay outside the judicial system. An elementary fact about the nature of capitalist societies has to be acknowledged. Most organizations are businesses, even in countries that have strong labour unions and thriving social movements. A ratio indicating litigation propensity can be formulated if we estimate the number of associations and the number of court challenges they mount.

What do we find? On the one hand, there are at least 180,000 businesses generating more than 500,000 dollars in revenue annually.[76] They bring 468 claims. On the other hand, Aboriginal peoples, Charter Canadians, civil libertarians and new left activists are represented by only 1,600 organizations.[77] They participate in 234 cases. This comparison suggests that corporations do not display a propensity to litigate. Table 3 confirms what many already suspect. The interests that conservative critics blame for the expansion of judicial power are far more inclined to litigate than other groups.

UNDERSTANDING INTEREST GROUP LITIGATION

Developing an Explanation

The real task for Canadians who want to understand interest group litigation is to figure out why most of the controversial claims are brought by organizations that share few similarities. A good explanation has to tell us why the judicial system attracts interests that are almost diametrically opposed – reformers who want to expand the scope of state intervention and big corporations determined to knock down laws that frustrate free enterprise.

This study emphasizes a crucial distinction. The propensity to litigate is elevated by three *stable characteristics*: impressive legal resources, identities bolstered by rights, and normative visions that demand judicial activism. Groups that do not display these stable characteristics still end up in court, however, because three *changing circumstances* can make legal action seem attractive or even essential. Organizations not inclined to litigate can take advantage of interpretive opportunities, counter immediate threats, and move policy battles into the court-room when their political resources wane. Using this distinction, we can find out why groups participate sporadically or frequently. It also reveals which interests have the greatest potential to influence public policy through litigation – those affected by both the stable character-istics and changing circumstances that pull and push organizations into the judicial system.

Stable Characteristics

Legal Resources. One stable characteristic that affects the propensity to litigate is the possession of legal resources. Such resources are not distributed evenly. Instead, governments have encouraged certain in-terests to litigate by dispensing new legal resources selectively. We know that courts have made our judicial system more accessible by lowering some of the old common law barriers; the law of standing has been liberalized and the requirements for intervening have been relaxed. Courts have also affected the distribution of legal resources by defining the purpose and scope of statutory rights and constitutional guaran-tees. This fascinating political process has produced winners and losers.

Groups that have limited legal resources bring a small proportion of the cases that take on cabinet decisions and public policies. Consider these examples. Labour unions can initiate constitutional challenges, but the argument with the greatest potential to help workers has not been accepted by the Supreme Court.[78] In a trilogy of cases, it decided that freedom of association does not create the right to bargain collec-tively or the right to strike.[79] The Supreme Court has also discouraged opponents of abortion by refusing to declare that section 7 gives a fetus the right to life.[80]

Some of the interests that display a propensity to litigate secured im-pressive legal resources during the patriation round in 1982. Charter Canadians can base their claims on guarantees that were designed to protect their interests. Most are "named" in section 15, the equality provision that prohibits discrimination based on race, national origin, colour, religion, sex, age and disability. Women and ethnic minorities can also invoke declarations that are supposed to guide the interpre-tive process; section 27 acknowledges the value of multiculturalism and section 28 reinforces the importance of gender equality. The 1982 constitution also helps minority language groups.[81] The Charter guarantees the use of French and English in public institutions in Canada and New Brunswick and minority language education in every jurisdiction. Civil libertarians have impressive legal resources because the Charter entrenches guarantees that have been recognized and respected by common law courts for centuries. They can talk to judges about a range of issues by asserting fundamental freedoms, democratic rights, and rights that protect the criminally accused.

Some of the interests that display a propensity to litigate have improved their legal resources in court. Gays and lesbians have achieved dramatic victories invoking the guarantee of equality because the Supreme Court was willing to extend the scope of section 15 by adding sexual orientation to the list of prohibited grounds.[82] The Supreme Court has developed the legal resources Aboriginal peoples now employ. They can protect activities, customs, and practices integral to their culture by asserting inherent rights and establish title to their ancestral lands by presenting oral histories.[83] First Nations can also challenge provincial laws that undermine their treaty rights and invoke a broad fiduciary duty that requires the federal government to act in their best interests.[84]

Businesses do not display a propensity to litigate because they lack the impressive constitutional weapons that some interests enjoy, but they participate more than labour unions, professionals, and social conservatives because they do have solid legal resources. On the one hand, the Charter does not entrench property rights, arguments that use section 7 to defend economic liberties have been rejected, and a number of rights protect individuals not corporate entities. On the other hand, business interests can advance claims that assert freedom of expression, mobility rights in section 6, and some of the legal rights, including the guarantee against unreasonable search and seizure and the guarantee of a fair trial without unreasonable delay.[85] Corporations can also devise a wide array of arguments when they are scrutinized by the state. The Supreme Court has decided that any Charter provision can be invoked as a defence, in criminal proceedings and in civil proceedings against public agencies that exercise coercive powers.[86]

We cannot understand why groups litigate just by looking at the distribution of legal resources. New left activists display a propensity to litigate, but anti-poverty advocates, environmentalists, and economic nationalists have weak constitutional resources. They cannot invoke Charter guarantees that have been designed to protect their interests. They can try to persuade courts to alter the scope and purpose of existing provisions, but most of their arguments have been rejected.[87] These new left activists have to be creative and tenacious to win – they have to devise innovative claims with very little. To appreciate why they persist in their efforts, we must consider other interest group characteristics conducive to litigation.

Identities Energized by Rights. Rival political actors construct collective identities to affect the way we see the world. They are animated by ideas, problems and tasks that give meaning, purpose, and a sense of belonging. Union leaders, for example, hope to inspire their members by talking about the virtues of solidarity and the need for fairness in the workplace. Some environmentalists place the notion of preserving at the centre of their collective identity. They tell us about species and experiences that have been lost forever because of our failure to protect the "gifts of nature." Saving is an idea that inspires pro-life groups. Their goal is not simply to oppose a public policy or a medical procedure. It is far more profound. They are determined to rescue endangered lives.

Rights have attractive qualities for interests trying to build collective identities, especially if they are determined to transform society. Because rights have a certain majesty they can turn ordinary political demands into principles that have to be respected. Because rights have been invoked to counter great evils, from racial segregation in the United States to genocide in Europe, they are emotionally charged. Rights also provide a source of unity; they seem to have a magnetic pull that can draw individuals together. Outside the courtroom, the language of rights can be used creatively and forcefully to rally supporters, frame arguments, and criticize threatening policies.

These attributes suggest that rights are more than mere utilitarian instruments that can be invoked to win legal remedies. However, interests that have identities sustained by rights are determined to explore the possibilities of litigation. The courtroom is an institutional site that offers litigants the opportunity to present claims based on rights. It is also a stage that gives the players a chance to publicize their concerns and promote their values. They can win credibility and legitimacy by convincing judges to accept their principled arguments. Litigation is also attractive because courts exercise authority; their decrees can direct other state institutions. Social activists who feel ignored by political elites can oppose unfavourable policies and Aboriginal peoples can force governments to respect the terms of treaties.

In Canada, the interests that display a propensity to litigate do have collective identities sustained by rights. Civil libertarians harness this novel source of energy to protect individuals from the state. Named for their enterprise, they mobilize the law to guard basic civil liberties.

Aboriginal peoples, Charter Canadians, and new left activists crave the power that rights can generate even more because they want to transform major social, economic, and political institutions. To achieve their ambitious goals, these interests "deconstruct" cultural conventions, undermine deeply rooted attitudes, and build alternative systems of meaning. Gays and lesbians want to redefine our understanding of marriage and family. Environmentalists conduct their own science and apply standards of proof that shift the onus from citizens concerned about the effects of toxic substances to corporations producing an endless flow of chemicals. Feminists confront bureaucrats who claim to be objective and devise interpretations of history that rival official accounts. Aboriginal peoples defend cultures that challenge western notions of property, community, and sovereignty.

The rights that energize collective identities in Canada have distinguishing features; their nature, history, and status vary. The rights that civil libertarians celebrate have a prestigious lineage. Fundamental freedoms and guarantees that protect the criminally accused have been recognized for centuries by judges following the common law tradition. Aboriginal peoples struggling to achieve self-determination and self-government assert inherent rights that can be acknowledged or rejected by courts. Rights are at the centre of the collective identities that bind Charter Canadians. They derive meaning, purpose, and influence from entrenched guarantees that were intentionally designed to protect their interests. The depth and intensity of their attachments became very apparent when coalitions formed to oppose the Meech Lake Accord and the Charlottetown agreement. They feared that major provisions in both packages jeopardized "their" rights.[88] Most new left activists are inspired by broadly defined rights that are not formally recognized. Some insist that our constitution is incomplete without a declaration that protects the natural environment and human health. Others want positive rights that would force governments to establish a welfare state that promotes human dignity and social equality. We know that judicial intervention has helped gays and lesbians. They can base their legal claims and political appeals on the promise of equality in section 15.

Businesses cultivate identities based on a range of values, including efficiency, prudence, and innovation. However, they can succeed without the power that rights can produce. Corporations do not encounter persistent organizational problems.[89] The incentive to pursue collective action is strong because the costs they try to avoid and the benefits they try to secure are usually concentrated and exclusive. Companies facing the same threats and the same opportunities tend to see their common interests. They also derive influence from their role in the economy.[90] Politicians know that businesses generate wealth. They create new technologies, attract foreign investment, support philanthropic endeavors, employ millions of workers, and pay billions of dollars in taxes.

Entering the Courtroom to Enhance Democracy. Aboriginal peoples, Charter Canadians, civil libertarians and new left activists share another characteristic that predisposes them to litigate: they are judicial democrats. These groups believe that litigation has the potential to make our public institutions more accessible, transparent and responsive, if courts hear from a diverse range of interests, guard fundamental social values and protect disadvantaged minorities. We know that some activists agree with the neo-Marxists and critical legal scholars who warned social movements to resist the lure of constitutional litigation. They doubt that lawyers and judges are the real champions of democracy. We also know that Aboriginal peoples, Charter Canadians, civil libertarians and new left activists make shrewd strategic calculations to improve their chances of success. However, the normative assertion that is embedded in their legal claims and political appeals is a crucial distinguishing feature. These interests display a greater propensity to litigate because the architects who design campaigns and the allies who work outside the courtroom believe that judicial review can enhance democracy. They are moved by this conviction.

Judicial democrats emphasize a structural defect that all liberal democracies confront. Without courts enforcing constitutional guarantees, governments can make choices that harm minorities, especially if they are vulnerable or unpopular.[91] This threat is serious, they argue, because our representative institutions do not reflect the diversity of Canadian society. For example, a growing number of women sit in Parliament and the provincial legislatures, but men still dominate these chambers; we see few visible minorities and even fewer Aboriginal peoples.[92] This deficiency raises the possibility that policies will not reflect the interests of "weaker voices" that struggle for recognition. Moved by public sentiments, ideological preoccupations or financial pressures, governments might be tempted to impose limits on the rights that minorities assert. This problem exists, we are told, even when politicians do not intend to discriminate.[93] The men who dominate our representative institutions often fail to appreciate the deleterious effects of laws that appear to be fair.

Judicial democrats who believe that courts should protect minorities suggest that majorities are more apparent than real. They identify faults acknowledged by political scientists and disenchanted voters.[94]

Elections are blunt instruments for registering preferences. During campaigns, personality is more important than policy and debates lack substance. Parties usually win control of the state by securing the support of pluralities, not majorities. After taking office, a new government with only a general mandate can decide to pursue a disruptive legislative agenda that most citizens oppose. Because party discipline is so strong, it is difficult to know how many representatives actually support a proposed policy.

The activists who offer this critical assessment also tell us that democracy is weakened by a persistent bias. Interests trying to shape public policy do not enjoy the same opportunities.[95] Some have access to the cabinet ministers and bureaucrats who exercise real power. Others are excluded or ignored because they question deeply held attitudes and practices that have been accepted for generations. Corporations are privileged because of their role in the economy. Worse, their influence has been bolstered by the pressures of globalization.[96] Groups concerned about public problems are often dismissed when they demand expensive social programs and strict regulations that penalize important industries. The judicial democrats who see this bias do not believe that our institutions are open and transparent.[97] Elite accommodation leaves little room for public deliberation and bureaucrats draft thousands of regulations away from the scrutiny that shapes the legislative process – they write "secret laws."[98]

Aboriginal peoples, Charter Canadians, civil libertarians and new left activists who want courts to enforce fundamental values find cautionary narratives in our past. They tell us that federal officials undermined Aboriginal culture and suspended basic human rights. Adults did not enjoy the privileges of citizenship and children were sent away to residential schools, wrenched from their families and communities. Voters could have objected to these practices in general elections, but they did not. In Manitoba, the Protestant Anglophone majority failed for more than a century to respect rights designed to protect the Catholic Francophone minority. During the 1940s, Japanese Canadians were taken to detention camps. Civil libertarians also remember the 1950s, when religious minorities in Quebec were subjected to a campaign of harassment, orchestrated by the Premier and carried out by the police. In several provinces, mentally disabled women were forced into sterilization programs. During the 1960s, the RCMP investigated thousands of civil servants to root out homosexuals. Feminists were still fighting blatant forms of discrimination in the 1970s, opposing social policies that stopped pregnant women from receiving unemployment benefits, provisions in the Indian Act that stripped Aboriginal women of their status and a family law regime that hurt women by discounting their contributions.

Judicial democrats display a propensity to litigate because they still believe that courts have to counter grave threats. Civil libertarians have to be vigilant because police officers who resent the Charter and politicians who promise law and order are tempted to limit fundamental guarantees.[99] Aboriginal women who want to advance their interests have to litigate to win access to constitutional conferences.[100] Legal action is still an essential strategy for environmental groups because provincial officials eager to promote economic growth sometimes leave pollution laws unenforced.[101] Coalitions of anti-poverty activists feel compelled to litigate when governments pass laws that stigmatize and harass homeless people.[102] Francophones in English Canada and Anglophones in Quebec have to invoke education rights to secure good facilities and autonomous school boards. Governments are willing to draft comprehensive agreements, Aboriginal leaders tell us, because courts continue to enforce Aboriginal rights.

Unlike these judicial democrats, the executives and lobbyists who represent corporations and entire industries do not believe that active courts should try to enhance democracy. In certain contexts, they say the very opposite. When litigation has hampered their ability to generate profits, businesses espouse an argument that is also made by conservative critics. They admire the virtues of majoritarian democracy and lament the loss of legislative supremacy. This defence becomes apparent when governments try to improve access to legal remedies. In Ontario, coalitions organized to stop the Class Proceedings Act during the late 1980s and the Environmental Bill of Rights during the early 1990s. To oppose these threatening measures, businesses questioned the legitimacy of judicial review, criticized the institutional capacity of courts and emphasized the disruptive effects of litigation.[103] What did they fear? Mischievous activists would "flood" the judicial system with "frivolous" claims. Because courts would become partners in the regulatory process, it would become less flexible and more cumbersome. Favourable decisions made by politicians who appreciate the central role that corporations play would be overturned by judges who are shielded from the realities of a competitive global economy.

Changing Circumstances

Interpretive Opportunities. Corporations do not share the stable characteristics that draw judicial democrats into the courtroom. However, this study also reveals an important similarity – corporations and

Figure 4
Targeting Elected Officials

Source: Court Challenges Database.

judicial democrats both encounter the changing circumstances that make legal action seem attractive or even essential. For example, these interests enter the courtroom when interpretive uncertainty creates opportunities that are difficult to resist. It can take several years for courts to define the terse declarations that governments write. Rival interests understand the importance of shaping this incremental process. Judges can accept or reject their arguments, expand or diminish their resources and improve or reduce their chances of success. Favourable decisions also create opportunities. When a single group pulls off an unexpected victory by persuading a court to accept a new interpretation of a statutory provision or a constitutional guarantee, other organizations will be tempted to reap the same rewards. We can see some of the effects in Figure 4. After the Charter was introduced, businesses tested legal arguments based on fundamental freedoms, legal rights and the guarantee of equality in section 15. Encouraged by several early victories, they challenged inquiry powers exercised by public agencies, Criminal Code provisions allowing publication bans, provincial taxes and measures frustrating commercial expression.[104] The pace of participation declined in 1991 because obstacles erected by the Supreme Court blocked off a number of possible strategies.

Judicial democrats also fought interpretive battles during the first decade. Charter Canadians were determined to shape the development of their constitutional rights and new left activists were eager to persuade the Supreme Court to extend the scope of existing provisions. Groups representing disabled people countered rules that restricted voting and environmental groups invoked the promise of life, liberty, and security to prevent toxic substances from damaging

Table 4
Hostile Actions

Organized Interests	No. of claims	Percentage of total claims brought by groups in each category
Charter Canadians	27	34
New Left Activists	7	19
Civil Libertarians	6	15
Aboriginal Peoples	10	13
Corporate Interests	25	5

Source: Court Challenges Database.

human health.[105] Several streams converged to produce the wave evident in Figure 4 between 1989 and 1992. Feminists launched an ambitious campaign in 1982 after leaving the patriation round triumphant. They achieved an important victory in 1989, when the Supreme Court agreed that section 15 mandates "substantive equality." The majority concluded that judges have to consider both the purpose and the impact of a law to stop the "differential treatment" that causes discrimination.[106] This precedent was crucial because it raised the value of constitutional litigation for interests advocating equality. Charter Canadians and new left activists launched a number of challenges to reveal how policies that are ostensibly neutral actually hurt women, gays and lesbians, visible minorities and poor people. Environmental groups started to litigate in 1970 to enforce a new generation of pollution laws, but their big break came in 1989 when the Federal Court decided that guidelines for environmental assessments created mandatory duties that constrain the Crown.[107] This single decision encouraged activists across the country to devise similar claims.[108]

Countering Immediate Threats. Judicial democrats and corporations also encounter immediate threats that push them into the courtroom. Table 4 reveals an inescapable strategic problem. Organizations have to target hostile actions to defend public policies, Criminal Code provisions, common law standards, judicial interpretations and administrative orders that favour their interests. It is startling to see that 34 percent of the claims brought by Charter Canadians are intended to counter these threatening claims. Critical legal scholars and neo-Marxists predicted this trend. After the patriation round, they warned social reformers who were dazzled by the possibilities of constitutional litigation that time and money would have to be spent reacting to claims brought by their enemies. Feminists intervene to protect Criminal Code provisions governing sexual assault, hate speech and pornography.[109] Groups representing the disabled support policies that mandate special education.[110] A growing number of issues pull competing organizations into the courtroom: cases that implicate the fetus attract pro-choice activists and pro-life groups;[111] fishing companies and Aboriginal peoples fight over valuable natural resources;[112] some Aboriginal bands oppose Aboriginal women who challenge residency requirements;[113] rival drug manufacturers try to secure and block the notices that allow companies to produce pharmaceuticals;[114] new left activists and businesses defend or attack measures designed to protect the natural environment.[115]

Corporations face another threat that can only be countered through litigation. Governments conduct inspections, initiate civil actions and bring criminal charges to enforce a range of laws. We already know that businesses raise the Constitution as a sword to cut away policies that constrain their activities. Corporate litigants also hold up the Constitution as a shield to block the state from scrutinizing their affairs. Businesses can devise a wide array of legal arguments because the Supreme Court has decided that any Charter guarantee can be invoked as a defence. To advance their interests, businesses attack a wide range of government powers: procedures allowing authorities to conduct searches and seizures; general inquiry powers; and regulatory measures that restrict the right to counsel in the old Combines Investigation Act, the new Competition Act, the Income Tax Act and laws governing the banking industry.[116] This desire to obstruct scrutiny will always be an important source of litigation.

Diminished Political Resources. Organizations also enter the courtroom when contextual changes diminish the level or value of their political resources. Their fortunes can be affected by the rate of economic growth, unemployment, environmental disasters, the appointment of new cabinet ministers and international conflicts. Because influence is not a fixed characteristic, all interests can be placed at a disadvantage – even huge industries that employ thousands of workers and generate billions of dollars in revenue. We know that tobacco companies have been hurt by compelling scientific evidence and adverse public opinion for more than a decade. Governments have introduced a number of measures to restrict the use of their product. Jurisdictions in Canada and the United States have also initiated civil claims to recover health-care costs.[117] This hostility makes litigation an attractive strategy. For example, RJR Macdonald won an impressive victory in a decision that has been denounced by health-care advocates, groups representing victims and new left activists who feel that corporations wield too much power.[118] Invoking the guarantee of free expression, it persuaded the Supreme Court to remove an advertising ban. The other cases are less dramatic. For instance, fishing companies on both coasts have been hit hard because federal officials have taken remedial steps that restrict commercial enterprises to halt the decline of stocks. Businesses unable to secure favourable policies have responded by pressing their claims in court.[119]

Only ideologues believe that corporations are invincible. Still, in a world shaped by the pressures of globalization, businesses that can survive in the international economy enjoy an advantage. Governments determined to eliminate annual deficits and tackle accumulated debts now support policies that favour competitive corporations. They are promoting the benefits of trade liberalization, deregulation, and tax reduction. This shift has undermined other interests. Politicians trying to reduce the size of the state are less willing to agree with activists who demand expensive national programs and onerous regulatory regimes. In this climate, judicial democrats find litigation even more compelling, especially when they encounter indifference and hostility. After failing to win in the legislative arena, Charter Canadians can mount legal challenges to reform the Income Tax Act and expand the scope of social services. When federal officials fail to implement the core recommendations of a royal commission that examines the plight of Aboriginal peoples, First Nations can ask judges to hear their concerns.[120] New left activists ignored by political elites can knock down policies that exclude homosexuals and demand the strict enforcement of environmental laws. Governments that have achieved a budget surplus have more room to consider policy options, but judicial democrats have learned an important lesson during the past decade: litigation is indispensable when the country is toiling through tough times.[121]

INTEREST GROUP LITIGATION AND CANADIAN DEMOCRACY

This study tells us what we need to know to contemplate the effects and implications of interest group litigation.

- The central insight is that Aboriginal peoples, Charter Canadians, civil libertarians, and new left activists are drawn into court by the stable characteristics that elevate the propensity to litigate and by the changing circumstances that make legal strategies seem compelling. These are the judicial democrats. They will continue to generate a steady stream of controversial claims because they believe that democracy can be enhanced by judicial review.

- Judicial democrats are not in court alone. The judicial system is filled with a wide array of groups that express a broad range of values. This diversity is a triumph for citizens who struggled for decades to win new opportunities to participate in our public institutions.
- Some organized interests are reluctant litigants. Professionals, social conservatives and victims mobilize the law sporadically. Although groups that represent workers are more willing to bring legal claims, they usually attack bureaucratic officials, leaving major public policies unscathed.
- Corporations do not display a propensity to litigate, but they do encounter the changing circumstances that push interests into the courtroom. They ask judges to overturn cabinet decisions and laws passed by both levels of government, often to resist state intervention.

The purpose of this study is to understand a controversial form of collective action, but it can also help us assess the current relationship between citizens, legislators, and judges. In the debate over judicial activism, most commentators exaggerate the hazards and underestimate the rewards. Courts interpreting cryptic constitutional declarations and treaties signed centuries ago do make decisions that cause turmoil. They can disrupt legislative agendas, strain regulatory regimes already burdened by arduous responsibilities and force governments to adjust the allocation of resources. Our political life, as a consequence, is probably less tranquil and more uncertain today. However, we now have a judicial system that responds to a diverse range of interests. Judges hear from professionals advancing pecuniary claims, Aboriginal peoples who want their treaty rights respected, and environmentalists who monitor the erosion of important ecosystems. Courts enforcing the Charter help businesses trying to protect commercial expression, homosexuals who want the family law remedies that heterosexuals expect and linguistic minorities struggling to preserve their culture. That so many groups are able to advance their claims through the courts is an accomplishment that Canadians should celebrate.

Critics troubled by active courts want to restore the relative calm we once enjoyed by resurrecting "traditional judicial review."[122] What do they propose? The Supreme Court has to bring back the old standing requirements, discourage interests from intervening, consider only narrow legal questions raised by live controversies and question the value of extrinsic evidence. They resent judges who allow political adversaries to clutter the courtroom, evaluate policy alternatives with misplaced confidence and try to settle future disputes in a single decision. Conservative critics believe that prudence should replace arrogance. It is too easy for judges to advance their personal preferences, they insist, if the "living tree metaphor" can be invoked as a license to alter the meaning and scope of enumerated guarantees. The Supreme Court has to remember the primary purpose of a liberal democratic constitution: (to protect individuals by placing limits on the state) Legal remedies should not increase the presence of the state. Judges should never punish governments for failing to act by filling perceived omissions. They should also resist the temptation to expand services, benefits, regulatory regimes and Aboriginal treaties.

This argument can sound appealing, especially when the Supreme Court delivers a decision that divides the country. Still, the measures that conservative critics propose have a distinct bias that Canadians should know about. Resurrecting traditional judicial review would filter out certain interests and values. Returning to the old rules governing standing and intervenor status would hurt public interests unable to demonstrate a direct stake in a dispute. Excluding extrinsic evidence would make it more difficult for litigants who want to trace the adverse effects of a law. Freezing the meaning and scope of constitutional guarantees would leave judges unable to address new social problems that create discrimination. If courts only placed limits on the state, litigation would be a poor strategy for citizens who want to bolster regulatory regimes or expand social services. Taken together, these obstacles would hinder interests concerned about racism, homophobia, gender inequality, environmental degradation, poverty, the lives of the disabled and the plight of Aboriginal peoples. Traditional judicial review would not, however, frustrate litigants advancing conventional pecuniary claims and legal action would still be an effective strategy for interests that want to resist state intervention.

Although constrained courts would cause fewer disruptions, we would pay a price. Litigation would help corporations but not groups trying to address public problems. Critics of judicial activism stumble here. They want to stop social reformers from seeking the legal remedies that businesses have always requested. Seen from this perspective, the current relationship between citizens, legislators, and judges is attractive because it meets a basic requirement of democracy that many Canadians embrace. Nations composed of diverse interests should not have institutions that respond to some and ignore others.

NOTES

1 Robert Matas, "Legal to Possess Child Porn, B.C. Court Rules," *Globe and Mail,* July 1, 1999, p. A3.
2 Kirk Makin, "Top Court Protects Disabled Rights," *Globe and Mail,* October 10, 1997, pp. A1 and A11.
3 Henry Hiss, "Women's Groups Applaud Ruling," *Globe and Mail,* February 26, 1999, p. A7.
4 Kirk Makin, "Court Puts Mothers Before Fetuses," *Globe and Mail,* November 1, 1997, pp. A1 and A14; Erin Anderssen, "Child Harmed in Womb Can't Sue Mom, Top Court Rules," *Globe and Mail,* July 10, 1999, p. A3.
5 John Saunders, "Ottawa Can't Block Benefits to Gay Survivors, Judge Rules," *Globe and Mail,* April 24, 1998, p. A5; Kirk Makin, "Gay Couples Win Rights," *Globe and Mail,* May 21, 1999, p. A1; Richard Mackie, "Ontario Bill Called Sexual Apartheid," *Globe and Mail,* November 25, 1999, p. A25.
6 Kirk Makin, "Donald Marshall Wins Again," *Globe and Mail,* September 18, 1999, pp. A1 and A3.
7 Alanna Mitchell, "Alberta Court Backs Ottawa on Gun Law," *Globe and Mail,* September 30, 1998, p. A3; "Hunters Challenge Bear Ban," *Globe and Mail,* February 20, 1999, p. A13.
8 Lila Sarick, "Supreme Court Ruling on Bernardo Tapes Sparks Anger," *Globe and Mail,* April 23, 1999, pp. A1 and A4; Paula Arab, "Stiff Sentence for Killing Own Children Draws Praise," *Globe and Mail,* June 23, 1999, p. A9.
9 Richard Mackie, "Education Bill on Trial Again in Appeal Court," *Globe and Mail,* November 12, 1998, p. A8; Kirk Makin, "Union Activists Can Hand Out Leaflets, Supreme Court Rules," *Globe and Mail,* September 10, 1999, p. A2; Daniel LeBlanc, "Public Service Workers Sue Over Pension Grab," *Globe and Mail,* November 9, 1999, p. A4.
10 Kirk Makin, "Top Court Tackles Freedom of Press," *Globe and Mail,* May 29, 1998, p. A4; Kirk Makin, "Ruling Gives Corporations New Charter Protections," *Globe and Mail,* November 6, 1998, p. A13.
11 Anne McIlroy, "Fisheries Minister Faces Lawsuit," *Globe and Mail,* February 19, 1998, p. A8; Thomas Claridge, "Federal Court to Hear Environmental Challenge," *Globe and Mail,* January 12, 1999, p. A5.
12 Andrew Petter, "The Politics of the Charter," *Supreme Court Law Review,* Vol. 8 (1986), pp. 473–505; Allan Hutchinson, "Charter Litigation and Social Change: Legal Battles and Social Wars," in Robert Sharpe (ed.), *Charter Litigation* (Toronto: Butterworths, 1987); Leo Panitch and Donald Swartz, *The Assault on Trade Union Freedoms* (Toronto: Garamond Press, 1988); Michael Mandel, *The Charter of Rights and the Legalization of Politics in Canada* (Toronto: Wall and Thompson, 1989).

13 George Koch, "Rise of the Court Party: Activists Are Abusing the Charter for Their Own Ends," *Western Report*, November 18, 1991, pp. 10–11; "Feminists Take Over," *Western Report*, September 6, 1993, pp. 30–31; Edward Greenspon, "Reform Seeks Curbs on Judicial Powers," *Globe and Mail*, June 9, 1998, p. A4; Jeffrey Simpson, "Reform Prepares to Mount Attack on Judicial Power," *Globe and Mail*, June 12, 1998, p. A16; John Ibbitson and Steven Chase, "Ontario Joins Alberta: Rein in Top Court," *Globe and Mail*, October 25, 1999, pp. A1 and A7.

14 Erin Anderssen, "Judges Wonder How to Respond to Attacks," *Globe and Mail*, August 25, 1998, p. A3.

15 F.L. Morton and Rainer Knopff, "The Supreme Court as the Vanguard of the Intelligentsia: The Charter Movement as Post-Materialist Politics," in Janet Ajzenstadt (ed.), *Canadian Constitutionalism* (Ottawa: CSPG, 1992); F.L. Morton, "The Charter Revolution and the Court Party," in Patrick Monahan and Marie Finkelstein (eds.), *The Impact of the Charter on the Public Policy Process* (North York: Centre for Public Law and Public Policy, 1993).

16 This term, coined by Alan Cairns, refers to interests that enjoy an advantage. Their rights are explicitly recognized in the Charter. See *Reconfigurations: Canadian Citizenship and Constitutional Change* (Toronto: McClelland & Stewart, 1995).

17 I was helped by two enthusiastic research assistants at the University of Toronto, Antonio Raviele and Samer Musallam.

18 This is the second phase of the Court Challenges Database. The first phase gathers together every claim supported by feminists and environmentalists between 1970 and 1995. See Gregory Hein, "Social Movements and the Expansion of Judicial Power: Feminists and Environmentalists in Canada (1970–1995)," Ph.D. Dissertation, University of Toronto, 1997.

19 J.R. Mallory, "The Courts and the Sovereignty of the Canadian Parliament," *Canadian Journal of Economics and Political Science*, Vol. 10 (1944), pp. 165–78.

20 *Employment and Social Insurance Reference* [1937] A.C. 355; *Labour Conventions Case* [1937] A.C. 377.

21 *Union Colliery v. Bryden* [1899] A.C. 580; *Cunningham v. Tommy Homma* [1903] A.C. 151; *Quong Wing v. The King* (1914) 18 D.L.R. 121 [S.C.C.]; *Alberta Press Case* [1938] S.C.R. 100.

22 Kent Roach, "The Role of Litigation and the Charter in Interest Advocacy," in F. Leslie Seidle (ed.), *Equity and Community: The Charter, Interest Advocacy, and Representation* (Montreal: Institute for Research on Public Policy, 1993).

23 *Edwards v. Canada* [1930] A.C. 123.

24 *Saumer v. City of Quebec* [1953] 2 S.C.R. 299; *Switzman v. Elbling* [1957] S.C.R. 285; *Roncarelli v. Duplessis* [1959] S.C.R. 121.

25 David Beatty, *Putting the Charter to Work* (Kingston: McGill-Queen's University Press, 1987).

26 Kenneth McNaught, "Political Trials and the Canadian Political Tradition," in Martin Friedland (ed.), *Courts and Trials: A Multidisciplinary Approach* (Toronto: University of Toronto Press, 1975).

27 Robert Presthus, *Elite Accommodation in Canadian Politics* (Toronto: Cambridge University Press, 1973); Hugh Thorburn, "Canadian Pluralist Democracy in Crisis," *Canadian Journal of Political Science*, Vol. 11, no. 4 (December 1978), pp. 721–38.

28 I recorded the number of claims not the number of groups. When groups from the same category present separate legal arguments as parties and intervenors, I recorded two claims.

29 *Calder v. British Columbia* [1973] S.C.R. 313.

30 William Bogart, *Courts and Country* (Toronto: Oxford University Press, 1994).

31 *The Queen v. Drybones* [1970] S.C.R. 282.

32 *Attorney General of Canada v. Lavell and Bedard* (1974) 38 D.L.R. (3d) 481 [S.C.C.]; *Bliss v. Attorney General of Canada* [1979] 1 S.C.R. 190.

33 The National Citizens Coalition and REAL Women have participated in several cases, but these organizations are not legal advocacy groups.

34 Erin Anderssen, "Class Actions Expected to Grow with Residential School Claims," *Globe and Mail*, July 10, 1999, p. A7.

35 Cairns, *Reconfigurations: Canadian Citizenship and Constitutional Change.*

36 *Thorson v. Attorney General of Canada* [1975] 1 S.C.R. 138; *Nova Scotia Board of Censors v. McNeil* [1976] 2 S.C.R. 265; *Minister of Justice v. Borowski* [1981] 2 S.C.R. 575. This rule was expanded to cover a broader range of remedies in *Minister of Finance of Canada v. Finlay* [1986] 2 S.C.R. 607. The requirements were reaffirmed in *Canadian Council of Churches v. Canada* [1992] 1 S.C.R. 236.

37 Ian Brodie, "Intervenors and the Charter," F.L. Morton (ed.), *Law, Politics, and the Judicial Process in Canada* (Calgary: University of Calgary Press, 1992).

38 *Dennison Manufacturing v. Canada* [1988] 1 F.C. 492; *Distribution Canada v. Canada* [1991] 1 F.C. 716.

39 *Mahé v. Alberta* [1990] 1 S.C.R. 342; Stephen Scott, Factum for Alliance Quebec and Alliance for Language Communities in Quebec, 1990; *Public Schools Act Reference* [1993] 1 S.C.R. 839.

40 *Eldridge v. British Columbia* [1997] 3 S.C.R. 624.

41 *Schachter v. Canada* [1988] 3 F.C. 515; [1992] 2 S.C.R. 679; *Thibaudeau v. Canada* [1994] 2 F.C. 189; [1995] 2 S.C.R. 627.

42 *International Fund for Animal Welfare v. Canada* [1988] 3 F.C. 590; *Canadian Wildlife Federation v. Canada* [1989] 3 F.C. 309; *Friends of the Oldman River So-*

ciety v. Canada [1990] 1 F.C. 248; [1992] 1 S.C.R. 3; *Angus v. Canada* [1990] 3 F.C. 410; *Edmonton Friends of the North Environmental Society v. Canada* [1991] 1 F.C. 416; *Tetzlaff v. Canada* [1991] 1 F.C. 641; *Friends of the Island v. Canada* [1993] 2 F.C. 229; *Vancouver Island Peace Society v. Canada* [1994] 1 F.C. 102; *Friends of the West Country Association v. Canada* [1998] 4 F.C. 340.

43 *Egan v. Canada* [1995] 2 S.C.R. 513; *Vriend v. Alberta* [1998] 1 S.C.R. 493.

44 *R. v. Sioui* [1990] 1 S.C.R. 1025; *R. v. Sparrow* [1990] 1 S.C.R. 1075; *R. v. Howard* [1994] 2 S.C.R. 299; *R. v. Nikal* [1996] 1 S.C.R. 1013; *R. v. Badger* [1996] 1 S.C.R. 771; *R. v. Pamajewon* [1996] 2 S.C.R. 821; *R. v. Côté* [1996] 3 S.C.R. 139; *Union of New Brunswick Indians v. New Brunswick* [1998] 1 S.C.R. 1161.

45 *R. v. Keegstra* [1990] 3 S.C.R. 697; *R. v. Andrews* [1990] 3 S.C.R. 870; *Canada v. Taylor* [1990] 3 S.C.R. 892; *R. v. Butler* [1992] 1 S.C.R. 452; *R. v. Zundel* [1992] 2 S.C.R. 731; *R. v. Lucas* [1998] 1 S.C.R. 439.

46 *Black v. Law Society of Alberta* [1989] 1 S.C.R. 591; *Rocket v. Royal College of Dental Surgeons of Ontario* [1990] 2 S.C.R. 232.

47 *Irwin Toy v. Quebec* [1989] 1 S.C.R. 927; *R. v. Canadian Pacific* [1995] 2 S.C.R. 1028; *Archibald v. Canada* [1997] 3 F.C. 335; *Thomson Newspapers v. Canada* [1998] 1 S.C.R. 877; *Canadian Egg Marketing Agency v. Richardson* [1998] 3 S.C.R. 157.

48 *Public Service Alliance of Canada v. Canada* [1989] 1 F.C. 511; *Nova Scotia Nurses' Union v. Canada* [1990] 3 F.C. 652; *Alberta Union of Provincial Employees v. University Hospitals Board* [1991] 2 S.C.R. 201; *Upper Lakes Group v. Canada* [1995] 3 F.C. 395; *Telecommunications Workers' Union v. Canada* [1995] 2 S.C.R. 781; *Newfoundland Association of Public Employees v. Newfoundland* [1996] 2 S.C.R. 3; *Public Service Alliance of Canada v. Canada* [1996] 3 F.C. 789.

49 *National Bank of Canada v. Atomic Slipper* [1991] 1 S.C.R. 1059; *Bank of Nova Scotia v. Dunphy Leasing* [1994] 1 S.C.R. 552; *Continental Bank v. Canada* [1998] 2 S.C.R. 298.50.

50 *R. v. Prosper* [1994] 3 F.C. 236; *R. v. Matheson* [1994] 3 F.C. 328.

51 *Young v. Young* [1993] 4 S.C.R. 3; *Fire v. Longtin* [1995] 4 S.C.R. 3; *Michaud v. Quebec* [1996] 3 S.C.R. 3.

52 *R. v. Sullivan* [1991] 1 S.C.R. 489.

53 *Norberg v. Wynrib* [1992] 2 S.C.R. 226; *K.M. v. H.M.* [1992] 3 S.C.R. 6; *R. v. M.L.M.* [1994] 2 S.C.R. 3; *R. v. Whitley* [1994] 3 S.C.R. 830; *R. v. O'Connor* [1995] 4 S.C.R. 411; *L.L.A. v. A.B.* [1995] 4 S.C.R. 536.

54 *R. v. R.D.S.* [1997] 3 S.C.R. 484; *R. v. Williams* [1998] 1 S.C.R. 1128.

55 *Vickery v. Nova Scotia Supreme Court* [1991] 1 S.C.R. 671; *Canadian Broadcasting Corporation v. Lessard* [1991] 3 S.C.R. 421; *Canadian Broadcasting Corporation v. New Brunswick* [1991] 3 S.C.R. 459; *Dagenais v. Canadian*

Broadcasting Corporation [1994] 3 S.C.R. 835; *Hill v. Church of Scientology of Toronto* [1995] 2 S.C.R. 1130.

56 *R. v. Stillman* [1997] 1 S.C.R. 607; *R. v. Cuerrier* [1998] 2 S.C.R. 371.

57 *Borowski v. Canada* [1989] 1 S.C.R. 342; *Tremblay v. Daigle* [1989] 2 S.C.R. 530; *McKinney v. University of Guelph* [1990] 3 S.C.R. 229; *International Longshoremen's and Warehousemen's Union v. Canada* [1992] 3 F.C. 758; [1994] 1 S.C.R. 150; *United Nurses of Alberta* [1992] 1 S.C.R. 901.

58 *Grant v. Canada* [1990] 2 F.C. 351; *Ontario v. Bear Island Foundation* [1991] 2 S.C.R. 570; *Blueberry River Indian Band v. Canada* [1993] 3 F.C. 28; *Samson Indian Band v. Canada* [1996] 2 F.C. 483; *Semiahmoo Indian Band v. Canada* [1998] 1 F.C. 3.

59 *Delgamuukw v. British Columbia* [1997] 3 S.C.R. 1010.

60 *Canadian Wildlife Federation v. Canada* [1989] 3 F.C. 309; *Friends of the Oldman River Society v. Canada* [1990] 1 F.C. 248; [1992] 1 S.C.R. 3; *Angus v. Canada* [1990] 3 F.C. 410; *Edmonton Friends of the North Environmental Society v. Canada* [1991] 1 F.C. 416; *Tetzlaff v. Canada* [1991] 1 F.C. 641; *Friends of the Island v. Canada* [1993] 2 F.C. 229; *Vancouver Island Peace Society v. Canada* [1994] 1 F.C. 102; *Friends of the West Country Association v. Canada* [1998] 4 F.C. 340.

61 *National Anti-Poverty Organization v. Canada* [1989] 1 F.C. 208; *Finlay v. Canada* [1993] 1 F.C. 1080.

62 *R. v. Morgentaler* [1993] 1 S.C.R. 462; *R. v. Morgentaler* [1993] 3 S.C.R. 463.

63 *Dehghani v. Canada* [1993] 1 S.C.R. 1053; David Matas, Factum for the Canadian Council for Refugees, 1993; *Liebmann v. Canada* [1994] 2 F.C. 3.

64 *R. v. Swain* [1991] 1 S.C.R. 933.

65 *Provincial Electoral Boundaries Reference* [1991] 2 S.C.R. 158; *Sauvé v. Canada* [1996] 1 F.C. 857; *Thomson Newspapers v. Canada* [1998] 1 S.C.R. 877.

66 *R. v. Pearson* [1992] 3 S.C.R. 665; *R. v. Morales* [1992] 3 S.C.R. 711.

67 *R. v. R. D. S.* [1997] 3 S.C.R. 484; *R. v. Williams* [1998] 1 S.C.R. 1128.

68 *Symes v. Canada* [1993] 4 S.C.R. 695; *Thibaudeau v. Canada* [1995] 2 S.C.R. 627; Katherine Hardie, Factum for the B.C. Public Interest Advocacy Centre, 1995; *Eldridge v. British Columbia* [1997] 3 S.C.R. 624.

69 *Egan v. Canada* [1995] 2 S.C.R. 513; *Vriend v. Alberta* [1998] 1 S.C.R. 493.

70 *Friends of the Oldman River Society v. Canada* [1992] 1 S.C.R. 3; *Quebec v. National Energy Board* [1994] 1 S.C.R. 159; *Canadian Egg Marketing Agency v. Richardson* [1998] 3 S.C.R. 157; Gregory McDade and David Boyd, Factum for Sierra Legal Defence Fund and Council of Canadians, 1998.

71 *C.E. Jamieson v. Canada* [1988] 1 F.C. 590; *General Motors of Canada v. City National Leasing* [1989] 1 S.C.R. 641; *Quebec Ready Mix v. Ricois Construction* [1989] 1 S.C.R. 695; *Goods and Services Tax Reference* [1992] 2 S.C.R. 445; *Trans-Gas v. Mid-Plains Contractors* [1994] 3 S.C.R. 753; *R. v. Canadian Pacific* [1995] 2 S.C.R. 1028; *Ontario Home Builders' Association v. York Region Board of Education* [1996] 2 S.C.R. 929.

72 *Archibald v. Canada* [1997] 3 F.C. 335; *Canadian Egg Marketing Agency v. Richardson* [1998] 3 S.C.R. 157.

73 *R. v. Canadian Newspapers* [1988] 2 S.C.R. 122; *Edmonton Journal v. Alberta* [1989] 2 S.C.R. 1326; *Pacific Press v. Canada* [1990] 1 F.C. 419; *Toronto Star Newspapers v. Kenney* [1990] 1 F.C. 425; *Armadale Communications v. Canada* [1991] 3 F.C. 242.

74 *Thomson Newspapers v. Canada* [1998] 1 S.C.R. 877.

75 *Irwin Toy v. Quebec* [1989] 1 S.C.R. 927; *Rothmans, Benson, and Hedges v. Canada* [1990] 1 F.C. 84; [1990] 1 F.C. 90; *R.J.R. Macdonald v. Canada* [1995] 3 S.C.R. 199; *Association of Canadian Distillers v. Canada* [1995] 2 F.C. 778.

76 The Corporate Income Tax Administrative File, 1996, Industrial Organization and Finance Division, Statistics Canada.

77 To reach this estimate, I consulted directories of associations, directories published by social movements, telephone directories, government statistics, and the minutes of legislative committees. I encourage readers who find this figure low to conduct their own search.

78 Margaret Philp, "Court Asked to Overturn Repeal of Employment Equity Law," *Globe and Mail*, April 7, 1998, p. A8; Nahlah Ayed, "B.C. Fitness Standards for Firefighters Eyed," *Globe and Mail*, February 23, 1999, p. A4; Richard Mackie, "Ontario Teacher Unions Win Legal Skirmish," *Globe and Mail*, July 7, 1999, p. A4.

79 *Public Service Alliance of Canada v. The Queen* [1986] 1 S.C.R. 424; *Alberta Labour Reference* [1987] 1 S.C.R. 313; *Saskatchewan v. Retail, Wholesale, and Department Store Union* [1987] 1 S.C.R. 460.

80 *Morgentaler v. The Queen* [1988] 1 S.C.R. 30; *Tremblay v. Daigle* [1989] 2 S.C.R. 530. It is worth noting that the Supreme Court has not delivered a definitive opinion on this issue.

81 Minority language groups can also seek the protection of the 1867 constitution.

82 *Egan v. Canada* [1995] 2 S.C.R. 513.

83 *Calder v. British Columbia* [1973] 2 S.C.R. 313; *Guerin v. The Queen* [1984] 2 S.C.R. 335; *R. v. Sparrow* [1990] 1 S.C.R. 1075; *Delgamuukw v. British Columbia* [1997] 3 S.C.R. 1010; Robert Matas, Erin Anderssen, and Sean Fine, "Natives Win on Land Rights," *Globe and Mail*, December 12, 1997, pp. A1 and A10; Jeffrey Simpson, "Oral Evidence Finds a Protector in the Supreme Court," *Globe and Mail*, February 18, 1998, p. A16.

84 *R. v. Sioui* [1990] 1 S.C.R. 1025.

85 *Hunter v. Southam* [1984] 2 S.C.R. 145; *R. v. CIP* [1992] 1 S.C.R. 843.

86 *R. v. Big M Drug Mart* [1985] 1 S.C.R. 295; *Canadian Egg Marketing Agency v. Richardson* [1998] 3 S.C.R. 157.

87 *Operation Dismantle v. R.* [1985] 1 S.C.R. 441; *Masse v. Ontario* (1996) 134 D.L.R. (4th) 20.

88 Ann Rauhala, "Women's Groups are Mobilizing to Hold up Constitutional Accord," *Globe and Mail,* June 25, 1987, p. A5; Stevie Cameron, "Women Say Equality Unquestionably at Risk in Accord," *Globe and Mail,* August 27, 1987, p. A2; Susan Delacourt, "Women's Group Sees Shades of Meech," *Globe and Mail,* May 5, 1992, p. A4; Paul Moloney, "Women's Coalition Calls For No Vote," *Toronto Star,* September 14, 1992, p. A1.

89 Mancur Olson, *The Logic of Collective Action: Public Goods and the Theory of Groups* (Cambridge: Harvard University Press, 1965).

90 William Coleman, *Business and Politics: A Study of Collective Action* (Montreal: McGill-Queen's Press, 1988).

91 This concern is expressed in almost every legal argument. Consider these cases. *Canadian Council of Churches v. Canada* [1992] 1 S.C.R. 236; Mary Eberts and Dulcie McCallum, Factum for LEAF and the Canadian Rights Disability Council, 1992; *Egan v. Canada* [1995] 2 S.C.R. 513; *Eldridge v. British Columbia* [1997] 3 S.C.R. 624; David Baker and Patricia Bregman, Factum for Canadian Association of the Deaf, Canadian Hearing Society, and Council of Canadians with Disabilities, 1997; *Vriend v. Alberta* [1998] 1 S.C.R. 493; Cynthia Paterson, Factum for Equality for Gays and Lesbians Everywhere, 1998.

92 Ovide Mercredi and Mary Ellen Turpel, *In the Rapids: Navigating the Future of First Nations* (Toronto: Penguin, 1993).

93 Mary Eberts and Gwen Brodsky, *LEAF Litigation Year One* (Toronto: LEAF, 1986); *Andrews v. Law Society of British Columbia* [1989] 1 S.C.R. 143; Mary Eberts and Gwen Brodsky, Factum for LEAF, 1989; "LEAF Sponsors Major Symposium on Equality Rights," *LEAF Lines* (Summer 1992).

94 For example, see Harold Clarke, Jane Jenson, Lawrence LeDuc, and Jon Pammett, *Absent Mandate: Interpreting Change in Canadian Elections* (Toronto: Gage, 1991).

95 Christine McLaren, "Fund to Help Groups Fight Environmental Court Cases," *Globe and Mail,* November 26, 1985, p. A2; "The Innu Struggle: Low Flights, High Price," *CEDF News* (Fall 1989); Kathleen Ruff, "The Charter of Rights and Freedoms: A Tool for Social Justice," *Perception,* Vol. 13, no. 2 (1989); B.C. Public Interest Advocacy Centre, *Ten Year Report* (Vancouver: BC PIAC, 1991); Greg McDade, *Sierra Legal Defence Fund Newsletter,* Vol. 11 (1995).

96 Maude Barlow and Tony Clarke, *MAI: The Multilateral Agreement on Investment and the Threat to Canadian Sovereignty* (Toronto: Stoddart, 1997); Shawn McCarthy, "Threat of NAFTA Case Kills Canada's MMT Ban," *Globe and Mail,* July 20, 1998, p. A1.

97 Franklin Gertler, Marcia Valiante, and Paul Muldoon, "Public Access to Environmental Justice," *Sustainable Development in Canada: Options for Law Reform* (Ottawa: Canadian Bar Association, 1990); Rick Lindgren, "Intervenor Funding: Common Sense for the Common Good," *Intervenor,* Vol. 20, no. 6 (1995).

98 Paul Muldoon and Rick Lindgren, "Minutes of the Task Force on the Ontario Environmental Bill of Rights," 1992.

99 Sean Fine, "He Is Out to Rearm a Force Under Fire," *Globe and Mail*, February 15, 1999, pp. A1 and A7; Jane Armstrong, "Rights at Heart of Porn Argument," *Globe and Mail*, July 1, 1999, p. A3; Kirk Makin, "Ontario Focus of Suit by Lawyers' Group," *Globe and Mail*, October 27, 1999, p. A2.

100 *Native Women's Association of Canada v. Canada* [1992] 2 F.C. 462; [1992] 3 F.C. 192; [1993] 1 F.C. 171; [1994] 3 S.C.R. 627.

101 Anne McIlroy, "Pollution Cases Not Prosecuted," *Globe and Mail*, January 22, 1998, p. A4; Martin Mittelstaedt, "Water Polluters Escaping Prosecution," *Globe and Mail*, March 1, 1999, p. A1; Martin Mittelstaedt, "Criminal Polluters Finding Canada the Promised Land," *Globe and Mail*, March 23, 1999, p. A7.

102 Graham Fraser, "Poverty Advocates Vow to Challenge New Ontario Law," *Globe and Mail*, November 16, 1999, p. A6; Richard Mackie, "Critics Attack Ontario Bill for Punishing Poor People," *Globe and Mail*, November 30, 1999, p. A25.

103 George Miller, "Environmental Bill of Rights a Dangerous Precedent," *Northern Miner*, November 26, 1990; Martin Mittelstaedt, "Environmental Bill of Rights Delayed," *Globe and Mail*, December 14, 1990, p. A14; Dianne Saxe, "Environmental Bill of Rights Will Open Pandora's Box," *Financial Post*, April 11, 1991.

104 *R. v. Canadian Newspapers* [1988] 2 S.C.R. 122; *Edmonton Journal v. Alberta* [1989] 2 S.C.R. 1326; *Air Canada v. British Columbia* [1989] 1 S.C.R. 1161; *Irwin Toy v. Quebec* [1989] 1 S.C.R. 927; *Thomson Newspapers v. Canada* [1990] 1 S.C.R. 425; *Stelco v. Canada* [1990] 1 S.C.R. 617.

105 *Canadian Disability Rights Council v. Canada* [1988] 3 F.C. 622; *Waste Not Wanted v. Canada* [1988] 1 F.C. 239.

106 *Andrews v. Law Society of British Columbia* [1989] 1 S.C.R. 143.

107 *Canadian Wildlife Federation v. Canada* [1989] 3 F.C. 309.

108 *Friends of the Oldman River Society v. Canada* [1990] 1 F.C. 248; [1992] 1 S.C.R. 3; *Angus v. Canada* [1990] 3 F.C. 410; *Edmonton Friends of the North Environmental Society v. Canada* [1991] 1 F.C. 416; *Tetzlaff v. Canada* [1991] 1 F.C. 641; *Friends of the Island v. Canada* [1993] 2 F.C. 229; *Vancouver Island Peace Society v. Canada* [1994] 1 F.C. 102; *Friends of the West Country Association v. Canada* [1998] 4 F.C. 340.

109 *Canadian Newspapers v. Canada* [1988] 2 S.C.R. 122; *R. v. Seaboyer and Gayme* [1991] 2 S.C.R. 577; *R. v. Keegstra* [1990] 3 S.C.R. 697; *R. v. Butler* [1992] 1 S.C.R. 452.

110 *Eaton v. Brant County Board of Education* [1997] 1 S.C.R. 241.

111 *Tremblay v. Daigle* [1989] 2 S.C.R. 530; *R. v. Sullivan* [1991] 1 S.C.R. 489; *R. v. Morgentaler* [1993] 3 S.C.R. 463; *Winnipeg Child and Family Services v. D.F.G.* [1997] 3 S.C.R. 925.

112 *Pacific Fishermen's Defence Alliance v. Canada* [1988] 1 F.C. 498; *Tsartlip Indian Band v. Pacific Salmon Foundation* [1990] 1 F.C. 609; *R. v. Sparrow* [1990] 1 S.C.R. 1075; *R. v. N.T.C. Smokehouse* [1996] 2 S.C.R. 672.

113 *Batchewana Indian Band (Members) v. Bachewana Indian Band* [1997] 1 F.C. 689.

114 *Glaxo Canada v. Canada* [1988] 1 F.C. 422; *Pharmacia v. Canada* [1995] 1 F.C. 588; *Apotex v. Canada* [1997] 1 F.C. 518; *Merck Frosst v. Canada* [1997] 3 F.C. 752.

115 *Pulp, Paper, and Woodworkers of Canada v. Canada* [1992] 1 F.C. 372; *Carrier-Sekani Tribal Council v. Canada* [1992] 3 F.C. 316; *R. v. Canadian Pacific* [1995] 2 S.C.R. 1028; *MacMillan Bloedel v. Simpson* [1996] 2 S.C.R. 1048; *R. v. Hydro-Quebec* [1997] 3 S.C.R. 213.

116 *Stelco v. Canada* [1988] 1 F.C. 510; [1990] 1 S.C.R. 617; *F.K. Clayton Group v. Canada* [1988] 2 F.C. 467; *YRI York v. Canada* [1988] 2 F.C. 504; *Thomon Newspapers v. Canada* [1990] 1 S.C.R. 425; *McKinlay Transport v. Canada* [1990] 1 S.C.R. 627; *Solvent Petroleum Extraction v. Canada* [1990] 1 F.C. 20; *R. v. Wholesale Travel Group* [1991] 3 S.C.R. 154; *Kourtessis v. Canada* [1993] 2 S.C.R. 53; *Groupe Tremblay Syndics v. Canada* [1997] 2 F.C. 719.

117 John Ibbitson and Richard Mackie, "Power to Sue Big Tobacco Tucked into Health Bill," *Globe and Mail*, December 3, 1999, p. A8.

118 *R.J.R. Macdonald v. Canada* [1995] 3 S.C.R. 199.

119 *Comeau's Sea Foods v. Canada* [1992] 3 F.C. 54; *Antonsen v. Canada* [1995] 2 F.C. 272; *Carpenter Fishing Corporation v. Canada* [1998] 2 F.C. 548.

120 Most of the recommendations of the Royal Commission on Aboriginal peoples, delivered in 1996, have been ignored by the federal government.

121 Other studies demonstrate the importance of litigation when political resources wane. See Sylvia Bashevkin, *Women on the Defensive: Living Through Conservative Times* (Toronto: University of Toronto Press, 1998).

122 Rainer Knopff and F.L. Morton, "Canada's Court Party," in Anthony Peacock (ed.), *Rethinking the Constitution* (Toronto: Oxford University Press, 1996), pp. 73–80.

Public Opinion and Canada's Courts

JOSEPH F. FLETCHER
AND PAUL HOWE

INTRODUCTION

Lately, newspaper columnists and editorial writers have been picking up on an issue that has been simmering ever since the Charter of Rights and Freedoms came into effect in 1982: What is the appropriate role for Canada's courts in the Charter era? Some critics of the courts in post-Charter Canada claim that judicial rulings on a variety of contentious matters, from gay rights to police procedures, are effectively making law that would better be left to our democratically elected representatives. Supporters of the post-Charter courts, however, see judicial review of legislative and executive action under the auspices of the Charter of Rights as a safeguard of our democratic rights. While critics of the courts recognize that fundamental individual and minority rights have a place in any democratic society, they typically contend that the pendulum has swung too far and that policies favoured by a majority of Canadians are regularly thwarted by an overzealous judiciary. Supporters, on the other hand, argue that the courts are properly carrying out their assigned role under the Charter of Rights and Freedoms.[1]

There is a question at the heart of this debate that to date has not been adequately addressed: What do Canadians think about the Charter and the new responsibilities of the courts since 1982? Are they satisfied or dissatisfied with the judicial politics of post-Charter Canada? Would they like the courts to show greater deference toward governments and legislatures? Or, are Canadians on the whole happy with the

Charter and the work of the courts? If citizens are largely satisfied, it would seem difficult to sustain the critics' objections, which are, after all, grounded in the supposition that the views of the majority should be accorded greater weight.

Surprisingly, there has been relatively little investigation of Canadian attitudes toward the courts and the Charter of Rights, particularly in recent years. To help fill this gap, the Institute for Research on Public Policy commissioned a national survey of 1,005 Canadians on these issues.[2] In several respects, this work draws upon earlier studies using similar questions. Two studies are particularly relevant. The first is the Charter Project based on a series of 1987 surveys.[3] The second is a series of cross-national studies on attitudes toward national high courts.[4]

In the first portion of the paper, we offer comparisons across time on questions relating to the Charter. In the second portion, we turn to attitudes regarding the courts in general and Canada's Supreme Court specifically, considering the latter in a cross-national context. The third section analyzes support for the courts by looking at public attitudes on some recent controversial Supreme Court rulings, to see how these relate to court support more generally. Finally the paper examines the views of Canadians on possible reforms to the current appointment procedure for Supreme Court Justices.

AWARENESS AND IMPRESSIONS ·OF THE CHARTER

What do Canadians know about the Charter of Rights and Freedoms? How many have even heard of it? And among those who have heard of the Charter, what are their impressions of it? Do they regard it as a good thing for Canada or a bad thing? Have awareness and attitudes changed appreciably since the Charter's inception? These questions provide a starting point for our inquiry.

To look at awareness, several minutes into nationwide telephone interviews conducted in 1987 and in 1999, a random sample of Canadians were asked, *"Now I would like to ask you whether or not you have heard of the Canadian Charter of Rights?"* The results are reported in Figure 1.

Looking first at the 1987 results, it is clear that the Charter quickly became a familiar feature of the political landscape in Canada. Nearly 84 percent of ordinary Canadians reported having heard of the Charter; only 15 percent had not. A handful of respondents refused to answer the question. There may be, of course, some degree of over-reporting reflected in these positive responses. Still, the figures are impressive. Only a few years after its proclamation a very substantial portion of Canadians recognized that there was something out there

Figure 1
Awareness of the Charter of Rights and Freedoms in 1987 and 1999

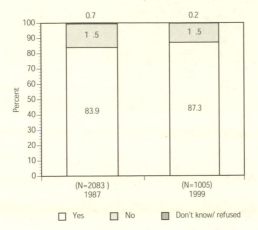

☐ Yes   ☐ No   ■ Don't know/ refused

known as the Charter of Rights. The results obtained by repeating the question in 1999 are similar. A few more Canadians say they are aware of the Charter; a few less report they have not heard of it. Very few respondents refused to answer. Awareness continues, in short, to be very high.

The next question gauged Canadians' impressions of the Charter. In both 1987 and 1999, everyone who claimed to have heard of the Charter was next asked, *"In general, do you think the Charter is a good thing or a bad thing for Canada?"*

The results, reported in Figure 2, make it clear that the Charter was and remains to most Canadians not only familiar but also much admired. Over 80 percent of those who have heard of the Charter in both 1987 and 1999 say it is a good thing for Canada. Only a small number of Canadians are willing to say the Charter is a bad thing, with no substantial change in views over time. Of course, a portion of citizens are unwilling to commit themselves one way or another, but this too has remained essentially unchanged. Taken together with the questions on awareness of the Charter, these evaluations enable us to succinctly summarize the distribution of opinion on the Charter: Most Canadians know about the Charter and they like what they see.

A question of particular interest to observers of Canadian politics is how the Charter has "played" across the country. Are people in one region more (or less) aware of the Charter than those in other regions? Are those who think poorly of the Charter disproportionately concentrated in one particular region?

The results bearing on regional variation are reported in Figure 3. The figures show the proportion of the population in each region that

Figure 2
Impressions of the Charter of Rights and Freedoms in 1987 and 1999

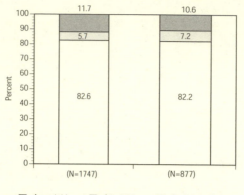

□ A good thing   □ A bad thing   ▢ Don't know/refused

regards the Charter as a good thing, or a bad thing, as well as those aware of the Charter but without an opinion. The proportion in each region who say they have not heard of the Charter is also included.

The first result of note in looking over Figure 3 is that irrespective of time period, the Charter is regarded as a good thing by strong majorities in every part of the country. The only substantial change comes in the province of Quebec. But that change takes a very particular form. In 1987, more than one in four Quebecers said they had not heard of the Canadian Charter of Rights; now it is one in five. The proportion of Quebecers reporting no awareness of the Charter has clearly declined, in tandem with a small increase in both the percentages viewing the Charter as good and bad. It is important to recognize, however, that the Charter is nevertheless as highly regarded in Quebec as it is elsewhere in Canada.

Regarding the responses in the other regions, the picture remains essentially unchanged between 1987 and 1999. The small fluctuations over time in observed percentages are more apparent than real, for none of them are statistically significant. So the substantive finding remains unchanged: The Charter is well known and well liked all across Canada. There are, of course, those who do not concur. Their numbers do not vary greatly, but the percentage appears to be highest in BC and lowest in the Atlantic region. But nowhere does the percentage of negative impressions break into double digits.

Partisan Differences

Given the clear partisan origins of the Charter, it is also important to note the distribution of opinion by party identification. Of course, the

Figure 3
Attitudes toward the Charter by Region, 1987 and 1999

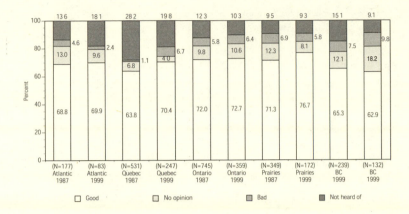

13.6	18.1	28.2	19.8	12.3	10.3	9.5	9.3	15.1	9.1
4.6	2.4	6.8 1.1	6.7	5.8	6.4	6.9	5.8	7.5	9.8
13.0	9.6		4.0	9.8	10.6	12.3	8.1	12.1	18.2
68.8	69.9	63.8	70.4	72.0	72.7	71.3	76.7	65.3	62.9
(N=177) Atlantic 1987	(N=83) Atlantic 1999	(N=531) Quebec 1987	(N=247) Quebec 1999	(N=745) Ontario 1987	(N=359) Ontario 1999	(N=349) Prairies 1987	(N=172) Prairies 1999	(N=239) BC 1999	(N=132) BC 1999

□ Good   □ No opinion   ▨ Bad   ■ Not heard of

federal party scene is now more complicated in 1999 than it was in 1987, with five rather than three federal parties. Yet even a glance at Figure 4 shows an already familiar story. Among partisans of every stripe in both survey years, we find strong majorities saying the Charter of Rights is a good thing. This is not to say that party affiliations do not have an influence on views of the Charter. In fact, in the 1987 results we note that simply reporting any party affiliation appears to be associated with positive regard for the Charter. The most important contrast within Figure 4 is not between supporters of different parties but rather between partisans and the one-quarter of respondents who do not express a partisan preference. The latter are substantially less likely to report they have heard of the Charter or to have an opinion about the Charter if they have heard of it. Still, most of them see the Charter as a good thing. The differences among those who do identify with the three major political parties are rather small, with Progressive Conservatives only slightly less likely to see the Charter as a good thing and just a bit more likely to see the Charter as a bad thing.

In 1999, as Figure 4 shows, those without a party preference remain less aware of the Charter than other groups and, if aware, less likely to have an opinion about it. Yet even most non-partisans still say the Charter is a good thing. Among supporters of the three older parties, there are no substantial changes over time. The percentages may seem to suggest that the PC and NDP supporters are more favourable toward the Charter now than they were in 1987, but the differences are not significant. The real changes over time come with the addition of two new partisan groupings, Reform and Bloc supporters. Although the sample in each case is very small, the general tendency of each newer party is

Figure 4
Attitudes toward the Charter by Partisanship, 1987 and 1999

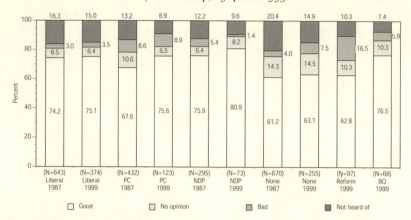

clear. Reform supporters, with just over sixteen percent answering that the Charter is a bad thing, are somewhat less enamoured with the Charter than other partisans. Nevertheless, a very clear majority of Reformers see the Charter as a good thing, though a substantial number either have no opinion or say they have not heard of it. For their part, partisans of the Bloc Québécois view the Charter in much the same way as their counterparts in the three older parties do.

Summing up our findings, it is apparent that the Charter was and remains widely known and highly regarded by Canadians generally. Most say they have heard of the Charter and, moreover, that they think it is a good thing for Canada. These findings hold true right across the country and across all major partisan groupings, including those without a partisan preference. Only a very few Canadians express a negative view regarding the Charter. And even in the regions and parties where they are most numerous, those who say the Charter is a bad thing are clearly in the minority.[5]

CANADIAN ATTITUDES
TOWARD THE COURTS

While current debates about judicial politics sometimes revolve around the merits and shortcomings of the Charter, critical assessments often focus on the courts. Much of the problem, it is said, lies in the expansive interpretation of the Charter by an overzealous judiciary. A closer examination of public support for the courts sheds light on how Canadians in general, along with various sub-groups of the population, feel about this claim.

Figure 5
Who Should Have the Final Say, 1987 and 1999

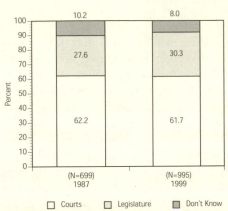

To find out what Canadians think of judicial power, respondents on both the 1987 and 1999 surveys were asked: *"When the legislature passes a law but the courts say it is unconstitutional on the grounds that it conflicts with the Charter of Rights, who should have the final say, the legislature or the courts?"* The results appear in Figure 5. In 1987, roughly 60 percent of Canadians preferred that the courts have the final say, whereas just about 30 percent favoured the legislature.[6] The results are virtually the same in 1999 with people continuing to favour the courts over the legislature by a two-to-one margin. The proportion who say they do not know remains essentially constant as well.

It would be anticipated that attitudes toward judicial power would be correlated with opinions on the Charter. In the debate leading up to the Charter and in the years since its adoption, critics of the Charter have charged that a constitutional bill of rights gives too much power to the courts in making decisions about the meanings and limits of rights and freedoms. Charter defenders, on the other hand, have tended to favour the courts. The Charter itself embodies something of a compromise in the form of the section 33 override (the "notwithstanding clause"), but this has been rarely used.

The relationship between two variables can be succinctly summarized using a measure of overall association, Cramer's V. A value of zero indicates no correspondence, with higher values indicating increased correspondence. There has been a substantial change in the correlation between responses to the "courts versus the legislature" question and assessments of the Charter. In 1987, preference for the courts or the legislature was only weakly related to evaluations of the

Charter (Cramer's V=0.12). In 1999, the correspondence shoots up considerably (Cramer's V=0.23). Favouring the courts as the ultimate decision-making body on rights issues now corresponds more closely with assessments of the Charter.

One way of understanding this finding is that the institutional implications of the Charter have begun to penetrate the thinking of the citizenry. This is not to say, of course, that there is a perfect correspondence between these different attitudes. Nothing could be further from the truth. The coefficients are not only far from the perfect score of 1.00 but also must be seen within the overall context of widespread support for the Charter. Thus even those who prefer the legislatures to the courts are still overwhelmingly (76 percent) of the opinion that the Charter is a good thing. It is just that they are less likely to hold that view than those who favour the courts (88 percent).[7] What this correspondence does indicate though is that opinions about the courts do influence Charter assessments, and more so today than in 1987.

Regional and Partisan Differences

We have seen that when respondents were asked who should have the final say, the courts or the legislatures, they favoured the courts by a two to one ratio in both 1987 and 1999. Figure 6 shows the regional breakdown in these attitudes. The overall pattern is similar to the regional breakdown in Charter support, described above in Figure 3. In both 1987 and 1999, there is majority support for the courts over the legislature in every region of the country.

No statistically significant regional difference emerges in either the 1987 or 1999 data, but the percentages appear to move somewhat in certain regions. The majority in favour of the courts may seem bigger in Atlantic Canada, and in the Prairies and BC it may seem smaller; however, these changes are not statistically significant with samples of these numbers. In Quebec and Ontario the percentages remain more or less constant. Overall, the majority in every region favours the courts.[8]

Turning to partisan breakdowns, Figure 7 reveals that supporters of most federal parties also strongly favour the courts over the legislature. But there has been some change over time: Progressive Conservatives are now less likely to reserve judgment and more likely to support the courts. The views of Liberals, NDPers and non-partisans have not changed significantly.

To no great surprise, the one group that shows marked opposition to judicial authority is Reform supporters, who split down the middle on the courts versus legislatures question in 1999. Others, including potential allies on the right of the political spectrum, do not share this

Figure 6
Who Should Have the Final Say by Region, 1987 and 1999

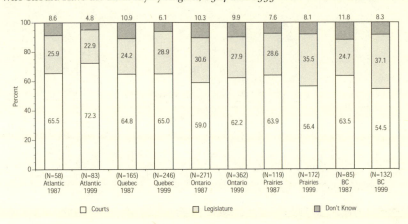

sentiment: 66 percent of Tory supporters favoured the courts in 1999, compared to only 44 percent of Reformers. The sample sizes are small, but this difference is statistically significant. The power of the courts, it would appear, is an important issuing dividing partisans of the two conservative parties.[9]

Taking the Measure of the Courts: Comparisons with Other Countries

The analysis to this point has focused on Canadian attitudes over time, the most striking result being the absence of change from 1987 to 1999 in the substantial public support for both the Charter and the courts. Another useful type of comparison is cross-national, for the debates taking place in Canada about the place of the courts are echoed in other countries where the judiciary wields a certain influence. Canadians are probably most familiar with the stir this issue has caused in the United States, where the practice of judicial review originated and where the Supreme Court has, to mixed reviews, played a pivotal role in shaping public policy on a variety of contentious issues over the years. But the practice of judicial review, along with debates about its merits, are nowadays widespread, and there is insight to be gained from comparing the Canadian experience to developments in a variety of different countries.[10]

It is only in the past few years that researchers have started to undertake systematic comparisons of public opinion toward the courts in different countries.[11] For the present survey, a series of questions identical to those used on surveys conducted elsewhere was included

Figure 7
Who Should Have the Final Say by Partisanship, 1987 and 1999

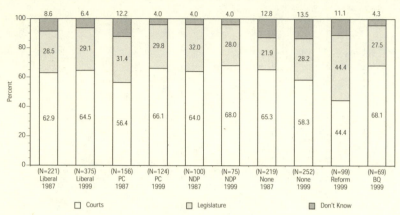

| | Courts | | Legislature | | Don't Know |

in order to see how Canadian opinion ranks cross-nationally. These questions focus on the highest court in each place – the Supreme Court in the Canadian case – rather than the courts more generally.

The first comparison concerns levels of awareness. Respondents were asked, *"Would you say that you are very aware, somewhat aware, not very aware, or have you never heard of the Supreme Court of Canada?"* The results, shown in Figure 8, indicate that comparatively speaking Canadians are quite aware of their highest court. Fully three-quarters indicate that they are somewhat or very aware.[12] Awareness levels are slightly lower than in the United States, Germany and Britain, but considerably higher than in many other countries.

Levels of awareness are not, however, consistent across the country. Of the questions on the 1999 survey, this one offers up one of the more striking differences between Quebec and the rest of Canada (ROC): only 42 percent in Quebec count themselves among the somewhat or very aware compared to 87 percent in the rest of Canada. While the sample size for Quebec is small, and it would be wrong to put too fine a point on the matter, it is clear that levels of awareness in that province fall well below those in other parts of the country.[13,14] It is also apparent that awareness levels in the rest of Canada are as high as anywhere else in the world.

The lower level of awareness in Quebec is not entirely surprising. Studies of Court rulings have found that Quebec generates a relatively small proportion of Charter appeals to the Supreme Court.[15] At the same time, Charter cases may be less salient in Quebec, given the particular concerns that drive political debate in that province. The

Figure 8
Awareness of National High Courts

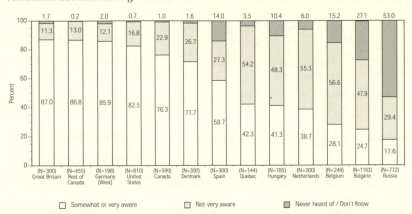

Source for all except Canada: Gibson, Caldeira and Baird, "On the Legitimacy of National High Courts."

division of powers between the provinces and the federal government is a more pressing concern in Quebec than the balance of power between the judicial, legislative and executive branches of government. While the Supreme Court continues to rule on a variety of different issues, its public prominence nowadays is largely a reflection of its role in shaping public policy through its interpretation of the Charter of Rights. It is perhaps not surprising, then, to find that levels of Supreme Court awareness are lower in Quebec – though the magnitude of the difference is quite striking.

Survey respondents were next asked to indicate how satisfied they were with the way the Supreme Court has been working: very satisfied, somewhat satisfied, not very satisfied or not satisfied at all. As Figure 9 indicates, Canada again fares well, sitting third from the top among a cluster of established democracies where satisfaction with the operation of each country's highest court is very high. Satisfaction is lower in Quebec than in other parts of Canada, though not markedly so. As with the earlier question about who should have the final say in cases of conflict, the courts or the legislatures, we find no evidence in Canada of widespread dissatisfaction with the courts.

Canadians, then, report high levels of awareness of their highest court and are generally satisfied with the way it has been doing its job. Despite this strong show of support, however, they are not opposed to the idea of reducing the Court's power. The survey asked respondents whether they agreed with the proposition that *"the right of the Supreme Court to decide certain controversial issues should be reduced."* The results,

Figure 9
Satisfaction with National High Courts (among those aware of highest court)

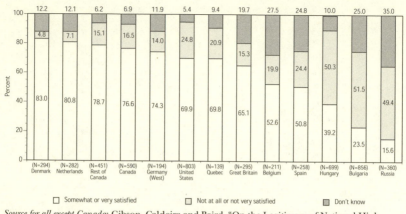

☐ Somewhat or very satisfied   ▨ Not at all or not very satisfied   ▨ Don't know

Source for all except Canada: Gibson, Caldeira and Baird, "On the Legitimacy of National High Courts."

shown in Figure 10, reveal that Canadians are about evenly split on the idea: 42 percent agree, 43 percent disagree, while 15 percent are undecided. Again, there is a difference between Quebec and the rest of Canada on this question, with Quebecers in this case showing somewhat less support for the Court's right to decide controversial issues than other Canadians.

In other countries, there is greater resistance to the idea of reducing the power of the highest court. In the US, only 36 percent favour tightening the reins on the Supreme Court, while 53 percent are opposed. Hungary, Denmark, and the Netherlands show a similar division of opinion. Among those living in the former West Germany, support for leaving the highest court's authority untouched is even greater, with only 22 percent favouring a reduction compared to 58 percent opposed to the idea. On this count, then, Canadians are somewhat less supportive of their highest court, comparatively speaking.

The next question on the survey asked people whether they agreed with a more radical – albeit hypothetical – statement about altering the Supreme Court's authority: *"If the Supreme Court started making a lot of decisions that most people disagreed with, it might be better to do away with the Supreme Court altogether."* While this draconian proposition is clearly not part of serious public debate about Canada's Supreme Court, it nonetheless serves as a useful barometer of any acute discontent that might exist in the general public. It turns out, not surprisingly, that Canadians are significantly less apt to support this radical proposal than the

Figure 10
The Right of the Supreme Court to Decide Certain Controversial Issues Should
Be Reduced (among those aware of highest court)

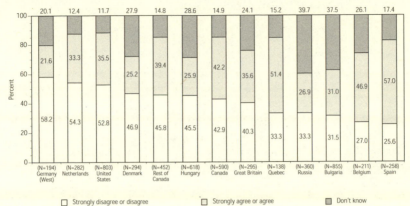

☐ Strongly disagree or disagree   ☐ Strongly agree or agree   ■ Don't know

Source for all except Canada: Gibson, Caldeira and Baird, "On the Legitimacy of National High
Courts."

more modest one noted above. Just over a third of Canadians agree
with the idea of doing away with the court should it consistently run
afoul of public sensibilities (36 percent), while a majority (53 percent)
are opposed (see Figure 11).

Of course, the same is true in most other countries: the radical proposal has less support than the more modest proposal to reduce the
court's authority to rule on controversial issues. The upshot is this: Canadians show greater support for their highest Court in their responses to the radical proposal, yet still lie in the middle of the pack,
lagging behind other countries such as Denmark and the United
States, where opposition to the idea of doing away with the highest
court is more solid.

As with the other measures of Supreme Court support, however, a
Quebec-ROC difference is apparent in Figure 11. Quebecers are markedly more open to the idea of eliminating the Supreme Court altogether if its decisions consistently run counter to Canadian public
opinion. Indeed, a majority support the idea, while only 31 percent are
opposed. Outside Quebec, 31 percent support the idea and 60 percent
are opposed; ROC is almost on a par with Denmark and the Netherlands, though still somewhat less supportive of their Court than the
Americans. Caution is in order, due to the relatively small sample sizes
involved, but the difference between Quebec and the rest of Canada is
sufficiently large that it cannot be explained by random error alone.[16]

Figure 11
If the Supreme Court Started Making a Lot of Decisions That Most People
Disagreed with, It Might Be Better to Do Away with the Supreme Court
Altogether (among those aware of highest court)

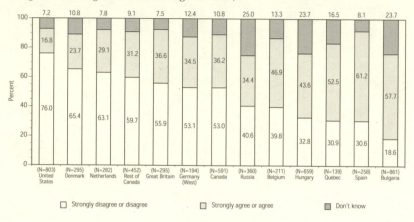

☐ Strongly disagree or disagree   ☐ Strongly agree or agree   ■ Don't know

Understanding Quebecers' Attitudes
toward Canada's Supreme Court

The gap between Quebec and the rest of Canada on these various
comparative measures of support for highest courts reveal a marked
Quebec-ROC difference in attitudes toward Canada's Supreme Court.
This contrasts with the uniformity in attitudes across the country on
the earlier question concerning who should have the "final say" in
cases of conflict, the courts or the legislatures (see Figure 6). On that
question, Quebecers were just as likely to favour the courts as other Canadians. This inconsistency is something of a puzzle: why does Quebec
stand apart on certain measures of support for the courts, but not on
other, seemingly similar, ones?

The difference likely lies in the details of the question wordings. The
earlier question asked respondents whether the *"courts"* should have
the final say when they rule a law *"unconstitutional on the grounds that it
conflicts with the Charter of Rights."* The questions used in the comparative analysis in this section ask about the *"Supreme Court,"* and are less
specific about the type of Court rulings in question, employing catch-
all phrases such as rulings on *"controversial issues"* and *"decisions most
people [disagree] with."* Both differences likely have an effect on responses. Mentioning the Supreme Court, rather than simply "courts,"
may evoke the image of federal power, since the Supreme Court is an
important symbol and instrument of federal authority. And using
catch-all phrases instead of asking specifically about the role of the

courts in applying the Charter of Rights may invite some respondents to reflect on the Court's role in division of power cases and reference cases, such as the 1998 ruling on the legality of Quebec secession.

This reasoning may help explain why the comparative questions reveal considerable differences between Quebec and the rest of Canada. Federal authority and the Supreme Court's role in division of power and reference cases are contentious issues in Quebec. Many Quebecers likely oppose the Supreme Court not because it sometimes strikes down legislation passed by elected bodies, but because they reject federal authority. When presented with the more generic phrase, "the courts," Quebecers show they are just as supportive as other Canadians of the general principle of judicial authority.[17]

These findings suggest that the Canadian results in our comparative analysis should be interpreted cautiously. In other countries, the questions about the highest court likely tap into the attitude they are principally designed to measure: support for the authority of courts to strike down legislation deemed incompatible with a bill of rights. In Canada, other issues of little significance elsewhere – federalism, regionalism and nationalism – conflate the results.[18] The same is probably true of Belgium and Spain, two other established democracies among the surveyed countries where regionalist discontent runs high. It is interesting to note that in Figures 9 to 11, these two countries consistently show lower levels of support for their highest courts than the other established democracies, including Canada.[19]

The upshot is this: there may be somewhat lower support in Canada (and other unstable federations) for the highest court of the land on certain measures, but this does not necessarily translate into lower support for the courts or the judicial branch more generally.

Summary of Cross-National Findings

The overall story that emerges from this comparative analysis is confirmation of considerable satisfaction with the courts in Canada. Canadians are relatively aware of their highest court and strongly supportive of how it has been working. On the question of eliminating the Supreme Court altogether, Canadians, especially outside Quebec, are also fairly committed to the Court. However, when asked if they would like to see the Court's right to decide controversial issues reduced, Canadians do split down the middle, suggesting that support for Canada's highest court is somewhat softer than in a number of other countries. We would reiterate, however, that there is reason to think that a lower level of support for our Supreme Court on certain measures partly represents opposition to centralized, federal power rather than judicial power.

UNDERSTANDING ATTITUDES TOWARD
CANADA'S JUDICIAL INSTITUTIONS

To this point, we have seen that Canadians are aware of the Charter and the Court and hold them both in high esteem. These findings are important for they show that recent critical commentary on the Charter and the Court in both the popular and academic press has little resonance with the Canadian public.[20] This section investigates why this is the case by examining what Canadians know and think about several recent and highly controversial Supreme Court rulings that figure prominently in contemporary Court and Charter criticism.

Our analysis is embedded in a more general theoretical framework that has been applied to a variety of political institutions to understand how legitimacy is built and sustained. In this approach, a distinction is conventionally drawn between specific support and diffuse support. The first refers to support for the policies and actions produced by a given institution. When applied to judicial institutions, specific support is usually conceived as attitudes toward specific cases or issue areas where the courts have ruled. Diffuse support refers to support for the institution itself. Typically, the supposition is that specific support is quite variable, while diffuse support is more stable and somewhat insulated from the vagaries of specific support.[21]

Research into the relationship between specific and diffuse support for the US Supreme Court has produced mixed results.[22] Early US findings suggested that specific and diffuse support were closely linked – a worrying finding for many since it suggested that a surfeit of unpopular decisions could seriously undermine the basic legitimacy of the US Supreme Court.[23] More recent research suggests, however, that the linkages are not as strong as previously suggested.[24] The analysis below reveals that in the Canadian case, there is, generally speaking, a modest linkage between specific support, as measured by attitudes towards specific Supreme Court rulings, and diffuse support, as measured by general attitudes toward Canada's judicial institutions. Moreover, we find that the linkages between specific and diffuse support vary across different issue areas in ways that help to explain the continued high levels of support for the Canadian courts.

Liberty, Equality and Legitimacy
before the Supreme Court of Canada

The cases selected for study here are among the most controversial in recent Canadian jurisprudence. They touch upon fundamental aspects of liberty, equality and political legitimacy in modern Canadian life. They were selected because of the substantial publicity surrounding each and their considerable influence on debate over judicial politics in Canada. As such they are not necessarily representative of the larger docket of items handled by the Supreme Court of Canada. Nevertheless they do represent three main areas of jurisprudence.

The first set of cases touches on freedom from unreasonable search and seizure, the second case on equality in employment opportunity and the third on the legitimacy of the secessionist enterprise in Quebec. The cases also involve different types of Supreme Court activity. The first involves the judicial oversight of police action, the second involves judicial review of provincial legislation, and the third is a reference case where the sitting government asked the Court's advice on a pressing constitutional matter. While the focus in what follows is primarily upon questions asked about the issues raised in these particular cases, we will also from time to time take advantage of other questions in the survey that lend some further perspective to the issues at hand. In particular, we draw comparisons between the current survey results and those from the 1987 Charter Project to assess changes in attitudes that help shape opinion on Court cases.

Freedom from Unreasonable Search and Seizure: R. v. Feeney[25]

A police officer investigating the murder of Mr. Frank Boyle on the morning of June 8, 1991 went to Michael Feeney's place of residence, an equipment trailer. He knocked but when the door was not answered, he entered. Finding Mr. Feeney asleep, the officer woke him and told him to move to a brighter area at the front of the trailer where he could ask him some questions. Upon observing blood on Feeney's shirt, the police officer seized the shirt and took Feeney to the local police detachment for further questioning. The officer had no warrant and Feeney had no lawyer. Based upon the interrogation, a warrant to search Feeney's trailer was obtained and additional incriminating evidence was found there the following day. At trial, the evidence against Feeney was admitted and he was found guilty of second degree murder.

Feeney appealed under the Charter. On May 27, 1997, the Supreme Court handed down a split (5–4) decision that the police had violated his rights. The Court further applied the standard remedy prescribed by the Charter for such violations: it excluded the evidence.

The *Feeney* case has strong similarities to one of the earliest Charter cases, *R. v. Therens*.[26] In a (6–2) ruling, the Supreme Court confirmed the rulings of two lower courts excluding breathalyzer evidence on the grounds that Therens had been detained without being informed of his right to counsel.

In 1987, we asked a general question about the right to counsel and found very nearly unanimous support among Canadians for the right of a person who has been arrested or detained by the police to consult a lawyer. Using a question based on the *Therens* case, we further learned that support for the right to counsel plummets when an infringement of this right entails, as the Charter requires, the exclusion of evidence in court.

Since the general question about the right to consult a lawyer had produced no variance in 1987, we repeated only the more specific question. This question – based upon the facts of the *Therens* case – weaves together concerns over the exclusionary rule contained in section 24(2) of the Charter as well as the right to counsel in section 10. It reads as follows:

Consider this case: The police asked an obviously drunk driver to take a breathalyzer test without telling him that he had a right to consult a lawyer. Should a judge allow the breathalyzer evidence to be used in court or should he exclude it even if the driver may go free as a result?[27]

The results for 1987 are presented in the first column of Figure 12.[28] What we see is that two-thirds of our sample indicated that the breathalyzer evidence should be allowed in court. Just over one-quarter agreed with the Court that it should be excluded. When we repeated the *Therens*-based question in 1999 we found essentially the same results, as shown in the second column of Figure 12. Clearly, things are little changed by the passage of a dozen years. Most Canadians believe that evidence obtained in a situation like *Therens* should be admissible in Court. Relatively fewer say that the evidence should be excluded at trial.

A question concerning the exclusion of evidence loosely based on the facts of the *Feeney* murder case produces, once more, almost identical results. The results appearing in the third column of Figure 12 were obtained using the following question. *Consider this case: A murder suspect is inside a house that has been surrounded by the police. The police are supposed to wait for a warrant before entering the house, but instead they go in immediately and find clear evidence that the suspect committed the crime. Should a judge allow this evidence to be used in court, or should he exclude it?* Again, two-thirds of Canadians say the evidence should be allowed in Court, and roughly one third say it should be excluded. Very few reply they do not know or refuse to answer the question.

The data in all three columns suggest that the Court's exclusion of evidence in these cases is clearly counter-majoritarian. It thus makes some

Figure 12
Should Improperly Obtained Evidence be Allowed in Court?

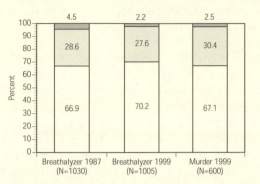

□ Allow evidence   □ Exclude evidence   ■ Don't know/Refused

sense that critics of judicial activism might seize upon the facts of a case like Feeney's to lambaste the Court and the Charter that inspires such rulings.[29] They reasonably assume that most Canadians, if aware of the Court's actions, would not be pleased. Before looking at how these results relate to diffuse support for Canada's judicial institutions, we turn to another recent ruling by the Court, this time in the area of equality.

Equality in Employment: Vriend v. Alberta[30]

Delwin Vriend began working in 1988 as a chemistry lab instructor at Edmonton Alberta's King's University College (a post-secondary college affiliated with the Christian Reformed Church). In early 1990, officials at the school learned that Mr. Vriend was openly living as a homosexual. The school president asked Vriend to resign in 1991. When he refused, he was fired for not complying with the college's policy on homosexuality. After complaining to the Alberta Human Rights Commission only to discover that homosexual behavior was not protected under the provincial human rights code, Vriend took his case to court.

The Supreme Court ruling on the matter came in November of 1998. In its decision, the Court ordered (8–1) the Alberta provincial government to add sexual orientation to the list of characteristics specifically protected under the province's human rights law.

The ruling met with vehement public reaction in Alberta, with thousands of phone calls and letters to the Premier's Office. So swift and strong was this apparently widespread negative public reaction that many observers expected the Alberta government would use the Charter of Rights' notwithstanding clause (section 33) to override the

Court's decision. In the end this did not happen. After some apparent wavering on the matter, Alberta Premier Ralph Klein declared: "I will accept the ruling, I think it's morally wrong to discriminate on the basis of sexual orientation."[31]

We began discussing this case with our respondents by asking how much they had heard about the *Vriend* decision. Our question was: *The Supreme Court also issued a ruling not too long ago in the case of Delwin Vriend, a teacher who was fired from his job at a private religious school because he is gay. Have you heard a lot, a little, or nothing at all about this ruling?*

Fewer than 10 percent of Canadians reported hearing a lot about the *Vriend* case, and 30 percent said they had heard a little. A full 60 percent admitted they had heard nothing at all about the case. Despite the publicity and the uproar, the decision was obviously not widely known among Canadians. There are clear differences on this count, however, across regions and partisan groupings. Where the case arose, on the Prairies, the number who had heard a lot about the case approached 15 percent, while among Reform party identifiers it was slightly over 20 percent.

Respondents were next asked whether they agreed or disagreed with the Court. Our wording was as follows: *In its decision, the Court ruled that a province must provide protection for homosexuals in its human rights legislation. Thinking about this ruling, would you say that you agree or disagree?* The results are in Figure 13.

The first thing to note is a substantial majority of Canadians support the decision rendered by the Court in the *Vriend* case.[32] Moreover, a majority in every region of the country favours the Court's ruling. There are regional differences, to be sure, with those living in Quebec most favourable to protecting the rights of gays and lesbians and those on the Prairies least favourable.[33] Similarly, when we break down responses by party affiliation, supporters of the BQ and NDP stand out as most in accord with the Court, while Reform supporters, evenly divided on the issue, are at the other extreme (the sample sizes are small, but the differences between these groups are large and statistically significant). Interestingly, too, awareness of the case makes no difference to opinion about the case: levels of support for the decision are the same among those who had heard nothing of the decision as they are among those who had heard a little or a lot (results not shown here). Such results perhaps highlight the political wisdom of Premier Klein's acceding to the Court's will in the *Vriend* case, despite the vocal protests.

The Supreme Court's decision in the *Vriend* case clearly forced the hand of Alberta's government on the issue of gay rights. And the ruling had a real impact on other provincial legislatures as well. Shortly thereafter, Newfoundland and Prince Edward Island, the two

Figure 13
Providing Protection for Gays in Provincial Human Rights Legislation, 1999
(Percentage agreeing)

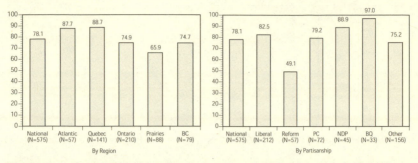

Three percent who replied "don't know" and one percent refusals have been excluded from this table. Including them would bring the national "agree" figure to 74.8 percent.

provinces that had not previously guaranteed equal protection for gays, quickly amended their provincial human rights codes. For critics, these political consequences of the Supreme Court decision represented a judicial trumping of legitimate provincial policy choices, but our findings of popular majorities concurring with the Court suggest otherwise. The legislatures that had refused to protect gay rights through human rights legislation were clearly out of line with public attitudes.[34]

The widespread support for gay rights manifested in public opinion on the *Vriend* ruling is a relatively recent development in Canadian society. This is the conclusion suggested by some comparisons across time we are able to draw, thanks to a general question we asked in 1987 which was available for replication in 1999. In both surveys we asked: *Do you approve or disapprove of allowing homosexuals to teach in school in (respondent's province)?* The results are presented in Figure 14.

What we see here is very nearly a sea change in attitudes toward gay teachers in Canada. A more than 20 point increase in support in twelve years is very significant, perhaps even more so politically than statistically. The rough 50–50 split on this issue in 1987 left open the democratic viability of discriminatory practices like that faced by a Delwin Vriend. The heavy preponderance of opinion today accepting and indeed approving gay teachers in schools presents political leaders with an entirely different political climate, one in which prejudice and discrimination are simply no longer acceptable.

We find, then, a significant difference in public opinion toward Supreme Court rulings in the areas of legal rights and equality rights. Most Canadians disagree with the gist of the *Feeney* decision and other search and seizure rulings, while most agree with the essence of *Vriend*.

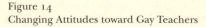

Figure 14
Changing Attitudes toward Gay Teachers

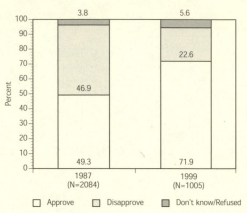

Before examining how these attitudes relate to general opinion on the courts and the Charter, we first consider another type of case, the Quebec secession reference, which has elicited a more mixed response from the Canadian public.

Political Legitimacy: Reference re Secession of Quebec[35]

In August 1998, the Supreme Court of Canada handed down its ruling in the Quebec secession reference. The Court had been asked by the federal government to rule on three questions: 1) whether Quebec could declare independence unilaterally under Canadian domestic law; 2) whether it could do so under international law; and 3) in case of conflict, which law was to take precedence? The Court ruled that Quebec could not legally secede unilaterally under either domestic or international law, rendering the third question immaterial.

But the ruling did not end there. The Court added some unexpected elements to its decision, going beyond the three specified questions to render a much broader judgment. One important added component that took most observers by surprise was the Court's pronouncement that the rest of Canada had an obligation to negotiate the terms of Quebec's departure following a clear referendum vote in favour of sovereignty.

The ruling in the Quebec separation reference, widely seen as one the most important in the Court's history, generated much media coverage and seemed to attract considerable public attention. The results in Figure 15 confirm this impression.[36] Asked whether they had heard a lot, a little or nothing at all about "the ruling a few months ago on

Figure 15
Awareness of Ruling on Quebec Secession

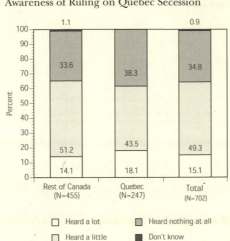

* In order to derive totals for the figures reported in this section, the Quebec
and ROC values were weighted in accordance with population proportions
(roughly 25 percent to 75 percent).

the legality of Quebec secession," 15 percent said they had heard a lot,
while close to 50 percent had heard a little.[37] One-third reported they
had heard nothing at all. Self-reported awareness of the secession reference was, then, relatively high – certainly compared to the *Vriend* decision, of which more than 60 percent of respondents said they had
heard nothing at all.

Respondents were next asked whether they agreed with each element of the Court's decision: the legality of unilateral secession and
the rest of Canada's obligation to negotiate. The overall division of
opinion is quite predictable. Quebecers are ambivalent about the first
part of the Court's ruling and highly supportive of the second, while
other Canadians strongly endorse the first part and are less sure about
the second.

Figure 16 reports attitudes toward the Court's ruling on the legality of unilateral secession. The question to respondents read as follows: *As part of its decision, the Court ruled that Quebec did not have the
legal right to secede from Canada unilaterally. Thinking about this part of the
decision, would you say that you agree or disagree?* The table shows that
there is solid support outside Quebec for this part of the decision,
with nearly three-quarters of respondents in agreement. In Quebec,
by contrast, the Court's ruling on unilateral secession is more divisive. Overall, 41 percent of Quebecers agree with the Court, while 52
percent disagree.

Figure 16
Opinion on Quebec's Right to Secede

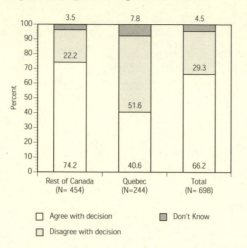

Figure 17
Opinion on Rest of Canada's Obligation to Negotiate

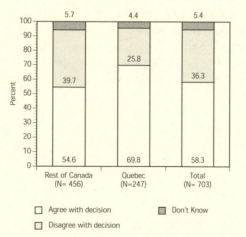

Figure 17 reports attitudes toward the second main component of the Court's decision. Respondents were read the following question: *In another part of its decision, the Court ruled that the rest of Canada had an obligation to negotiate with Quebec after a clear referendum vote for sovereignty. Do you agree or disagree with this part of the decision?*[38] Opinion on this matter is somewhat divided outside Quebec, with 55 percent agreeing with the Court and 40 percent disagreeing. In Quebec, the Court's decision is more uniformly endorsed, with 70 percent backing the ruling.

Table 1
Combined Opinions on Quebec Secession Decision

	Rest of Canada	Quebec	Total
Agree with neither*	13.1	18.6	14.3
Agree secession illegal only	31.6	9.7	26.4
Agree with obligation to negotiate only	11.8	39.4	18.4
Agree with both	43.4	32.2	41.0
(N)	(449)	(236)	(685)

*Includes respondents disagreeing with both parts of the decision, or disagreeing with one part of decision and responding "don't know" to the other; excludes those who responded "don't know" to both questions.

Thus, opinion on the obligation to negotiate is, in some measure, the mirror image of opinion on the right to secede – though significantly there is, in this instance, majority agreement with the Court both inside and outside Quebec.

Attitudes toward each part of the Supreme Court ruling considered in isolation tell us something about the level of support for the decision, but perhaps more telling are the results of the two questions considered in combination, as shown in Table 1. The table confirms the substantial, though far from overwhelming, public support for the secession ruling. In both Quebec and the rest of Canada, only a small minority reject both aspects of the Court's ruling. Naturally, there is a solid minority in both places that agrees with only the part of the decision favourable to "their side" – 32 percent in ROC agree with only the illegality of unilateral secession; 39 percent in Quebec agree with only the obligation to negotiate. But a clear plurality in ROC (43 percent) and a very substantial minority (32 percent) in Quebec agree with both parts of the decision. Only small percentages in both places concur with only that aspect of the ruling favourable to the other group.

Also relevant to the structure of public opinion on the secession reference are levels of awareness of the case. It will be recalled that awareness of the *Vriend* decision – whether the respondent had heard a lot, a little, or nothing at all about the ruling – had no bearing on attitudes toward the decision. The same is not true for the secession reference. Consider the figures shown in Table 2, which reports opinion on the decision broken down by awareness level. In ROC, those relatively aware of the Court ruling – those who had heard a lot or little about it – are considerably more supportive. Indeed, among this group, there

Table 2
Awareness and Attitudes on Quebec Secession Decision

	Heard lot or little about decision	Heard nothing at all or don't know
REST OF CANADA		
Agree with neither*	10.9	17.6
Agree secession illegal only	27.6	39.2
Agree with obligation to negotiate only	9.9	15.0
Agree with both	51.7	28.1
(N)	(294)	(153)
QUEBEC		
Agree with neither*	12.7	29.1
Agree secession illegal only	10.0	9.3
Agree with obligation to negotiate only	41.3	36.0
Agree with both	36.0	25.6
(N)	(150)	(86)

*Includes respondents disagreeing with both parts of the decision, or disagreeing with one part of decision and responding "don't know" to the other; excludes those who responded "don't know" to both questions.

is majority support for both parts of the ruling, compared to just over one-quarter support among those who have heard nothing at all about it. A similar pattern is apparent in Quebec. Those who have heard a lot or a little about the decision are somewhat more likely to agree with both parts of the decision, and considerably less likely to reject both.

Opinion on the Quebec secession reference is then nuanced and uneven, varying between Quebec and the rest of Canada and across respondents with different awareness levels. In the aggregate, it is also relatively neutral, unlike attitudes toward the other rulings discussed above. While there is overwhelming public agreement with the *Vriend* decision enforcing equal employment rights for homosexuals, and generally strong opposition to court rulings upholding civil liberties such as the freedom from unreasonable search and seizure, the state of public opinion on the secession reference is more evenly split.

But as we will see below these negative, positive and more neutral attitudes toward specific cases do not have equal impact on public sentiment toward the courts more generally. Instead, some exert more influence than others. The next sections examine these linkages and assess their implications for the future evolution of Canadian attitudes toward the courts.

Feeney, Vriend, Secession of Quebec and Support for the Court and the Charter

How do opinions on the cases we have examined relate to more general sentiments about Canada's courts and the Charter? Table 3 summarizes the relationship between the five different measures of Charter and court support described previously in this paper and opinion on three cases – *Feeney*, *Vriend* and the Quebec secession reference – by showing the percentage supporting the Court broken down by respondent opinion on the three cases.

Scanning the overall results reveals one immediate and important difference: of the three cases, it is clear that opinions on the *Feeney* ruling are not strongly linked to general assessments of the Charter or Canada's courts. None of the differences observed between supporters and opponents of the *Feeney* ruling is large or achieves statistical significance. The same is not true of *Vriend* and the Quebec secession reference; attitudes toward these decisions show stronger linkages to diffuse support for Canada's judicial institutions. For example, in the case of satisfaction with the Supreme Court, there is a significant linkage with both of the latter cases. The secession ruling has the larger effect of the two, with a satisfaction gap of 20 points between those in agreement with both parts of the decision (86 percent) and those in agreement with neither (66 percent).[39] In the case of *Vriend*, the gap is slightly smaller, with supporters of the decision showing a satisfaction level of 81 percent compared to 66 percent among opponents of the ruling. For *Feeney*, the difference on this item is insignificant. It would seem then that opinions on this controversial case, where most people disagree with the judicial ruling, have relatively little impact on diffuse support for the courts, whereas the decisions enjoying greater public support have more influence.

It would also seem to be true that the case involving civil liberties (*Feeney*) is less closely linked in the public mindset to the Charter and the practice of judicial review than the case involving equality rights

Table 3
Percentage Support for the Charter and Courts
by Opinion on Three Supreme Court Cases

Response	Feeney Decision		Vriend Decision		Quebec Secession Reference		
	Agree	Disagree or don't know	Agree	Disagree or don't know	Agree with both parts	Agree with one part	Agree with neither part
Charter	81.6	81.6	84.8*	72.0	84.1	79.0	83.6
(N=)	(152)	(354)	(388)	(118)	(251)	(271)	(73)
Final Say	60.7	65.0	66.4*	54.2	64.1	61.8	68.0
(N=)	(174)	(403)	(436)	(138)	(281)	(304)	(97)
Satisfaction	76.7	76.6	80.6*	66.0	86.3**	72.9	65.9
Trust	77.0	70.7	77.1*	60.9	74.2	69.7	70.4
Reduce	48.0	40.4	45.7*	34.0	48.4	41.1	37.0
Do Away	53.1	52.3	53.0*	52.1	58.4**	57.0**	42.0
(N=)	(174)	(403)	(436)	(138)	(256)	(270)	(81)

* Significantly different from "disagree or don't know" (p. <.05).
** Significantly different from "agree with neither part" (p. <.05).

Charter: Charter a good thing (excludes those who have not heard of Charter)
Final Say: Courts should have final say not legislature
Satisfaction: Satisfied with the way the Supreme Court has been working
Trust: Agree that the Supreme Court can usually be trusted to make decisions that are right for the country as a whole
Reduce: Disagree that right of the Supreme Court to decide certain controversial issues should be reduced
Do Away: Disagree that if Supreme Court started to make a lot of decisions most people disagreed with it might be better to do away with it altogether.

(*Vriend*). This finding is in keeping with previous analyses which have found equality rights in the Charter to be especially salient to the general Canadian public[40] – this despite the fact that at the Supreme Court level there have been more Charter challenges involving legal rights in the 1990s and these have enjoyed higher rates of success.[41]

It is interesting to note, however, that the type of considerations invoked by *Feeney* – the relative importance of civil liberties and efficacious law enforcement – are significant for some. For Reform party supporters, in particular, opinions on the *Feeney* case have a strong impact on diffuse support for judicial institutions. This relatively small group in our survey sample, mostly opposed to the *Feeney* ruling, are also on most measures considerably less supportive of the courts and the Charter. Among those for whom a particular issue is salient, the linkage between specific cases and more general support can be quite strong. But the number of Reformers in the sample is relatively small and their atypical attitudes do not therefore affect the overall result. In the population at large, it is *Vriend* and the secession reference that are more closely linked to Charter evaluations and court support.

The impact of issue salience on attitudes is also evident when the *Vriend* results shown in Table 3 are broken down by awareness level. Among those who have heard a lot or little about the ruling, the linkage between feelings about the case and diffuse Court support is considerably stronger than it is among those who have heard nothing of the case. For example, while Table 3 shows a 12 percent gap in court support (on the "final say" item) between opponents and supporters of the *Vriend* ruling, further analysis reveals an 18 percent gap among those with some awareness of the decision and only a nine percent gap among those unaware. Similarly, the 13 point gap in Charter support is a more impressive 22 percent in the aware group and only six percent in the unaware. The expected connections between specific cases and general attitudes are present in our survey sample and are, in some sub-groups, of considerable magnitude. But in the population at large, these connections are attenuated by the weakness of attitudinal linkages among Canadians with low awareness levels about judicial decisions, coupled with relatively high levels of unawareness.

In sum, Court decisions that Canadians oppose in the area of civil liberties seem to have less impact on general attitudes toward Canada's judicial institutions than do rulings in other areas that are more favourably received. Moreover, awareness of specific cases can be an important mediating factor, for the connection between specific and diffuse support is often stronger among those with some awareness of a given ruling.

The Cases in Combination

Our analysis to this point has examined a variety of court cases largely in isolation from one another, addressing two basic questions: what is the level of public support for case X and how does this relate to more general attitudes toward Canada's courts? There is, however, something to be gained from analyzing respondents' combined attitudes toward these cases to see how various combinations interact and condition general attitudes.

Slightly over 10 percent of the population is opposed to all three of the prominent Court rulings we asked about on our survey.[42] At the same time, an equal percentage is supportive of all three decisions. This means, of course, that the largest group – fully three-quarters of respondents – is of mixed opinion, finding only some Supreme Court decisions to their liking. As others have previously noted, public opinion on Court rulings seems to comprise a large band of ambivalent opinion, bracketed by opposing minorities more firm and consistent in their views.[43]

How do the three groups measure up in their general attitudes toward the courts and the Charter? Since we know opinions on the three cases – in particular *Vriend* and the Quebec secession reference – have some impact on general attitudes, clearly some differences are to be expected. The relevant comparisons are summarized in Table 4.

Some of the differences apparent in the figures in Table 4 are considerable. On two measures – satisfaction with the Supreme Court and a desire to see the Supreme Court's right to decide controversial issues reduced – the gap between consistent supporters of Court rulings and consistent opponents approaches 30 percent. On one other measure – Charter support – the gap is on the order of 20 percent. These figures exceed by a fair margin the differences previously seen for the individual cases (see Table 3). The cumulative effect of consistent disagreement with Court rulings is markedly greater than the impact of single decisions in isolation.

Yet this cumulative impact should not be overstated. Consistent opponents of Court decisions may be less supportive of Canada's judicial institutions than those happy with recent rulings, but they are hardly inveterate foes. Most pick the courts over the legislature when asked who should have the final say in cases of a Charter conflict (58 percent pick the courts, 35 percent the legislature, and seven percent do not know). Half would not countenance dispensing with the Court altogether (Do Away) even if it were consistently to make a lot of decisions with which most people disagreed; only 29 percent would, while 16 percent are undecided. Three-quarters, moreover, regard the Charter as a good thing (Charter). On only one measure, Reduce, is there even plurality support for an anti-Court sentiment: 47 percent would like to see the right of the Supreme Court to decide controversial issues reduced, compared to 28 percent who would not and 25 percent who are undecided. Thus, aversion to Supreme Court rulings does have a considerable impact on attitudes toward the institution more

Table 4
Percentage Support for the Charter and Courts by Combined Opinion
on Three Cases

Response	Agree with all three (%)	Mixed opinion (%)	Disagree with all three (%)
Charter	92.1*	82.1	74.6
(N=)	(63)	(368)	(59)
Final say	62.9	65.1	57.7
Satisfaction	88.6*	77.8*	60.8
Trust	81.2*	74.6*	59.7
Reduce	55.7*	42.8*	27.8
Do away	62.3	51.5	50.0
N=	(70)	(429)	(73)

*Significantly different from the third column (p.<.05).

Charter: Charter a good thing (excludes those who have not heard of Charter)
Final Say: Courts should have final say not legislature
Satisfaction: Satisfied with the way the Supreme Court has been working
Trust: Agree that the Supreme Court can usually be trusted to make decisions that are
right for the country as a whole
Reduce: Disagree that right of the Supreme Court to decide certain controversial
issues should be reduced
Do Away: Disagree that if Supreme Court started to make a lot of decisions most
people disagreed with it might be better to do away with it altogether

generally, but there remains a large reservoir of support even among
the small portion of respondents consistently opposed to recent high-
profile decisions.

Broadly speaking, then, public opinion toward specific decisions of
Canada's courts is fairly symmetrical, with a broad band of mixed opinion at its centre, and small minorities on either side who differ considerably in their feelings about specific rulings from the Court. As to
diffuse support for the courts and the Charter, both remain high. The
spectrum of diffuse support is thus not centred on the mid-point, it is
shifted decisively toward the positive end of the scale. Even consistent
opponents of Supreme Court rulings are modestly favourable in their

assessments of Canada's judicial institutions, while those more positive about the Court's recent work are stalwart supporters.

Understanding Attitudes Toward Canada's Judidical Institutions: Summary of Findings

In this section, we have considered why Canadians continue to hold the Charter and the courts, including the Supreme Court, in high regard by examining some contentious cases that have made waves in legal and political circles. The analysis points to several conclusions:

- The level of public support for specific Supreme Court rulings varies considerably from case to case. In cases involving civil and legal rights, such as *Feeney* and *Therens*, Canadian opinion largely runs counter to judicial determinations. However, in the prominent *Vriend* case, involving equality rights for homosexuals, public opinion is highly supportive of the Court's ruling (protestations from its Alberta opponents notwithstanding[44]). Meanwhile, attitudes toward the Court's ruling in the secession reference are mixed. Support in Quebec is probably higher than would have been expected before the ruling came down, but nevertheless lower than in the rest of the country where a majority supports each principal part of the decision.
- Awareness of Supreme Court rulings is on the whole quite low, though this too varies from case to case. Only seven percent of Canadians have heard a lot about the *Vriend* decision and another 30 percent have heard a little, leaving over 60 percent who say they have heard nothing at all. Awareness of the secession reference is considerably higher, however, with two-thirds having heard something of the case and about a third of Canadians reporting they have heard nothing at all.
- The linkage between opinions on particular cases and diffuse support for the courts and Charter varies considerably. In the case of *Feeney*, for example, these connections are weak, whereas for *Vriend* and the secession reference, they are considerably stronger. This helps explain continued high levels of support for the Charter and Canada's courts: the judicial decisions of which Canadians approve have greater leverage over their general feelings toward the Charter and courts than do those they oppose.
- Combined attitudes toward the three cases offer insight into the overall configuration of public opinion toward the courts. Only a small minority opposes all three decisions, and only a small minority supports all three; most people are of mixed opinion. The impact of these aggregate opinions on diffuse support is marked. Consistent

opponents and consistent supporters of Court rulings are far apart on some measures of general court and Charter support. Thus, opinions about the Court's work do bear upon perceptions of its deeper institutional legitimacy. But at the same time, there remains a considerable reservoir of diffuse support even among consistent opponents of Supreme Court rulings.

APPOINTING SUPREME COURT JUSTICES

If Canadians are more supportive of the Charter, the courts and particular rulings of the Supreme Court than recent media coverage might give us to believe, this does not mean they are opposed to any and all changes in the way the judicial system operates. One potential court reform that has received some attention is altering the method of appointing judges to the Supreme Court of Canada. Currently the Prime Minister chooses them. There is, of course, some consultation with the Justice Minister and other officials behind closed doors, as well as a certain amount of lobbying from the legal community, but the final decision is the Prime Minister's.

Various alternative appointment methods have been proposed. Some would like candidates to be put forward by a nominating committee that would include representatives from constituencies such as the legal community, elected legislators and the lay public. Others would like to see parliamentary hearings held to assess a candidate's judicial philosophy and qualifications, akin to the Senate hearings that take place in the United States.[45] Those who advocate the decentralization of power would prefer that the provinces put forward nominations for the Court. Combined approaches – a nominating committee and parliamentary hearings, for example – have also been advocated.[46]

Before asking survey respondents their views on this issue, they were first asked whether they knew who currently selects judges for the Supreme Court of Canada. The results, shown in Figure 18, come as no great surprise: only 13 percent of Canadians know that it is the Prime Minister who makes the selection.[47] This finding is in keeping with the results of many surveys that have found Canadians are not especially well-informed about the detailed workings of their political institutions. The level of knowledge surrounding a particular issue is always an important mediating factor to bear in mind when assessing the likely impact of public attitudes on the political agenda.

Respondents were then asked the following question: Supreme Court judges are chosen by the Prime Minister. Some people think the provinces should be allowed to name them instead. Other people say

Figure 18
Who Chooses the Judges for the Supreme Court?

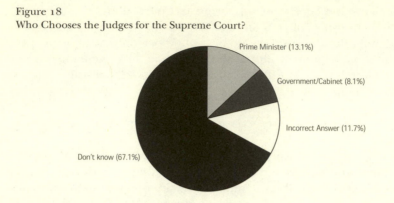

the Parliament in Ottawa should hold hearings to help choose them. Who do you think should choose Supreme Court judges: the Prime Minister, the provinces, or Parliament?

The question did not offer combined methods as an alternative, though if respondents volunteered such a response, it was recorded as such. The objective was simply to get a rough sense of people's relative preferences for the different players that might be assigned a role in the appointment process.

The results, shown in Figure 19, clearly indicate that most Canadians would prefer some type of change to the current method. Only eight percent think the Prime Minister should choose Supreme Court judges. Nearly half would prefer that the provinces make the choice, while more than a third would like Parliament to be involved in the decision.

In assessing the significance of this result, however, it is important to come back to the awareness factor. Many Canadians may not like that the Prime Minister is responsible for Supreme Court appointments, but the overwhelming majority are unaware that this is the current selection method. It is not surprising, therefore, that this has been an issue at the margins of public debate, where it will likely remain despite persistent efforts to highlight the issue and stoke public discontent.

If discontent does rise, however, it is not clear that provincial input will necessarily be the reform of preference. For there are significant differences of opinion concerning appointment procedures among those with different levels of awareness about the Supreme Court – specifically, between those aware and those unaware of the current method of appointment. This is apparent in the results shown in Figure 20, where the data on appointment method preferences are broken down according to whether or not respondents were aware of how Supreme Court justices are chosen at present. Included in the aware

Figure 19
Who Should Choose Supreme Court Judges?

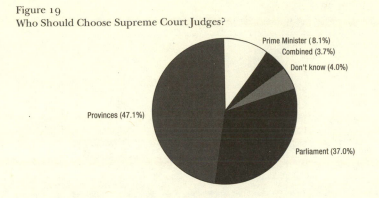

group are the 79 respondents who said the justices are appointed by the Prime Minister and the 49 respondents who were not far off the mark in saying they are selected by the government or cabinet.

Among those unaware of the current method of appointment, over 50 percent think there should be provincial input, while 35 percent think Parliament should make the choice. Among those who know how the judges are picked, however, just over one-quarter opt for the provinces, compared to 45 percent who choose Parliament. A further 14 percent think the Prime Minister should continue making the appointments, compared to only six percent among the unaware group. Breaking down the sample by awareness level makes the sample sizes rather small; nevertheless, it is highly unlikely that the observed differences are simply due to random error.[48]

The impact of awareness on appointment method preferences is likely to have some effect on any public debate that might unfold around the issue. Inevitably, such debate will be more heavily influenced by keen court watchers than less interested parties. We would anticipate, therefore, that the proposals most likely to get the wind in their sails are those calling for some manner of Parliamentary input to the appointment process.

CONCLUSION

These results from IRPP's national survey on the courts and the Charter of Rights shed considerable light on the ongoing debate over the role of Canada's judiciary in the Charter era. They suggest that staunch critics who decry the judicial activism they see in recent Supreme Court decisions and call for greater deference from the courts have yet to win Canadians over to their point of view. Some controversial rulings, especially in the area of civil liberties, are

Figure 20
Preferred Appointment Method by Awareness of Appointment Method

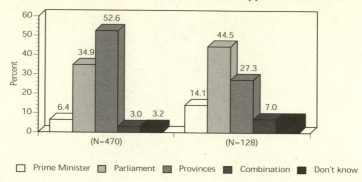

opposed by many Canadians, but others, such as the *Vriend* decision, are widely endorsed. The Charter of Rights and Freedoms enjoys as much popular support as ever, as much as in 1987. At the same time, support for courts over legislatures, when the two are at odds, has remained steady since that date. It is still the case today that twice as many Canadians pick the courts over the legislatures, suggesting that the regular recourse to the notwithstanding clause advocated by some is not likely to win public favour. In light of all the publicity surrounding the courts lately, much of it negative,[49] it is noteworthy that Canadians continue to show strong respect for the right of the courts to strike down legislation they deem unconstitutional.

Based on these findings, there is no evidence that a groundswell of opposition to judicial authority is in the offing. Nor is there any strong indication that courts in Canada are less highly regarded than the courts in other countries. Canadians, if a bit more willing to consider reducing their highest court's right to rule on certain controversial issues, are relatively supportive of the Supreme Court on other measures. It is also important to remember that evaluations of Canada's Supreme Court likely represent a blend of two sentiments: feelings toward judicial authority and feelings about federal authority. In many other countries, this is not the case. Therefore, support for judicial authority in Canada – as opposed to the Supreme Court – is likely underestimated by our comparative data.

Still, there is room for reform. Canadians do feel that the method used to appoint Supreme Court justices is in need of alteration. Many Canadians would look favourably on some change to the appointment procedure – provincial input for some, Parliamentary input for others, especially the more highly aware. While this would probably not silence the most vocal critics of the courts, it would likely enhance public confidence in the judicial system. Giving other players some say in appointments to Canada's highest court would be one constructive response to critics' concerns about judicial power.

NOTES

1 For statements of the contending positions see other essays in this collection. For a more detailed treatment see, Joseph F. Fletcher (ed.), *Ideas in Action: Essays on Politics and Law in Honour of Peter Russell* (Toronto: University of Toronto Press, 1999).

2 The survey was commissoned by the Institute for Research on Public Policy; the questionnaire was developed by Paul Howe and Joseph Fletcher. The fieldwork was carried out by Opinion Search, an Ottawa-based polling firm and took place from March 1 to March 20, 1999. The sample size of 1,005 produces results accurate to within ± 3.1 percent, 19 times out of 20. Potential respondents were called up to ten times to try to secure an interview. The response rate of 30 percent, while low by the standards of an academic survey, is not uncommon for a commercial survey, as response rates have been declining in the past few years throughout the polling industry. In an effort to ensure that the comparisons we draw below with a 1987 academic survey are sound, we compared respondents in the earlier study who had been easy to reach with those more difficult to reach – and found no significant differences in their opinions. Thus, we can say with certainty that if the response rate in 1987 had been comparable to that of the current survey, there would have been no difference in the results. We can also say (with slightly less confidence) that had the response rate of the current survey been higher, the results would not have differed in any significant way.

3 Paul M. Sniderman, Joseph F. Fletcher, Peter H. Russell and Philip E. Tetlock, *The Clash of Rights: Liberty, Equality and Legitimacy in Pluralist Democracy* (New Haven: Yale University Press, 1996).

4 James L. Gibson, Gregory A. Caldeira and Vanessa A. Baird, "On the Legitimacy of National High Courts," *American Political Science Review*, Vol. 92, no. 2 (June 1998), pp. 343–58.

5 Breakdowns in Charter support by age, level of education, place of birth (in Canada or elsewhere) and sex, for both the 1987 and 1999 surveys reveal a greater incidence of "do not know" and "never heard of" responses among certain categories of respondents, such as women and the less educated. For the most part, however, the proportion offering these responses has diminished over time. Aside from this, there are no salient differences across social and demographic categories, thus confirming our basic finding: most Canadians know and like the Charter. For further details, see

Joseph F. Fletcher and Paul Howe, "Canadian Attitudes toward the Charter and the Courts in Comparative Perspective," *Choices*, Vol. 6, no. 3 (June 2000), p. 26.

6 This question was used for a wording experiment in 1987, permitting a precise comparison with only one third of the 1987 respondents. See Sniderman *et al.*, *The Clash of Rights*, pp. 163–68.

7 For more detail on the determinants of Charter support, see Fletcher and Howe, "Canadian Attitudes toward the Charter and the Courts in Comparative Perspective," pp. 11–12.

8 A comparison of this regional breakdown with figures from a November 1999 Angus Reid poll reported in *The Globe and Mail* (Kirk Makin, "Opinion Mixed on Power of Judges," *The Globe and Mail*, November 23, 1999, p. A5) reveals some interesting differences. Whereas we find the highest level of support for the courts in the Atlantic region, the *Globe* poll – which asked if people felt that judges in Canada have too much power – finds support in that region to be the lowest. And whereas we find support in BC to be lower than elsewhere, the *Globe* poll puts BC in the middle of the pack. Why these differences? Most likely, the apparent upswing in opposition in Atlantic Canada in the November 1999 poll represents dissatisfaction with the *Marshall* decision concerning aboriginal fishing rights (handed down in September), while the BC result in our March 1999 poll represents negative reaction to the *Sharpe* decision on child pornography handed down by the BC Supreme Court in January 1999. These regional fluctuations point to the significant impact specific cases can have on general attitudes toward Canada's courts and judges, a theme we take up in more detail later in this paper.

9 Breakdowns on the courts versus legislature question by age, level of education, place of birth (in Canada or elsewhere) and sex, for both the 1987 and 1999 surveys reveal higher levels of "do not know" responses for certain categories of respondents such as women, the less educated and older Canadians. In addition, there seems to be a slightly stronger preference for the courts among younger Canadians and a greater tendency to favour the legislature among Canadians with more formal education. But these differences are small and the results principally confirm that a majority of Canadians across virtually all social and demographic strata, when asked who should have the final say, the courts or the legislature, express their support for judicial authority. For further details see Fletcher and Howe, "Canadian Attitudes toward the Charter and the Courts in Comparative Perspectives," p. 27.

10 Essays on the role of the courts in various countries around the world can be found in C. Neal Tate and Torbjörn Vallinder (eds.), *The Global Expansion of Judicial Power* (New York: New York University Press, 1995).

11 A comprehensive summary of the results of many of these surveys can be found in Gibson, Caldeira and Baird, "On the Legitimacy of National High Courts."

12 A random sub-sample of 600 respondents was asked this particular set of questions. The margin of error for a sample this size is ± 4.0 percent, 19 times out of 20.

13 Given the samples sizes for Quebec and the rest of Canada, we would expect – were there, in reality, no difference between the two regions – to see a difference of less than nine percent, 19 times out of 20. The actual difference of over 40 percent far exceeds this margin or error.

14 We were concerned that this result might simply reflect nationalistic Quebecers willfully understating their awareness of the Supreme Court in order to make a political statement of sorts. To check if this was the case, levels of awareness among supporters of different federal political parties were examined. It was found that Bloc Québécois supporters were no more and no less aware of the Supreme Court than supporters of the other parties, which suggests there was no willful understatement at play.

15 See F.L. Morton, Peter Russell and Tory Riddell, "The Canadian Charter of Rights and Freedoms: a Descriptive Analysis of the First Decade, 1982–1992," *National Journal of Constitutional Law*, Vol. 5 (1995), Table 3, p. 9. For an update, see Patrick J. Monahan, "The Supreme Court of Canada's 1997 Constitutional Decisions: A Statistical Overview," *Canada Watch*, Vol. 6, nos. 4, 5, & 6 (October 1998), Table 6, p. 105.

16 More precisely, if there were, in reality, no difference between Quebec and the rest of Canada, we would expect to see a difference of less than 10 percent, 19 times out of 20. The actual differences of approximately 20 percent considerably exceed this margin of error.

17 The same is true of Bloc Québécois supporters: they support "the courts" as much as supporters of other parties, but are much less supportive of the Supreme Court.

18 These difficulties of interpretation and comparability are, of course, unavoidable. In order to even begin to draw comparisons between support for the courts in Canada and in other countries, use of identical question wordings is essential, even if caveats must be attached after the fact.

19 As a pair of disgruntled Basque nationalists noted: "We are seeing a judicialization of Spanish policy with respect to the Basque question...When we decide something, Madrid opposes it and refers the question to the Constitutional Tribunal, which always renders a judgment in its favour." Cited in Claude Lévesque, "Le Parti Herri Batasuna cite l'exemple irlandais," *Le Devoir*, May 28, 1999, p. A5 (translated by current authors).

20 In the popular press, see Preston Manning, "Parliament, Not Judges, Must Make the Laws of the Land," *The Globe and Mail*, June 16, 1998, p. A23;

Filip Palda, "Nine Despots are the Best We Can Do," *National Post,* July 14, 1999, p. A18; and Ian Hunter, "Taking the Law in Vain," *National Post,* July 29, 1999, p. A19. In response to these criticisms, Canada's Supreme Court justices have begun defending themselves publicly, as in Janice Tibbetts, "Politicians duck divisive issues, chief justice says," *National Post,* July 12, 1999, p. A1.

21 This theoretical approach was pioneered by David Easton in *A Systems Analysis of Political Life* (New York: John Wiley and Sons, 1965). See also David Easton, "A Re-Assessment of the Concept of Political Support," *British Journal of Political Science,* Vol. 5 (October 1975), pp. 435–57.

22 A comprehensive overview of the American literature on Supreme Court support can be found in Lori Hausegger and Troy Riddell, "The Changing Nature of Public Support for the Supreme Court of Canada," paper presented at the 1998 Annual Meeting of the Canadian Political Science Association, Ottawa, May 31-June 2, 1998, pp. 2–5.

23 Walter F. Murphy and Joseph Tanenhaus, "Public Opinion and the United States Supreme Court," *Law and Society Review,* Vol. 2, no. 3 (May 1968), pp. 357–84.

24 Gregory A. Caldeira and James L. Gibson, "The Etiology of Public Support for the Supreme Court," *American Journal of Political Science,* Vol. 36, no. 3 (August 1992), and Gibson, Caldeira and Baird, "On the Legitimacy of National High Courts."

25 *R. v. Feeney* [1997] 2 S.C.R. 13. The rulings are also available through the Supreme Court of Canada website at: www.scc-csc.gc.ca

26 *R. v. Therens* [1985] 1 S.C.R. 640.

27 In 1987, half of the respondents were randomly selected to hear a slightly different version of the question, which said that the driver "might have consulted a lawyer" to see whether explicitly framing the matter as one of right in any way affected responses. We found no significant difference then, so we decided this time to ask only the "had a right" version of the question.

28 Questions replicating items from the 1987 study were asked of all respondents in the present survey. For reasons of economy, questions with no 1987 comparison were posed to a randomly selected 60 percent of the respondents in the 1999 study. Thus the number of respondents for these items is 600.

29 It is perhaps worthwhile to note, since it is rarely mentioned in criticisms of the ruling, that despite the exclusion of the evidence Feeney was convicted at retrial.

30 *Vriend v. Alberta* [1998] 1 S.C.R. 493.

31 Joe Woodard, "Ralph Gets Moral, and Alberta Gets Gay Rights: How Klein Snookered Public Opinion to Satisfy Homosexuals, the Supreme Court and the Media," *Alberta Report,* April 20, 1998, p. 12.

32 These results correspond to those of a September 1998 Angus Reid poll showing 80 percent of Canadians believe that gays should be protected against discrimination.

33 These Prairie results square with an April 1998 Angus Reid poll that found 64 percent of Albertans agreed when asked: "Do you, yourself, agree or disagree that human rights legislation in Canada should protect gays and lesbians from discrimination based on sexual orientation?" Kevin Steel, "The Poll that Wasn't," *Alberta Report,* May 25, 1998, p. 9.

34 It is worth noting that in its submission to the Court the province of Alberta never stated what societal objectives it intended to advance by denying equal rights protection based on sexual orientation.

35 *Reference re Secession of Quebec* [1998] 2 S.C.R. 217.

36 Insofar as we anticipated that there may well be differences on these items between respondents in Quebec and the rest of Canada (ROC) we made sure that these questions were posed not only to the random 60 percent of our sample but also to all respondents in Quebec. The sample size for these items is therefore 705, composed of 247 Quebecers and 458 from the rest of Canada.

37 The exact wording of the question was: *The Supreme Court issued a ruling a few months ago on the legality of Quebec secession. Have you heard a lot, a little, or nothing at all about this ruling?*

38 This question, of course, simplifies the Court's ruling. Rather than mentioning the "clear majority" and "clear question" conditions specified by the Court, it uses the more ambiguous phrase "a clear referendum vote for sovereignty." Nevertheless, it was felt to be a reasonable approximation of the Court's decision.

39 To check whether the differences in Panel C of Table 3 are simply reflections of differences between Quebecers and other Canadians, OLS regression was used to isolate the effect of opinion on the secession reference independent of a Quebec-ROC variable. When this was done, all the statistically significant differences reported in Panel C remained significant at the same levels.

40 Paul M. Sniderman, Joseph F. Fletcher, Peter H. Russell and Philip E. Tetlock, "Political Culture and Double Standards: Mass and Elite Attitudes toward Language Rights in the Charter of Rights and Freedoms," *Canadian Journal of Political Science,* Vol. 22, no. 2 (June 1989), pp. 259–84.

41 See the statistics on Supreme Court Charter review cases in Peter H. Russell, "The Supreme Court and the Charter: Quantitative Trends – Continuities and Discontinuities," *Canada Watch,* Vol. 6, nos. 4, 5 and 6 (October 1998), pp. 61–64 and Patrick Monahan "The Supreme Court of Canada's 1997 Constitutional Decisions: A Statistical Overview," in the same volume, pp. 102–07.

42 For the analysis in this section, we have treated all those who disagreed with one of the elements in the secession reference as opponents of the ruling. Only those agreeing with both are coded as supporters.

43 See F.L. Morton's essay in this collection.

44 See, for example, Woodard, "Ralph Gets Moral, and Alberta Gets Gay Rights," pp. 12–17.

45 Owen Lippert, "It's Time Parliament Reviewed Supreme Court Appointments," *Fraser Forum* (March 1998), pp. 24–25.

46 See for example, the essays by Jacob Ziegel and Peter Russell in this volume.

47 Again, a sub-sample of 600 respondents was asked the set of questions about appointment procedures.

48 More precisely, if there were, in reality, no difference between the unaware and the aware groups, we would expect to see differences of less than 10 percent, 19 times out of 20.

49 Just prior to the survey there were two highly publicized incidents that might well have undermined Canadians' confidence in the courts. In January, the BC Supreme Court ruled, to much public outcry, that the law making possession of child pornography a criminal offence was unconstitutional, and in February, Alberta Court of Appeal Justice John McClung wrote his scathing missive to the *National Post* lambasting Madame Justice Claire L'Heureux-Dubé for the commentary she attached to the Supreme Court's ruling in the *Ewanchuk* case. That these two incidents do not seem to have dented public confidence underlines the resilience of Canadian support for the courts.

Section 33, The Notwithstanding Clause: A Paper Tiger?

HOWARD LEESON

INTRODUCTION

Any discussion about section 33 of the *Constitution Act, 1982*, the so-called notwithstanding clause, involves notions about how power ought to be shared in a society, about sovereignty and the role of the individual, and about how these arrangements should be set out in written or conventional constitutional arrangements. As Peter Russell said in his book, *Constitutional Odyssey*: "As people on other continents at other times have learned before us, the ideal of self-determination is as challenging as it is alluring ... When constitutional legitimacy comes to rest on the sovereignty of the people, the threshold question becomes just who these people are who are capable of sharing a common constitution based on their mutual consent."[1]

In particular, in an era when individual rights have been expanded and safeguarded in law and the ability of governments to interfere with them has been circumscribed in constitutions, the question of who should safeguard rights is far from trivial. The approach of Britain, until its increasing entanglement with the European Union, was to locate ultimate power in Parliament. The American response, albeit appropriated by the courts themselves after 1803, has been to give ultimate power to the courts. Increasingly in liberal democratic societies, the American model, that the courts should be entrusted with this responsibility, has been adopted. For a number of reasons, they are perceived as best able to arbitrate questions of rights, especially when it involves the state or its agents. Usually, however, judges are not democratically chosen and lack the legitimacy of having been elected. As well, they most often come from privileged academic or social backgrounds, rendering the courts unrepresentative of the general population. For these and other reasons, there is a reluctance on the part of many to give the courts the final say in questions that may be fundamental to the functioning of society.

In Canada, with the adoption of the Charter of Rights and Freedoms in 1982, an attempt was made to balance the two approaches. This was done through the insertion of a *nonobstante* clause, section 33, which allows the legislatures and Parliament of Canada, in certain instances, to override the provisions of the Charter. As might be expected, this attempt at compromise has drawn criticism from both sides of the debate about how best to protect rights. Supporters of the judicial approach are outraged that legislatures may still apply majoritarian standards to questions of fundamental rights, while supporters of parliamentary sovereignty consider any devolution of sovereignty to nonelected judges to be a violation of democratic principles. Those who support the clause point out, however, that it is the quintessential Canadian compromise, a compromise that leaves no one happy, but no one hurt. As Donna Greshner and Ken Norman have observed: "The foundational issue brought into sharp relief by the question [about section 33(1)] is the balance of power between the judiciary and democratically elected legislatures."[2]

The story of how we came to adopt this provision is an interesting one. The conceptual origins of section 33(1) are found in earlier arrangements of the role of governments and bills of rights. However, the particular version that emerged in November 1981 and was ultimately enacted in 1982 had more to do with the raw politics of bargaining and chance phone calls late at night than with reasoned debate about what might constitute a rational compromise between democracy and constitutional law. Some may see this as an unacceptable way to write the most fundamental document of Canadian society. It was, as is often the case, the best that could be done at the time.

Whatever the process or motivations in 1981, section 33 is part of the constitution of Canada and has been used by more than one legislature. However, it has been used sparingly, raising questions about the efficacy of the compromise and the continued usefulness of this provision. Some believe that it will become like the power of disallowance – the federal government's power to veto any provincial act – theoretically available but never used.[3] Others argue that as the courts become more active, blurring the lines between the powers of the legislature and the courts, section 33 ought to be used more.

This article traces the origins of section 33, discusses the historic compromise reached in November 1981 from the viewpoint of a participant in the negotiations, and looks at the instances and arguments surrounding its use since 1982. Finally, it comments on the proper role of the judiciary and legislatures in interpreting the Charter of Rights and Freedoms.

THE PHILOSOPHICAL ROOTS OF SECTION 33

Given the controversial nature of section 33, one might expect its origins to be clothed in anonymity. However, there is no shortage of people claiming authorship of both the idea and the specific form of this clause in the existing constitution. Such attention may reflect only the number and zeal of those who seek social prestige and attention in claiming credit for obscure causes. More likely, it reflects the firm and widely held belief that this particular section is not only a good addition to our constitution, but absolutely necessary to the health of Canada's democracy.

It should be pointed out that section 33 is not the only "notwithstanding clause" in the Charter. There is also section 28, which states "Notwithstanding anything in this Charter, the rights and freedoms referred to in it are guaranteed equally to male and female persons." However, section 33 is the only one that deals with the question of whether the courts or the legislatures shall have ultimate authority for a decision regarding the rights and freedoms elaborated under sections 2 and 7–15.

While the origins of this particular clause are fairly recent, debate over it is not. When Hume said "Every man must be supposed to be a knave,"[4] he was expressing the view that because of self-interest, no individual can really be trusted to make decisions about the public good. Thus, Hume concluded: "Good constitutions will not depend on the existence of great private virtues; they will ensure that the private interests of men, even bad men, will be so controlled and directed as to serve and produce the public good."[5]

In short, good government will depend on institutions that provide checks and balances on all decision-makers. Of course, in his era the concern in Europe was not with tyrannical elected officials or party discipline in parliaments, but with monarchs and the heads of churches.

The debate about who should make the final decision on any issue on behalf of the group or society has a long history. The exercise of this power has most often been associated with religious agencies, but secular authorities have often contested the right of churches to arrange "earthly" affairs. This clash continues in many societies in the 21st century, modern Iran being a good example of a state where the religious and secular authorities continue to debate their respective roles.

For countries like Canada with a parliamentary system, the contest between the monarchy and parliament has long been settled. Indeed, the contest between the executive and parliament seems to have shifted to become a contest between the cabinet and the House of Commons, which many believe has been won not only by the cabinet but by the prime minister. Thus, in most parliamentary systems the judiciary has come late to the struggle, and has only recently been armed with written bills of individual rights that give it immense constitutional power.

Although this dimension of the struggle is quite recent in Canada, it is now fully engaged. It rests on the principle that no agency of the state, whether religious or secular, ought to be able to interfere with the individual's right to conduct his or her affairs in certain matters. This kind of prohibition has some parallel in human history, but the force with which it is asserted in modern society can be traced to two principles inherent in the notions of classical liberalism: the rule of law and democracy. The latter ensures that only elected bodies pass constitutional amendments that set the parameters of individual rights. The former restrains the zeal of elected bodies. Together they underwrite the powers inherent in modern constitutions. Patrick Monahan puts it this way: "A country's constitution is the set of fundamental principles that together describe the organizational framework of the state and the nature, the scope of, and the limitations on the exercise of state authority."[6]

Thus, the making of laws may only be undertaken according to law, and not simply at the whim or behest of individuals with private power. Put another way, no one can make law who is not delegated to do so by constitutional arrangement, and no one is above the law.

However, written constitutions with bills of rights are not compatible with the British concept of parliamentary supremacy. In the parliamentary system the definition of rights still resides in a majoritarian body. For those who worry about this kind of concentration of power, bills of rights seem most appealing: "The alternative approach...is to constitutionally entrench certain substantive limits on the manner in which state power can be exercised. We say that rights or norms are *entrenched* [emphasis in original] when they are set out in a fundamental constitutional document that takes precedence over all other laws and that cannot be amended through the ordinary process of law making."[7]

But a constitution is not a body of people. It cannot come to its own defence. Who should determine when there has been a transgression against constitutional values, and who should have the power to remedy such a transgression? In short, who should be the guardian of the constitution, and how will breaches be remedied?

While the answer to this question may seem self-evident today, it was not so in the United States when that country faced this matter in the early nineteenth century. In *Marbury v. Madison* in 1803, the Supreme Court of the United States "read into" the constitution a duty and right on its part to review the constitutionality of laws and actions of the President and Congress. But the elected officials of the time did not accept this unofficial role of the court. They insisted that each branch of the government was co-equal and the sole judge of the constitutionality of its own actions.[8] The precedent of judicial review became firmly entrenched in the United States, however, and was exported to many other countries.

One of the countries that quickly adopted this principle was Canada. In interpreting the *British North America Act*, both the Supreme Court of Canada and the Judicial Committee of the Privy Council had no difficulty in declaring acts of either the Parliament of Canada or the provincial legislatures to be *ultra vires*. Frederick Vaughan has summed it up this way: "[W]hile Canadian courts in the past demonstrated a pattern of judicial deference to the will of the legislature, their role in the division of powers and reference cases did offer some scope for an early judicial activism of sorts. Thus, the judiciary has played an important role in the constitutional life of the country, although in the past it did so anonymously, and judges only rarely met with criticism."[9]

John Whyte, former constitutional adviser to the Saskatchewan government, argues this view even more strongly: "Judicial control over governmental authority and legislative choices is no alien concept for Canada. We are a nation in which past solemn commitments are allowed to work to the disadvantage of current preferences. For instance, perfectly clear legislative preferences about the administration of laws are frequently frustrated by the prior constitutional commitment to separation of powers."[10]

The courts in Canada early and often exercised their authority to be the final arbiter as to whether or not a particular power was federal or provincial in character. However, they lacked the power to set aside actions of Parliament or the legislatures on the basis that they violated fundamental rights or freedoms.

EARLY VARIATIONS OF NOTWITHSTANDING

The concept of notwithstanding began as a legal drafting technique. It was employed to overcome inconsistencies in legislative provisions so that one of the inconsistent provisions would prevail. For example, in sections 91, 94 and 101 of the BNA Act, 1867, there are elements of federal power over matters that would ordinarily be considered provincial, such as the federal power over patents which can infringe on provincial authority over property and civil rights. In the case of section 101, the federal government's power to create a system of courts is a subtraction from the provinces' general power to constitute courts under section 92(14). Thus, the notwithstanding formulation was used to "clarify" which section predominated.

It is not surprising, then, that this concept entered into discussions about the amending formula. The idea that an act or power should continue to exist in one part of Canada, despite the passage of a law or constitutional change that declared it null or void in other parts of the country, first arose in 1935 in discussions about an amending formula for Canada after the passage of the Statute of Westminster. In these discussions in the Continuing Committee on Constitutional Questions, the possibility for provinces to opt out of constitutional amendments that encroached on provincial power was first floated. A 1965 summary of the opting out formula said: "In respect of most matters concerning the federal government and all of the provinces, by an Act of Parliament and the assent by resolution of the legislative assemblies in two-thirds of the provinces representing at least 55 percent of the population of Canada [in relation to matters enumerated in clauses 13 and 16 of section 92]...the legislature of any province...which has not approved...may continue exclusively to make laws in relation to the subject matters coming within such enactment."[11]

Thus, a province could continue to exercise power *notwithstanding* the constitutional change under the general amending formula, either by specific dissent or by inaction. In this regard, the concepts of opting out and notwithstanding are very similar. A law remains valid despite the action of another agency of government that has the power to declare it invalid.

The concept of notwithstanding was brought sharply into focus by the Canadian Bill of Rights, passed in 1960. Space does not permit a full history of the development of rights and their constitutional entrenchment in Canada. Suffice it to say that throughout the twentieth century the concept of constitutionally entrenched rights was vigorously advocated by many, including John Diefenbaker, Tommy Douglas and Pierre Trudeau. During the two decades after the Second World War, there were several unsuccessful attempts to entrench a bill of rights in Canada. The major problem was the need for provincial approval. The provinces were disinclined to accept a charter of rights without resolving the problems of the amending formula and distribution of powers.[12] In 1960 the Diefenbaker government put before Parliament the Canadian Bill of Rights. Its passage marked the first time that comprehensive legislation of this type had been adopted at the federal level.[13]

The Bill of Rights was unique in many respects, but for our purposes section 2 is most important.

Every law of Canada shall, unless expressly declared by an act of the Parliament of Canada that it shall operate notwithstanding the Canadian Bill of Rights, be so construed and applied as not to abrogate, abridge, or infringe...any of the rights or freedoms herein recognized and declared...[14]

This was the first insertion of a notwithstanding or *nonobstante* clause. Its purpose was to ensure that Parliament could still exercise sovereign authority in situations where this sovereignty might be challenged. But despite its addition, some were concerned that Parliament was in danger of losing its sovereignty. Commenting on this, Bora Laskin, later Chief Justice of the Supreme Court of Canada, noted that Parliament was hardly under siege:

There has been some concern that the judicial elevation of the Canadian Bill of Rights to the position of being a statute that can effectively sterilize other federal legislation, has abrogated the doctrine of parliamentary supremacy. In the words of Abbot J., dissenting in *Drybones*..."it necessarily implies a wide delegation of the legislative authority of parliament to the courts."

It may perhaps be stated somewhat differently that the Canadian Bill of Rights provides a prescriptive standard against which all federal legislation past and future must be measured, unless Parliament chooses to avail itself of the exception in s. 2 of the Bill and declare otherwise. Resort has been had to the so called "*nonobstante* clause" only once...but its very existence in what is still, after all, only a federal statute capable of being repealed, is at least some evidence that legislative supremacy in Canada has not as yet been imperilled.[15]

Whatever was said about the use of section 2 of the Bill was ultimately of little consequence. As many authors have noted, judicial interpretation of the Bill was "cautious and restrictive."[16] Since the Bill applied only to federal institutions and the courts were extremely deferential, there was little imperative for Parliament to "declare" a bill under section 2. The real importance of section 2 lay in the precedent that it established for later discussions.

DEVELOPING THE CHARTER OF RIGHTS

Many believe that the attitude of the Supreme Court toward the Canadian Bill of Rights is a major reason for the push toward an entrenched charter of rights. Ian Greene is one of them: "A major impetus for a constitutional charter of rights came from those who were disappointed with how the Supreme Court had interpreted the Bill of Rights. For them, the only solution was the replacement of the legislative supremacy approach under an entrenched charter of rights."[17]

Supporters of a charter of rights received a boost in 1968 with the election of Pierre Trudeau. There is little doubt that without Pierre Trudeau the movement to adopt a charter would have failed. Immediately after becoming Prime Minister in 1968, he initiated the process that resulted in what is now referred to as the Victoria Charter. It was the most extensive process of constitutional review ever undertaken in Canada. The centrepiece of this effort was the entrenchment of a new charter of rights that would include language rights.[18] The result, as we know, was failure to come to an agreement in 1971. However, the development of the texts for an entrenched charter, resulted in what some call a "soft *nonobstante.*" The proposed charter stated:

Nothing in this Part shall be construed as preventing such limitations on the exercise of the fundamental freedoms as are reasonably justifiable in a democratic society in the interests of public safety, order, health or morals, of national security, or the rights or freedoms of others, whether imposed by the Parliament of Canada or the legislature of a province, within the limits of their respective powers, or by the construction or application of any law.[19]

A "soft *nonobstante*" was a direction to the judiciary to be respectful of the need to consider reasonable limits on individual rights in society.[20] It preserved judicial supremacy, while leaving the impression that the courts ought to be extremely deferential to Parliament. There was no "hard *nonobstante*" clause similar to section 2 of the Bill of Rights. It is significant that the negotiators thought that some kind of limit on judicial discretion was needed. No one, apparently, felt that a charter could be entrenched without some safeguard or check on the courts.

FEDERAL-PROVINCIAL
NEGOTIATIONS, 1978–81

Although the Victoria Charter was not adopted, the Trudeau government did not abandon its efforts at constitutional change. These attempts were sporadic until 1976, when the election of the Parti Québécois government in Quebec gave an enormous impetus to finding solutions to the problem of national unity. However, by this time Quebec represented only one of several challenges to national unity, and the entrenchment of a charter of rights was no longer perceived to be paramount. As Roy Romanow said in his book two years after patriation: "The irony of Canada's most recent constitutional agreement [1981] is that it was not, in fact, driven by the modern conception of the state as articulated by Trudeau. On the contrary, the period of constitutional negotiations, which began after 1976, was entirely the product of older, communitarian impulses. It was the convergence of forces brought about by the OPEC oil cartel and the election of the Parti Québécois in Quebec.... The immediate cause of the struggle to produce a new constitution was the conjoining of regional/economic and regional/ethnic forces."[21]

The period 1978–81 was a watershed for many reasons. Of course, the most important issue in 1978 was the impending referendum in Quebec. The Parti Québécois had adopted an official policy of "*étapisme*," a step-by-step progression toward independence. Essential to this policy was the promise to hold a referendum on sovereignty during its first term in office. Only after a "yes" vote in that referendum would the Parti Québécois proceed to negotiate with the rest of Canada on sovereignty with some form of economic association. The PQ was strong, reformist and brimming with confidence.

By contrast, the Liberal federal government was in a period of decline. Trudeau had been Prime Minister for ten years and was widely disliked in parts of Canada. He lacked the political authority that a recent election would have given him. Indeed, the government was in its fourth year and appeared to be avoiding a date with the electorate.

In western Canada the sudden rise in natural resource and grain prices had precipitated an economic boom, unprecedented in the region's history. Enormous amounts of wealth were flowing into the provincial treasuries. In order to "moderate" the flows of capital in Canada and to "protect" consumers from high prices, the Trudeau government had brought in fiscal policies that many in western Canada saw as extremely discriminatory. Western alienation was alive and well during this period.

This new array of regional forces left the federal government with no option but to try and fold all of the elements of constitutional change into one package, including a charter of rights. In June 1978 the federal government tabled Bill C-60, a comprehensive package of constitutional proposals that included an entrenched charter of rights. The procedure for adoption was incremental, with the charter to apply first to the federal government and any provinces that chose to adopt it. Bill C-60 contained the "soft *nonobstante*" of the Victoria Charter. There was no notwithstanding clause.

In August 1978 the provincial governments responded by offering to negotiate an entire package of constitutional changes. The details of these negotiations are well documented.[22] In order to deal with the large number of issues, the first ministers struck a committee of ministers called the Continuing Committee of Ministers on the Constitution (CCMC). It was co-chaired in 1978–79 by Roy Romanow, Minister of Intergovernmental Affairs and Attorney General of Saskatchewan at the time, and Marc Lalonde, representing the federal government. Of the fourteen items to be discussed by the CCMC, three dominated the negotiations. They were patriation with an amending formula, a charter of rights with language rights, and natural resources. Eventually, these three items came to form the essential trade-off for agreement in 1981.

The CCMC met three times in late 1978 and early 1979. The charter of rights put forward by the federal government at the first meeting was the charter contained in Bill C-60. Throughout the negotiations the participants took the position that nothing was agreed to until everything was agreed to. Thus, the negotiations on any particular item were always conducted with an eye to progress on other items.

On the matter of an entrenched charter, the choices had been narrowed realistically to three options. These were a full charter (fundamental, democratic, legal, mobility and equality rights) with a "soft *nonobstante*" clause, a limited charter (fundamental and democratic rights) with no *nonobstante* clause, or a full charter with a hard notwithstanding clause. However, some governments, like that of Manitoba under Sterling Lyon, were adamantly opposed to any entrenched charter with or without a *nonobstante* clause, a position that they maintained throughout. Lyon, a traditional conservative, believed fervently in parliamentary supremacy. Saskatchewan, headed by New Democrat Allan Blakeney, also opposed the entrenchment of a charter. Blakeney believed in legislative supremacy too, but for reasons that were exactly the opposite of Lyon's. He believed that the courts were essentially the most conservative institutions in society and would use a charter to block the expansion of social entitlements. His government was willing to accept a charter with a *nonobstante* clause and entrenched language rights. He agreed with the latter as part of the "confederation bargain." By contrast, several provinces, New Brunswick for example, were enthusiastic supporters of entrenched rights. Finally, a third group of provinces was ranged between these two views, some arguing for a limited charter and others withholding their support pending the outcome of other items on the agenda.

The concept of a *nonobstante* clause had not been discussed for ten years. The Trudeau government, while opposed to it in principle, agreed to consider it in 1978. Briefing notes from Saskatchewan had the following to say:

Several provinces were opposed to an entrenched Charter of Rights although there was an indication that entrenchment would be acceptable provided that an appropriate override clause were included.

The federal government suggested that such a clause could be made optional. Most provinces did not favour this. The federal government was clearly anxious that there be some progress toward the adoption of a Charter.[23]

By the time the first ministers met in February 1979 there had been some shifts amongst the provinces. Two important things had happened. First, many of the provinces had agreed to entrench a limited charter, i.e., one dealing with fundamental freedoms, democratic rights, and language rights. They only agreed to the latter if appropriate safeguards could be worked out. A Saskatchewan briefing note confirms this:

Most provinces seem to be prepared to accept the entrenchment of fundamental freedoms (speech, religion, association), democratic rights (universal suffrage, 5 year parliaments, annual sessions) and language rights (the nature and extent of which would have to be carefully considered) if the federal government will defer the remaining portions of its proposed Charter...for consideration in a later stage of constitutional discussions.

The feds [*sic*] are attracted by the possibility of a deal along these lines, but would rather inscribe the entire Charter in the revised constitutional bill, and allow provinces to opt into remaining portions as and when they see fit.[24]

The federal government agreed to the possibility of opting in at various times to some sort of charter of rights, a sort of smorgasbord approach, and, surprisingly, it agreed to consider the insertion of an override or *nonobstante* clause.[25] The notwithstanding clause would apply to legal, nondiscrimination, and mobility rights. In addition the "soft *nonobstante*" clause would remain, that is, the "reasonable and prescribed by law" clause.

At the First Ministers' meeting in February of 1979, the matter of the charter was discussed both privately and publicly. When the Prime Minister called for positions, the provinces were split on the various portions of the charter. All but Manitoba agreed to entrench fundamental and democratic rights.[26] (This is remarkable, given the disagreement at the CCMC discussions in December.) No province indicated that these should be subject to a *nonobstante* provision. (This is quite different from 1981, as we will see) On other parts of the charter the first ministers were split, with only five supporting entrenchment of language rights and most opposing the entrenchment of legal and nondiscrimination rights.[27]

That no agreement resulted from the FMC did not surprise most observers at the time. The fact that the Parti Québécois government was unlikely to agree to anything prior to its referendum, the lack of agreement on sharing oil revenues, and the length of the list of items up for negotiation all militated against any agreement. As noted by some participants, the political climate and timing were all wrong: "Finally, although the governments generally endeavoured to submerge their political and ideological differences while engaged in federal-provincial discussions at the CCMC level, by February, 1979, with a general election only weeks away and the defeat of the Trudeau government looming as an increasingly important political event, the policy of non-partisanship evaporated."[28]

As we know, the political climate did change. In the spring of 1979 the Liberals were defeated by the Conservatives under Joe Clark, who formed a minority government. This government only lasted nine months. In February 1980 the Liberals, once again led by Pierre Trudeau, were returned with a majority government.[29]

THE PATRIATION OF THE CONSTITUTION

The turbulent political events of 1980 and 1981 mark a significant watershed in the history of Canada. It was an extraordinary time. In Quebec, the federal Liberals were returned with almost every seat, the first referendum on sovereignty was held and defeated, the Parti Québécois was re-elected in 1981, and patriation of the constitution was agreed to over the objections of the Quebec legislature. In BC, Alberta and Saskatchewan, no MPs from the governing party were elected, the National Energy Policy was met with a firestorm of protest that led to reductions in oil deliveries to eastern Canada, and separatist parties were founded. In the end, however, the western provinces signed an energy pricing deal and agreed to the constitutional package negotiated in November 1981.

It is difficult to overestimate the impact of the conjunction of these events. By the summer of 1980 the political situation of 1979 had effectively been reversed, and this was crucial to the patriation efforts. It was now the Trudeau Liberals who had successfully defeated the Parti Québécois in a referendum in Quebec and who had a new majority mandate, while the Parti Québécois had lost the referendum and were clinging to power in their fifth year. To use sports parlance, momentum was on the Liberal side. As we now know, the Prime Minister had decided to proceed with patriation and a charter, even if it meant acting unilaterally.

The process proposed by the federal government in June of 1980 was not new. The reconstituted CCMC, now co-chaired by Jean Chrétien and Roy Romanow, would meet through the summer and present their best efforts at a First Ministers' Conference in the fall. Trudeau made it abundantly clear that he was prepared to proceed with or without the provinces. In the subcommittee studying the charter of rights, ministers and officials started from familiar proposals. Indeed, although they laboured mightily throughout the summer, little had changed. The federal charter looked much like C-60 and the proposals of the 1979 First Ministers' Conference.

There was discussion of the *nonobstante* clause, initiated mainly by Saskatchewan, but the federal officials and ministers did not even agree to consider it. This was quite different from the negotiations in 1979, when the federal government agreed to its inclusion and use in regard to judicial and nondiscrimination rights. As they were fond of saying that summer, "That was then and this is now."

In the leaked strategy document developed by the federal government for the First Ministers' Conference in September 1980, dubbed the "Kirby memorandum" after the official who had drafted it,[30] the legislative override clause is referred to as follows:

Federal officials raised doubts respecting the necessity for an override clause but suggested that if there should be one, it should be restricted by requirements that any law enacted under an override provision be adopted by a 60 percent majority of the legislative body and expire after a specified time (e.g., 5 years).[31]

Later in the document, the federal government outlined its preferences. These did not include the notwithstanding clause.

As we know, the First Ministers' Conference of September 1981 failed to produce an agreement and the federal government proceeded unilaterally with a package of proposals that included a charter of rights but no *nonobstante* clause. It did not surface again until November 1981, when, after the Supreme Court decision in September declaring the

federal action unconstitutional in the conventional sense, the first ministers assembled in Ottawa for one last attempt to secure agreement on a
package.[32]

In the raw bargaining of the First Ministers' Conference between
November 2 and 5, 1981, it became apparent that if there was to be
an agreement there would have to be a charter with language rights
that was acceptable to the federal government, an amending formula that was acceptable to the provinces, and "something" on natural resources. Within each of these sections there would also have to
be provisions to make it more palatable to the party being forced to
compromise. Thus, within the natural resources section the federal
government retained considerable control. Within the amending
formula several provisions mitigated the original formula put forward by Alberta.[33] Within the charter, the notwithstanding clause
was reintroduced.

At the beginning of the conference there was pessimism about the
ability of the participants to overcome the negative influences of the
previous year. Harsh words and entrenched positions had become the
order of the day. Indeed, it was widely believed that both Prime Minister Trudeau and Premier Lévesque would have preferred to see the
conference fail in order to continue their respective fights.[34] Not surprisingly, many of the objections to an entrenched charter of rights remained unchanged. Manitoba was unprepared to accept any
entrenched charter, while several provinces wanted an override clause
for some sections.

Most of the conference was *in camera* with no minutes. Our knowledge of what went on is limited to the personal notes of those of us
who were there. It is fair to say that most of the discussion surrounded
the amending formula, but there was a fair amount on the charter.
Generally, everyone knew that one part of an agreement depended on
progress in another area. Real bargaining began on the second day
and was most intense on the Wednesday afternoon. At that point, the
Prime Minister and the Premiers of Alberta and Saskatchewan had an
exchange on the integration of the amending formula with a charter
that had a notwithstanding clause. Trudeau attempted to point out
what he considered a logical inconsistency in Blakeney's position, that
is between his argument to make the charter more flexible with a notwithstanding formula and his support for a fairly rigid amending formula. As well, Trudeau obviously thought that the combination of the
opting out portion in the amending formula and the notwithstanding
clause in the charter was too much. The following are excerpts from
that discussion:

Blakeney: As to *nonobstante* [for the charter] I think that is a long way ahead –
it would be a long step forward and would gain some support.

Trudeau: I think that we would quickly find objectors. My view is that if you
have a notwithstanding in the part on Education, you have *nonobstante* and opt
out. You get us coming and going.

Lougheed: But opting out has to do with jurisdiction and being able to do
something that others want but we don't. *Nonobstante* is different.[35]

The rest of the afternoon did not go well. The first ministers agreed
to break until the morning, at which point they would resume in public, presumably to report failure.

As we know, during the night a series of negotiations took place that
eventually resulted in the package of proposals that became the patriation package. These negotiations on the night of November 4, 1981
did not include the Premiers of Quebec and Manitoba. Both were considered unlikely to agree to a package, the former because of Quebec's
stand on sovereignty and the latter because of his inflexibility on an
entrenched charter of rights. In anticipation of a conference failure,
the Premier of Manitoba had already returned the previous day to
campaign in the provincial election. Officials, ministers and some of
the other Premiers met and spoke on the phone during the night.
They managed to put together a compromise package.[36]

In effect, the provinces traded the amending formula for the charter.
There were already some changes to the charter that had been accepted
in Parliament in the unilateral action period in 1981; the major change
of the November 1981 First Ministers' Conference was the inclusion of a
notwithstanding clause, section 33. This was a *sine qua non* for most of the
provinces that had opposed Trudeau. The matter of its ambit was unde-
termined, however. In the original draft of a compromise document,
both Saskatchewan and Newfoundland restricted its application to sections 7–15, legal and nondiscrimination rights. This was consistent with
the proposals of the previous three years. Alberta insisted, however, that it
apply as well to section 2 pertaining to fundamental rights and freedoms.
The others agreed. This proposal was communicated to Ontario, and
through them to the federal government. At 3:00 a.m. on November 5,
1981, members of the Ontario delegation contacted the author to determine whether or not Alberta was firm in the application of the notwithstanding clause to fundamental rights and freedoms. I indicated that I
thought that they were and that it would have to stay. Jean Chrétien and
the federal delegation were furious at this.[37]

At the private meeting of first ministers the next day, the subject of the *nonobstante* clause was one of three important issues. Trudeau tried to raise the legislative majority required to opt out, a time limit on the *nonobstante* clause and a First Ministers Conference on aboriginal rights:

Trudeau: I'll tell you my opinion. I deeply feel that it is a mistake not to be able to go to the people. But I'm prepared to swallow too. [On the opting out] I put a suggestion to you. When it was considered by you, [earlier in 1981] you considered a two-thirds vote [in the legislature] but it's a bit late in the day. [On notwithstanding] Let's give it the test of time. A compromise came to me. I propose a compromise to you. That the *nonobstante* have a five-year sunset clause. I don't think that we can drop aboriginal rights out completely. My suggestion. Put in a First Ministers Conference for the future.[38]

All these suggestions were accepted by the nine provinces that had agreed to the morning's proposals. Quebec refused to agree to the package. The inclusion of a notwithstanding clause in the charter of rights had become a reality.

REACTION AND FURTHER CHANGES

The first ministers knew that the original accord was a fragile deal. Indeed, at the end of the private session Trudeau held up the copy signed by the nine premiers and said, "I better take this and run." They had agreed on two key issues: first, that the legal drafting should take place immediately, and second, that no substantive changes would be made to the accord without the agreement of all. The latter point became important when women's and Aboriginal groups reacted strongly against the accord. Aboriginal groups were outraged that a section dealing with Aboriginal rights had been taken out at British Columbia's insistence. They demanded that it be reinstated. Women's groups reacted strongly against the ambit of the notwithstanding clause. Chaviva Hosek, Vice-President of the National Action Committee on the Status of Women at the time, outlined this reaction:

The fears [of women's groups] were justified. In the final desperate negotiations to achieve substantial agreement between the federal and provincial governments, women's interests were sacrificed, almost by neglect.... Confusion reigned. The Accord was reached on November 5. But when the Prime Minister was asked in the House of Commons whether section 28 would be subject to the override, he was unable to answer. It was not until November 9 that he made clear that it was. Women's groups were appalled.[39]

As already discussed, section 28 is a "directional clause" that states "notwithstanding anything in this charter, the rights and freedoms referred to in it are guaranteed equally to male and female persons." The question raised after November 5, 1981 was whether or not section 28 would be subject to section 33. The reason for the delay in the Prime Minister's response was simply that no one had considered section 28. It was not, as Hosek stated, that women were unimportant, but that all attention had been concentrated on sections 2 and 7–15. The dispute arose when it became clear to the legal drafters that it would be necessary to determine the interaction of these clauses. The Saskatchewan government believed that section 28 as it stood could endanger affirmative action programs. Others, including the federal government, dismissed these fears. The Premier of Saskatchewan was unfairly branded as being "against women." Given the government's legislative record on women's issues, this was patently absurd.

The matter was further complicated by the Saskatchewan position that if the "deal" of November 5 was re-opened to change section 28, Saskatchewan would insist on the reinstatement of the provisions on Aboriginal rights. This caused concern in Alberta and British Columbia. Eventually both demands, that section 28 remain as it had been before the November 5 draft and that Aboriginal rights be reinstated, were acceded to. As Hosek said in 1983, "the power of section 28 in relation to other sections is not clear..."[40]

USE OF SECTION 33 AFTER 1982

Given the ferocity of the debate about the inclusion of a *nonobstante* clause, one might have expected its use to be frequent and controversial after the proclamation of the Charter of Rights and Freedoms in 1982. Such has not been the case. It has only been used by two legislatures, Quebec and Saskatchewan. Not unexpectedly, the use of section 33 by the Quebec legislature was controversial. In 1982 the Parti Québécois government secured passage of Bill 62 in the legislature, which added a standard notwithstanding clause to each of the statutes in force in the province. As well, it became standard practice to add the clause to each new bill. This use of section 33 was in protest against the fact that Quebec had not agreed to the constitution in 1981. The practice continued until 1985, when the new Quebec Liberal government discontinued it. This blanket use was challenged in court on several grounds. The Quebec Court of Appeal struck down this use of section 33, but its decision was reversed by the Supreme Court of Canada.[41]

The Liberal government of Quebec used section 33 on five different occasions. Four appear to have been uncontroversial.[42] The fifth, in

1988, was extremely controversial. In that year the Supreme Court of Canada struck down a portion of Bill 101, Quebec's language law, which dealt with the use of languages other than French on commercial signs.[43] In effect, the court said that the law in question was an infringement of the Charter right to freedom of expression. A majority of francophone Quebecers still felt that this portion of Bill 101 was necessary to protect the French language in the province. The Liberal government was forced to respond by reinstating the portion of the law dealing with exterior signs, using section 33 to exempt it from the Charter.

While this action was popular in Quebec, the use of the notwithstanding clause in this manner provoked a negative reaction in the rest of Canada. Many believe that this action was mainly responsible for the defeat of the Meech Lake Accord, because it allowed some provincial governments (Manitoba in particular) to procrastinate and build opposition to the agreement.

The Prime Minister at the time, Brian Mulroney, made it quite clear that he believed section 33 was both unacceptable and a mistake. In a speech to the House of Commons in 1989 he said: "The framers of the flawed Constitution Act of 1982 inserted the notwithstanding clause which limits our most fundamental freedoms...never before nor since in our history has a Prime Minister of Canada made a concession of such magnitude and importance. Never before has the surrender of rights been so total and abject."[44]

After the defeat of Meech Lake, the Mulroney government made some half-hearted efforts at seeking the repeal or modification of the clause, but they came to nothing.

The use of section 33 in Saskatchewan was less spectacular, but equally controversial in the province. The specific case involved a labour dispute between the government of Saskatchewan and its workers, represented by the Saskatchewan Government Employees' Union (SGEU). In the fall of 1985, in an attempt to put pressure on the government, the SGEU had commenced rotating strikes. In January a mediator released a report, which the union rejected. The government of Premier Grant Devine decided to end the dispute by legislation. On January 30, 1986, it recalled the legislature and introduced Bill 144, an act that forced the union back to work and provided the terms of a new collective agreement. The act was remarkable in one respect: it contained a clause exempting it from the Charter of Rights and Freedoms.[45]

The reason for doing so was rooted in a 1984 court decision, in which another piece of labour legislation had been struck down. That legislation had ordered the dairy workers in the province back to work, but had been struck down by the Saskatchewan Court of Appeal on the basis that it infringed on freedom of association as guaranteed in the Charter.[46] (Eventually the Supreme Court reversed this decision.)

The addition of the notwithstanding clause was challenged on several bases, but one in particular was novel. It was the first time outside Quebec that the notwithstanding clause had been used prospectively, that is, not in response to a court decision, but in anticipation of it. Interestingly, many who had agreed with the insertion of a *nonobstante* clause in 1981 had not anticipated that it would be used to "bullet-proof" legislation. As we know, the use of the clause in this way is not prohibited, and one can anticipate that it might be used this way again in the future.

These are the only actual uses of the notwithstanding clause since 1982. It has been 12 years since Quebec used it. As we will see in the following discussion, its use has been urged many times and has even been publicly contemplated by the Premier of Alberta, but to no avail.

POST-PATRIATION ARGUMENTS ABOUT
SECTION 33

Arguments about section 33 inevitably involve rights and the best way to protect them. That is, everyone is in favour of rights, no one is against them. Thus, when reduced to its essence, the debate raises two basic questions: what should be considered a right, and which institution can best protect those rights, the courts or the legislatures? Left out of the equation for the most part is any suggestion that rights ought not to be protected, that is, that certain social attitudes and practices should not be placed in a special category when it comes to political claims in our society. Those who argue against entrenched charters do so from the perspective that the list of rights ought to be very limited, and that these rights are better protected by legislatures. In particular, they reject "expanded" charters as devices designed to raise the profile of what are really only political claims. What we are left with they argue, when you have an expanded charter, is a process that looks suspiciously like the political process except that some matters are now of a "higher order" and get priority. More will be said about this later.

Most of the arguments about section 33 are set out in two articles, one by John Whyte and the other by Peter Russell, both published by the *Alberta Law Review*, in 1990 and 1991, respectively.[47] Whyte vigorously attacks the insertion of the clause, despite the ironic fact that he was the chief constitutional advisor to Premier Allan Blakeney at the time of the adoption of the clause in 1981.[48] Whyte quite forcefully rejects the argument that justifications for section 33 can be found in Canadian constitutional principle, opting instead for a more relativist foundation anchored in social policy needs: "In my view these attempts to locate a justification for the override procedure in Canadian constitutional theory are wrong for two reasons. First, the principles at work in the design of the Canadian state support not allowing any legislative exemptions from court enforced rights at least as powerfully as they support including such a power in the constitution. Second, arguments rooted in constitutional principle distract us from enquiry into the actual social goods and bads that are likely produced by the practice of exercising the legislative power to override Charter rights. In short, this sort of debate keeps us from choosing a policy that is good because it reflects the actual aspirations of the community."[49]

Whyte goes on to outline these arguments in detail, citing the three constitutional principles which, he says, have been used to argue for a *nonobstante* clause. These are legalism, democracy and federalism. He argues that the rule of law is a widely accepted principle whose ultimate expression is constitutionalism. Constitutionalism is "[the] process by which political expressions from one age can bind future ages unless equally formal political processes are mustered to remove the constitutional constraint. In short, Canadian constitutionalism is not in thrall to the idea that populations are free to determine their own best interests from moment to moment. Judicial control over governmental authority and legislative choices is no alien concept to Canada."[50]

He also points out that courts have more often than not been entrusted with the ultimate right to adjudicate constitutional arguments in Canada.

In dealing with the argument that charters erode majoritarian control, he expresses the view, albeit somewhat weakly, that democracy is not solely about majorities. Indeed, he proposes a more profound concept of democracy that includes political participation, equality, autonomy and personal liberty. He goes on to say that "the point that needs to be made is that the democratic principle provides a powerful pedigree for judicial control over political choices that erode some fundamental human rights."[51] He also dismisses arguments based on federalism, largely because of the idea that the courts have been heavily involved in making final decisions that bind parliaments.

Whyte's argument rests primarily on the assumption that the judiciary is not as subject as Parliament or a legislature to political whim, that it is a more trustworthy agency when dealing with individual rights: "The primary reason for wishing to do away with the override clause is that the anxiety that produced the political demand for entrenched rights cannot be rationally calmed in the face of the legislative power granted by section 33. That anxiety is simply this: political authority will, at some point, be exercised oppressively; that is, it will be exercised to impose very serious burdens on groups of people when there is no rational justification for doing so."[52]

He goes on to list examples of this oppression, many of which are familiar.

In answering the challenge, Peter Russell avoids wholehearted support for the *nonobstante* clause. Indeed, he has been criticized by some for being so lukewarm that he does more damage than detractors do.[53] However, in examining the substance of the arguments, while rejecting what he calls Whyte's "disdain for democracy," he correctly defines the main issue as the choice between judicial and legislative supremacy, and concludes that Whyte is wrong. Russell argues strongly that legislative and judicial supremacy are both wrong. In effect, he seeks the middle ground between those who see no role for the legislature in defining and enforcing rights and those who abhor entrenched charters for detracting from parliamentary sovereignty: "In a nutshell, the argument about the substance of decision-making is as follows. Judges are not infallible. They make decisions about the limits and nature of rights and freedoms which are extremely questionable. There should be some process, more reasoned than court packing and more accessible than constitutional amendment, through which the justice and wisdom of these decisions can be publicly discussed and possibly rejected. A legislative override clause provides such a process."[54]

He goes on to enlarge on this argument and provide examples. Finally, he concludes: "Are the judiciary and the judicial process so inherently superior to the legislature and the processes of ordinary politics that we are justified in running these risks? Professor Whyte apparently thinks they are....I would submit that judicial review of legislation under the Charter, in turn, has its own limitations and blind spots. Judges often fail to take into account, and indeed sometimes are exposed to the scantiest submissions on, the relationship of challenged law to its total social or political context."[55]

In effect, Russell is arguing for a "common sense" policy of sober second thought, allowing each branch of government to correct the deficiencies in the work of the other.

There are others who take stronger positions on both sides, but they add little except heat to the debate. There is one exception. In a 1983 article, Donald Smiley raises some interesting questions about patriation. He examines the Charter of Rights and Freedoms and is critical of both supporters and opponents of the Charter. He rejects as "indefensible" the argument by Lyon and others that entrenchment of the Charter was a renunciation of our monarchical and parliamentary traditions. He also ridicules the argument that rights have now been fully guaranteed through entrenchment. He indicates that a better name for the Charter would be "A Constitutional Enactment for the Better Protection of Certain Rights and Freedoms in Canada."[56] His most trenchant argument surrounds the types and numbers of rights that have been entrenched:

Because of their traditions and experience, judges may be assumed to have some capacity for wisdom in ranking the competing claims of individual freedom and effective law enforcement. There is less reason to believe that judicial procedures will be an effective means of resolving intricate questions of social policy involving for example, "equality rights," the native peoples, and the official language provisions. *The fault of the process by which the Charter came into effect was not that it resulted in entrenchment per se, but rather the indiscriminate entrenchment of a large number of individual and group claims without sufficient discussion of the expected impact of constitutional recognition on particular kinds of rights or the political culture more broadly* [emphasis added].[57]

Thus, he questions not only the ability of the courts to handle complex social issues, as does Russell, but also the wisdom of entrenching so many new rights without consideration of how they will be reconciled without social confusion or upheaval. Unresolved in his mind is the matter of the *nonobstante* clause.

As we can see, arguments about section 33 have more to do with assumptions than practice, with personal judgement and deference than evidence.

SECTION 33 – A PAPER TIGER?

Whatever the expectations of those who supported or opposed the inclusion of section 33 in the Constitution Act, it is probably fair to say that no one could have predicted the lack of enthusiasm shown by Parliament and the provincial legislatures for its use. As noted above, it has only been used in two provinces, and it has never been used by Parliament. This is not because of a lack of controversy surrounding some of the decisions by the Supreme Court.

How can we explain what has not happened? One way would be to say that legislatures are being deferential to the courts in their new role, that they understand and accept the new relationship between the two institutions, a relationship in which the courts have the lead in matters relating to rights. This is unlikely. As Peter Russell points out, legislatures have not exactly been deferential in the past, and there is no evidence to suggest that this attitude has changed. That is, one cannot point to a series of debates in Parliament or the legislatures centred on this issue in which the houses came to the conclusion that they needed to accept a new role.

However, it is possible that attitudes toward the courts are being shaped in a more subtle way. In most matters, legislatures are subject to tight party discipline. This restricts the ability of members to express a legislative view on judicial decisions, apart from the view expressed by the executive branch of government. Recommendations on how to respond to court decisions come from ministers of justice on the advice of government lawyers. It is part of the system and culture that these officials are used to being deferential to courts and inclined to see their own future career options in that field. It is quite possible that this has an impact on decisions about the use of section 33.

Another explanation might lie in public perceptions. That is, judges are held in much higher esteem than legislators, who are viewed as "politicians." Recent polls indicate that the public not only rejects the idea that judges have too much power, they actually believe that judges should have more power.[58] Thus, in any fight between the two branches the legislators are unlikely to win. While this may seem plausible and have some impact on a decision about the use of section 33, it is probably not the major variable involved. Any fight between the two branches would involve a specific case or issue, which usually focuses the dispute away from the legitimacy of the protagonists. Put another way, being on the "right side" of the issue is more important than who you are in most cases.

A third explanation is that the use of section 33 might cause such a public outcry that legislators are afraid to use it. Again, this seems like an attractive explanation. Amongst the "chattering classes" there is substantial opposition to the very existence of section 33. Surely legislators would be reluctant to incur public wrath for its use. Again, however, the evidence is at best mixed in this regard. When section 33 was used in Quebec, public opinion was either favourable or neutral. Most of the informed public inside Quebec was also supportive. Outside the province opinion was generally opposed, but it made little difference. By contrast, in Saskatchewan in 1986 most of the informed opinion was fiercely opposed to the way that section 33 was used. The general public seemed apathetic. The government proceeded in spite of the opposition of the "chattering classes."

In Alberta section 33 was not actually used, but it was contemplated. In the *Vriend* case,[59] the Supreme Court "read in" a new section to Alberta human rights legislation protecting individuals from discrimination based on sexual orientation. The government of Alberta briefly considered using section 33 to exempt the legislation from the court decision, but decided not to do so. This was not because the legislature would have demurred. There was some political pressure not to use the clause, both from inside and outside the province, but there was also pressure in favour of its use. The consensus in the media seems to be that negative pressure caused the government to back down, but we have no way of really knowing this.

A better case for the use of section 33, one where public opinion seemed to be strongly behind government policy, involved the Supreme Court decision on tobacco advertising. In 1995 the Supreme Court held that the Tobacco Products Control Act violated section 2 of the Charter, because it forbade the advertising of tobacco products.[60] The court held that a total ban was too drastic, and indicated that a "targeted" ban might be acceptable.[61] The decision caused a political furor because there was considerable social support for the control of this deadly product. The government responded by deferring to the court and redrafting legislation. Janet Hiebert is right to state that the Court's decision was flawed: "The Charter, like other bills of rights, was intended to protect citizens and other human members of the polity. Thus, the Court's elevation of a corporate economic interest to the same status as individuals' constitutional rights, and its protection of that interest, are ill-conceived."[62]

This was hardly a case of an embattled minority needing court protection for its right to free speech. These were wealthy and powerful corporations using the courts to accomplish a commercial objective that they could not accomplish through the political process. The Parliament of Canada ought to have used the notwithstanding clause, if for no other reason than to buy time to sort out its legal situation. But despite many calls for its use, and powerful public support, the government decided to defer to the court.[63]

It is not clear that public opinion was a determining factor in the cases we have studied.

Three other explanations for the reluctance to invoke the notwithstanding clause need to be considered. The first is the "nuclear bomb" theory. That is, that the use of section 33 would be considered in most cases to be radical overkill, the equivalent of dropping the nuclear bomb in a war. There are other, less costly ways for legislatures to achieve their objectives. This may be a consideration, but only in marginal cases. Another explanation is that the use of section 33 is not a long-term solution to a problem involving a court decision on a Charter right, since the problem will return again in five years. This might be a small consideration, but it would not explain the federal government's reluctance in the case of the tobacco advertising decision. Finally, it could also be argued that in most cases the courts have been on the right track and that there has been no need for greater use of section 33. This is an interesting argument, which may in general be true. However, there are far too many specific cases where it could have been used for us to conclude that courts have been near perfect.

Since no single explanation seems powerful enough to fit each case, we are left with the rather weak conclusion that it is a combination of all of the above (and perhaps others not mentioned here), and that further study is needed to refine possible explanations.

If the legislatures have been reluctant to use section 33, the courts have not been reluctant to expand their role. Indeed, in the last decade they have been aggressive in enlarging their role and increasing their power in many respects. Courts seem inclined to go beyond what had been the established boundaries between the legislature and the judiciary.[64] They follow a pattern set by the Supreme Court itself. The most flagrant example of judicial expansion came in the so-called "Judges' Pay" decision.[65] In this judgement the Supreme Court rendered a decision involving remuneration schemes for provincial court judges in four provinces. The provincial judges had asked that various statutes freezing or reducing their remuneration be declared unconstitutional on the basis that they violated the independence of the judiciary.

In summary, the Supreme Court ruled, Justice La Forest G. dissenting, that the actions and statutes involved were unconstitutional. Some of the pronouncements in the judgement are breathtaking in their ambit. Not only did the Court strike down pay decisions, it went on to prescribe how such matters must be handled in the future:

However, to avoid the possibility of, or the appearance of, political interference through economic manipulation, a body, such as a commission, must be interposed between the judiciary and other branches of government. The constitutional function of this body would be to depoliticize [sic] the process of determining changes to or freezes in judicial remuneration.[66]

There is no constitutional basis for this type of body, nor any authority for the court to create it. The Court simply "read in" a constitutional amendment creating commissions. The decision goes on to say, "*Any changes to or freezes in judicial remuneration made without prior recourse to the body are unconstitutional* [emphasis added]."[67]

The Court based its judgement on the Preamble to the Constitution Act of 1867, and section 11(d) of the Charter. In his dissent, Justice La Forest G. disagreed with the majority on their interpretation of the preamble and with their conclusion that commissions are somehow mandated by section 11(d) of the Charter: "Judicial independence must include protection against interference with the financial security of the court as an institution. However the possibility of economic manipulation arising from changes to judges salaries as a class does not justify the imposition of judicial compensation commissions as a constitutional imperative."[68]

Several things are noteworthy about this case. First, there is no apparent recognition by the court that it was in a conflict of interest. In the case of members of the legislatures, although they are allowed to set their own remuneration levels, members are subject to election within five years. Nor are there constitutional provisions that ensure that pay levels for members will not be reduced. That the court decided this matter as it did, without recognizing a conflict, is unacceptable. Second, the judicial scholarship involved in asserting that the Preamble to the Constitution Act of 1867 contemplates judicial independence of the type asserted in this judgement is questionable, to say the least.[69] Finally, while judges may incidentally "fill in the gaps" in the constitution through the extension of principles, this decision does much more. It actually creates new institutions. The issue here, however, is that none of the legislatures involved contemplated using the notwithstanding clause in this case. It should have at least been discussed, since the case turned in part on section 11(d).

CONCLUSIONS

Three important conclusions can be drawn from this discussion. The first is that section 33 now appears to be a paper tiger. It may become the equivalent of the powers of reservation and disallowance, available in theory, but not used in practice. This is, in part, due to the reasons argued above. It is also true that the less it is used, the less likely that it will be used.

Second, as anticipated by Professor Smiley, the courts have wandered deeply into social decisions that they are ill-equipped to address.

Although they did not ask for this power, they must be restrained in their use of it.

Section 33 is not the instrument to correct this problem in the long run. It is at best a temporary stopgap to enable more dialogue. But it should not be abandoned.

Finally, given the power of the courts, we must think more about reform of the judiciary. This has to include appointment procedures, tenure, and the relationship between the courts and legislatures. If nothing is done, the observation by American jurist Charles Evan Hughes that "we are under a constitution, but the constitution is what the judges say it is" will be true.

NOTES

1 Peter Russell, *Constitutional Odyssey*, 2nd ed. (Toronto: University of Toronto Press, 1993), p. 6.
2 Donna Greshner and Ken Norman, "The Courts and Section 33," *Queen's Law Journal*, Vol. 12, no.2 (1987), p. 163.
3 Sir John A. Macdonald thought that the power of disallowance was crucial for ensuring the supremacy of the federal government, but it has not been used since 1938.
4 Quoted in Leo Straus and Joseph Cropsey, *History of Political Philosophy*, 2nd ed. (Chicago: University of Chicago Press, 1973), p. 526.
5 Straus and Cropsey, *History of Political Philosophy*, p. 526.
6 Patrick J. Monahan, *Constitutional Law* (Toronto: Irwin Law, 1997) p. 3.
7 Monahan, *Constitutional Law*, p. 5.
8 This is an interesting point, not only in the current context, but because it raises the question of who watches the watchers. That is, if the Supreme Court of Canada reviews all actions of the executive and legislative branches, who reviews the actions of the courts? The answer is, at present, the Court itself, which is unacceptable to many. It would be interesting to see what would happen if a House of Commons committee attempted to review and declare particular actions of the court unconstitutional.
9 Frederick Vaughan, "Judicial Politics in Canada: Patterns and Trends," *Choices*, Vol. 5, no. 1 (June 1999), p. 9. This essay is reproduced in this collection.
10 John D. Whyte, "On Not Standing For Nothwithstanding," *Alberta Law Review*, Vol. 28, no. 2 (1990), p. 351.
11 Honourable Guy Favreau, Minister of Justice, *The Amendment of the Constitution of Canada* (Queen's Printer, 1965), p. 22. This is an interesting proposal in light of the recent discussion about proper majorities in the

Clarity Bill introduced in 1999. The figure of 55 percent appears to have some historical precedent.

12 For a full discussion of this matter, see Peter Hogg, *Constitutional Law of Canada* (Toronto: Carswell, 1997), pp. 605–17.

13 Several provinces, for example Saskatchewan, passed bills of rights as early as 1947.

14 As quoted in Bora Laskin, *Canadian Constitutional Law* (Toronto: Carswell, 1975), pp. 946.1–946.2.

15 Laskin, *Canadian Constitutional Law,* pp. 900.31–900.32.

16 Gerald A. Beaudoin and Ed Ratushny, *The Canadian Charter of Rights and Freedoms,* 2nd ed. (Toronto: Carswell, 1989), p. 58.

17 Ian Greene, *The Charter of Rights* (Toronto: James Lorimer & Co., 1989), p. 33.

18 There are many good descriptions of this three-year effort. Donald Smiley, in *Canada in Question,* 2nd ed. (Toronto: McGraw-Hill Ryerson, 1976), summarizes the effort quite well in chapter 2. He notes that the federal government was uneasy about broadening the process beyond patriation, an amending formula, and a charter of rights, but finally agreed to discuss institutions and the division of powers in stages two and three.

19 As quoted in Smiley, *Canada in Question,* p. 76.

20 A variation of this became section 1 of the Charter of Rights in 1981.

21 Roy Romanow, John Whyte, and Howard Leeson, *Canada Notwithstanding* (Toronto: Methuen, 1984), p. xvii.

22 Romanow, Whyte and Leeson, *Canada Notwithstanding.* Other good accounts are Robert Sheppard and Michael Valpy, *The National Deal* (Toronto: Fleet Books, 1982) and Keith Banting and Richard Simeon, *And No One Cheered* (Toronto: Methuen, 1983).

23 Briefing notes, *Continuing Committee of Ministers on the Constitution,* December 6, 1978, Charter of Rights section.

24 Saskatchewan Briefing Note (February 1979).

25 Several people have come forward to claim some credit for the inclusion of the notwithstanding clause. One prominent academic, Paul Weiler, writing in the Michigan Law School journal in 1984, outlines his meetings with various politicians and officials. It is clear that the possibility was "in the air" as we used to say. Paul Weiler, "Rights and Judges in a Democracy: A New Canadian Version," *Michigan Journal of Law Reform,* Vol. 17 (Fall 1984), p. 80, note 97.

26 Author's notes. Given the final positions of the provinces two years later, this is quite remarkable.

27 Author's notes.

28 Romanow, Whyte, and Leeson, *Canada Notwithstanding,* p. 54. Indeed, some Premiers like Sterling Lyon could hardly conceal their disdain for Trudeau, preferring to wait for a new Conservative government.

29 This is really an amazing period in Canadian political history. Trudeau had resigned as leader of the Liberal party in November of 1979, but was convinced to return after the Tory budget was defeated in the House in December 1979.

30 Michael Kirby, then Secretary to the Cabinet for Federal-Provincial Relations and now a Senator, was the chief strategist for the federal government on this matter. His "eyes only" memo was leaked by a federal civil servant to the Quebec government.

31 "Kirby Memorandum," Federal Government Secret Memo, p. 5.

32 For more detailed accounts of this period, see Romanow, Whyte and Leeson, *Canada Nothwithstanding*; Sheppard and Valpy, *The National Deal*; and Banting and Simeon, *And No One Cheered*.

33 The important elements of the Alberta formula were a general amending clause that required that any amendment have the support of the Parliament of Canada and two-thirds of the provinces representing 50 percent of the population, with the right to opt out of any amendment that derogated from the powers or privileges of the provinces; compensation for provinces opting out of any amendment where the federal government assumed the financial responsibility for a program; and a small list of items (matters like the monarchy) requiring unanimity.

34 Few believed that the PQ could agree to something that would damage their chances of attaining sovereignty-association in the future.

35 Author's notes.

36 The author was one of the four deputy ministers who negotiated the original package early in the evening, with other deputies from the provinces of Alberta, British Columbia and Newfoundland. The package was based on a possible compromise scribbled out on an envelope earlier in the day by Jean Chrétien and Roy Romanow in a kitchen off the meeting room.

37 Interestingly, my estimation was wrong. In a conversation some 10 years later, the former Deputy Minister of Intergovernmental Affairs in Alberta, Dr. Peter Meekison, indicated that they did not have strong feelings about this. It was a bargaining point for them and they would have accepted a proposal to remove section 2 from the application of section 33 if asked. No one did.

38 Author's notes.

39 Chaviva Hosek,"Women and the Constitutional Process," in Banting and Simeon, *And No One Cheered*, pp. 291–92.

40 Hosek, "Women and the Constitutional Process," p. 295.

41 Hogg, *Constitutional Law of Canada*, pp. 731–41.

42 For a discussion of this see J. Bayefsky, "The Judicial Function under the Canadian Charter of Rights and Freedoms," *McGill Law Journal*, Vol. 32 (1987), pp. 791–833.

43 *Ford v. Quebec (Attorney General)*, [1988] 2 S.C.R. 712.

44 Canada *House of Commons Debates*, April 6, 1989, pp. 152–53.

45 "Pursuant to subsection 33(1) of the Canadian Charter of Rights and Freedoms, this act is declared to operate notwithstanding the freedom of association in paragraph 2(d) of the Canadian Charter of Rights and Freedoms."
The bill was also exempted from the Saskatchewan Human Rights Code.

46 *Retail, Wholesale and Department Store Union (RWDSU) v. Saskatchewan* [1985]
5 W.W.R. 97 (Sask. C.A.). For a good discussion of this case see Greshner
and Norman, "The Courts and Section 33," p. 155.

47 John D.Whyte, "On Not Standing For Notwithstanding"; Peter H. Russell,
"Standing Up For Notwithstanding," *Alberta Law Review*, Vol. 29, no. 2
(1991), pp. 293–309.

48 I was one of the other chief advisors who also initially had misgivings, but
succumbed to the logic of our Premier's arguments.

49 Whyte, "On Not Standing for Notwithstanding," p. 349.

50 Whyte, "On Not Standing for Notwithstanding," pp. 350–51.

51 Whyte, "On Not Standing for Notwithstanding," p. 352.

52 Whyte "On Not Standing for Notwithstanding," p. 355.

53 See Michael Mandel, *The Charter of Rights and the Legalization of Politics in
Canada*, 2nd ed. (Toronto: Thompson Educational Publishing, 1994),
p. 89. He lumps Russell in with Alan Borovoy and others.

54 Russell, "Standing Up for Notwithstanding," p. 295.

55 Russell, "Standing Up for Notwithstanding," p. 308.

56 Donald Smiley, "A Dangerous Deed: The Constitution Act, 1982," in
Banting and Simeon (eds.), *And No One Cheered*, p. 91.

57 Smiley, "A Dangerous Deed: The Constitution Act, 1982," p. 92.

58 Luiza Chwialkowska, "Poll Shows Canadians Divided on Judges' Power to
'Make Law'" *National Post*, February 18, 2000, p. A4.

59 *Vriend v. Alberta* [1998] 1 S.C.R. 493.

60 *R.J.R.-MacDonald v. Canada (Attorney-General)* [1995] 3 S.C.R. 199.

61 Hogg, *Constitutional Law of Canada*, p. 843.

62 Janet L. Hiebert, "Wrestling With Rights: Judges, Parliament, and the Making of Social Policy," *Choices*, Vol. 5, no. 3 (July 1999), p. 11. This essay is
reproduced in this collection.

63 In the discussions about possible uses of the *nonobstante* clause in 1981, the
tobacco case was one that came up. There was concern that although section 2 was supposedly drafted so as to exclude corporate free speech, there
would come a time when the court would ignore the intentions of the
drafters and find in favour of an ill-advised social practice on the basis of
corporate free speech. It was thought that Parliament would have no trouble using the *nonobstante* clause in such a case. Alas, the drafters were wrong
in both respects.

64 For example, in Saskatchewan a provincial judge thought nothing of ordering a new social program to be established in the province to meet the needs
of her judgement, despite the fact that no monies had been voted for this

purpose by the legislature. In this case, the program ordered has a social purpose that most would agree with, the treating of fetal alcohol syndrome. However, she seemed oblivious to the fact that it was not within judicial power to order the legislature to spend money to implement programs.

65 *Reference re Remuneration of the Judges of the Provincial Court of Prince Edward Island* [1997] 3 S.C.R. 3 [hereinafter *Reference re Remuneration of Judges*].

66 *Reference re Remuneration of Judges* [1997] at p. 13.

67 *Reference re Remuneration of Judges* [1997] at p. 13.

68 *Reference re Remuneration of Judges* [1997] at p. 21.

69 This is only the latest example of such a questionable judgement. In the recent *Secession Reference*, the Court asserted that "the 1982 amendments did not alter the basic division of powers in ss. 91 and 92 of the Constitution Act." This extraordinary claim is made as if section 92A, altering powers over natural resources, did not exist.